Forward Everywhere

HER MAJESTY'S TERRITORIALS

Also from Brassey's

BATES
Japan and the British Commonwealth Occupation Force 1946–52

BAYNES
Urquhart of Arnhem
The Life of Major General R E Urquhart CB DSO

CLAYTON
Forearmed
A History of the Intelligence Corps

GRAHAM & BIDWELL
Coalitions, Politicians and Generals
Some Aspects of Command in Two World Wars

HARTCUP
The Silent Revolution
The Development of Conventional Weapons 1945–85

O'BALLANCE
Afghan Wars 1839–1992
What Britain Gave Up and the Soviet Union Lost

RAUGH
Wavell in the Middle East 1939–1941
A Study in Generalship

Forward Everywhere

HER MAJESTY'S TERRITORIALS

Stanley Simm Baldwin

BRASSEY'S (UK)
London • New York

First English edition 1994

UK editorial offices: Brassey's, 165 Great Dover Street, London SE1 4YA
orders: Marston Book Services, PO Box 87, Oxford OX2 0DT

USA orders: Macmillan Publishing Company,
Front and Brown Streets, Riverside, NJ 08075

Distributed in North America to booksellers and wholesalers
by the Macmillan Publishing Company, NY 10022

Library of Congress Cataloging in Publication Data
available

British Library Cataloguing in Publication Data
A catalogue record for this book is available
from the British Library

ISBN 0-08-040716-1 Hardcover

Typeset by M Rules
Printed in Great Britain by
BPCC Wheatons Ltd, Exeter

AD PATREM

In loving memory of Dobson Baldwin of Tow Law, never a Territorial but a volunteer for the field, who survived the slaughters of the Somme and for the remainder of his days said an enthusiastic yes to life; my father and exemplar.

Foreword

By Field Marshal Lord Bramall
KG, GCB, OBE, MC, JP

Any student of defence affairs will appreciate that if you are forced for political or economic reasons to run down your Regular front line armed forces, even though the international scene remains essentially dangerous, volatile and unstable, your reserve forces assume increasing importance. Moreover, if you continue that Regular rundown to a point, as will shortly occur in this country, when our front line forces will be incapable of sustained action in any conflict worthy of the name, without reinforcement by reserves, these reserves, of which the Territorial Army is, by far, the most effective element, become even more important still. Stanley Baldwin's book, *Forward Everywhere*, which is a highly authoritative history of our Militia and Territorial forces over the years, is, therefore, most topical and government ministers would benefit by reading it.

Baldwin writes with humanity and humour and his analysis of the conflicts that confronted Britain over the ages and our country's response to them is most instructive. I believe he has also captured the spirit of the periods of which he writes. We feel ourselves among the stolid Yeomen, the reluctant Militiamen, the earnest Volunteers of 1859, the self-sacrificing Territorials of 1914–18, the well-travelled 'Terriers' of 1939–45 and the fit technocrats of today. Even more, he has succeeded in letting us feel just what it was like to stand in waterlogged, amateurish trenches in the winter of 1914–15, then climb out of a trench and go over the top with some of your comrades cursing, others making the sign of the Cross, and three or four kicking a football across no-man's land, seemingly with the insouciance of a Saturday afternoon's recreation. He lets us endure the freezing hopelessness of Gallipoli and introduces us to the conviviality of summer camps of long ago. The reader can experience the frustration of Territorials standing by their ack-ack sites during the Munich crisis and wondering whether their jobs will still be waiting for them when and if the crisis passes, and can learn what it was like to be mobilised and to fight with weekend comrades.

And when it is peace again we go through the Aladdin's cave of a demobilisation centre, choosing a civilian outfit and hoping that not too many workmates will have selected the same pattern chalk-striped suit and the porkpie trilby that we fancied. The research has been prodigious; the author has persuaded leading public figures to tell us their experiences in the Territorials and he has dug deep in official archives. All in all, Baldwin has produced an important social document that could hold its place in the history and sociology faculties of universities as well as in military libraries.

Like many regular soldiers I may from time to time have wondered what motivated the Territorials and, indeed, how efficient they would be if put to the test in action. When I became Commander-in-Chief of the United Kingdom Land Forces and had more dealings with the TA I found the answers, but I wish I had had the benefit of reading this book all those years ago.

Baldwin has an immense zest for the TA tradition. He started as a 17-year-old undergraduate in Durham University Senior Training Corps, saw active service in the Middle East and since then has served his country in a part-time capacity in the Ministry of Defence, Headquarters United Kingdom Land Forces, Horse Guards and the Cabinet Office, as well as soldiering at brigade and regimental level. Additionally he was a colleague of mine at the Greater London TA&VRA. I am delighted, therefore, to write this Foreword to such a well-rounded account of the weekend warriors and I wish it well.

Bramall
Field Marshal
House of Lords
15 September 1993

Preface

The first time you throw a live grenade your hands tremble. The awesome thought that so much destructive power is about to explode a few yards away turns to fear when you realise that there are only two people in the throwing bay. If anything goes wrong, only you and the instructor will be killed.

Most Territorials go through it, but what of the instructor through whose hands pass so many apprehensive trainees? Usually a sergeant, he will not be a full-time soldier. He may, for example, work in an advertising agency (to cite from my first TA experience on a grenade range). Even if the nervous recruit lobs the grenade successfully over the blast wall and he and his instructor have ducked in the manner approved by the manual, there may still be peril. Occasionally you get a 'blind', that is, the grenade fails to explode. It cannot be left there. The senior instructor present must make it safe. That he accepts such duties cheerfully, says much for the Territorials.

I cannot remember when it first occurred to me that to be a Territorial – a weekend soldier entrusted with military weapons and professional duties – is something special. I had respect for these part-timers when I watched my first mobilised TA unit under fire from machine gun and air attack. That grew into admiration as I saw them on security patrols through Jerusalem and hunting fanatical Irgun Zvai Leumi terrorists in the Judaean hills. But perhaps the greatest realisation of what the TA is about came some years later when I stood on a range and observed a white-haired colonel, his battledress chest resplendent with campaign ribbons, lying on the ground scrupulously polishing the ammunition for a young lance corporal, number one on the Bren in the brigade headquarters shooting team.

My admiration for the Terriers increased in the years following the end of the old TA in 1967, when members of the T&AVR's category III soldiered on with only cursory official encouragement. Many of these men were the last of the stalwarts who had helped to win the war, and their loyalty and experience were impressive. But with hindsight, we can see that the changes worked and the far smaller, more professional part-time element of the so-called 'one Army' is highly deserving of the nation's respect. It may be that the military planners require too much of these weekend soldiers (wastage is a constant problem) but the fact remains that in them Britain has a cost-effective reserve that is fit and knows its job. A Territorial costs only a sixth of what it takes to fund a regular soldier, and the TA, which provides approximately one third of the whole Army, takes only five per cent of the entire Army budget.

Part-time soldiering seems over the years to have attracted people who were leading or who were destined to lead interesting lives. You will read of the youth who joined the new-born Territorial Force at 17 after serving before the mast of a windjammer from the age of 15, who rounded Cape Horn thrice in sail and who in his mid-nineties was piloting a glider, having meanwhile fought at Gallipoli, commanded a battery at Passchendaele and managed to spend a night as a prisoner in the Tower of London. You will read of another lad of 17 who joined the Finsbury Rifles and rose to be Britain's senior non-royal field marshal, and of the woman recruit who went on to become the wartime and immediate postwar director of the Auxiliary Territorial Service (ATS). You will discover the British driver who struck Hitler and lived to tell the tale; the officer who brought Mussolini's pet dog back to Britain after the Duce and his mistress had been executed by partisans; the Roman Catholic who was ordered by his commander-in-chief to call on the Pope and apologise for the destruction of Monte Cassino's Benedictine monastery; the stockjobber whose weight fluctuated so wildly that he maintained three complete wardrobes of different sizes, who lived in a suite at the Savoy during the week and who owned and raced cars, powerboats and horses.

The man who gave his name to a widely used weapon of the Second World War, the Blacker Bombard, not forgetting its stablemate the PIAT (Projector Infantry Anti-Tank) was a Territorial. You will be reminded of the four part-time soldiers whose literary works are classics and still in print many generations after being written, one of the three being Scotland's national poet, who has the rare distinction of having a night of the calendar named after him. There is the private in the London Scottish whose ankle was smashed by a German shell in the TF's baptism of battle and who counted it as a blessing because he was invalided and went on to become a Hollywood star in the interwar years, Oscar winner and the world's screen epitome of an English gentleman. You will encounter the young Terrier who became an archbishop, the Yeoman who failed to become prime minister but was viceroy of India, foreign secretary and Britain's wartime ambassador to the United States at a time when we needed the resources of that mighty nation.

You will read of the Territorial who rose to the pinnacle of the legal profession, and of another, who achieved immense dignity as the holder of three of the great offices of state and, later, as speaker of the House of Commons but who, in his TA days, was treated with less respect and suffered the indignity of being 'debagged' in the open air and having beer swilled over his naked parts for military ignorance coupled with pomposity. There are those who became deputy speakers, others who became secretaries of state for defence or war ministers (one of whom managed, in a less demanding age, still to be serving as a Yeomanry captain while holding his War Department portfolio). There is the archaeologist and brigadier who became the television age's first idol of the intellectual panel game. He was a gunner, and one of the NCOs in his unit when he was a battery commander went on to achieve a more substantial fame, gaining such eminence in his profession and in matters of state that a newspaper described him as 'one of the three most important persons in the country' – the others being the prime minister and the head of MI5. Incidentally both men were awarded titles and both became Companions of Honour, not bad for Terriers who served together in the same unit.

You will come across the Scotsman with the very English name who founded the Boys' Brigade on the lines of his old Volunteer unit and the Volunteer a generation later who, during the First World War, decided to join the colours and took hundreds of his work colleagues with him (those were the days). On the eve of the next war, an enterprising Territorial officer, a Fleet Street reporter in civilian life, brought together an unlikely company of journalists and actors who trained in the afternoons because they worked in the evenings (his initiative earned him fame within London's TA circles and years later his administrative skills went on to gain him international status in the world of Olympics). You will meet the august companionages of those who became prime minister and of those who won the VC.

A history of part-time soldiering is a social history of Britain. For instance, which service department today would dare to advertise for 'respectable' recruits as was the practice of Volunteer units? Which government would dare to allocate military command according to a scale of land ownership or filial expectations of the same, as was the system in the Militia? When the TF was founded, women were considered not sufficiently responsible to vote. When the ATS helped Britain to win the Second World War (as far as AA Command was concerned, largely enabling 60 per cent of the command's male strength to be transferred overseas) they did so, rank for rank on only two-thirds of the male pay scales. Today there is parity in pay. Incidentally, I have not devoted a separate chapter to women, but have treated the subject organically, tracing their military ascent from the days when the ATS were allowed to work at only five trades in 1939 to more than 100 by 1945. Today women command mixed units, are proficient in weapons and are musicians in infantry bands. The TA has a woman who can disarm bombs and another who marshals helicopters. In 1992 the first woman to join the Parachute Regiment directly from civilian life enlisted; she was recruited into 4 Para(TA).

During the years that I have been preparing this book, it has been my privilege to study hundreds of units, not all in the flesh but many through the archives of regiments, cities, livery companies and associations, or by the experiences of former part-time soldiers. Have I a favourite unit? If I could step back in time, I would join the Working Men's College Corps of Rifle Volunteers of 1859, studying and training (each as a spare-time pursuit) under the enthusiastic command in both activities of his Honour Thomas Hughes, QC, author of *Tom Brown's Schooldays*, paying my weekly mite towards a uniform, economising to go to the Easter training, and learning drill and physical training (PT) from Philip Read, DCM, who was invalided after being wounded as a sergeant major at the Redan. A close second in my choice would be the Queen's Westminsters of 80 years later, but it would have to be in that company of West End show business and Fleet Street characters who, because they worked at night, paraded in the afternoon. They included such people as the men's front row chorus from Ivor Novello's *The Dancing Years*, who drilled with such precision at rifle pace on the square at Wellington Barracks that they made the Guards there look like maladroit amateurs and who, in those days of shortages of uniforms as well as weapons, annoyed the professionals by such outrages as going on parade in sandals; people like the film stars and matinée idols whose sternness on sentry duty was undermined by children who approached them shyly with autograph books.

Millions of people have been Territorials. Their story is worth relating and I have tried to tell it from the inside against a background of social change. Many of them fell in great wars (129,806 in the First World War alone), a few died in minor campaigns, but to the combatants the effect of the bullet is the same whether it be fired in a great or minor conflict. Britain owes much to them. Every autumn we celebrate the valour of the Few in the Battle of Britain. They deserve our most sincere respect, but how often is today's public reminded of the debt due to the many thousands of soldiers, men and women, largely Territorials, who were responsible for the ground defence of Britain against air attack? Not only did they play their part in the attrition of the enemy's air arm but they provided a boost for morale when weary and frightened civilians saw '*our*' searchlights clamp on to the enemy bombers and heard '*our*' guns defending the homeland.

For us in Britain today the times are less anxious but there is evil in many parts of the world and a potential for widespread delivery of death. Thrice in the past nine decades the United Kingdom was ill-prepared. More recent transgressions of frontiers leave the public with little confidence in our intelligence information or the diplomatic readings therefrom.

Could it happen again? The Secretary of State for Defence announced in Parliament on 10 December 1991 that the TA (which then had a recruited strength of about 73,800) would be reduced to a ceiling of about 63,500 by

1995. The cuts could have been worse. But it is valid to wonder whether the government has considered fully the Commons defence committee's observation last autumn that military operations of the type undertaken in the Gulf War could be mounted in future only with considerably greater dependence on reserve forces. The fighting and brutality in Bosnia following the break-up of Yugoslavia could be negligible when compared with what might happen all around the perimeter of the former Soviet Union. The fragmentation of what was once the largest state in the world is a Pandora's Box of colossal proportions. There are troubles in Georgia, Armenia, Azerbaijan and in the northern Caucasus. And who dare predict what could develop in South Africa within the next three years? However, let us be positive. Here stands Her Majesty's Territorial Army; at 67,812 strong (and soon to be smaller still) it is tiny when set against the TA of 1939 and microscopic compared with the Militia, Yeomanry and Volunteers of old. Nevertheless, it is efficient, enthusiastic and ready to go, in the words of the top medical category, Forward Everywhere.

SSB
VJ Day 1993

Contents

MY THANKS

I should like to express my gratitude to Major R A G (Rags) Courage, CVO, MBE, Grenadier Guards, for his constant support during my years at the Horse Guards; to Major M C (Felix) Jaffé, TD, Major C H A Skey, TD, and all members of the Fire Escape club for keeping alive the spirit of 47 Infantry Brigade (TA) for 27 years to date; and Sergeant A H Mayle, the Royal Regiment of Fusiliers (V), for devotion to his regiment and his ready help to its sons whether in-pensioners or recruits fresh from taking their oath. I must mention, too, the memory of the late Henry Howell, editor for many years of *The Territorial*.

I am most grateful to the many scores of people who have helped me in the preparation of this book, and particularly Britain's most distinguished contemporary soldier, Field Marshal Lord Bramall, KG, GCB, OBE, MC, JP, Lord Lieutenant for Greater London, for adding lustre with his foreword. My thanks are due also to Major Herbert Sawyer, Rough Rider and veteran of the Burma campaign, for his copious knowledge of Army regulations and customs, dress and of matters military east of Aden, and to Major G W (Robbie) Robertson, MC, Royal Artillery, author and historian, for generous help. I also thank Bruce Hobbs, MC, youngest winning rider of the Grand National, celebrated trainer and worthy North Somerset Yeoman and Yorkshire Dragoon, for sharing his wartime experiences. I must thank too John Whitmore Esq, tireless worker for the Royal Fusiliers Veterans, and Major Malcolm Smith, TD, Royal Logistic Corps (V), both of whom supplied details of worth. I am grateful also to the eminent and busy persons, including a former prime minister, other ministers, peers of the realm of first creation, figures of world status, including an outstanding Irish peer, proconsuls of high colonial office, and generals, who have generously given me the benefit of their experiences. I should like to thank the ever helpful staff of the Ministry of Defence library, including Mrs Judithe Blacklaw, for digging out dusty documents, the staff of the National Army Museum and the trusty librarians of *The Times*, in particular Ronald

King, former late-night librarian of that celebrated newspaper, for his skilled advice in years past while London slept. I am grateful to the TA's near contemporary the Automobile Association for permission to reproduce photographs and in particular to Mr R J Flavel, its archivist, for research on the patriotic contribution made to part-time soldiering by the AA and its employees. I thank my son Julian, for his skilled help with photography.

My gratitude is due to the secretaries of the TA&VRAs, all of whom gave me data about their associations, and in particular I thank Brigadier Peter Bowser, CBE, DL, of the TA&VRA for Greater London, who so kindly read my chapter on this important and often overlooked aspect of the TA and made helpful suggestions (though I alone remain responsible for any errors that might arise). I am indebted to the TA&VRA for Northern Ireland and their invaluable book, *An Account of the Territorials in Northern Ireland 1947–1978*, compiled by Colonel I B Gailey, Colonel W F Gillespie and Lieutenant Colonel J Hassett. I am grateful to Simon Jenkins, editor of *The Times*, and James Bishop, editor-in-chief of the *Illustrated London News* Group, for permission to reproduce illustrations from their famous journals, and to Major General Bryan Dutton, CBE, director of public relations (Army), for facilitating my use of official photographs. I must express my thanks to the clerks and archivists of livery companies who so generously supplied details of their relationships with units (and refreshed me with tea during my research), and to the livery companies themselves for their support of the Territorials. In particular I wish to record my gratitude, if I may presume to speak for my own regiment, to the master, wardens, liverymen, clerk and staff of the Worshipful Company of Cordwainers for their outstanding loyalty and hospitality to their unit over many years. Two works that I found invaluable in compiling my chapter 'Soldiers Supreme' are *The Register of the Victoria Cross* and *The Register of the George Cross*, published by *This England*, of Cheltenham, an admirable organ of that often-scarce sentiment national pride. I must express my appreciation of Terriers' families and employers for tolerance of weekend and summer absences. Finally my thanks are due to the weekend warriors themselves, whose story this is.

Author's Note

Echoing that other ex-serviceman Thucydides in his introduction to his great history of the Peloponnesian War (Book I, 22), I shall be satisfied if these pages are of use to readers who seek to understand past events. But, unlike him, I have tried to indicate the romance and human interest of my subject. The rebarbative Athenian, writing 2,400 years ago, testily opined that his work was fashioned not for the moment but for eternity. In this respect my aim is precisely the opposite of his.

A word on style: I have eschewed formality and have described regular regiments and corps by their popular titles, the way in which their members would describe them to other persons. Thus the Black Watch is described as such, not the Black Watch(the Royal Highland Regiment), and the Rifle Brigade is simply that, not the Rifle Brigade(the Prince Consort's Own). An exception occurs in describing some Territorial units, for example, those in that sprawling organisation the London Regiment. The reason for this apparent inconsistency is that the regiment existed in a vital period and its geographical appellation must be retained. Nevertheless, it is equally necessary to remind readers of the richly varied parentage of individual battalions. Within the metropolitan trawl were Scotsmen, Irishmen, outer Londoners, riflemen and those whose allegiance was to the City. Accordingly the 2nd Battalion of the capital's regiment is described as the 2nd Battalion of the London Regiment(the Royal Fusiliers). At second mention, the nickname, the Second to Nondons, is used. A generation on, the Second World War brought the need to convert many TA units, particularly infantry and yeomanry, to other arms of the service. I would have been unfaithful to their memory if I had failed to preserve their original title.

I have used a lower case 't' in the definite article preceding the names of infantry regiments, although in formal terms official usage insists on the capital letter. Where part of the title of a unit is enclosed in brackets, the opening bracket is typeset close to the previous word. The reason for this is that some

Territorial titles are long and contain three sets of brackets. I hope that, visually, the condensation is more satisfactory than a string of spaces.

In describing two regiments of the Principality of Wales I have spelt them as the Royal Welsh Fusiliers and the Welsh Regiment up to 27 January 1920. Thereafter they are Welch. I realise that this usage may appear inconsistent and that there is ancient authority for the 'c'; nevertheless my style is in step with War Office communications, *The Army List* and the descriptions impressed on medals and embroidered on colours.

List of Illustrations

Glossary of Abbreviations

AA	Anti-aircraft
AAC	Army Air Corps
ACC	Army Catering Corps
AER	Army Emergency Reserve
AM	Albert Medal
ASC	Army Service Corps
AT	Anti-tank
BEF	British Expeditionary Force
BEM	British Empire Medal
CB	Companion, Order of the Bath
CBE	Commander, Order of the British Empire
CGM	Conspicuous Gallantry Medal
CH	Companion of Honour
CMG	Companion, Order of St Michael and St George
CVO	Commander, Royal Victorian Order
DCLI	Duke of Cornwall's Light Infantry
DCM	Distinguished Conduct Medal
DLI	Durham Light Infantry
DSO	Distinguished Service Order
EGM	Empire Gallantry Medal
EM	Edward Medal
ERD	Emergency Reserve Decoration
GBE	Knight Grand Cross, Order of the British Empire
GC	George Cross

GCB	Knight Grand Cross, Order of the Bath
GCMG	Knight Grand Cross, Order of St Michael and St George
GCVO	Knight Grand Cross, Royal Victorian Order
GM	George Medal
HAA	Heavy Anti-Aircraft
HAC	Honourable Artillery Company
HG	Home Guard
HSF	Home Service Force
KBE	Knight Commander, Order of the British Empire
KCB	Knight Commander, Order of the Bath
KG	Knight Companion, Order of the Garter
KOSB	King's Own Scottish Borderers
KCVO	Knight Commander, Royal Victorian Order
KOYLI	King's Own Yorkshire Light Infantry
KP	Knight Companion, Order of St Patrick
KT	Knight Companion, Order of the Thistle
KSLI	King's Shropshire Light Infantry
LAA	Light Anti-Aircraft
LDV	Local Defence Volunteers
LF	Lancashire Fusiliers
LMG	Light Machine Gun
LVO	Lieutenant, Royal Victorian Order
MBE	Member, Order of the British Empire
MC	Military Cross
MEF	Middle East Forces
MGC	Machine Gun Corps
MM	Military Medal
MMG	Medium Machine Gun
MVO	Member, Royal Victorian Order
MX	Middlesex Regiment
OBE	Officer, Order of the British Empire
OCA	Old Comrades' Association
OM	Order of Merit
PAD	Passive Air Defence
QGM	Queen's Gallantry Medal

RA	Royal Artillery
RAC	Royal Armoured Corps
RAMC	Royal Army Medical Corps
RAPC	Royal Army Pay Corps
RASC	Royal Army Service Corps
RCT	Royal Corps of Transport
Recce	Reconnaissance
RE	Royal Engineers
REME	Royal Electrical and Mechanical Engineers
RF	Royal Fusiliers
RFC	Royal Flying Corps
RIrF	Royal Irish Fusiliers
RLC	Royal Logistic Corps
RNF	Royal Northumberland Fusiliers
RRF	Royal Regiment of Fusiliers
RSF	Royal Scots Fusiliers
RTC	Royal Tank Corps
RTR	Royal Tank Regiment
RWF	Royal Welch Fusiliers
SL	Searchlight
SLI	Somerset Light Infantry
SMG	Sub-Machine Gun
SR	Special Reserve
SWB	South Wales Borderers
TA	Territorial Army
T&AVR	Territorial and Army Volunteer Reserve
TA&VRA	Territorial, Auxiliary and Volunteer Reserve Association
TAER	Territorial Army Emergency Reserve
TD	Territorial Decoration/Efficiency Decoration Territorial
TEM	Territorial Efficiency Medal
(V)	(Volunteer)
VAD	Voluntary Aid Detachment
VC	Victoria Cross
VD	Volunteer Decoration
VF	Volunteer Force

1

The Originals

Every man thinks meanly of himself for not having been a soldier or not having served at sea.

DR SAMUEL JOHNSON, 10 APRIL 1778[1]

The Territorial Force came into existence on 1 April 1908 as a result of the Territorial and Reserve Forces Act of the previous year. Edward VII was on the throne; the Prime Minister, Sir Henry Campbell-Bannerman, was dying and when the force was exactly a week old his place was taken by Herbert Asquith. It was a memorable year for that irrepressible Yeomanry officer, writer and rising young Liberal politician Winston Churchill: no sooner was Asquith appointed to form a new administration than he gave Churchill his first cabinet post, as president of the Board of Trade with the rank of a secretary of state; and in September Churchill married.

The Boy Scouts movement had been formed on New Year's Day and retirement pensions, payable at 70 for men, were introduced later in the year. The year also saw the first powered flight in England by a man in a heavier-than-air machine. In America the United States Navy designed the first specification for a military aircraft. Germany, making it plain that she sought greater international muscle, enacted legislation enabling her navy to be enlarged and, in the meantime, launched her first Dreadnought-class warship, the *Nassau*. Professor Ernest Rutherford (who would be knighted in 1914, ennobled in 1931 and commemorated by having the artificial element rutherfordium named in his honour), received the Nobel prize for chemistry for his research into radioactivity, which would later contribute to the splitting of the atom.

'The Mother Country' was an affectionate concept in the dominions of the Empire. Although Canada, Australia and New Zealand were mature nations they accepted Britain's lead in many aspects of life, from defence to law, Britain having the final appeal tribunal on points of law in the Judicial Committee of the Privy Council. The House of Commons was populous; its 670 members included MPs from constituencies throughout Ireland. In the general election not much more than two years earlier, the Liberals had whirled to success with the biggest party majority since the passing of the Reform Act of 1832 had brought some semblance of democracy to the polls. In 1908, women would have to wait for another decade before they could vote – at the age of 30 – and yet another decade before their qualifying age was reduced to equality with that of men, 21. The House of Lords, which had only a handful of life peers, the law lords, and was as unrepresentative then as it is now, had powers equal to those of the Commons.

Atlases at that time were dominated by the comforting pink of the Empire. The Union flag, in either pristine or heraldically reduced form, flew over about 11 million square miles of territory and protected a quarter of the world's population. But an ominous indicator was emerging: Britain, after more than half a century as the world's leading manufacturer, had been overtaken by the United States. Nobody realised it then, but the world had moved into the American century.

Although 1908 marked so precisely the foundation of the Territorial Force, we must go back a few years to understand why it was necessary to form a new type of military reserve – after all, Britain had had part-time soldiers for centuries and had relied heavily on them in some periods. For instance, during the reign of James I, as Macaulay remarked in his *The History of England*, there was no standing army and 'the defence of our island was still confided to the militia'.

At the time that Queen Victoria and her subjects were celebrating her diamond jubilee, Britain was the superpower of the world, confidently dispensing her institutions around the greatest empire in history. It was thoroughly in keeping with this grandeur that, as a matter of policy, the Royal Navy kept equal in power to the combined strength of the two next greatest navies. But two and a half years later, the nation's confidence was shaken by events in South Africa, where farmer soldiers of the two Boer republics gave Britain some costly lessons in warfare.

Britain's regular Army was tiny in comparison to its imperial commitments. Professional, constantly tested by native emergencies yet unaided by conscription, it was a masterpiece of economic and humane equilibrium. Kaiser Wilhelm II of Germany might well think it 'contemptibly small'[2] but, with the delicate strength of an eggshell, it did its job admirably, embracing every continent. Tribal unrest from within and foreign ambitions at the frontiers were unable to distort the serenity of the ovoid. But the South African War demonstrated that external pressure, if sufficiently concentrated and with modern weapons, could pierce the shell; Britain had used 448,435 troops, 256,645 of them regular soldiers, to win. There were fears on the north west frontier of India about Russian ambitions and continental Europe was in an arms race in which the major powers there were amassing the biggest peacetime armies ever known. The war was a jolt and it was soon followed by another: there was a period in 1900 when Britain was virtually without any regular unit to defend the homeland. Describing the home defences after reinforcements had been rushed to South Africa, Hugh Arnold-Forster, Secretary of State for War, pointed out on 1 February in the Commons:

> We shall have only six battalions of infantry of the line and three battalions of Guards, all under strength, and as far as the line battalions are concerned largely composed of men who are not fit to take part in active operations. We shall have nine cavalry regiments, some without horses and all under strength. Beyond that we have nothing, nothing at all . . . We have got the whole organised Army out of the country, and the War Office is face to face with the problem of how to make an army to take its place.

If a foreign country had invaded at that time, Britain's defence, apart from the Fleet, consisted of the unconvincing force described by Arnold-Forster plus an inefficient and depleted Militia and the Volunteers serving at home. Emergency measures were taken; Militia battalions not already embodied (46 had been called out by the end of November) were immediately embodied too, the establishment of the Volunteers was increased and they were given extra training. In May retired Volunteers were asked to join a Volunteers reserve to help to defend the country against invasion. The Queen appealed to retired regulars to rejoin the colours in so-called royal reserve battalions for home service or garrison duty overseas. They were offered a £22 bounty. It attracted 24,130 of those veterans.

Soon after the war, the public received another shock, this time about the quality of the auxiliary forces. The Royal Commission on the Militia and Volunteers, which was set up on St George's Day 1903 under the Duke of Norfolk, examined its first witness, Lieutenant General Sir William Nicholson, Director General of Military Intelligence and Mobilisation, on 19 May. And many more witnesses later, in May 1904, it reported critically: 'We are forced to the conclusion that the Militia, in its existing condition, is unfit to take the field for the defence of this country. We think, however, that its defects arise from causes beyond the control of its officers and men.'[3] As for the Volunteers, the commission commented: 'We are agreed in the conclusion that the Volunteer Force, in view of the unequal education of the officers, the limited training of the men, and the defects of equipment and organisation is not qualified to take the field against a regular army.' The force 'owed its origin and continuance mainly to the energy and goodwill of its officers and men, and the fact that it does not attain to the standards imposed by war conditions is in no way attributable to them.' The fact remained that 'neither the musketry nor the tactical training of the rank and file would enable it to face with prospect of success, the troops of a Continental army'.[4]

The commission had acknowledged that the Militia and all types of

Volunteers had 'earned the approval of those under whose command they served' in the war. This was gracious enough but it did not tell the whole story; in most cases those who had served in that theatre were carefully selected after they had been keen enough to volunteer for active service in the first place, so they were not typical. The defects, which included transport, equipment and artillery *matériel*, were all beyond the control of the members of these forces. For instance the Militia had only three batteries of field artillery.

One of the politically unacceptable findings of the commission was about the length of training needed. It commented:

> For an increase of efficiency in the Militia we must look in the first instance to an increase in the period of training. The evidence satisfies us that the principal part of this increase must be given during the recruit stage, and in view of the opinions expressed by a large majority of those officers who have appeared before us, we cannot recommend less than six months of continuous training for the militiaman in his first year of service.
>
> This should be followed in the second, third and fourth years by not less than six weeks' training.[5]

The commission criticised the system of funding under which commanding officers were forced by economic considerations to recruit quantity rather than quality to qualify for as big a capitation grant as possible. Today it may not be generally appreciated that the CO of those times was personally liable for his unit's debts, so no one could blame him if he placed a high priority on numbers. Years after the commission's findings, the case in 1907 of *Samuel* v. *Whetherley* (LR 1907, 1KB, 709) illustrates the point: the estate of a deceased CO was held liable for debts incurred by his corps, although the property in the goods concerned had passed to his successor in command.

The implications of the commission's report were alarming, even though the strength of the Volunteers stood at 250,226 and that of the Militia at 93,873. (In considering the country's defences we must add to these figures the strength of the Yeomanry, but the latter was not within the parameters of the inquiry). The commission had done its work thoroughly. It examined 134 witnesses over 82 sittings, studied questionnaires returned from every unit of Militia and Volunteers and considered memoranda from scores of officers in the two forces and from other interested persons. The evidence filled two enormous volumes plus one of appendices.

The government did nothing about the findings, and the main recommendation, that training in one or other of these forces should be made compulsory for the country's young men, was not implemented (or at least not until 35 years later in the more frightening world of 1939). As the Secretary of State for War said when answering a question by Herbert Samuel in the

Commons on 2 June 1904: 'The government does not intend to make any proposals to the House in favour of a system of conscription'. Six days later the Prime Minister reiterated the government's position against conscription in a similar answer to Sir Frederick Banbury.

Despite the international arms race, government reasons against conscription were electoral unpopularity and expense, estimated by Balfour at £25,900,000. It would take a change of government and four years from the publication of the commission's report before any substantial benefit to Britain's defence forces of those Edwardian days could come into effect.

A different kind of inquiry had been set up in 1902; this was Viscount Esher's War Office (Reconstitution) Committee. As a result of its recommendations, early in 1904, which were accepted by the government, the venerable office of commander-in-chief was abolished. It was unfortunate that the appointment vanished during the tenure of 'Bobs', the nation's most distinguished soldier and darling of the newspapers, Field Marshal Earl Roberts of Kandahar, VC. He would be replaced by an Army Council of civilian as well as military members, the chairman being the Secretary of State for War. Work started on setting up an outline General Staff. The Esher committee, contrasting War Office organisation unfavourably with that of the Board of Admiralty, commented:

> The Admiralty system of higher administration is absolutely sound in principle. It has been handed down without material change from the period of great naval wars. It may be said to have been founded on the proved requirements of wars, and although it has not recently been put to the supreme test, it has smoothly and successfully met new demands as they have arisen, including the enormous increase in personnel and *matériel*. It conforms closely to the arrangements under which the largest private industries are conducted. Finally, it has retained the confidence of the Navy and of the nation.
>
> This cannot be said of the War Office, where great changes have been frequent and where stability of administration has never been attained. The complex system which prevailed at the time of the Crimean campaign broke down completely under the stress of war, after bringing the nation to the verge of disaster. The changes that followed were important, and in some respects beneficial. The conception of a War Office for dealing with the whole business of the Army dates from 1855; but a dual system, involving great disadvantages, prevailed till 1870 . . . But when in 1890 the Hartington commission urged a drastic measure of reorganisation nothing was done. It has followed that the War Office has been subjected to successive tinkering processes, by which improvements in minor matters may occasionally have been accomplished, but which left great principles entirely out of sight.[6]

The Army was to be reorganised into six corps but in fact only one of these, a corps of three divisions based on Aldershot, was created. Apart from this the Army retained its six independent divisions and four cavalry brigades. However satisfactory the system was in peacetime, there were numerous shortages that with the creation of an expeditionary force would have to be made good on mobilisation.

The big changes came when the Liberals swept convincingly into power early in 1906. The task of reshaping the Army for the 20th century was entrusted to a lawyer MP with a taste for philosophy, Richard B Haldane, KC, who had previously been appointed Secretary of State for War in late December, and who, apparently, during the general election campaign of the new year, had devoted his time to electioneering during the day and was able to get around to military matters only after dinner. He had a hard look at the Norfolk and Esher findings and one result of his endeavours was the passing of the Territorial and Reserve Forces Act of 1907, which brought into existence the Territorial Force on 1 April the following year. This organisation, now the Territorial Army, has fought victoriously in the two most terrible wars that the planet has ever known and individual members have engaged the enemy in lesser actions; at the time of writing, more than 900 Territorials, having volunteered, were serving in the Gulf War.[7]

As Secretary of State for War, Haldane applied himself to other aspects of reform. For instance, he organised the regular Army into a ready-for-action operational force of one cavalry and six infantry divisions, insisted on a strong General Staff embracing the defence needs not only of Britain but also of the independent dominions, the Imperial General Staff (which had been established in a previous government), and set up specialist training schools.

Army reform had, of course, been in the air since the start of the 1870s, and welcome progress had been made by Cardwell in his days at the War Office. After Cardwell, the movement continued, but it came to fruition only in Haldane's tenure. His success almost certainly lay in the diplomatic way this lawyer and philosopher handled potential conflict between military men, civil servants and politicians. The Prime Minister, Campbell-Bannerman, himself a former Secretary of State for War, had advised Haldane that whatever he did he must 'give the credit of it to the soldiers'.[8]

Haldane was a long-serving war secretary, having six and a half years with the portfolio and he left his stamp on the regular Army before becoming Lord Chancellor. But we are concerned with his creation of the Territorial Force and, to a lesser extent, of the Special Reserve out of the existing part-time forces of the day. First, however, we must trace the history of part-time military service.

2

The Militia

> *. . . by your obedience to my general, by your concord in the camp and your valour in the field we shall shortly have a famous victory over the enemies of my God, my Kingdom and my People.*
>
> ELIZABETH I AT TILBURY, 1588

Of the three elements of part-time soldiering, the Militia, the Yeomanry and the Volunteers, the first is by far the most ancient. The concept of the Yeomanry is easy to grasp but the terms Militia and Volunteers are often misunderstood because their roles overlapped and, at some periods, their memberships were similar. Originally and for most of its life, the Militia was a compulsory organisation, whereas the Volunteers were always simply volunteers, just as the membership of the Territorial Army is today. Complications arose because, eventually, some Militia sub-units had members who volunteered and, later, whole units were volunteers. Finally, in 1852, the Militia as a whole was made a voluntary organisation (more accurately, the Militia had fallen into disuse but it was revived in that year under its old title but as a purely voluntary force).

Yet another complication was that some members of the Militia – usually the keenest – saw their service in it as a way into the regular Army. This produced some distinguished officers and brave men, with VCs to prove it (*vide* Chapter 17 Soldiers Supreme). But apart from the value to the Army of such individual beacons, the upward movement from Militiaman to regular soldier was one of the factors that made the Militia so ill-prepared to take on a foreign foe at the turn of the century: as soon as the career-minded members became efficient, they moved into the pensionable Army. The Militia was thereby systematically losing many of its best men. The War Office, which from 1799 had encouraged the practice, later sent strict instructions about this switching when it discovered that some units had personnel on strength who were simply names, the men themselves had enlisted in the regular force.

Another difference between the Militia and the Volunteers was social: the corpus of the former was usually formed from the labourer grouping, whereas the latter had a higher standing in society. For instance, the statesman

Charles James Fox was content to be a private in the Chertsey Volunteers. Also, in the decades of the ballot, a large number of Militiamen were serving because they had been hired to do so by men who had been ballotted to serve but had exercised their right to provide a substitute; by contrast, no one was a Volunteer's substitute. The Militia officers tended to be the large landowners or their sons, and they had a powerful lobby in both the House of Commons and, particularly, in the House of Lords. The former was, of course, nowhere near as representative a chamber as it is today, and the latter has never represented anyone but its members. It goes without saying that the gap between the Militia officers and their men was far wider than that between the Volunteer officers and their men. For long centuries the relationship between the Militiaman and his officers was feudatory, and despite the statute that in Victoria's reign had paved the way for ending this local command element, Militia commanding officers in conference with Haldane in 1906 made it clear that they preferred not to serve in the force that would replace the Volunteers. In the event, they transferred to the Special Reserve in 1908.

Over a number of decades, governments had tried to run the Volunteers, in the phrase that echoes down the years and is still with us, 'at no extra cost to public funds'. This meant that the Volunteers paid from their own pockets to play their part in national defence – it was a favour to the country, and some governments took advantage of their willingness. 'A costless disciplined army of 150,000 marksmen' was how *The Times* described the Volunteers in 1867. Because of this financial independence, the Volunteers had far more freedom than is usual in military organisations: they elected their own commanding officers, voted on the type of uniform they should adopt, worked out their own terms of service and commitments governed by civil law contracts for their units, and paid for their own instruction, ranges, ammunition and field days. It was different with the Militia. As to the roles of the two forces, the Volunteers' was simply to support the regular forces in defending the United Kingdom. The Militia, too, had this task plus that of supplementing the regular Army during war for garrison duties, overseas as well as in Britain, and they might even be called on for field service abroad. Militiamen recruited from 1811 onwards, for instance, could be posted to Ireland (51 Geo III c 118, c 128).

THE HISTORY

This auxiliary role of Britain's Militia is a modern concept; a true militia (from *miles*, Latin for soldier) comes to us from far back in the history of nations. Originally it was the fatherland in arms. There were no standing armies: when defence was needed, it was the obligation of free men to provide it. The militia was the army of the day. Even in Tudor times, the only formation approaching a permanent army was often a mere 200 strong; it was formed of the Yeomen of the Guard whose duty it was to protect the monarch. James I relied on his militia. In Saxon England the militia was known as the *fyrd*, a force levied locally for the defence of the area. Its other names were the *ban* or the *host*. The light cavalry of the *fyrd* were called *hobelars*. In Saxon times, we learn from Grose:

> All qualified to bear arms in one family were led to the field by the head of the family, and every ten families made a Tything commanded by a Borse-holder, ten Tythings constituting a Hundred under the Chief Magistrate of the Hundred, and several Hundreds a Trything, and the force of the county or shire commanded by the Heretoch or Duke, under the supreme command of the King's Lieutenant or General whose office lasted only during any war.[1]

When the Normans imposed their institutions on England, a complicated system of feudal duties (some titular remnants of which still exist and some others of which were robustly vulgar) largely replaced the *fyrd*; this took perhaps two decades. In its stead there came the *posse comitatus* (county force), which incidentally gave its name many generations later and thousands of miles distant to the summarily assembled civilian force under the sheriff that became so necessary in the policing of the vast spaces of a United States county.

The ancient obligation of free Englishmen to help in the defence of their country was confirmed by the Statute of Winchester of 1285. Under its provisions, males aged between 15 and 60, with certain exceptions, were required to rally to the country's standard. Every such person in those days of Edward I had to arm himself on a scale determined by the amount of land he held or the value of his movable possessions.

At various periods, the militia system was made obsolete because it was overtaken by technical developments on the battlefield but it seems to have been curiously adept at surviving. After centuries of effective use, it became clear that the *host* armed with pikes and swords was no match for a force of armoured horsemen. But the fortunes of war turned with the advent, early in the 12th century, of the powerful longbow and the discovery that well trained bowmen shooting rapidly at a range of 200 yards could stop those armoured knights thundering down on them – provided the archers kept their nerve. Chain mail, as was demonstrated at Crécy and Agincourt, could not stop an arrow from a longbow nor, at short range, could armour plate, beaten light enough for its wearer to engage in combat; an iron-tipped arrow, striking the armour at the right angle, could penetrate it far enough to be effective. With the general encouragement – amounting in some reigns to compulsion – of archery practice, peasants, tradesmen, indeed most men, could be quickly trained for successful military action in time of national peril and could engage the enemy at a distance,[2] after which armour-clad foot soldiers could move among the fallen cavalry, despatching them.

The introduction of artillery, that expensive and wayward technology that only monarchs could afford in any strength, on the field at Crécy pointed the way of future warfare. But its deployment there was insignificant compared with the deadly practicality of the archers. After many years of development of the new weapon, however, the doctrine evolved that guns emplaced beyond the range of arrows could kill the archers with impunity, as was demonstrated at Formigny in 1450 and Castillon three years later. These large guns and the arrival later of hand-held firearms meant that the militia system fell into desuetude again, because the technology was too complicated for rapidly assembled part-time troops to operate. But the militiamen made a comeback when the weapons became cheaper, lighter and easier to master. The senior, by military precedence, of today's Territorial units dates from this era. The direct ancestor of the Royal Monmouthshire Royal Engineers (Militia) was a group that became a train band in 1577.

Elizabeth I spoke encouragingly to the country's 'milecia' at Tilbury when its members assembled with the rest of the English forces, including noblemen's troops, to meet the invasion threat of the Spanish Armada on 8 August 1588. In lapidary phrases, the Queen told the troops she had no doubt that 'by your obedience to my general, by your concord in the camp and your valour in the field, we shall shortly have a famous victory over the enemies of my God, my Kingdom and my People'.

The Spaniards did not get the chance to invade. In the next reign the militia was Britain's only army. After James I, there followed the upheavals of the Civil War. After the restoration of the monarchy, the Militia, now titled as such and dignified with a capital M, entered the period by which it is usually remembered.

In Scotland, a Militia was created by the Parliament in Edinburgh, the Scotch Estates, through a statute of 1663. It offered to furnish Charles II with 20,000 foot soldiers and 2,000 cavalrymen, all provisioned for 40 days. The force, raised from the counties according to their populations, was to be ready for the king's use. In 1668, the Privy Council decided to pay the Militia for 10 days a year, enabling them to exercise for five days every year, the extra days' pay being to allow for travelling time. Each infantryman would receive six Scottish shillings a day; cavalrymen would get 18 shillings. Ten years later, the Estates approved a proposal by the king that, instead of paying 22,000 for 10 days, it would be better to train the whole force for two days and spend the money saved on training 5,500 of the troops for 32 days. He gave an assurance that if experience revealed that the mass of troops needed more than two days then he would find the money from his own resources to pay them for any extra training. The programme was implemented by the commissioners of Militia in each county. The instructions to the commissioners began:

> His Majesty, taking into consideration the great dangers which threaten his sacred person and government and all his good and faithful subjects, both from foreign and intestine designs, and especially from the hellish plot of Jesuits and Papists and turbulent commotions of seditious people . . .

Following the outbreak of the Seven Years War, Britain had deployed many of its regular forces overseas, so the Militia was reorganised. This was done by the Militia Act of 1757 (30 Geo II); section 70 repealed all previous legislation on the force. Instead of property owners supplying men, horses and arms under a graduated scale (the principle of the General Levy and the 1662 statute) it introduced a system under which counties would be liable to raise quotas of men aged between 18 and 50 on a parish basis. Each county's quota would be chosen by ballot. The men would serve part-time for three years. Another ballot, three years after the first, would bring in a fresh draft in substitution for the first. The total strength demanded for England and Wales was 32,040. As examples of county quotas, Monmouthshire was required to produce 240 and Breconshire 160. A later statute (2 Geo III) set full-time training at 28 days and made the force liable in actual or threatened invasion or rebellion to be embodied for service anywhere in the kingdom.

Because of memories of the 1745 rebellion the 1757 Militia Act did not apply to Scotland. Many Scots, however, thought it should do so, and lobbying took place in an attempt to bring it about. An example of this was the Poker Club, formed in 1762, by a group of private citizens. The name was chosen so as not to antagonise people who opposed the Militia, but to those in the know it implied a stoking of national spirit as a poker stirs a fire.

The Gordon riots of June 1780, instigated by Lord George Gordon led to an unprecedented loss of life and destruction of property in London. Militiamen guarded the Bank of England and clerks there were reduced to melting down pewter inkwells to fabricate musket balls for them when standard ammunition was spent. The example of the HAC and the City's old train bands, as disciplined groups standing for law and order, led to the formation of part-time bands of citizens called armed associations, springing up all over the country, rather like an unofficial Home Guard.

During the wars that followed the French revolution, Britain, again faced with the threat of invasion, raised extra forces. By 1794 French expansionism made Britain increase the Militia. A statute of that year authorised lord lieutenants to raise volunteer companies or individuals for service with the force during its embodiment, on the same conditions as to pay, bounty, clothing and the like as the ordinary Militia (34 Geo III). Meanwhile, in 1793–95, the train bands of London were abolished and their members were formed into six Militia regiments (33 and 35 Geo III). In 1795 too, up to 10 per cent of the Militia were permitted to join the Navy or the Artillery, such transferees being replaced by recruits gathered by beat of drum and receiving 10 guineas bounty (35 Geo III). Two years later the Militia of Scotland was reorganised and that of England and Wales was augmented by a Supplementary Militia (37 Geo III). A proclamation stated:

> Defence against Invasion. The necessity of having on the shortest notice the numbers required, properly armed and clothed, as defence against invasion by France, to leave no doubt that if any attempt should be made, of the contest being brought to a speedy and successful issue, and of the Country being delivered from all the Miseries and Horrors which would arise from the landing of the enemy.

The establishment of the Supplementary Militia was set at 63,878 and the commitment of the men who joined it was for 21 consecutive training days in their own counties at one shilling a day plus allowances for dependants. Two years later it was decided to reduce the Supplementary Militia; voluntary transfer of its men into the Army was encouraged by the offer in 1799 of a 10 guineas bounty. The period of regular service was for five years or duration of war plus six months afterwards, whichever was the longer. An individual county that had attained its quota was permitted to transfer a quarter of its men into the Army. The size of the Militia itself was cut to 76,566 by the offer of transfers into regular units in return for a 10 guineas bounty for service in Europe. Again the limiting factor for each county was a quarter of its quota.

OVERSEAS SERVICE

After the short-lived Peace of Amiens and troop stand-downs, hostilities with France were resumed in 1803; the government had to assemble again the force it had disbanded. Its measures included a statute to raise 50,000 men by ballot, members of the HAC and the Yeomanry being exempt. Another measure passed that year was the Levy en Masse Act, which empowered the authorities to arm and train men aged between 17 and 55. But in areas where Volunteer corps had been formed, or individual Volunteers offered their services, the ballot would be suspended, provided these Volunteers were prepared to serve anywhere in Britain. This brought a big increase in the number of Volunteers – by the end of the year they totalled 380,000.

A constant force, renewing itself every four years, was envisaged by the Local Militia Acts of 1808. The local Militia was distinct from the general

Militia. Under these provisions men from 18 to 30 would be chosen by ballot to serve in the Militia locally for their four-year period. Volunteers would be invited to come forward and the quota set by the legislation would be enforced in every area except those in which voluntary service reached the quota. By 'local' the legislation meant service in the Militiaman's own or a bordering county in the normal course of events. But the exigencies of an invasion or of a large-scale insurrection could mean that his service could legally be extended to any part of Britain where troops might be needed. The local Militia were commanded by regular officers or those from the general Militia.

The increased tempo of the war resulted in a change in the terms of service in 1811: Militiamen could be sent to Ireland and they were allowed to enlist in the Army. By 1812, the local Militia was 214,418 strong. Two years later, Parliament decided that complete regiments or companies of Militia could transfer to the Army. This opened the way to foreign service for Militia units. Some fought with distinction against superior numbers of French in the Iberian Peninsula and earned the approval of the Duke of Wellington, who said so 40 years later in a speech in the Lords on June 15 1852, three days before his Waterloo Day celebrations (Hansard p 730). Victory at Waterloo in 1815 had meant that the force was no longer needed; both it and the general Militia were disembodied and even annual training was discontinued. A year later, both the ballot and voluntary enrolment were suspended by an order in council of 27 June 1816, following a statute passed previously that year (56 Geo III c 38). Subsequent orders were made every year until 1832, after which they were discontinued. The underlying statutory provisions for raising both the general and the local Militia again remained but because of the long period of peace that followed Waterloo they were not invoked.

When the Militia returned, in 1852, it was as a voluntary body, and it remained so in spite of the three main emergencies of the latter half of the 19th century: the Crimean War, the Indian Mutiny and the South African War. In the 1852 reconstitution, the government set the establishment at 80,000 and retained the power to recruit compulsorily by ballot if sufficient numbers of volunteers were not forthcoming. The training commitment was 21 paid days a year. In extreme emergency, the government was enabled to increase the establishment to 120,000 and the commitment to 56 paid days. The oldest documented unit of them all, the Royal Monmouthshire Militia, was retitled the Royal Monmouthshire Light Infantry Militia.

The Militia's revival, as a volunteer force, in 1852 followed a threat of invasion from France, the second of the so-called Three Panics. There it stayed, contributing solidly to the nation's military effort in the Crimean War, the Indian Mutiny, in the wake of which it relieved regular forces needed in the sub-continent, and the South African War, until dismissed in 1908 by the statute that established the Special Reserve (and also the Territorials). Little more than a generation later, the Militia was back in its original compulsory role. In mid-1939 Britain was breathless with preparations for war and in May of that year the formation of a new force called the Militia was established by Parliament. Fit young men were registered and subsequently conscripted into the Militia for six months' military training. Incidentally, Territorials were exempt from the scheme, just as generations of earlier Volunteers who were rated efficient had been exempt from the ballot of compulsion. In fact, those young conscripts of 1939 did not serve long as Militiamen. Well before the members of the first intake were due to be released, the war started and, by a subsequent statute, they were subsumed into the Army proper. Instead of serving six months, they were in uniform for more than six years.

In less egalitarian days than our own, the practice of substitution, under which a person drafted by the ballot could pay someone to do his service meant, once this was taken up on a large scale, that many of the men who formed the Militia should really have been in the Army as professionals. To some extent, therefore, the Militia and the Army were competing for the same recruits. Needless to say, there was no question of substitution in the Militia of 1939.

THE IRISH EXPERIENCE

Part-time soldiering in Ireland evolved through political and religious pressures along different lines from those of the other parts of the United Kingdom. Across the Irish Sea, the prototype of militiamen appeared with the stipulation that those 'undertakers' who had been the beneficiaries of land grants during the plantation of the north of the island in 1608 had to provide stocks of weapons for emergencies. Along with the arms, the undertaker had to provide a body of troops 'which may be reviewed and mustered every half-year, according to the manner of England'. By 1631, the number of such men exceeded 12,000 throughout the ancient province of Ulster, which was larger than what today we know as Northern Ireland. These private arrangements continued and entered a period of rapid voluntary expansion with the advent of the American War of Independence, which had led to depleted garrisons of regular troops, who were needed to fight across the Atlantic. The opportunism of France in entering the war on the side of the colonists also posed a threat to Ireland. Irish Protestants, determined to defend the country, formed their own companies of troops, but these were volunteers rather than compelled men.

In 1793, Westminster passed the Militia Act which set quotas of Militiamen to be raised by each county. The total was 21,660. In that year, the 27th Royal Cork City Regiment was founded from a reorganisation of the Militia of the

County and the City of Cork. According to the *Records of the Royal Longford Militia*:

> The State of Ireland in 1792 was most disturbed, midnight marauding to obtain arms, and local risings etc, openly usurped the freedom of the Government, whilst in 1793 the outbreak of war with France and the Country stripped of regular soldiers though in a state of rebellion, brought about a reorganisation of the Irish Militia to stop the tide of anarchy.

As in England, Wales and Scotland, men of military age were registered on a parish basis and a ballot, taking usually rather less than a quarter of the registered names in the county, under the supervision of the lord lieutenant, determined who should serve. Substitution was allowed, as was paying a fine to postpone service. Nevertheless, as would happen in Scotland four years later, the registration for the ballot resulted in riots. The statute made no distinction between Protestants and Roman Catholics, which was the first formal recognition of equality in the military sphere. Cavalry units too were raised against the threat of a French invasion.

In 1809, the peacetime quota of the Militia in Ireland was set at 30,000, with an additional 15,000 in the event of war (49 Geo III).

After Waterloo, the Militia in Ireland, as in the rest of the United Kingdom, fell into disuse, remaining only in name, each regiment maintaining a tiny staff. The government did not use its powers to expand the force. However, in 1852, renewed fears about France's ambitions led to the reconstitution of the Militia as a voluntary body. In 1854, the 27th Royal Cork City Regiment was converted to a gunner Militia unit as the Royal Cork City Artillery, subsequently it became 3 Brigade of the Southern Ireland Division, RA. The year also saw the raising of the Antrim Militia Artillery, which, during the Crimean War and the aftermath of the Indian Mutiny, was called out to release regulars from garrison duties in Britain and the Mediterranean.

When the South African War started, the Antrim Militia Artillery volunteered for overseas. Following the practice in the rest of the United Kingdom, a composite service company of 158 chosen members was formed for the field. With a similar company from the Donegal Royal Garrison Artillery, they together formed an artillery brigade (what we would describe as an artillery regiment today). The Antrims' first duty in the war was the unexpected one for gunners of taking a draft of Boer prisoners to a camp in remote St Helena.[3]

Northern Ireland was again treated differently from the rest of the United Kingdom when the last Militia statute of all, that of 1939, was passed. The province, by now reduced to the six counties that comprise Northern Ireland today, was excluded from its provisions.

COLENSO 'WAS LOST AT ALDERSHOT'

As far as Britain's reserves in 1904 were concerned, the Norfolk commission's report posed the problem succinctly:

> Each of the five great Powers of Europe has abandoned the once prevalent idea that war is the exclusive business of a limited class, and has subjected its male population to a thorough training either naval or military. Accordingly, each of these nations is today ready to employ in war the greater part of its able-bodied male population between certain ages, under the guidance of a specially trained body of officers and N.C.O.s . . . Each of the great States has also, with a view to war, so organised its material resources, and in particular its means of communication, that they may be fully utilised for naval or military purposes from the very beginning of hostilities.
>
> The consequences of this change, which was undertaken more than thirty years ago, even by those Powers which were the last to adopt it, and has long since been completed, is that in a war against any of them Great Britain would be in one respect at a grave disadvantage. For while her antagonist by previous organisation would be enabled to devote to the struggle the greater part of its resources both in men and in material, Great Britain would not at the beginning have at her disposal in any effective form more than a fraction of her population, and her material resources could be very imperfectly applied. Thus at the present time the organised energy of which Great Britain can dispense for her defence and for that of her Empire is, proportionately, but a fraction of that which a Continental great Power can avail itself.
>
> The number of fully trained men who are available in first line in the event of mobilisation is in France rather more, in Germany slightly less, than two millions. In the United Kingdom, besides the regular Army and the first-class reserve – which together number about 200,000 and which alone have had a training in any way comparable to that given to the millions of France and of Germany – there are only the Auxiliary Forces which, though they number altogether about 380,000, have none of them received anything approaching one year's continuous training.[4]

The commission pointed out that the number of men in France and Germany who had had two or three years', and in a few instances one year's, service in the army was considerably more than three millions. Excluding the war years 1900–02 as extraordinary, the average effective strength of the Militia over the 10 years 1891–99 was 113,554. The total enrolled strength on 1 April 1904 was 93,873. The average effective strength of the Volunteers over the same period was 223,589. The total enrolled strength on 1 April 1904 was 250,226.

HRH the Duke of Connaught, commander of the forces in Ireland and of III Army Corps, said in evidence:

> I do not know what the War Office intend to be the role of the Militia. I have never been officially informed of the role of the Militia beyond being responsible for the 27 days' training; I know nothing more.[5]

The report was scathing about the type of training, the training areas and, in the case of the Militia at depots, the pointlessness of the training. It said:

> To quarter troops upon a manoeuvring ground where they will never fight and exercise them there until they know every yard of it is a violation of every principle of sound training; it is as great a violation to exercise men in larger formations from which few but the staff and senior officers derive much practice, until the company and battalion training has been perfected.[6]

The Duke of Bedford told of his experience: 'If you go to a great military centre you find very little training ground there, and such great competition for it.'

Another Militia commanding officer pointed out: 'I trained at Salisbury Plain in 1902 and a more wicked waste of public money I never saw in my life. I suppose it cost £1,000 to take us down there.'

Colonel Horsley believed he could bring his battalion to a standard fit to oppose foreign troops within a month, but with this caveat: 'You must not go down to Aldershot and do nothing.'

Lord Clifford, who commanded a Volunteer brigade, commented of the average Volunteer: 'If he was only taught on Salisbury Plain I do not think he would be worth much, but if you taught him to fight in the hedges and ditches and cultivated country I believe he would be a very serious obstacle.'

Sir William Butler reinforced these views: 'Neither do I see any necessity for assembling men who are only half trained, and can only be half trained, in large masses in isolated and desert places like Salisbury Plain. You kill recruiting by it.'

From Scotland, Colonel Mackenzie brought further information: 'At Stobs this year we were too crowded and there was no room practically to allow the Volunteers to train by themselves . . . the General wished to have all the troops under his eye there.'

Captain Turner Lee, on his return from active service in South Africa, told of his experience:

> The last time I was at Aldershot . . . I had to walk up and down a road and imagine that I was an advanced guard, and that both sides were shut in; the men could not understand that they were supposed to be in the woods on either side of the road, and you would never have marched up that road with an advanced guard to attack a picket at the top. The whole thing was stupid.

Sir William Butler's opinion was:

> Take Aldershot. Does any man mean to say that Colenso was lost on the Tugela? It was lost at Aldershot; let us face it. Magersfontein was elaborately prepared for on the Fox Hills. I will go further. Colonel Long's eleven guns were lost in the Long Valley, and Colenso was disastrously rehearsed for twenty years on the banks of the Basingstoke Canal.

Worse was to come. The old-time training of the Militia was praised in contrast with the contemporary course. Formerly, the recruit was usually trained at his battalion headquarters under the preliminary drill system, for periods of 49 days, afterwards increased to 56, and later in the few cases where it was continued, to 63, which included a special course on musketry or gunnery. On its termination, the recruit passed directly into his battalion to receive 27 days' battalion training. This made a total of 90 consecutive days' training in his first year. All COs spoke highly of the system. (German recruit training lasted 112 days, after which a recruit was posted into battalion.)

But in the contemporary Militia a system of drill on enlistment was established. A recruit could enlist at any time of year. The bona fide Militia recruit who elected to attend preliminary drill, if any was held at his unit, received no inducement, in contrast to:

> the unemployed wastrel who only wants to be fed and drilled for a few weeks in order to come up to the line standard – the line being his ultimate destination, makes what is in truth a fraudulent enlistment into the Militia, often under the advice of the Depot Staff; at the end of 49 days he gets a special bounty of 10s. and if he enlists into the Regular Army he can anticipate this bounty by a week. Meanwhile his pay, his rations, his bounty, his clothing and those of the Regular sergeants who drill him, are all debited to the Militia and go to swell the average cost per head of the Militia as prepared for the edification of the public, and the only contribution of such men to the force to which they fraudulently and by connivance belong is that the real Militia is left to wear out their soiled clothing.
>
> There is, however, another class of Militia recruit who joins these depots for instruction, he does so either to see how he likes soldiering or because he really intends to remain in the Militia, but cannot help going there and the treatment which he receives demands consideration. Charges have been made before us that he is often unfairly treated at these places, that he is put on an undue proportion of fatigues, that his drill is neglected, and that he is partly teased and partly bullied into joining the line. These charges have also been strongly and categorically denied, but the weight of evidence goes to show that in many cases they are far from unfounded, and that so far as that is so a grave abuse exists. Colonel Fryer says: 'Young men who join the

Militia when they go to the depot are rather looked down upon, they are called "half-soldiers" and the consequence is that they go straight through to the line. They are rather laughed out of being Militiamen, I gather . . . Of course it is only in very few cases that that [extra fatigues] does happen, and it gets about and does harm; I have served at the depot myself.'

Colonel North speaks even more strongly: 'The great idea of everybody at the depot is to get the Militiaman to enlist in the line and very often they give them a very hot time, and although lots of people deny it, it is a very well-known thing.'

Lord Algernon Percy's evidence is: 'They are looked down upon by the line recruits . . . their whole uniform and everything else is different . . . they are nobody's child and very often they are absolutely uninstructed.'

In Colonel Courtenay's opinion: 'The Militiaman at the depot does not get looked after as he ought to be.'

Colonel Cooke-Collis' evidence is very decided: 'They get really no training, if a recruit says he intends to stay in the Militia he does coal fatigue and nothing else . . . here is a note from a man at a depot, he says, "Unless the recruit says he is going to join the line, he leads a dog's life and learns nothing". That is in plain language what I think is the general opinion.'

Colonel Legard expresses the belief that: 'The real secret at the bottom of that system [is] to enable the Army to get recruits out of the Militia.'

All of the last four witnesses quoted were members of the Militia Advisory Board.[7]

LOSING ITS ROLE

The Militia, the constitutional force, had done well for the country over the centuries. As we have seen, for many years it was Britain's only land defence force. In 1588 it stood ready at Tilbury. In the more recent eras, for instance on 23 February 1797, it helped to defeat an invasion of Wales. To be sure, it was a half-hearted invasion, consisting of only about 1,200 Frenchmen who landed at Fishguard. But Militiamen from Pembrokeshire and bordering counties with the local part-time cavalry, the Castlemartin Yeomanry Troop of the Pembrokeshire Yeomanry, and led by Lord Cawdor of Stacpole so frightened the invaders, who for the most part had split into small groups, that they surrendered at Goodwick Sands without loss of life.

In 1811 the Duke of York, Commander-in-Chief, described the Militia as 'a never failing resource on every occasion of difficulty and danger'. Lord Castlereagh, Secretary of State for Foreign Affairs, in referring in the Commons on 13 November 1813 to the 100,000 Militiamen who fought in the Peninsula said:

> We could not have kept possession of Portugal, or have sent forces to co-operate in the deliverance of the Peninsula at large, and taken up that menacing position on the frontiers of France which our Army now occupies; we should have been shut up within the bounds of our insular policy, and could not have set that glorious example to other nations, or borne our share in the general exertions which have been made for the deliverance of Europe. Parliament ought always, therefore, to bear in recollection that it is to the Militia we owe the character we at present enjoy in Military Europe, and that without the Militia we could not have shown that face which we have done in the Peninsula.

But the problem of the Militia as it stood at the turn of the century was that it was disintegrating and was losing its role. Admittedly it had supplied 1,691 officers and 43,875 men forming 60 complete Militia battalions actually in the South African theatre; and this was in addition to 10 battalions of Militia who manned garrisons in Egypt, the Mediterranean stations and other bases. Besides these, some 14,000 Militia reservists served in their parent line regiments in the war zone; and finally there were embodied Militiamen serving at home (and this was all achieved out of a total Militia strength of 109,551 of all ranks in 1899). But the policy of enabling Militia officers to gain regular commissions and the offer of bounties to men who transferred to the Army had resulted in the departure of the best soldiers. The situation had been aggravated by the formation of the Militia Reserve in 1867; despite its name, this was a reserve not for the Militia but for the regular Army. It consisted of Militiamen who undertook to serve in the Army in the event of war; in return they received an annual bounty of £1. All these factors converted the Militia into a sort of depot which supplied personnel for the line regiments.

Commanding officers were remote figures who usually saw their men once a year; at other times, as the Norfolk commission pointed out, they entered the headquarters on sufferance of their own adjutants. COs had no control over promotion of deserving men, and if they visited the depot, they were expected to do little more than to arrive in plain clothes and have luncheon. Additionally, as Militia officers were no longer supplied exclusively from the unit's county, the local character had disappeared. As far back as the Crimean War, some 50 Militia battalions had volunteered for the theatre and some battalions were on garrison duties in Gibraltar and elsewhere in the Mediterranean. The original concept of the Militia as a home defence force had vanished. The ineptly titled Militia Reserve (see above) was abolished in April 1901 and two years later a genuine reserve for the Militia was founded.

Even such a senior figure as the Duke of Connaught, commander of the forces in Ireland and of III Army Corps (who had been a strong candidate for the post of commander-in-chief of the British Army, on the recommendation of his mother, Queen Victoria) admitted in his evidence to the Norfolk commission on the auxiliary forces that he was unaware of the exact functions of the Militia. The commission's impression that the officers were insufficiently trained and that the force was completely unorganised for war made inevitable the conclusion that it was unfit to take the field in the defence of Britain.

The problem was: should the Militia move closer to the regular Army or should it be put into the second line with the soon-to-be-formed Territorial Force? At a conference of Militia commanding officers held in July 1906 and attended by Haldane, the officers made clear their determination that the Militia should not become what we understand today as Territorials. Haldane decided to change its character and make it a true reserve for the regular Army; he conceded that existing units should preserve their identity in the new force, to be called the Special Reserve. Of the 124 Militia battalions, 101 were retained, the 23 others being disbanded. Of the 101 survivors, 70 amalgamated with the existing depots of line regiments and, Haldane said in a memorandum on the Army Estimates for 1908–09, 'will drill both Line and Special Reserve recruits, four will form a depot for Special Reserves of Rifle Regiments, and 27 will form Extra Reserve battalions'. These Extra Reserve battalions were from well recruited regiments that already possessed a Special Reserve battalion.

The establishment for the Special Reserve was 80,300. Recruiting began on 16 January 1908; and by New Year's Eve of that year it had attracted 67,740 members.

And so the story of the old constitutional force is nearly ended, apart from the need to note the terminal service of a few hundred men from the Militia and even fewer from the Militia Reserve who declined to join the Special Reserve but who served on until the run-out of their engagements. The force's long history can best be summed up in the irresistible phrase of Colonel GJ Hay at the turn of the century: 'The equipment of the people's force throughout nearly 20 centuries seems to have been divided into the skin, iron, leather and cloth ages.'[8] Bearing in mind the return of the Militia in mid-1939, perhaps one may add that there was to follow the oilskin and rubber age (for protection against poison gas); and now, half a century beyond that, soldiers find themselves in the plastic and impregnated charcoal age.

3

The Volunteers

Let your reforms for a moment go!
Look to your butts and take good aims!
Better a rotten borough or so
Than a rotten fleet and a city in flames!
Storm, Storm. Riflemen form!

Ready, be ready against the storm!
Riflemen, Riflemen, Riflemen form!

ALFRED LORD TENNYSON,
Riflemen Form, 1859

The Volunteers are junior to the Militia in historical terms, but there is documentary evidence as far back as 1537 that the voluntary military movement was developing independently. First London, it seems, and then other cities had from early times at their disposal trained groups of military enthusiasts, known as train companies, train bands, trainbands or trained bands, who volunteered to make themselves proficient enough to defend their localities. The Honourable Artillery Company, for instance, has a charter granted by Henry VIII to its ancestor the 'Fraternitie or Guylde of Saint George' granting a licence to successive 'Maisters Rulers Cominaltie and Brethern of the saide Fraternitie or Guylde' for the 'better encrease of the defence of this o[r] Realme and Maynetennce of the Science & Feate of Shoting in Longbowes Crosbowes and Handgonnes'. The document refers to the 'Maisters and Rulers of the saide science of Artillary' being 'rehersed for Longbowes Crosbowes and Handgonnes'.

That was sealed on 25 August 1537, which makes the HAC senior in date of formation as an identifiable unit to every other regiment in the Army, regular or part-time, and perhaps to every regiment in the world. The word artillery in those days was applied to any missile, including arrows and small arms. It is mentioned in the Old Testament, where the Authorised Version in the English of James I refers in the first book of Samuel (xx: 40) to Jonathan, who after releasing arrows as a prearranged signal to be understood by David, who is hiding from Saul, hands his 'artillery unto his lad', a servant. Both the Revised

Version and the Revised English Bible, in referring to the bow and arrows, translate the original Hebrew word as 'weapons' in that context, though it has a more general meaning as 'instruments'.

The HAC's bows have long since been discarded but it is still 'rehersed' in hand guns though today it relies on more powerful weapons. There is a school of thought that maintains that the HAC's ancestor, the Guild of St George, must have been in existence before the granting of the charter, which merely regularised rather than inaugurated the guild, and this is probable. But on the evidence, we can say with certainty that today's HAC is a unit whose direct ancestor was in existence in 1537. The name has altered – in fact through the centuries it has had at least 27 names, including the Societie of Citizens of London practizinge Arms and military discipline, London's Hopefull Infantrie, and the Martiall Company exercising Arms in the Artillery Ground. Time and again it will be necessary to refer to 1537 as the known starting point of voluntary part-time service. The HAC was the model on which other volunteer service forces were based. Furthermore, it has traditionally provided officers for other forces. The historian of London, John Stow, writing in the 16th century, tells us that there were members of the Artillery Garden and of the Artillery Company who were appointed officers in command of the feverishly assembled units in Elizabeth's famous military camp at Tilbury, where they gathered to defend England against the threatened Armada invasion in 1588[1]. There is a close link between today's HAC and the Ancient and Honorable Artillery Company of Boston, Massachusetts which, as the Military Company of the Massachusetts, was copied from the HAC when the latter entered its second century of chartered existence[2]. In Britain, a similar unit was set up in Colchester in 1621, with other boroughs, including Bury St Edmunds, Bristol and Chester, following.

The HAC does not have the field of ancient lineage to itself. Another unit prominent in the Army's order of battle today is the Royal Monmouthshire Royal Engineers (Militia), which celebrated its 400th birthday in 1977. Its members are prepared to take on the HAC and argue all night over which is the older directly descended regiment. The argument stems from the fact that although the HAC has earlier documentation, the Monmouthshire Engineers, which have been a unit of the Royal Engineers for well over a century, appear before the HAC in *The Army List*. This is because prominent members of the latter fought for Parliament in the Civil War; in one engagement, troops commanded by an HAC member drove off the Royalist forces of Prince Rupert, Count Palatine of the Rhine, at Windsor. Again, there were HAC members among the train bands that deployed at Turnham Green to defend London from threatened Royalist attack. Interestingly, Rupert joined the HAC in 1664, after the Restoration. His signature is in the possession of the HAC. Another valuable document is a company warning order of 1682 which states:

SIR,

It is ordered, that on *Tuesday* the 5th of this instant *September*, 1682, the *Artillery-Company* shall perform an Exercise at Arms at *Baumes* or the fieldes leading to it. You are therefore earnestly desired to make your appearance in the *Artillery-Ground*, by Nine of the Clock on the day aforesaid precisely, in your compleatest Arms and Habit, with Red Feather. Pray fail not, as you value your own Honour and the interest of the Society.

You are desired to be punctual at the time, because the Company entends to March early.

Those Gentlemen that on that day handle Muskets, are desired to take care that their Arms are clean and well fixt, and that they bring with them fine dry Powder and even Match.

William Pemberton, Beadle

The voluntary train bands of Edinburgh appear to date from the closing years of the 16th century. The certain documentation includes the minute book of the captains of 'the toun's traine bands', which begins in 1676[3]. It seems that from time to time the town council elected 16 citizen representatives of the merchants and craftsmen each to be a captain of a company of the regiment. Every captain had under him a lieutenant, an ensign and two sergeants. Every year the captains elected two of themselves for higher office: one to be the commandant (later called the moderator) and the other to be the clerk. The bands were established on military lines though they seem to have been used as associations more concerned with watch duties than with guarding the capital from a foreign enemy. We have evidence from City of London livery companies of payments being made for the train bands of their locality. Among the requirements to be held for these bands were stocks of powder, shot and bows and arrows – *matériel* designed to use in the field against an invader rather than to police the city.

VOLUNTEERS MIXED WITH MILITIA

Volunteers joined Militia units and for a number of years there were tangled relationships between the two types of part-time soldiers. A statute of 1758 allowed Militia units to have Volunteers operating with them on active service. The captain of a Militia company could recruit such Volunteers provided the lord lieutenant gave his consent and the individual reached an acceptable standard of training and discipline and was ready to provide himself with the correct weapons, equipment and uniform. The practice continued and during the American War of Independence, commanding officers of Militia regiments were permitted to recruit men to form into Volunteer companies with their own identity within the units. Lord lieutenants were allowed to grant commissions to qualified Volunteers to lead these companies. Such Volunteers qualified for Militia weapon and uniform allowances. In such mixed units the dominance of the Militia was guaranteed by the regulation that the total of Volunteers in a battalion must not exceed the strength of any one company in the battalion.

In 1780 lord lieutenants were empowered to accept for Crown service independently raised companies of Volunteers, to incorporate them within the county regiment and to give commissions so that they could have their own officers. But they were still subject to Militia discipline and allowances and could be stood down or reduced according to the demands made on the Militia. Soon the popularity of the Volunteers and the difference in outlook and social standing between the men who were serving because they were compelled to do so, or because they were being hired as substitutes for those balloted, and those who had volunteered for the role led to official recognition of the need for separate part-time forces. This need was seen to transcend the benefit of economies inherent in a shared infrastructure.

Parliament passed the first of the Volunteer acts in 1782, and many corps were formed. The statute gave the right to regular Army levels of pay for Volunteer companies on active service in national defence or against rebellion. They were, of course, subject to military discipline while on such service and an indication of the independent standing of the Volunteers, as distinct from the Militia, is seen in the provision that when a Volunteer appeared before a court martial, the court should consist solely of Volunteer officers if this were operationally possible. The Volunteers were thus recognised officially as separate but the advance was of short duration. The statute was for 'the present war' and peace meant that the independent corps had to be disbanded in 1783.

However, the Revolutionary wars with France again brought the threat of invasion. In 1793 the situation was serious and the Volunteer Act of 1794 resurrected the corps. In the haste and uncertainty, powers already contained in a statute of 1779, by which lord lieutenants could raise companies of Volunteers in the Militia, were re-enacted. Within weeks, a new statute (34 Geo III c 31) set up an organised Volunteer force. This could legally be embodied if invasion was considered imminent. Internally, it could be embodied to deal not just with rebellion but against riots. The majority of corps formed were infantry but volunteer horsemen came forward too and they became known as the Yeomanry Volunteer Cavalry. Bona fide membership of a Volunteer unit gave exemption from Militia obligations. The Queen's Westminster Volunteers date from this period, when they were founded by Lord Grosvenor. In the City, which had long been used to having part-time volunteers, the units were raised on a ward basis. The ward is a tiny area, usually of a few streets. An example is provided by the formation of the Broad Street

Volunteers through the initiative of Alderman Richard Clarke in November 1797. The volunteering founder members gave their services free and agreed that they should themselves 'provide clothes, arms and accoutrements at their individual expense and serve within the City of London only, unless by their own consent'.[4]

In 1798, groups of another type, sometimes called armed associations, were established to undertake the role of anti-invasion saboteurs. They were extremely local groups led by a landed proprietor of the neighbourhood and chosen for their work skills. For instance, there would be boatmen, blacksmiths, horsemen, and builders, parish parties who knew their neighbourhood and could demolish bridges, make off with boats or horses to deny them to the enemy, block roads and so on, anything to impede the invaders. The government provided them with weapons and equipment but those volunteering had to supply their own uniforms, unless the parish or a public appeal could do so. Men who were members of one of these associations were exempted from the Militia ballot.

The Peace of Amiens, the definitive treaty of which was signed in March 1802, had brought a hope of peace when the preliminary articles were signed in October 1801 and units were disbanded. But in June 1802, the Yeomanry and Volunteer Act gave the government powers to accept service offers from Yeomanry and Volunteer units; this time there was no duration-of-war limit. Fighting restarted in May 1803 and the Crown began recruiting again from the forces it had disbanded. Three statutes were quickly passed: the Defence Act, which gave the king power to order lord lieutenants to appoint officers who could instruct volunteering citizens; the second had as its aim the creation of a reserve army of 50,000 by ballot (with effective members of the HAC, the Yeomanry and the Volunteers being exempt); the third, the Levy en Masse Act, was what today we would recognise as compulsory enrolment in the Home Guard. The intendment of this third statute was to train the male population aged between 17 and 55. It was a drastic measure but it remained unused, the reason being a clause providing that the act would not come into effect in areas where enough Volunteers willing to serve anywhere in the kingdom came forward. All over the country, the response was enthusiastic: by December, some 380,000 Volunteers were in uniform, and by 1804 there were 479,000. One unit, founded on 5 September 1803, was the Duke of Cumberland's Sharpshooters. They must be mentioned because they were one of the few units to survive (they did so as a rifle club with royal patronage) when the peace brought about by Waterloo led to the decline of the Volunteer corps. Typical of the military gestures of 1804 was a grand review of troops at Glasgow Green in the autumn. The Militia and Volunteers and the Glasgow Light Horse paraded after regular units.

The total of part-time soldiers dropped and James Wilson's *Roll of the*

Volunteer Army, published in 1806, showed that in the preceding year there were 328,956 infantry Volunteers, 31,771 cavalry and 10,131 gunners.

VOLUNTEERS DISBANDED, YEOMANRY SURVIVES

The initial victory over Napoleon brought an end to fears of invasion, and most of the foot corps were disbanded (the HAC, here as in many aspects of volunteer soldiering, was treated as an exception). Other units that survived included the Duke of Cumberland's Sharpshooters and corps in Exeter and Essex; like the Sharpshooters, they did so by becoming rifle clubs. The government viewed the Yeomanry, raised, supported and commanded on a county basis, in a different light from that of the Volunteers. The comfortably situated mounted troops, usually formed around the great landed estates, were seen as important for internal security, so they were retained, although in progressively reduced strength.

A period of social unrest occurred in 1820 when the Radical Rising brought the fear of revolution to Glasgow. Troops were used to quell disturbances in the city. A military review at Glasgow Green included local troops represented by the Glasgow Light Horse and the Glasgow Sharpshooters as well as regular units.

Although the victory at Waterloo had brought about a long period of peace there were invasion scares in the middle of the 19th century, one more serious than the others. Richard Cobden described in his *The Three Panics*, published in 1862, the alarm felt by the public in the 1840s and the 1850s. The first was in 1848 when fears about Britain's inadequate defences arose after a letter from the Duke of Wellington to Sir John Burgoyne advocating the immediate raising of 150,000 Militiamen for coastal defence was unintentionally published. Renewed apprehension of a French invasion arose in December 1851. The traditional fears of French intentions were increased when Napoleon's nephew became president of France following a *coup d'état*. The 1st Devonshire Volunteers were raised and the government accepted their services in 1852.

The year also saw the reintroduction of the Militia in England and Wales. This time, instead of being a compulsory force augmented by some men who gave voluntary service, it was a wholly voluntary body (though with the power (15 and 16 Vict) to recruit by ballot if sufficient volunteers did not come forward) with an initial establishment of 80,000 men. They would be expected to complete 21 days' paid training a year. These numbers could both be increased if necessary, the establishment to 120,000 in extreme emergency and the training extended to 56 days a year. In 1854, the Crimean War, in which France was one of Britain's allies, pushed apprehension about French ambitions into the background; nevertheless statutes (17 and 18 Vict) set up voluntary militias in Scotland and Ireland. But the third and most serious panic emerged in 1859 with a revived fear of invasion by another Emperor Napoleon. Lord lieutenants of counties were sent a letter dated 12 May by the Secretary of State for War permitting the raising of part-time voluntary forces under the 1804 statute (44 Geo III c 54) which had authorised the formation of voluntary forces against that earlier Napoleon. But the difference between the 1804 force and that of 1859 was that now the government envisaged the Volunteers as a cheap form of defence. Nevertheless, this was not how those volunteering saw it; they responded by the tens of thousands. This was when the Volunteer movement really took root, as an auxiliary to the Army and the Militia. Artillery Volunteers would be responsible for operating coastal batteries. Rifle Volunteers would be tasked with skirmishing against the enemy's regular forces. Engineers Volunteers were raised too, rapidly in Middlesex (the county was almost as quick in forming engineers as it was with rifle units, of which it raised a prodigious number) and Lanarkshire. The 1st Edinburgh Engineers Volunteers were raised the following year and, four years later, the 1st and 2nd Lancashire Engineers Volunteers and the Newcastle-on-Tyne Engineers Volunteers were formed.

At the beginning of 1859, the Duke of Cambridge, Commander-in-Chief, had pointed out in a Memorandum on Volunteer Organisation to the Secretary of State for War that to be efficient a Volunteer force 'must be subject, as far as practicable, to military discipline . . . at the same time there cannot be a doubt that the service should be made as little irksome to the men as possible'. The simplest way to achieve this was:

1 To make the lord lieutenants of Counties responsible to those persons who propose to raise such regiments, or companies of Volunteers.

2 To make Officers who command such regiments or companies responsible for the men they enrol in each corps.

3 To oblige all the men to take an Oath of Allegiance by which they would further bind themselves to be forthcoming on their services being required, and to obey the orders of their superiors when called out for duty.

4 To arm the force with some accoutrement from Government stores, or should they arm themselves, with the same class of weapons and more especially with regard to rifles of the same calibre.

'WITHOUT ANY COST TO THE PUBLIC'

When the Secretary of State for War issued a circular letter on 12 May 1859 to lord lieutenants authorising them to form rifle corps under the 1804 act, the government's permission to establish the corps was subject to a number of conditions. Not the least of these was that corps members must provide their own arms, uniforms and equipment and meet all expenses themselves except when on active service. Although the letter purported to be based on the 1804 act, which had not been repealed, the important condition about the corps being self-supporting was novel. A circular of 25 May outlined the scope and duties of the new corps, which were modest enough. Skill in handling a rifle and discipline modelled on that of the Army were sufficient; the corps were not to be organised like the Army – for instance, the largest formation would be a company (this was later withdrawn) – or to drill like regular soldiers. The government would provide ammunition and targets at cost price. The War Office sought to explain its parsimony in a somewhat fanciful further circular of 13 July. It regarded members of the corps as holding in civilian life 'important and often lucrative occupations' and pointed out that it understood the essence of a Volunteer force to be a willingness of its members 'to bear, without any cost to the public, the whole charges of their training and practice'. Having said this, it added that the government would supply 25 per cent of the total number of Enfield rifles needed by individual corps on condition that each corps would provide a place of safe custody and a storeman for them.

The system of raising corps was that public meetings would be held in cities or neighbourhoods and if decisions to form them were made, committees would be set up and a nominal roll of potential Volunteers would be prepared. This would be sent to the lord lieutenant, who, if he approved, would forward the request to the War Office. If accepted, the committee would be informed of the numbers authorised for the corps and would be given its precedence. The most senior corps was later established as that of Devon, which had survived from the days of the old Volunteers.

Whether or not the government considered that the HAC, the oldest of all units, sufficient in itself to cover the City of London we are not aware. All we know is that the City was not included in the circular letters. Consequently, it was not until 21 July that the lord mayor called a public meeting in Guildhall in response to a request by 152 representatives of business houses. The request for the meeting 'sharing in the unanimous determination of the Government and people of this country to maintain a strict neutrality during the present Continental complications', called for the 'establishment of a comprehensive and efficient Volunteer Rifle Brigade in the Metropolis'. The meeting decided in favour of the force, the lord mayor approved, forwarded the application to the War Office and the London Rifle Brigade was duly formed.

Under the brigade's constitution, the lord mayor for the time being was to be president; he would preside over a council of three field officers and nine others not on the effective strength of the regiment. This council would control everything 'not appertaining to military affairs'.

The title London Rifle Brigade was an unusual one compared to those of other corps rapidly forming around the country. And the War Office had something to say in the matter. A letter of 28 October stated:

> If the Corps now numbers 180 men the title 'London Rifle Volunteer Brigade' will be allowed at once. But the designation of a Brigade is only allowed to a Corps of more than one Battalion, and it is given in this instance on the distinct understanding that every endeavour will be made to enrol a thousand members. As soon as this number has been attained the establishment of officers will be 1 Colonel Commandant, 2 Lieut-Colonels, 2 Majors, 16 Captains, 16 Lieutenants, 18 Ensigns, 2 Adjutants, 1 Surgeon, 2 Assistant-Surgeons.

It concluded that the City was 49th in the Rifle Volunteer Force of Great Britain and that the brigade would rank as the first division of the force in the City. The LRB took as its motto *Primus in urbe*. It will be remembered that the HAC, although far more senior, stood aloof from the Volunteer Force, and so did not figure in the numbering. Years later the LRB, although retaining the *Primus* in its motto, lost its seniority to the Royal Fusiliers Volunteer battalions on the formation of the London Regiment; the first four battalions of Londons were provided by the Royal Fusiliers and their 2nd Battalion took as their jaunty nickname the Second to Nondons. The LRB was thus positioned fifth in the City, and the new sequence of seniority caused a bitterness among the LRB that apparently took years to overcome.

By autumn, the War Office was ready to give more help to the Volunteers. A circular to lord lieutenants of all counties in Britain stated:

> *War Office*
> *October 14th, 1859*
>
> My Lords,
>
> I have the honour to inform you that Her Majesty's Government have decided to issue immediately to Rifle Volunteer Corps an additional supply of long Enfield Rifles (pattern 1853) to the extent of 25% of the effective strength of the Corps. This supply will raise the aggregate issue to 50% in the effective strength of the force. I have to request that you will be good enough to communicate this decision of the Government to the Commanding Officers of the various Corps in your County, who should at once forward the prescribed request to this office for such portion of the supply as they may be entitled to under the regulations. At a later period I shall be prepared to issue a further instalment of arms of the same pattern as now granted.

I have the honour to be, My Lord,
Your obedient servant,
Sidney Herbert.

The HAC continued to go its own way and to behave as though the new units did not exist. For instance, in 1859 the LRB had the men, the command structure and the enthusiasm; what it did not have were drill halls or a range. An approach to the HAC for permission to use part of its land was rejected – though the HAC was willing to absorb the new body into its own ranks. (Applications from the LRB and several other City units for the use of HAC facilities continued to be made up to the 1880s but all were rejected). The LRB decided to create a range near the Crystal Palace and at the same time the regiment's council considered a move to have a national committee for organising an annual countrywide shooting competition. Lord Elcho offered his services and this was the start of the National Rifle Association.

THE GREAT RUSH

In 1859 the moment of recruiting was, perhaps, perfect: perception of a patriotic role against foreign aggression, the romantic age in literature had passed about a generation earlier but there was renewed interest in Arthurian legend of military daring in a noble cause; there were shorter working hours, the appeal of empire and the urgent Victorian dream of self-improvement. Perhaps Tennyson's poem, *Riflemen Form*, first published in *The Times* of 9 May in that year, caught the imagination. Credit must also go to Hans Busk. Captain Busk was a member of the Queen Victoria's Rifles, a Volunteer unit that had been formed on 5 September 1803 as the Duke of Cumberland's Sharpshooters which, as we know, had in practice, if not in title and establishment, survived the 1814 disbandments by carrying on simply as a rifle club. In 1835 it became the Royal Victoria Rifle Club. In the panic of 1852, civilian volunteering was looked on with government favour and the Club was officially recognised as the Victoria Rifles 1st Middlesex Rifle Volunteers in 1853. It had its own premises, a parade ground and range facilities. Busk had published the first edition of his manual, *The Rifle and How to Use It*, in 1857. He had named France as the enemy and in 1859 he published another book, *The Navies of the World*, which showed among other things the growing strength of the French navy. Busk travelled thousands of miles throughout Britain lecturing on the need for defence, and had the satisfaction of seeing Volunteer corps established in the towns at which he spoke. The Volunteers made part-time soldiering into a national movement. There were assertions that Busk was the father of the Volunteers, but others staked their claims, so much so that *The Times* published a leader on the subject in 1867:

> *The Origin of the Volunteer Movement.–*
>
> Several persons are vehemently contending for the honour of having taken the initiative in a movement which has had so signal a success as to have produced a costless disciplined army of 150,000 marksmen. We have been appealed to, and names we have never heard of have been placed before us, as deserving of public gratitude on this account. Of course no individual can have any claim to the merit of having originated this great work. It arose out of the circumstances and exigencies of the day, and it sprang from a unanimous feeling of the necessity of preparing for defence. Hans Busk was, as we know, for some time alone in pressing the subject upon the public notice, and to him, if to anybody, credit is due for having laboriously aided at the birth of the institution. The Volunteer army, however, is not an invention, and no one has a right to patent it.

CHOOSING A CORPS

The county or borough played their traditional roles in providing the basic administrative foundation for recruiting, but many Volunteer units based their appeal on members' jobs, social inclinations, ethnic origins, educational background or even attitude to alcohol. Did you work for the Civil Service or perhaps a bank? – You could join a Civil Service Corps or a Bankers' Corps respectively. Were you a barrister, or a railway worker? – You could join the Inns of Court Corps (recruited not only from the four London inns but also from King's Inn in Dublin and from among Scots advocates), or a Railway Corps respectively. Were you a Scots solicitor, or a Freemason? – You could join the Writers to the Signet, or a Freemasons' Corps respectively. There were Public School Corps and there were the Oxford University Rifles. A few years later there would be a corps formed almost entirely from printers; it was raised at the works of Eyre & Spottiswoode. The War Office had given permission for corps to be raised on a friendly society basis, so there were various friendly society corps. There were corps formed by teetotal groups. Several corps were formed in the working class district of Tower Hamlets; others were formed from the wealthy people working in the City.

An example of a borough corps is provided by the Queen's Westminster Volunteers. The corps had been raised in the previous century in response to the threat of invasion by France but was disbanded after Waterloo. In 1859 it was reconstituted by Hugh Lupus, Earl Grosvenor (later Duke of

Westminster). He commanded it for 22 years and thereafter was honorary colonel.

Leeds provides us with a typical proud provincial city corps. It was titled the 7th Yorkshire(West Riding) Corps when it was founded in 1859, but quickly became known as the Leeds Rifles. The corps was heavily recruited, became in 1908 a part of the TF and was an important focus for recruiting and fighting during the First World War. The descendant unit is training today.

An 1859 corps that had no geographical boundary but offered community of race was the London Irish Corps, which attracted some famous members. At its inaugural meeting in December 1859, the Marquess of Donegall took the chair, and an early but hardly realistic recruit was the Prime Minister, Palmerston, then busily engaged in his second administration and in his 76th year. The London Irish would always be a well recruited corps – about twice the strength of most other London units (this is in line with today's situation, where Northern Ireland TA units are, per head of population, nearly twice as well recruited as the TA in the rest of the United Kingdom). The London Irish's members would also prove ready volunteers for any action that was going, such as helping against the Fenians; furthermore, the savage test of the First World War would reveal that it had a fighting spirit second to none. Liverpool too had its Irish Corps.

For workers who knew their place in life, there were Artisans' Corps; for those individualists who did not recognise any such constraint, there was in London an Artists' Corps (and it attracted some celebrated names whose works would fetch huge sums; these artists included John (later Sir John) Millais, Frederick (later Lord) Leighton, Edward (later Sir Edward) Burne-Jones and the sculptor G W Watts). One unlikely corps was formed from part-time students intent on improving themselves by study and already committed to spending much of their spare time at evening classes.

The Working Men's College Corps, founded by Thomas Hughes, author of *Tom Brown's Schooldays*, the archetypal book on public school life, comprised three companies recruited from students and staff at the Working Men's College. It will be worth our while to spend some time on it to show how, in a movement in which the government and the military authorities seemed to assume that most members were comfortably placed, a corps comprising men of modest means developed. The inaugural meeting took place in the college coffee room and Hughes's was the first signature on a document petitioning for permission to raise a corps. They were so quickly off the mark that they applied to the lord lieutenant of Middlesex before the county authorities had shown themselves prepared to set up a scheme. Hughes received this cool reply:

Privy Council Offices, May 20th, 1859

Sir,– I am directed to acknowledge the receipt of your letter addressed to the Marquess of Salisbury as Lord-Lieutenant of the County of Middlesex offering your services in the formation of a Volunteer Rifle Corps among the Working Men's College, and informing his Lordship that you have a list of more than sixty names of those ready to join.

As no arrangements have been made for the formation of Rifle Corps in the County of Middlesex I have only to inform you that a note has been taken of your application.

I have the honour to be, Sir
Your obedient Servant
W. Franks

Considering that their hours of labour were longer than is customary today and that public transport was slower then, those men must have been truly inspired by the work ethic. We may wonder how they found the energy to be part-time soldiers as well as part-time students after the day's toil. Hughes, founder of the college, later became principal; he was captain commandant of the corps and when it expanded to 10 companies, he handed command to a regular soldier. Hughes went on to become a major and then to command the unit as a lieutenant colonel. On retiring he became honorary colonel. Sometimes training upset the study schedule and there were complaints from non-military students about noise. But unpromising though the arrangement of working men trying to improve themselves in their spare time and yet training to defend the country was, both the college and the descendant unit of its corps are functioning strongly today. The college has moved from Bloomsbury to Crowndale Road, near St Pancras, and the corps, which officially started life in the order of battle as the 19th Middlesex Rifle Volunteers of Great Britain, moved to Queen Street, then to the Apollonicon Hall, St Martin's Lane, to 33 Fitzroy Square, to Handel Street, near the British Museum, and finally to Balham High Road, south of the Thames. Its direct descendant, C(City of London Fusiliers) Company of the London Regiment, still trains every week at Fusilier House, Balham.

The line of descent is through the 1st Volunteer Battalion of the Royal Fusiliers of later Victorian times, to the 1st(City of London) Battalion of the London Regiment(Royal Fusiliers), which was created with the new-born TF and which fought in the First World War; through the disappearance of the original London Regiment in 1936–37 and the reemergence of the original battalion in the 8th Battalion of the Royal Fusiliers and then its 1939 offshoot, and the 624th Light AA Regiment, RA(Royal Fusiliers); through the postwar City of London Battalion of the Royal Fusiliers, which was formed when the 8th and 624th amalgamated; through the 1967 diminution and reshaping of the

TA, in which the battalion was reduced to a company of the Fusiliers Volunteers; through the large regiment era, when it became C(City of London) Company of the 5th Battalion of the Royal Regiment of Fusiliers, and so to a further change when it became C(City of London) Company of the 8th Queen's Fusiliers(City of London). Finally the company became C(City of London Fusiliers) Company of the London Regiment in 1993. Veteran members, who were Territorials of the Royal Fusiliers, are traditionally the most numerous group at the annual parade of the Federation of Old Comrades Associations of the London Territorial and Auxiliary Units, and additionally they exercise regularly their privilege of dining, lunching and holding their TA battalion reunions inside the Tower of London.

A glimpse of the period when the idea of forming a college corps was mooted comes to us through an account from Dr Frederick James Furnivall, English tutor and a senior member of the college, who became a captain commanding a company:

> When I told my Grammar Class what we meant to do, and asked its members to join our Corps, a quiet member at the back, whom I had then only just seen, said 'I shall be glad to give you any help I can Mr Furnivall'. I answered: 'Thanks Read, but do you know anything about soldiering?' 'Rather,' he said, 'I was wounded outside the Redan, and was Sergt.-Major of the 33rd Foot when I was invalided.' This young man was Philip Read, who had won the distinguished medal for his conduct at the Battle of Inkerman, and who was afterwards to exercise a great influence on the College Corps. He was at that time telegraph clerk in Buckingham Palace.[5]

Read was appointed drill instructor. When the corps moved to the Apollonicon Hall he took a course in physical training and thereafter oversaw exercises for the unit and went on to become a long serving stalwart, adjutant and a much respected major. Hughes was later to thank him publicly for his work generally and in particular for saving the corps money in its formative stages by taking on the duties of drill instructor. The drill seems to have been of a high standard. The corps was placed in Lord Elcho's brigade and Hughes's men were praised for their precision by *The Illustrated London News* reporting on a review of the Volunteers by Queen Victoria on 23 June 1860. It observed:

> Specially noticeable in this Brigade also was the 19th Middlesex, the Corps of the Working Men's College. Their step was as regular and their front as accurate as if it had been ruled by line.

At the review, in Hyde Park, 19,000 Volunteers paraded before the Queen. Was it through the enthusiasm of the Volunteers or was it the none-too-subtle hand of the Foreign Office seeking to impress foreign observers that the parade of these part-time troops, sadly underfunded and finding their own drill halls, ranges, uniforms and many of their weapons, should have been held only a year after foundation? Anyway, *The Illustrated London News* deemed the occasion important enough to publish a coloured supplement on it.

The Working Men's College, like other corps, spent time, discussing what sort of uniform to adopt. 'One set wished for an attractive ornamental uniform; one for an ultra plain outfit, Garibaldi shirt and belt, while another element desired a neat military cut suit with little in the way of ornamentation'. This last won the day and the corps chose grey for their neat suit, topped with a shako cut down so that it was more like a *képi* in grey with a scarlet and black band.[6]

A COUNTY AND A NUMBER

Those professional or group corps were popularly known by their group title, for example, the Post Office Rifle Corps, but for official purposes the War Office later gave them a county or city designation and a number within the designation. For instance the first county to furnish a corps that satisfied government requirements was awarded primacy of place; the second county to do so was numbered second. Thus Devonshire became the senior county and Middlesex second. The City of London started recruitment considerably later than the shires which is why, as we have seen, the War Office numbered it as the 49th in the precedence of the counties. Within each county were several corps, and each of these (regardless of whether it was raised from a town, professional or social group) was numbered in order of local seniority. Thus the Working Men's College Corps, although usually referred to as such or as Thomas Hughes's Corps, was listed officially as the 19th Middlesex Rifle Volunteer Corps in the Rifle Volunteer Force of Great Britain. The Artists', the Post Office and other group corps were similarly given a number.

In many ways, the Volunteers of Victorian days were the most interesting of all the part-time soldiers. There they were, populous and varied in education, job and economic circumstance to an extent far more stratified than are the part-time soldiery of today. Those Victorians seem to have been typically respectful of class divisions, accepting the *status quo* but appreciating the privilege of belonging to a clubable group permitted to bear arms and perhaps seeing their service as a way of rising in their corps and in society generally. They were also patriotic.

On the whole, those early Volunteers tended to be men who could afford to join their unit; like joining a club, you had to pay to belong to it. You had to pay your fare to the range and to camp and for your uniform and ammunition. If an individual did not have money he could in effect borrow it by being issued with his uniform and equipment and buy it at, in some instances, sixpence a week; but this was organised on a corps basis and did not involve government funds. Drill instructors had to be paid for out of a corps' funds. A number of Volunteers in some corps were prosperous and it was usually from them that the loans emanated, but sometimes appeals were made for support. In the case of corps such as the Artisans or the Working Men's College, the rank and file could not afford to pay and at first most of the income came from subscriptions by the officers. There was a lord mayor's fund that gave financial support in some areas. Most of the drill hall recruiting posters emphasised that the men the units wanted had to be respectable. (Even after the establishment of the TF in 1908 some units continued to demand subscriptions from all ranks. In the case of the London Rifle Brigade, the practice was stopped by the War Office in 1916 as being detrimental to wartime recruiting, and by then, of course, conscription had started in England, Wales and Scotland. In the inter-war years, many units maintained a subscription, for example, the HAC, the Inns of Court and the City of London Yeomanry [Rough Riders]. The Inns of Court were the most expensive.)

One problem for the authorities of the mid-19th century was, of course, the possible consequence of allowing a huge section of the public, for long periods a quarter of a million of them, to be armed. Ireland, for instance, was treated at arm's length: the Volunteer Act of 1863, which largely regulated the Volunteers right down to their becoming Territorials, excluded Ireland (sect 53). The century had witnessed violent revolutions in continental Europe. The industrialisation of the northern hemisphere, led by Britain, had brought social problems and labour unrest. In some instances workers' demonstrations had been put down by regular soldiers and prosperous part-time troops, the Yeomanry. The Manchester disturbances and, in particular, the Peterloo incident, in which deaths were caused by the use of Yeomanry units, are cases in point. But the authorities are usually ponderous and apprehensive if not always simply circumspect. With the perspective of history, we can see that those Volunteers of 1859 were motivated largely by the same sort of patriotism that 80 years later caused a similar rush into part-time soldiering, in the Britain of 1939, when practically everybody sensed, despite the Prime Ministerial assurance about 'peace for our time', the promises of Hitler and the proselytising of the Peace Pledge Union, that war was inevitable.

NINE DRILLS A YEAR

The Volunteer Act of 1863, while accepting the traditional premise that a corps should be led by its own officers, stipulated that when a number of corps were in a formation they should be commanded by a general or field officer of the regular Army. There must also be an annual inspection by a general or field officer of the regular Army. There were many other rules with which Territorials of today would be familiar. The act provided that standards of efficiency should be set by order in council. Any order in council had to be laid before both houses of Parliament for scrutiny for a month before the Crown could approve it. The first order (27 July 1863) set a minimum of nine drills a year for trained men. Of these, six must be battalion drills for members of consolidated corps, while three must be battalion drills for members of administrative regiments. Recruits had to complete 30 drills in their first year. Musketry tests had to be passed and members had to attend annual inspection unless officially excused. Standards of drill and exercises were set.

There was no statutory period of commitment, the position of a disenchanted soldier being determined by the rules of his corps. He was given an overriding statutory right to resign on the expiry of 14 days' notice provided he returned all weapons and other items of issue in good condition and paid any dues owed to the corps. If he wanted to transfer to the Army or the Militia, all he had to do was comply with the last two conditions and the need to give notice was waived. The right to resign on giving 14 days' notice was automatically suspended if he had been embodied.

The Militia and Volunteers moved a step nearer to the Army when, under the Regulation of the Forces Act, 1871, control of auxiliary forces was taken back from what had become the traditional leadership, the lord lieutenants, and exercised directly by the Crown. This revesting in the Sovereign, acting on the advice of the Secretary of State for War, came into effect by order in council dated 5 February 1872. From now onwards officers in the auxiliary forces would, like regular officers, receive commissions directly from the Sovereign. But the lord lieutenants would be permitted to nominate candidates for first commissions. Lord lieutenants were no longer allowed to exercise command. However, when the auxiliary forces of his own county or city were on parade or exercising on a field day he could take the salute.

The relationship with the Army became closer still in 1873 when a War Office circular of April brought unit by unit into attachment with the regular brigade of their military district. Efficiency was to be achieved by making the officer commanding each brigade depot responsible, from now on, not only for command, but also for training and inspection.

In 1875, the Volunteer Force was costing £458,189 a year on the Army Estimates. This was made up of: adjutants, including forage and lodging allowance, £75,701; permanent staff £59,158, capitation grant £296,130; miscellaneous £27,200. The capitation grant consisting of 30 shillings a year for each efficient Volunteer was paid by the government into the regimental fund. The fund was administered by the CO helped by a finance committee. The money was spent, subject to certain conditions, in the way that appeared to be best for maintaining efficiency.

The changes known as the Cardwell reforms after Edward (later Lord) Cardwell, Secretary of State for War, instituted many much needed improvements in military life, humanitarian and social as well as organisational, in the Army of mid-Victorian times in the 11 years culminating in 1881. For instance in 1870 there was introduced the system of shorter service with the colours (enabling a soldier who had completed his full-time service to be transferred to the reserve with a contingency commitment). The consequences of not having a proper reserve had been revealed during the Crimean War; in 1871 came the abolition of the practice of buying commissions and promotion (the artillery and the engineer arms had been free of this taint). Another reform was the abolition of flogging unless on active service. But we will interest ourselves in those reforms that touch on part-time soldiering; they drew the Volunteers closer to the Army.

After a 'localisation' report of the previous decade, Cardwell completed localisation by territorialisation in 1881. He grouped the infantry regiments numbered from 26th upwards (the senior 25 regiments already had separate battalions) into pairs and made each pair a brand-new regiment. Each new regiment was given a territorial (geographical) title and linked administratively with the county or city after which it was named. The older of the pair became the new regiment's first battalion, the junior became the second. For example, the 57th Foot and the 77th Foot became the first and second battalions respectively of the Middlesex Regiment. The numerical designations were retained but in general they were not often used, though some regiments persisted privately for generations in using their numerical as well as their territorial title. For example the Northumberland Fusiliers (the 5th) and the Lancashire Fusiliers (the 20th) proudly called themselves respectively the 5th Fusiliers and XX the Lancashire Fusiliers. Even to the present day the Cheshire Regiment retain 22nd in their title. The Guards regiments, the 60th Rifles and the Rifle Brigade were not included in localisation.

The Militia became the third and fourth battalions of the territorialised regiment, which necessarily gave them greater awareness of the regimental family, though they already had a stronger local tie than their regular counterparts. As for the Volunteers, they were gradually made Volunteer battalions of the regular regiment and with minor differences (such as white-metal buttons and badges instead of the regulars' brass, and where appropriate, silver lace instead of gold) had to wear uniforms identical to those of the rest of the family. A further move from individuality came with a provision of 1881 that Volunteer units could no longer necessarily expect to be led by their own officers. This promised greater efficiency and readiness.

Under the Cardwell system, one regular battalion would serve overseas on a long posting in, for instance, India or Africa; the other would stay in the United Kingdom. Both would provide companies to set up a regimental depot and the depot would supply both battalions with recruits or drafts of reinforcements as required.

The increasing propinquity between part-time and regular units was emphasised in 1882 when a small group of Volunteers offered to undertake active service in Egypt during the Mahdiist campaign. They were from the Post Office Volunteers and their offer was accepted. The men were deployed in their specialised role. The breakthrough had been made, and it gained not only their unit's but the whole of the Volunteers' first battle honour, 'Egypt, 1882'. (Eighteen years later the South African War would give the Volunteers their first large-scale opportunity to show the nation what they could do and they would take it by the thousand).

In 1886, the first Volunteer medical unit, the Volunteer Medical Staff Corps, was formed in Maidstone, Kent. Its strength was sufficient to allow the unit to be represented among the part-time troops taking part in the royal review at Aldershot of 1887 to celebrate Queen Victoria's golden jubilee as the world's leading monarch.

PRECEDENCE OF ARTILLERY UNITS 1885

In 1885 the precedence of the Artillery units was:

The Honourable Artillery Company of London of the Armoury House (revived in 1610).

The Artillery Volunteers by county seniority:

1 Northumberland
2 Hampshire
3 Devonshire
4 Sussex
5 Edinburgh (City)
6 Cornwall
7 Midlothian
8 Norfolk
9 Banff
10 Kent
11 Forfarshire
12 Essex
13 Lancashire
14 Kincardine
15 Cinque Ports
16 Renfrewshire
17 Dorsetshire
18 Fifeshire
19 Glamorganshire
20 Haddington
21 Lanarkshire
22 Yorkshire (East Riding)
23 Ayrshire
24 Argyll
25 Gloucestershire
26 Pembrokeshire
27 Yorkshire (North Riding)
28 Cheshire
29 Caithness
30 Lincolnshire
31 Aberdeenshire
32 Berwickshire
33 Kirkcudbright
34 Inverness-shire
35 Elgin
36 Stirlingshire
37 Wigtown
38 Dumbarton
39 Berwick-on-Tweed
40 Cumberland
41 Durham
42 Cromarty
43 Ross-shire

44 Orkney	50 Somerset	57 Isle of Man
45 Nairn	51 Middlesex	58 Staffordshire
46 Sutherlandshire	52 Suffolk	59 Carnarvon
47 Shropshire	53 Tower Hamlets	60 Bute
48 Yorkshire (West Riding)	54 Monmouthshire	61 London (City)
49 Newcastle-on-Tyne	55 Surrey	62 Worcester
	56 Anglesey	

Within the counties were local groupings. For example, Northumberland had 1st (Northumberland and Sunderland), located at Newcastle; and 2nd (The Percy), at Alnwick. Attached to 2nd (The Percy) were the 1st Berwick-on-Tweed Artillery Volunteer Corps.

In Yorkshire (East Riding) the 1st were at Scarborough and the 2nd were at Hull.

Cumberland had only one, the 1st, at Carlisle.

Newcastle had the 1st Newcastle-on-Tyne Artillery Volunteers and attached to them were the 3rd Durham Artillery Volunteer Corps.

THE RIFLE VOLUNTEER FORCE OF GREAT BRITAIN 1885

The Rifle Volunteer Force of Great Britain consisted in 1885 of the following Volunteer battalions, in county precedence:

1 Devonshire	22 Suffolk	43 Denbighshire
2 Middlesex	23 Stirlingshire	44 Hampshire
3 Lancashire	24 Buckinghamshire	45 Somersetshire
4 Surrey	25 Lanarkshire	46 Forfar
5 Pembrokeshire	26 Kent	47 Cambridgeshire
6 Derbyshire	27 Glamorgan	48 Shropshire
7 Oxfordshire	28 Nottinghamshire	49 London
8 Cheshire	29 Merionethshire	50 Yorkshire (East Riding)
9 Wiltshire	30 Yorkshire (West R)	
10 Sussex	31 Leicestershire	51 Hertfordshire
11 Edinburgh (City)	32 Midlothian	52 Perthshire
12 Essex	33 Aberdeenshire	53 Berwickshire
13 Northumberland	34 Roxburgh	54 Sutherland
14 Renfrewshire	35 Cinque Ports	55 Kincardineshire
15 Northamptonshire	36 Monmouthshire	56 Haverfordwest
16 Dorsetshire	37 Cornwall	57 Haddington
17 Norfolk	38 Ross-shire	58 Isle of Wight
18 Staffordshire	39 Worcestershire	59 Ayrshire
19 Berkshire	40 Inverness-shire	60 Dumfries
20 Gloucestershire	41 Warwickshire	61 Elgin
21 Brecknockshire	42 Lincolnshire	62 Argyll

63 Cardigan
64 Durham
65 Wigtown
66 Buteshire
67 Yorkshire (North Riding)
68 Cumberland
69 Herefordshire
70 Dumbartonshire
71 Huntingdon
72 Carnarvonshire
73 Montgomeryshire
74 Orkney
75 Carmarthen
76 Caithness
77 Kirkudbright
78 Westmoreland
79 Fifeshire
80 Bedfordshire
81 Newcastle-on-Tyne
82 Linlithgowshire
83 Selkirkshire
84 Banffshire
85 Radnorshire
86 Flintshire
87 Berwick-on-Tweed
88 Clackmannan
89 Tower Hamlets
90 Nairn
91 Peeblesshire
92 Isle of Man
93 Kinross-shire
94 Anglesey

SOME PARENT REGIMENTS OF VOLUNTEER BATTALIONS

At this period the Volunteer battalions' parent regiments, of which a limited selection is given, included:

The Royal Scots:
1st(The Queen's City of Edinburgh) Rifle Volunteer Brigade
Midlothian(32) 1st(Leith), 2nd(Midlothian and Peeblesshire)
Berwickshire(53) 1st Duns
Haddington(57) 1st Haddington
Linlithgow(82) 1st Linlithgow

The Queen's(Royal West Surrey Regiment):
1st VB (late 2nd Surrey), Croydon
2nd VB (late 4th Surrey), Reigate
3rd VB (late 6th Surrey), Bermondsey
4th VB (late 8th Surrey), New Street, Kennington Park
Cadet corps at Whitgift School and Charterhouse

The Buffs(East Kent Regiment):
1st VB (late 2nd Kent), Canterbury
2nd(The Weald of Kent) VB (late 5th Kent) (Kent and Cinque Ports), Cranbrook, near Staplehurst

The King's Own(Royal Lancaster Regiment):
1st VB (late 10th Lancashire), Ulverston

The Northumberland Fusiliers:
1st VB (late 1st Northumberland and Berwick-on-Tweed), Alnwick
2nd VB (late 2nd Northumberland), Walker-on-Tyne

The Royal Warwickshire Regiment:
1st VB (late 1st Warwickshire), Birmingham
2nd VB (late 2nd Warwickshire), Coventry

The Royal Fusiliers(City of London Regiment):
1st VB (late 10th Middlesex), Fitzroy Square
2nd VB (late 23rd Middlesex), Great Smith Street

The King's(Liverpool Regiment):
1st VB, Anne Street, Liverpool
5th VB, Prince's Park, Liverpool
13th VB, Southport
15th VB, Islington Square, Liverpool
18th(Liverpool Irish), Everton Brow, Liverpool
19th(Liverpool Press Guard), Everton Road, Liverpool

The Norfolk Regiment:
1st VB (late 1st Norfolk), Norwich
2nd VB (late 2nd Norfolk), Great Yarmouth

The Lincolnshire Regiment:
1st VB (late 1st Lincoln), Lincoln
2nd VB (late 2nd Lincoln), Grantham

The Devonshire Regiment:
1st(Exeter and South Devon) VB, Exeter
2nd(Prince of Wales') VB, Plymouth
3rd VB, Exeter
4th VB, Barnstaple
5th VB, Newton Abbot

The Royal Welsh Fusiliers:
1st VB (late 1st Denbigh), Wynnstay
2nd VB (late 1st Flintshire and Carnarvonshire), Rhyl

The Rifle Brigade(the Prince Consort's Own) (in the County of Middlesex):
7th(London Scottish), Adelphi
14th(Inns of Court), Lincoln's Inn
15th(The Customs and the Docks), Custom House
16th(London Irish), King William Street
18th, Greville House, Paddington
19th(St Giles's and St George's, Bloomsbury), the Foundling Hospital
20th(Artists'), Fitzroy Square

24th (General Post Office) (this battalion had telegraph companies).

Within the Rifle Brigade but unnumbered were:
1st (the Tower Hamlets Rifle Volunteer Brigade) Whitechapel Road

When Maidstone was creating the first Volunteer medical unit, a much older rifle corps, the Queen's Westminster Volunteers, was moving into a new and luxurious £10,000 headquarters, the Queen's Hall in James Street. By then recruits had to agree, under a four-year civil contract, to make themselves efficient (as certified by annual attendance) or pay a 35 shilling fine for each year of incomplete attendance.[7]

Recognition of the part-time soldiers' service came in 1892 with the introduction of the Volunteer Long Service Decoration (giving recipients the privilege of the postnominal VD) for officers who completed 20 or more years' service. Two years later, the Volunteer Long Service Medal was instituted to reward the non-commissioned ranks.

The Empire celebrated again with their monarch in 1897 in commemoration of her 60 years on the throne. Among the part-time forces' contributions was that of a group of Scots Volunteers, led by Lieutenant John Cameron. Braving dense mist, they marched from Fort William and ascended Ben Nevis. At the highest point in Great Britain, the slopes resounded with a *feu de joie* from their rifles, prolonged cheering and the playing of the national anthem on the pipes. The year brought a more sombre activity for the 11-year-old Volunteer Medical Staff Corps at Maidstone, where they helped the town to cope with a typhoid epidemic.

In July 1899, the Prince of Wales reviewed all the London Volunteer units on Horse Guards Parade to celebrate the 40th anniversary of the great volunteering rush. Although many a newspaper columnist and music hall entertainer had poked fun at the Volunteers, the press and the entertainment industry were among the most enthusiastic applauders of the sacrifice of the part-time soldiers when they volunteered for the South African War, which put Britain in such peril. Under the terms of their enlistment they could not be compelled to go overseas, but there was no shortage of volunteers for active service. To overcome the legal obstacles to overseas service, Volunteers and Yeomen who volunteered to serve in South Africa had to join the regular Army as private soldiers, albeit on a temporary enlistment. This rule also applied to Volunteer officers, who joined the regular Army as privates and were given temporary commissions. The Imperial Yeomanry and the City Imperial Volunteers are the names that spring to mind in connection with that war but in fact far more Volunteers fought there in active service companies than in the City Imperials. These companies were ad hoc groups of 116 Volunteers and five officers and they were posted into regular battalions already serving in the theatre; more than 18,000 Rifle Volunteers went to war in this way, out of the total of 19,856 Volunteers serving there.

One reason for the formation of the companies was the difficulty in expecting a whole Volunteer or Yeomanry unit to volunteer for South Africa; they had, after all, committed themselves only for home defence, and the term of the war enlistment was for one year or not less than the duration of the war. No prewar Volunteer unit served in South Africa as a unit. Another reason was that it was thought that these part-time soldiers would perform better if they served in a major unit alongside professional soldiers.

But the glamour adhered to the Imperials. The City Imperial Volunteers (CIV) were raised by the lord mayor of London, on Government authorisation, at the end of Black Week, in mid-December. The Court of Common Council and the Volunteers responded swiftly. The former provided money and the latter put in some hard training. Within a month their advance party was steaming to Africa. The CIV were formed by a royal warrant dated Christmas Eve and details were supplied by Army order of 6 January, Epiphany. The lord mayor provided clothing and equipment through public appeals and the War Office supplied weapons and ammunition, transport and camp facilities. The unit's total strength was 1,550 and it was very much a picked force. Members wore slouch bush hats with the left brim pinned up by black metal titles CIV an inch high.

The Imperial Yeomanry too was raised rapidly, thanks to the support of the counties for groups volunteering from local Yeomanry units and in the next two years, more than 6,000 in this category served in South Africa. In total the IY's numbers reached 35,520, but the vast majority of these were civilians who volunteered for the war only; they were not Yeomen in the prewar sense, nor did they have the standard demanded of the Rifle Volunteers, each of whom had to have been recorded as efficient in marksmanship and in training attendance for the two previous years.

In 1902, the War Office, worried about the paucity of reserves, set a higher commitment for Volunteers. An annual camp of at least six days was demanded and the number of drills was increased. But this had the opposite effect to that intended: many Volunteers found the higher commitment left insufficient time for job and family duties, so they resigned. Thus started a vicious circle: potential recruits apprehensive of the enlarged commitment, stayed away, so that in many corps there were not enough newcomers to replace those Volunteers who had resigned, which meant that those remaining found their subscriptions increased to pay for overheads from a smaller membership. To be a Volunteer became a bigger financial burden than ever. This was not so much of a problem for the Yeomanry with its comfortable rural background, but for many urban craftsmen and clerks it put the Volunteers out of reach.

4

The Yeomanry

And you, good yeomen,
Whose limbs were made in England, show us here
The mettle of your pasture.
SHAKESPEARE, KING HENRY IN *Henry V*

The word yeoman suggests the countryside and an interest in the land. In the *Shorter Oxford Dictionary* we are told that a yeoman is 'a freeholder under the rank of gentleman'; by Cobbett's definition 'those who till their own land are yeomen', or going back to the 15th century we learn from Mallory: 'The kyng called upon his knyghts squires and yemen'. These all give an indication of how the military force known as the Yeomanry came by its name.

The origins of the Yeomanry are to be found in the troops of horse militia and horse volunteers that appeared in the Civil War and, later, in the volunteer cavalry operating in the 1745 rebellion. But it was not until a statute of 1794 (34 Geo III c 31), during the French Revolutionary Wars, that the Yeomanry, as we know it, was raised under the name of Volunteer Cavalry. It must not be confused with the troops of light horse which were part of the Volunteers raised under the act of 1782 and successive statutes. Nor should the Yeomanry be confused with the fencibles (a word derived from the French *défensable*, and by derivation in Scots usage it came to mean capable of and liable for rendering defensive military service). The fencibles were full-time regiments raised for the duration of national emergency. The 1794 act resulted in the formation of 28 true Yeomanry regiments within a year. By the second year the number had risen to 34. Examples of those raised in 1794 are the Wiltshire, the Warwickshire, the Yorkshire Hussars, the Nottinghamshire (Sherwood Rangers), the Devon, the Staffordshire, and the South Nottinghamshire Hussars. Examples of those raised in 1795 are the Royal Gloucestershire and the Shropshire.

By the Provisional Cavalry Act, 1797, a provisional mounted force was authorised for defence during the wars. It was to be levied compulsorily from owners of horses but the act might be suspended in any sub-district where three-quarters of the required quota had registered as Volunteer Cavalry under the 1794 act. In fact the raising of the Volunteer Cavalry was so successful in every area, by now there were 65 regiments, that the provisional cavalry was unnecessary. Yeomanry corps were of two types according to the area of their service: mounted or dismounted. The mounted units were initially known as Yeomanry.

The Yeomanry were also called out to suppress riots. One series of disturbances arose from the passing of the Militia Act, 1797, one of the statutes to build up Britain's defences. They spread to Scotland when it was learned that that country had to provide 6,000 Militiamen. In consequence, the Western Troop of the Roxburghshire Yeomanry were called out when rioting broke out in Jedburgh.

One of the regiments raised in 1797 was the Lothians and Border Horse. It had a distinguished quartermaster who was a member of the bar, poet and novelist, Walter Scott. In that year he married Charlotte Mary Carpenter. The historical novels, *Ivanhoe* and *Quentin Durward* were yet to come, but he became very grand, a baronet of first creation, a publisher and printer and laird of Abbotsford. Another regiment raised in the same year was the Cheshire Yeomanry.

FIRST BATTLE HONOUR, 'FISHGUARD'

The Castlemartin Troop of Yeomanry, a sub-unit of the Pembrokeshire Yeomanry, helped to make history when they went into action against a French invasion force. Admittedly it was a mild, even eccentric invasion, consisting of only about 1,200 enemy, who had landed at Fishguard, Pembrokeshire on 23 February 1797. It was more of a raid than a serious invasion, but the aggressors were so surprised to find themselves opposed by the Militia of several Welsh counties and mounted troops that they surrendered without loss of life on either side. The action resulted in a unique battle honour 'Fishguard' being awarded to the unit designated the Castlemartin Yeomanry. The descendant unit, the 102nd Field Regiment, RA(TA), proudly displayed the honour, the first of many to be carried by Territorials.

Initially, Yeomanry units were recruited largely from farmers, and their officers were landed proprietors. As well as having a military role, they were relied on in the days before police forces existed as the most effective body to keep the peace (*vide Annual Register, 1799* p 27; *1815* p 89; *1816* p 174; *1817* pp 5 and 15). Thus, at the outset, the Yeomanry resembled a combination of the home defence units that would be created during the two World Wars and the special constabulary, essentially local in recruitment and legality. It would be many years before they acquired jurisdiction outside their own counties.

The basic unit of a Yeomanry regiment was the troop, which had a large measure of independence and was usually named after the area or estate on which it was based. It had its own quartermaster and ideally consisted of 50 troopers.

Dating from this fruitful period of recruitment a letter from Henry Glassford of Dougalstoun, who became an MP eight years later, gives us a flavour of the times. The wealthy Glassford, who was in the Baldernock Yeomanry Cavalry, Stirlingshire, writing to a tenant at Milngavie, John Galbraith, says:

To John Galbraith
Milngavie *Glasgow 3rd Nov 1798*

John,

I perfectly forgot to send you notice of Our first day of meeting for beginning to exercise the Troop of Yeomanry Cavalry – for which I was sorry – I shall be happy to see you with your Horse, on Thursday next at the drilling Ground near Baldernock Church, at eleven oclock, with your Horse. You will get a Saddle & Bridle, and other Accoutrements without any expense to you & you will find the exercise very easy.

I am John
Yours etc.
Henry Glassford[1]

The Yeomanry were embodied at various periods between their inception and April 1803. When war was resumed the next month, they were again embodied, and once more in 1815. With the defeat of the French there came the start of the long period of peace with its progressive reductions in Britain's defence forces. In 1816, the minimum training was lowered from 12 to five continuous or six individual days a year. There were, however, outbreaks of social unrest in some parts of the country. The most notorious was in Manchester, where at St Peter's Fields there occurred the Peterloo massacre in August 1819. The 15th Hussars, a troop of artillerymen with two field guns and contingents of the 31st and 88th Foot, along with the Cheshire Yeomanry and two troops of the recently formed Manchester and Salford Yeomanry were deployed to quell a crowd being addressed by Henry ('Orator') Hunt, a former Wiltshire Yeoman. While the deputy chief constable, protected by a troop of the Manchester and Salford, arrested Hunt, some of the Yeomen were separated from the main party and were in peril, so the Hussars and the Cheshire charged the crowd, estimated at about 60,000. The number killed varied from 11 to 15 according to different accounts and up to 420 were reported injured. One policeman was killed and 46 troops hurt. In Scotland, the Radical Rising of 1820 was seen as a danger to internal security; two troops of Lanarkshire Yeomanry were formed.

In 1828 the Yeomanry was partly disbanded and what was left was remodelled. Further cuts were made in 1838 but the Lanarkshire Yeomanry survived (and many decades later, despite an amalgamation with the Ayrshire Yeomanry to undertake a joint dismounted role as an infantry battalion in the First World War the Lanarkshire would endure as the 13th of the 14 Yeomanry regiments allowed to retain their horses in the massive reorganisation of 1920). Although the force reductions of 1838 reflected the fact that there was no apparent external threat, the expansion of a police force must have played a part. Nevertheless, the Yeomanry continued its existence, unlike most of the units of the Militia and of the Volunteers.

The People's Charter had appeared in 1838. It attracted support on a scale of millions throughout the country in its demand for a measure of parliamentary reform most of which today we take for granted: universal suffrage for adult men, a secret ballot, electoral divisions of roughly equal population, pay for MPs and the abolition of the property qualification for parliamentary candidates (allowing working men to offer themselves for election). It also called for annual elections. As the Yorkshire reformer Benjamin Wilson put it, working men wanted 'a voice in making the laws they were called upon to obey'.[2]

There was a tragic clash at Newport, Monmouthshire, in 1839 when about 7,000 manual workers, some of them armed, tried to free a Chartist speaker from prison. Troops fired on the crowd, killing 22. In the same year a gathering at Halifax attracted an estimated 200,000 protesters. The depression of three years later resulted in more tasks for the Yeomanry, particularly in the industrial areas. Some regiments now had carbines instead of pistols. Night demonstrations, an eye witness tells us, presented a fearsome spectacle: torches, protest banners and tens of thousands of men covered in grime and sweat who had joined the march straight from their jobs in the coalmines, iron foundries or workshops.[3] In 1848 a vast demonstration was planned for London. The Yeomanry were called out, about 150,000 special constables were sworn, and police from other parts of the country were drafted to the capital. The demonstration was contained and the protests quietened.

At the other end of the country, *The Glasgow Herald* of Friday 25 August 1848 reported:

> *Glasgow Yeomanry Cavalry:* We learn that a meeting of the Gentlemen interested in the formation of this Corps was held in the Council Chambers on Monday for the purpose of forwarding the necessary arrangements. His Grace the Duke of Hamilton, Lord Lieutenant of the County, having been pleased to intimate that previous to naming officers, he would be glad to receive through the Lord Provost a list of names suggested by the members of the Corps, a list was accordingly agreed upon and ordered to be transmitted to his Grace. The Marquis of Douglas intimated his willingness if

appointed, to take command. About 150 gentlemen belonging to the county have already enrolled themselves as members of the Corps.

Once the corps had been approved it became the Glasgow and Lower Ward of Lanarkshire Yeomanry Cavalry.

THE CRIMEAN WAR AND INDIAN MUTINY

Increased overseas commitments for the regular forces resulted in the Yeomanry being embodied in their local areas in 1854 during the Crimean War, and again from 1857 to 1858 during the Indian Mutiny.

In 1870, the War Office decreed that each Yeomanry regiment should be limited to eight troops for effectiveness of operation. Yeomanry regiments were issued with the Westley–Richards breech-loading carbine. (This would in turn be replaced in 1878 by the Snider carbine).

Along with the rest of the auxiliary forces, the Yeomanry was brought back under direct control of the Crown in 1871 by the Regulation of the Forces Act from the counties under lord lieutenants.

The Yeomanry was costing in 1875 a total of £83,086 a year on the Army Estimates. This was made up of: adjutants, including forage and lodging allowance, £9,194, sergeant majors £660; sergeants £9,052; trumpeters £1,460; training pay £37,305; extra pay £24,415; miscellaneous £1,000.

YEOMANRY CAVALRY 1885

In 1885 the Yeomanry Cavalry regiments, in order of precedence, were:

1 Royal Wiltshire
2 Warwickshire
3 Yorkshire Hussars
4 Nottinghamshire (Sherwood Rangers)
5 Staffordshire
6 Shropshire
7 Ayrshire
8 Cheshire
9 1st West Yorkshire
10 Leicestershire
11 North Somerset
12 Duke of Lancaster's Own
13 Lanarkshire
14 Northumberland
15 Nottinghamshire (Southern Nottinghamshire)
16 Denbighshire
17 Westmoreland and Cumberland
18 Pembroke
19 Royal East Kent
20 Hampshire
21 Buckinghamshire
22 Derbyshire
23 Dorset
24 Gloucestershire
25 Hertfordshire
26 Berkshire
27 Middlesex
28 Royal 1st Devon

29 Suffolk
30 Royal North Devon
31 Worcestershire
32 West Kent
33 West Somerset
34 Oxfordshire
35 Montgomeryshire
36 2nd West Yorkshire
37 East Lothian
38 Lanarkshire (Glasgow)
39 Lancashire Hussars

The troubles in Egypt led to the partial embodiment of the Yeomanry in 1885. Three years later, the Defence Act of 1888 enabled the War Office to embody Yeomanry regiments for service anywhere in Britain.

In April 1893, the War Office, to save money, reorganised Yeomanry regiments internally into squadrons and externally into brigades. A brigade comprised two regiments. These were to train together, share an adjutant and take part in a joint camp every third year. Within a regiment, the squadron became the basic unit instead of the troop. Each squadron would have 100 men. The troop had been self-sufficient with a pride and character of its own engendered by its distinctive geographical name, taken from the country town or estate from which it originated, and its own quartermaster. It was commanded by a captain. Under the new system, troop quartermasters had to be phased out by the end of the century. The early Yeomanry, as we have seen, was rooted in the land and could fairly be described as a contractual acceptance by free men of a feudal obligation. For instance, many large estates insisted in their agreements with their tenants that obligations of voluntary military service should be observed. The more substantial tenants would have to provide a man and a mount. A small tenant had the option of supplying one of the two.

In 1896, the Yeomanry were issued with Martini–Metford carbines, in good time for the forthcoming war against the Boers.

SOUTH AFRICAN WAR

Britain's setbacks of the early part of the South African War led to an appreciation of the mounted infantry role and there was unaccustomed rapidity in forming voluntary units. When the war passed into its unexpected second phase, volunteer units were raised specifically for the fighting. These included the City of London Yeomanry (Rough Riders), Paget's Horse, the Duke of Cambridge's Own, the Westminster Dragoons, the Sharpshooters and Lovat's Scouts. The name Rough Riders implied a response to what was seen as the rough tactics of the Boer farmer soldiers. The Sharpshooters implied a practised reaction to the sharp shooting of those same Boers, most of whom had been shooting for game for the pot since boyhood. But the term Sharpshooters also had an older, British derivation from the Duke of Cumberland's Sharpshooters and the Glasgow Sharp-shooters of several generations earlier.

General Sir Redvers Buller, VC, when commander-in-chief in South Africa, had appealed for some 8,000 irregular troops as mounted infantry in companies of 100 (see Chapter 3). On Christmas Eve the War Office announced the formation of the Imperial Yeomanry Committee, most of whose members had served or were serving in the Yeomanry. It comprised: Hon Colonel A G Lucas, of the Loyal Suffolk Hussars; Hon Lieutenant Colonel E W Beckett, of the Yorkshire Hussars; Hon Colonel Viscount Valencia, of the Oxfordshire Yeomanry; Colonel T A St Quinton, a retired regular officer; Hon Colonel the Earl of Lonsdale, of the Westmoreland and Cumberland Yeomanry; Captain W L Bagot, of the Reserve of Officers; and Colonel Lord Harris, of the Royal East Kent Yeomanry. A royal warrant promulgated in Army Order 1 of the following month authorised the committee to raise the initial contingent of the Imperial Yeomanry. About a month into the new year the early companies of the Imperial Yeomanry (IY) were steaming to South Africa.

The public responded enthusiastically with financial and moral support, augmenting the government grants of £40 for each IY mount and £25 capitation for each man. From this, the committee procured riding tackle, other equipment and uniforms. Weapons were provided by the War Office. The counties were to prove particularly generous in contributing to the Yeomanry funds.

The Imperial Yeomanry was consequently raised rapidly with the backing of the counties for groups volunteering from their local units, and in the next two years more than 6,000 in this category served in South Africa. The movement started just before Christmas when Northumbria took the lead with £1,000 from a Mr H H Scott, of Hipsburn, Northumberland. He told Earl Grey of his plan to raise enough money from Northumberland and the county of Durham to put into the field 100 well equipped mounted infantrymen. Grey got in touch with the Secretary of State for War and telegrams were sent to Northumbrian notables. Ultimately these two north-eastern counties donated £50,085 (£33,558 from Northumberland and £16,527 from Durham) to equip their Yeomen. In fact the number sent reached 335 men and their mounts. Scott's son was an early volunteer for the force. Volunteers who reported with their own chargers were allowed £40 a mount by the government. The Northumberland men who survived were granted the freedom of Newcastle upon Tyne on their return.[4]

Those Victorians rallying to the Empire's cause spent the first month of the new century in hectic preparation and they attended a departure service at the cathedral. On 1 February they were given breakfast in the Assembly Rooms at Barras Bridge, Newcastle. At 6.30pm they formed up at the Artillery Barracks, placed bridles on their mounts, sheeted them, marched in double file through the city and formed up in front of the curving façade of John Dobson's classical Central station. The next day they embarked in the SS *Monteagle* at Liverpool, and probably felt somehow at home during the voyage because the vessel had been built at Palmer's Yard, Jarrow. The two squadrons from Northumberland and Durham were grouped with the 13th Squadron (Shropshire) and the 16th Squadron (Worcestershire) to form the 5th Regiment of the Imperial Yeomanry.

In the north west of England, the Cheshire Yeomanry officers set out to raise enough money to equip two companies with uniforms, including wide-brimmed hats, accoutrements and horses. Money poured in: there was enough left over to give every volunteering son of the county a pair of binoculars, a compass and £1 to spend in the ship. The fund was not exhausted and a doctor was hired to accompany the companies at £150 a year with £200 for surgical equipment. The Cheshire companies were listed as the 21st and 22nd of the Imperial Yeomanry. On 29 January, there was a farewell service in Chester cathedral and the next morning the two companies paraded outside the town hall. The contingent was played off by the bands of the 1st Cheshire and Caernarvonshire Volunteer Artillery and the 2nd Volunteer Battalion of the Cheshire Regiment. At Liverpool, the contingent, with companies from the Lancashire Hussars and the Warwickshire Yeomanry, embarked in the SS *Lake Erie*.[5]

A total of 35,520 served in the Imperial Yeomanry in the war, but they were far from being all Yeomen. The early volunteers for South Africa were from existing Yeomanry units, but they were followed by men who were not Yeomen but who never the less volunteered for the fighting and served for the duration of the war in the IY. Their services were accepted with alacrity and without any requirement of previous military training, in contrast to the cool reception that had greeted the first Volunteers' offer of service in the autumn of 1899. In fact, the engines of the great recruitment that started at the end of that year and in early 1900 were the lord mayor of London and notables of the counties.

Because of the generosity of the public in responding to appeals, the Volunteers and the Yeomen had better uniforms and in some cases better equipment than regular troops and the Militia in South Africa. But after a few months in the field, clothing and other items in need of replacement had to be made good by ordinary issue stock.

The South Africa War was unusual: it was the first modern war, the first to be photographed in motion pictures, and the scale of operations was enormous. It took the troops weeks and thousands of miles of steaming to reach the theatre and, once disembarked, they soon discovered the vast landscape that had to be covered. Units kept records of how many thousands of miles they marched – excluding patrols. The Northumberland and Durham squadrons of the 5th Regiment of Imperial Yeomanry, for example, trekked 3,500 miles. The Cheshire Yeomanry companies, 21st and 22nd, marched 2,189 miles and were transported 2,844 miles by train, a total of 5,033 miles, which provided a title for a book, *5,000 Miles with the Cheshire Yeomanry in South Africa*, a compilation of articles and letters home, edited by H J Cooke, whose son was a trooper in the 22nd Company. The London Rifle Brigade contingent, part of 21 Brigade, covered 523 miles in 51 days in their advance on Pretoria, fighting in 26 engagements. They were on the move for 40 days, an average of 13 miles per day's march. Then there were diseases, which, striking unacclimatised troops, claimed far more British lives than did Boer bullets.

The War Office, realising how poorly defended against a possible continental invasion Britain itself had become as a result of the rapid deployment of troops to South Africa, started a recruiting campaign. In May 1900 it called on former part-time soldiers to join the Volunteer Reserve to defend the country. The upper age limit for other ranks was 55 and for officers 62. The other qualification for enlisting was certified efficiency as a Volunteer for six years.

The 72nd, 76th, 78th and 79th companies were all part of the 20th Battalion of the Imperial Yeomanry which sailed for South Africa in the April of 1900, after what had become the usual period of only a month's preparation. Once in the theatre the companies were attached to different units.

In Britain, the Yeomanry was embodied for home defence as part of the near-panic measures to make up for the critical shortage of regular troops to defend the country.

After the main phase of the fighting was over in 1901, a representative contingent of the Volunteers who had been returned home were invited to receive campaign medals from the hands of their sovereign. The King had said that he was prepared to hand their medals individually to one officer and 40 other ranks from each volunteering company that served in the war. In typical Army style, hurrying in order to hang around for one and a half hours, some 3,000 men assembled at 10.00am on Friday 26 July on Horse Guards Parade. The rain cleared in time for the King's arrival at 11.30 and they approached his dais in single file to receive their medals. Not all marched smartly: some had lost a leg, or an arm; others were presented to their monarch in wheelchairs; the jaw of one man had been shot away.

BIG CHANGES AND TWO UNITS FOR IRELAND

Lessons learned early in the South African War, coupled with the pressing need for a more realistic home defence against a background of continental countries with huge peacetime armies that were becoming more powerful every month, led to the formation of a Yeomanry committee to consider organisation and weapons. The committee consisted of Colonel Lord Harris (chairman), Major General the Earl of Dundonald, Major the Marquess of Bath, Captain Sir John Dickson-Poynder, Colonel Viscount Galway, Colonel L Rolleston and Colonel A G Lucas. As they all had Yeomanry experience they called no witnesses. They decided in favour of rifle and bayonet. Their recommendations, published on 2 January 1901, were rapidly incorporated in the Militia and Auxiliary Forces Act, of April 1901. The act and Army Order 109 laid down that the Yeomanry Cavalry should be named the Imperial Yeomanry. But this was the least of the changes. The Yeomanry's importance was emphasised by the provision that members who joined from 17 August on were made subject to many of the regulations pertaining to the Militia, except those relating to camp and preliminary instruction. The mounted infantry Lee-Enfield magazine rifle with bayonet became the standard weapon. Swords were withdrawn, apart from a few retained for ceremonial: officers and some NCOs were allowed to retain them on parade. The War Department would provide rifles, bayonets and saddles, leaving uniforms as the regiment's responsibility from capitation allowance. From the end of the year, khaki would be the official dress.

The Brigade organisation was abolished. Each regiment would have four squadrons, each under their own major and adjutant. A regiment's establishment would be 596, including 30 officers, plus a machine gun detachment of an officer and 16 other ranks. There would be permanent staff of a regimental adjutant and five sergeants.

Pay was generally improved and everybody taking a horse to camp would receive £5. At camp officers would be paid at the scale of their regular counterparts. A lieutenant colonel would receive £1 1s 6d a day and a second lieutenant 6s 8d. The veterinary officer would receive 13s 8d and the quartermaster 10s 6d. Interestingly (compared with today) the medical officer with his 15s would receive less than a major's 16s. All officers would qualify for an allowance of 10s a day. Perhaps to help pay for the war, the new scales for officers did not come into effect until 1903. For other ranks, pay would vary according to rank instead of the existing flat rate. A non-commissioned quartermaster would receive 10s, a regimental sergeant major 9s 6d and a trooper 5s 6d. At first sight, a trooper seemed worse off than when there had been 7s 6d for all. But he now received a horse allowance and more was provided: tents meant that he did not have to pay to be billeted privately. Anyone without a horse could hire one with his £5 allowance.

Higher training standards were demanded. Camp would last 16 days – two days for marching in and out plus 14 days' training. It must be held between 1 May and 30 September. To qualify as efficient, everyone had to attend a full camp, put in six drill nights (12 in his recruit year) and achieve a musketry rating of second class shot. A regiment with efficient members, or a squadron of fewer than 100, for two consecutive years, could expect disbandment.

A 1902 statute enabled the government to form a reserve division and it expressly stated that the Militia Act of 1882, which provided for maintenance, would apply to the Yeomanry. This and the 1901 statute related to the whole of the United Kingdom and under them two Yeomanry regiments were formed in Ireland. The North of Ireland Imperial Yeomanry was raised by the Earl of Shaftesbury on 7 January 1902; the South of Ireland Imperial Yeomanry was the other.

5

The New Force

It shall be lawful for His Majesty to raise and maintain a force, to be called the 'Territorial Force', and consisting of such number of men as shall from time to time be provided by Parliament.

SECT 6, THE TERRITORIAL AND RESERVE FORCES ACT, (7 EDW 7)

During a war we expect nearly everyone to become an armchair strategist. But well after the fighting in South Africa ended, Britain's clubs, drawing-rooms and public-houses buzzed with talk of defence. At one period hardly a month passed without a new book on the war being published. In spite of undoubted victory and ecstatic celebrations, there was a feeling that all was not well with the Army. In 1903, Mr L S Amery, friend of Churchill and later to be a minister of the crown, published in book form and under his own name a series of critical articles he had written for *The Times* and which were published in January and February of that year entitled *The Problem of the Army.*[1] And Germany was becoming stronger by the month. Relations with Germany had deteriorated because of its sympathy with and aid to the Boers. German field guns had proved effective against British troops.

The commander-in-chief who saved the situation in South Africa, the popular Field Marshal Lord Roberts, VC, who probably knew more about war and its prosecution than anyone else in Britain, understood the threat to the nation, and so did Richard B Haldane, KC, an MP with no military experience, but who had interested himself in defence debates. When he was appointed Secretary of State for War in late 1905 Haldane applied his intellectual powers to analysing what was wrong with the Army and identifying its needs to cope with continental warfare (see Chapter 1). While Roberts was using his prestige, popularity and experience to call for conscription as the solution (as recommended in the Norfolk commission's report in 1904), Haldane, whose intellectual approach served him so well in the law (having graduated with a first-class degree in philosophy he became a scholar of four Scots universities, went to the bar and later rose to the top of his profession as Viscount Haldane of Cloan, Lord Chancellor), in university administration and in cabinet office, aimed at reform. For a start he studied the German military staff system –

ironically this, coupled with his admiration for German philosophers of the past (he had studied at Göttingen University), was later to be held against him by fanatics during the wave of anti-German sentiment that built up in the First World War.

We need not examine all Haldane's reforms at too much length but he developed the General Staff system and strengthened the Imperial General Staff that had been set up during Balfour's administration to persuade the dominions to mesh their defence needs with those of Britain. The war against the Boers had shown that around the Empire was a body of military potential ready to come quickly to the help of Britain (examples of this are provided by the number of Canadians, Australians and New Zealanders in particular, as well as South Africans, who fought in the war). The principle of exchange postings of officers between the General Staff in Britain and the Australian General Military Staff was agreed at the Imperial conference of 1907, and the conference also resolved that defence within the Empire was not just a local responsibility but something that should be undertaken by this family of nations helping each other. By the following year, an Australian officer had already taken his place in Britain and a Canadian officer had been offered the post of commander of an infantry brigade at Aldershot.

The part of Haldane's reforms that concerns us is his radical reorganisation of the auxiliary forces. The Yeomanry and the Volunteers now became the Territorial Force (TF) and the Militia was transformed into the Special Reserve (SR). The SR had a split role: some elements would undertake lines of communications and garrison duties overseas, others would supply drafts of reinforcements for their parent regular units. The first line of defence was now the regular Army plus its Reserve (comprising former regulars who still had a commitment after leaving the colours) plus the SR; the second line was the TF.

The auxiliary forces in Ireland were treated somewhat differently. The Militia became part of the Special Reserve, as in the rest of the United Kingdom, but the North Irish Horse, as the North of Ireland Imperial Yeomanry had become, and the South Irish Horse, as the South of Ireland Imperial Yeomanry had become, were changed to Cavalry Special Reserve units and did not form part of the TF as was the case with all other Yeomanry regiments. The Antrim Militia Artillery, which after its South African War service had been renamed the Antrim Royal Garrison Artillery (Militia), became the Antrim Royal Garrison Artillery (SR).

A dapper Scots major-general called Douglas Haig, director of staff duties, was one of the professional experts on whom Haldane relied in reshaping the military strength of Britain and the Empire for the continental war that was soon to change the face of Europe. Haig probably never dreamed that within a decade he would be the field commander of the mighty armies that Britain and the dominions were to throw against the Central Powers on the Western battlefront and, by costly attrition, contribute to victory on this vital front.

Training, administration and commitments of the auxiliary forces were brought together by the Territorial and Reserve Forces Act, and with the linked regular battalions and the strengthened local associations, there now existed an efficient framework for building the sort of Army that the 20th century and a Europe of increasing industrial power demanded. A small infantry regiment would now consist of: 1st battalion (regular), 2nd battalion (regular), a depot, 3rd battalion (SR), 4th battalion (TF) and perhaps a 5th battalion (TF). There were of course some well-recruited regiments, for example the Middlesex, that had more than two regular battalions. The Royal Warwickshire Regiment, the Royal Fusiliers, the Lancashire Fusiliers, the 60th Rifles and the Rifle Brigade all had four regular battalions.

Some regiments had more than one battalion of the Special Reserve (these were known as extra reserve battalions); this meant that the regiment's TF element would be designated the 5th battalion or 6th and so on. The basic system applied to all the 74 line regiments serving overseas, and 14 cavalry regiments were in similar manner linked with 14 others serving at home.

Haldane's logic was that if a regular battalion suffered heavy casualties early in the fighting, the losses would be made good swiftly by drafts from the SR battalion. Subsequent losses could be met by customary recruiting. An assumption was made that after a year of full-scale continental warfare, only 20 per cent at most of the original personnel of the regular units in the expeditionary force would be still in action. Regiments with extra reserve battalions would stand by to operate as complete units or simply to provide reinforcements if further drafts should be needed.

As for the Territorials, on proclamation they would be embodied for intensive training, ideally for six months. So for them, mobilisation implied training, not fighting – at least for the early part of a war. As the Territorials' professionalism improved, more and more regulars could be spared from home stations and sent abroad. Overseas garrisons could be provided by the extra reserve battalions or by Territorials who might volunteer to serve abroad.

Much thought was given to the TF's home defence role and conflicting statements were made during the formative months leading to the passing of the 1907 Act, not the least being Haldane's view that the TF would need that six months' training to be efficient. But legally, at least, the force was for home defence only. Perhaps the shrewd lawyer realised that just as the Volunteers and Yeomanry had soon volunteered for South Africa, so could the nation rely on the Territorials to do so in any future conflict, and not to shelter behind their legal commitment to home defence only. In fact, when the great test came, 97 per cent of them volunteered to go overseas.

On New Year's Day 1908 the post of director of Auxiliary Forces was changed to the director general of the Territorial Force. The directorate was transferred from the adjutant general's department to that of the Army Council, the parliamentary under secretary of state.

Regular Army generals took command of the 14 infantry divisions into which the TF was formed. Regular officers too were put in charge of nearly all the infantry brigades (each of which had four battalions) and of the 14 cavalry brigades. Each cavalry squadron was allowed six scouts for reconnaissance, and at this period some Yeomanry regiments were lectured on the subject by no less a person than Lieutenant General Sir Robert Baden-Powell. The infantry divisions had artillery, engineers, ordnance and other supporting arms and services so that they could be quickly built into complete operational formations. The cavalry brigades had horse artillery to give a balanced force. How Lord Ranelagh, a leading Volunteer lieutenant colonel and (from the regular Army's point of view) troublesome advocate of big Volunteer formations, would have loved it. But all that had been two generations ago. Each battalion was 1,009 strong divided in eight companies. There were 204 battalions of infantry and there were supporting corps troops. The infantry included 10 battalions of cyclists. Some of today's artillery units date from this period when new batteries of Royal Horse Artillery were raised to provide guns for each of the cavalry brigades.

Oddly, for battalions that traced direct descent from the Volunteers of long ago and which, after Cardwell, were linked to regular units as Volunteer battalions, the London infantry units became battalions of a massive new formation, the London Regiment. But they retained their individual cap badges and other distinctions of dress. The HAC infantry were originally meant to be included in the new formation but they managed to retain their independence. This left 27 battalions, including one of cyclists, designated to comprise this biggest infantry regiment in the history of the Army. The arrangement also led to the creation of some of the longest titles. These included the 8th (City of London) Battalion the London Regiment (Post Office Rifles), the 15th (County of London) Battalion the London Regiment (Prince of Wales's Own Civil Service Rifles), and the 20th Battalion the London Regiment (Blackheath and Woolwich). The Inns of Court Volunteer Rifle Corps, after being earmarked as part of the new regiment, were left outside its scope and became an officer-producing unit, thereby reducing the Londons' battalions to 26.

In the TF of 1908, camp was cut from 16 to 15 days. A Yeomanry regiment's establishment was reduced from 30 officers to 25 and the number of other ranks was set at 449. The troops were paid 1s 2d per day plus a messing allowance of 1s a day and free rations. The horse allowance was £5 a day – a considerable sum at that time. Incidentally, until 1901, the pay for other ranks had been at a flat rate, regardless of rank. A newly commissioned TF officer could obtain a £20 outfit allowance provided that he qualified for confirmation of his commission within two years.

A change from the relaxed days of the Yeomanry and Volunteers was that officers were no longer able to claim honorary rank after a long period of commissioned service. For instance, a captain of 15 years' commissioned service had previously been able to claim an honorary majority.

The 'Imperial' was deleted from the Yeomanry's title in 1908, and on 17 August the Territorial Decoration award replaced the Volunteer Decoration (the letters TD after your name do not import the embarrassment caused by VD), though long-serving officers were still using the postnominal VD in the 1930s, some with a VD and a TD, and in Australia, for instance, it continued in use very much longer.

A War Office leaflet, *Service of the Imperial Yeomanry in the Territorial Force*, of March 1908 told members of the Yeomanry what their pay and allowances would be in the new force, 'during annual training in camp, and whilst called up for instruction'. It did not apply to the Irish Yeomanry. The rates were:

1. Pay.

	s	d
Quarter master serjeant	4	4
Farrier quarter master serjeant	4	0
Squadron serjeant major	4	4
Squadron quarter master serjeant	3	4
Saddler serjeant	3	8
Farrier serjeant	2	10
Serjeant	2	8
Shoeing smith	1	8
Saddler	1	9½
Trumpeter	1	4
Corporal	2	0
Private	1	2

2. Allowances &c.

Separation allowance at the following rates will be given for the families of all married non-commissioned officers:–

	s	d
Wife of quarter master serjeant or similar rank	2	1
Wife of squadron serjeant major or similar rank	1	4
Wife of non-commissioned officers of other rank	1	1
Each girl under 16 years, or boy under 14 years	0	2
Ditto, if motherless	0	4

Army rations will be issued free for all non-commissioned officers and men and these will be supplemented by regimental arrangement, each Officer Commanding being given 1s. a-day for each non-commissioned officer and man for this purpose. An equitation bounty of £1 will be paid to each soldier present at training for not less than 8 days, who is then certified to be efficient in equitation.

By Command of the Army Council,

E W D Ward

The War Office
2nd March, 1908

One important departure from tradition that was emphasised in the Territorial and Reserve Forces Act of 1907 that brought the Yeomanry into the Territorial Force was that Yeomanry units were no longer to be deployed to suppress civil disturbances. From now on they were simply soldiers.

SPECIAL PROVISION FOR THE HAC

The HAC were given permission in 1906 by their captain general, Edward VII, who was extremely interested in the TF, to use a distinctive ribbon for their long service awards, both the filigree-style decoration for officers and the medal for other ranks. Instead of the old Volunteer colour of green, or green and yellow as it became, the HAC's ribbon was of scarlet, blue and yellow, household colours of the monarch.[2] The privilege was confirmed in 1931.[3]

In 1908, the HAC gained a statute to itself, reminiscent of the grant of its ancient charter. The Honourable Artillery Company Act was passed safeguarding its property from the provisions of the Territorial and Reserve Forces Act, which had meant conveying most of its drill halls to the TF, and restating its civil rights. The HAC and its forebears, who for nearly four centuries had stood uniquely alone, had been invited to become part of the TF. A general meeting of the company agreed unanimously to join the new force provided the government introduced the protective bill. The government, with its massive party majority, had no trouble in obliging.

Although the Yeomanry was now grouped with the other arms in the TF, the years of independent existence had left their mark, so Yeomen still tended to regard themselves as different from the others. Camp, for instance, did not necessarily mean that the Yeomen had to rough it. They had far more tents than an infantry unit, because they were inclined not to sleep more than three in a tent; this view was accepted but they had to pay for the extra tentage out of their own pockets. Cookhouse and other fatigue duties were undertaken by civilian labour hired by the Yeomen, some of whom even took their own grooms to camp. Although khaki was by now the official working dress, these cavalrymen would dine in dress uniform.

THE FIRST AID NURSING YEOMANRY

A cavalry sergeant major lying wounded and horseless on a battlefield in the Sudan was the force behind the establishment of Britain's women's voluntary corps, the First Aid Nursing Yeomanry (FANY). He was Edward Charles Baker, known as the founder, and the moment of his inspiration is best recounted in his own words:

> During my period of service with Lord Kitchener in the Soudan campaign, where I had the misfortune to be wounded, it occurred to me that there was a missing link somewhere in the Ambulance Department, which, in spite of the changes in warfare, had not altered very materially since the days of the Crimea when Florence Nightingale and her courageous band of helpers went out to succour and save the wounded. On my return from active service I thought out a plan which I anticipated would meet the want, but it was not until September, 1907, that I was able to found a troop of young women to see how my ideas on the subject would work.[4]

Baker, who after his discharge from the Army became an employee of the Armour Meat Company at Smithfield market, in London, wanted horsewomen of sufficient firmness to allow them to ride to the battle, give first aid, and depending on the seriousness of the casualty's wounds, either carry him back to the field hospital, or stay with him and treat the wounds until the ambulance was able to arrive. Thus he would have supplied the missing link. He found his recruits after advertising in the newspapers and it is probable that the passage through Parliament of the Territorial and Reserve Forces Bill with its intendment of increasing the defence stance of the country added to the public interest in such a corps. Baker became commandant.

The FANY's constitution was registered in 1908. Baker was an impressive 6ft 7in tall and an imaginative organiser. His daughter Katie seems to have inherited his verve. She became a sergeant major in the corps and in February 1909, she attracted new members by selling the appeal of the FANYs in the company of regular Army recruiting sergeants in Whitehall.

In May 1909, Katie won the gold medal for jumping at the Territorial Forces Exhibition at the Royal Agricultural Hall. The next month, a music hall matinée by leading entertainers at the St James's Theatre yielded sufficient funds to buy their first ambulance, £83 5s 6d for the vehicle and £16 4s 6d for the harness, leaving more than £30 for the general fund. The heavy vehicle would be pulled by a pair of horses. That summer the corps had their first camp, on land owned by a supporter of the Territorials, Mr H Waechter, in the Chiddingfold area of Surrey.

By 1910, the FANY had sufficient members to rent a headquarters above

Gamage's store in Holborn. They were receiving their battle riding instruction through the good offices of the Surrey Yeomanry at Clapham Park, south west London, and they were publishing their own corps *Gazette*. The FANYs bought their own uniform of khaki tunic and skirt worn with wide-brimmed hat for the field. On dress occasions they wore a dark blue, bell-shaped skirt ornamented with three rows of white braid at the hem, short scarlet tunic with stand-up collar and white facings, scarlet forage cap with black patent leather peak, white gloves, black riding boots and white medical haversack.

THE FIRST BATTALION TO MOVE BY MOTOR TRANSPORT

On 17 March 1909, an exercise in public relations by the Automobile Association (AA), not yet four years old, whose secretary was a Territorial, resulted in a milestone for military planning. A complete battalion equipped for active service was moved from London to Hastings and back by motor. The resort, location of an earlier invasion and a landmark in English history, was chosen as the objective of a fictional invasion force and the manoeuvre was to demonstrate how efficiently defending troops, with everything they would need for their task, could be rushed to the coast. The equipment included guns, ammunition, limber waggons, water carts, food and medical supplies and an ambulance. The secretary of the AA, Stenson Cooke, was in the Essex Regiment and had many years' service as a Volunteer. The AA now wanted to convince those in authority that the motor car was not merely something with which to antagonise the police and frighten the horses but that it had military potential. The idea was put to the MP for Hastings, Arthur du Cros, a Territorial lieutenant colonel in the Warwickshires, who persuaded the War Office to lend a battalion for the experiment. It was large in every sense: a composite battalion 1,000-strong of Grenadier, Coldstream and Scots Guardsmen.

The 300 cars, provided by members of the association, were under the overall command of Colonel W J Bosworth, a military tutor and chairman of the AA. Heavy equipment followed in large waggons, provided by du Cros's brother. The vehicles mustered in three approach columns: from Chelsea Barracks, marshalled by du Cros, Wellington Barracks, marshalled by Sir Nevill Gunter, and the Victoria Embankment, marshalled by Mr F G Baisley, and they converged at Crystal Palace to begin the 54-mile run. Haldane, accompanied by his sister and Sir Edmund Ward, a member of the Army Council whose signature appears on many documents regulating the TF, witnessed the morning muster at Chelsea. Arrangements were made for the cooperation of police forces through whose areas the convoy passed. Association scouts manned crossroads to shepherd the seven sections into which the battalion had been divided in the right direction. Thousands of people lined the route. The *Hastings and St Leonard's Observer* reported:

> There was something to stir the blood in this swift rush of motor cars to the coast with soldiers all prepared to repel the imaginary invader. The rattle and dash of the cars flying by in seemingly endless succession, uniformed officers and men and the hugeness of the whole thing, seized the imagination, and set the pulse beating rapidly . . . Through the suburbs of London . . . up hill and down dale, now along a straight, even fairly dry piece of road, then through a pea-soupy kind of mud, along through melted snow between snow-covered banks . . . The wind blew off the caps of one or two of the men but there was no stopping . . . Outside every wayside inn there were little crowds of men who cheered lustily....At every farm the farmer and his family and all hands lined the walls and cheered and waved handkerchiefs . . . Opposite every country school the children were assembled with flags, or grouped around one large Union Jack . . . At Pembury there was a halt for 15 minutes. The men were glad to get out and stretch their legs, and have a little refreshment . . . then a signaller got to work from the roof of the commanding officer's brougham in the front, the cars were lined up end on, the bugles sounded the assembly and they were off again.

The first car arrived in London Road, Hastings, shortly after 1.00pm and was greeted by huge crowds, displays of bunting, and cheering from passengers on the top decks of trams. Music was provided by the Territorial bands of the 5th Sussex Battery of the 3rd Home Counties Brigade, RFA, and the 5th Battalion (Cinque Ports) of the Royal Sussex Regiment. However, it was not until 3.30 that the baggage waggons arrived. The Guards set off to march to the cricket ground but so many enthusiastic sightseers were pressing around them that the police and Territorials had difficulty in clearing the route. As it was St Patrick's Day, the mayor of Hastings provided Irish stew (the result of a public appeal) for the troops after they had piled their rifles and greatcoats. The experiment was hailed by the press, 150 of whose representatives were gathered in the town, as a triumph for automobilism. Among those accompanying the convoy were General Sir Frederick Stopford, General Lawson and General Heath, besides Captain Sloman, of the United States embassy, and two German embassy officials, Captain Wiedemann, naval attaché, and Major Ortertag, military attaché. The Army Council praised the 'public spirited generosity' of the owners of the cars. The *Hastings and St Leonard's Observer* noted that as soon as the crowds identified their MP, du Cros, who had donned khaki for the occasion, they gave him 'a rousing cheer, which he modestly acknowledged'.

RAISING THREE RESERVES

Once a Territorial battalion achieved three-quarters of its establishment, it was allowed the privilege of bearing colours. Recruiting was so successful that with the new force less than 15 months old, the monarch was able to hold a presentation parade on 19 June 1909 on the east terrace of Windsor Castle, the colour parties of the qualifying battalions parading in dress uniform to receive their colours from King Edward VII.

In 1910, recruiting began for three reserves. Two of them, the Territorial Reserve and the Technical Reserve, were necessarily small but the third, the Veteran Reserve, proved to have a popularity reminiscent of the Volunteer days. By 1 January 1913, it was 190,836 strong.

6

First Taste of Battle

You will be back home before the leaves are off the trees.
KAISER WILHELM II EXHORTING SOLDIERS
LEAVING FOR BELGIUM, AUGUST 1914

Members of the London Scottish, completing the first day of summer camp at Ludgershall on Salisbury Plain, on Sunday 2 August 1914, had their shortest night's sleep. Lights out had sounded at 10.30pm; reveille was blown 15 minutes later. A telegram ordered the unit to return immediately to the drill hall. Once they arrived back they had two days of inactivity.

As events turned out, the Territorials had been formed hardly a moment too soon. But the Army and its auxiliary forces were in a far better state of preparedness than they had been for the previous war. 'In every respect the Expeditionary Force of 1914 was incomparably the best trained, best organized and best equipped British Army which ever went forth to war'.[1] Britain declared war on 4 August and regular units had already been ordered to mobilise that day; an example of the relevant instruction is provided by the telegram sent to the 2nd Battalion of the Royal Dublin Fusiliers at Gravesend, received at 5.00pm on 4 August and bearing the message, 'Mobilize' (it can be seen in the National Army Museum). The next day, the Territorials were embodied and told where to report. Territorials of the Royal Garrison Artillery manned their heavy guns on the coastline. Mobile patrols were the responsibility of the Yeomanry. Infantry units were given guard duties.

On 2 August 1914, the London Rifle Brigade (LRB) had their shortest annual camp: it lasted three hours. A few days later, they had their longest: it lasted more than four years.

The LRB had gone to a tented camp at Whitebread Hole, Eastbourne, arriving there at 2.30pm. At 5.30 they started back to London because of the pace of international events but were allowed to return to their homes. The cabinet agreed on mobilisation the next day, ordered it on 4 August, and embodiment took place on 5 August. As they were served by good bus and train services (free travel for men in khaki) members of the LRB not on duty were allowed home to sleep at night. But this carefree state of affairs ended when a stand-to was ordered and few men reported back for duty. The dearth of people reporting was not the men's fault. Apparently, so many units had telephoned local police stations, requesting the police to alert troops in their area, that the lines became jammed.

The Cast Iron Sixth, the 6th(City of London) Battalion of the London Regiment too had a short camp. They arrived at Eastbourne on 1 August and that evening they were on their way back to London. They were embodied on the 5th with a strength of 1,029, but remained in London until the 19th when they moved to Bisley, East Grinstead and Crowborough.

Units of the 1st London Division departed from Waterloo station and travelled to the Wareham area of Dorset on 2 August for camp but were sent back immediately on arrival.

Mobilisation orders for the Sherwood Rangers Yeomanry meant that there would be no camp that year; they had been due to attend camp in September. Mobilisation orders arrived at unit headquarters on the night of 4 August and the regiment noted that by the following evening nearly every member had reported for duty. Embodiment was on a squadron basis; one officer in each squadron was authorised to buy horses from members of the regiment and the shortfall was made good by requisitioning chargers from the Remount Department. On the first Monday of the war, A, B and C squadrons left their headquarters at Newark, Mansfield and Worksop respectively and marched to regimental headquarters in Retford. The next day, with the war a week old, the Rangers took part in a farewell service in East Retford church, loaded the horses into rail trucks and arrived at Diss, Norfolk, where 3 Brigade, of the 2nd Mounted Division had its area. The Rangers' transport was a ragged collection of horse-drawn vehicles varying from a light dray to their heaviest, a two-wheeled coal cart. Whenever the regiment moved it had to rely on hiring more suitable vehicles.

Embodiments for these Yeomanry regiments had gone according to plan but there was indignation among the London Territorials and their families over the apparent slip-up of their units being sent to pointless camps, reporting there only to be sent back. There was however, good reason for the manoeuvre. Because of their geographical location and the unity of structure of their major units, as battalions of the London Regiment, Haldane's London divisions and brigades had been given a pivotal role complementing the immediate departure of the regular forces that comprised the BEF (in law, the TF was for home defence only). At the beginning of August, the British government wanted to give Germany time to consider its ultimatum and was anxious not to prejudice the situation by cancelling camps in case Germany saw this as an act of provocation and so an excuse for war.

The poster embodying Territorials stated:

Army Form E.634
[Form to be used when the whole of the
Territorial Force is Embodied]

TERRITORIAL FORCE

HIS MAJESTY THE KING having been graciously pleased to order by Proclamation that directions be given by the Army Council for Embodying the Territorial Force, all men belonging to the said Force are required to report themselves immediately at their Headquarters.

Forms
E.634
4

An example of the planning is provided by 1 London Infantry Brigade, consisting of four Territorial battalions affiliated to the Royal Fusiliers, in Haldane's titling the 1st, 2nd, 3rd and 4th (City of London) Battalions of the London Regiment. The brigade was tasked with security of the immensely important railway line between London and Southampton, the docks there, the line from the port to Amesbury, and the line from London to Newhaven. Southampton was the main departure point for troops and Newhaven was the principal port for embarking *matériel*.

The 2nd (City of London) Battalion, later to earn the nickname the Second to Nondons, proceeded to camp at Wareham on 2 August. By noon of that day, soon after marching into its location, it was ordered to head back to London, reaching its drill hall at about 11.00pm. It was a hungry battalion: it had been unable to obtain a meal at Wareham as the Navy had commandeered the rations set aside for the 1st London Division. But the CO, prepared for mobilisation, had previously stocked supplies for the battalion and additionally was able to obtain sufficient bread for the day. Providing loaves for 600 men at short notice on a Sunday night of a bank holiday weekend was no mean example of the quartermaster's art.

The battalion slept at the drill hall and because of its preplanned role as part of 1 London Brigade, it went through the preliminary stages of mobilisation the next day in Dean's Yard, Westminster Abbey. For its railway duties it was reorganised into four double-sized companies. In the words of a member of the unit, Second Lieutenant W E (Billy) Grey, 'Before the dawn of the 4th the railway was under strict surveillance, and the battalion was at its war station some 18 hours before Great Britain declared war – a minor manifestation of that triumph of efficiency, the mobilisation of the British armed forces.'[2]

NIGHT UNDER THE STARS

The 2nd Mounted Division's 3 Brigade, consisting of the Sherwood Rangers Yeomanry, the Derbyshire Yeomanry, the South Nottinghamshire Hussars and the Nottinghamshire Battery of the RHA, moved from its first wartime area at Diss, Norfolk, to the Thames Valley for more training and here, during a march from Reading to Wyfold Court, many Yeomen had their first experience of a night under the stars without benefit of bivouac. At Moulsford in September the regiment was asked whether it would volunteer as a whole to serve overseas. The few men who refused to serve beyond their original commitment (as was their legal right) were sent to the depot at Retford, where they formed the nucleus of the regiment's second line. On 8 October, the 2nd Mounted Division paraded on the Downs west of Moulsford in line for the King, who inspected them on horseback, probably the first time that a complete Yeomanry division paraded in line.

Two Yeomanry regiments not technically in the TF though part of it in spirit were the North Irish Horse and the South Irish Horse, both of which had been made Cavalry Special Reserve regiments. The North Irish were mobilised at 4.00pm on 4 August. On 17 August, their C Squadron sailed from Dublin to Le Havre. A few days later, they were joined by their A Squadron, accompanied by B Squadron of the South Irish Horse. Although the Special Reserve is beyond the scope of this book, these units deserve their place in this chapter because on 24 August they became the first part-time cavalry unit to engage the enemy in the war (see page 73).

THE CAVALRYMAN AND HIS HORSE 1914

In 1914 a mounted cavalryman carried his rifle slung over his left shoulder, the butt resting on the rifle bucket on the off side of the horse. His bandolier of 90 rounds of rifle ammunition was slung over the same shoulder, as was his waterbottle. His haversack was slung over the right shoulder. In addition to the rider, the horse carried:

Saddle
Saddle wallet

1. The first battle honour for part-time soldiers, 'Fishguard'. It was awarded to the Pembrokeshire Yeomanry for the work of its Castlemartin troop in repelling a French landing force in 1797.

2. A detail of the Working Men's College Corps with rifles. Members are seen here on the range. *(Archives of the WMC Volunteer Rifle Corps)*.

3. Rifleman Justin Miller in 1891 uniform and Lance Corporal Bob Shaun in present day chemical warfare kit and the plastic Mark VI helmet, both of the 4th Royal Green Jackets. Seen here in October 1989 beside the portrait of the Kaiser. *(Courtesy of The Times)*.

4. A company of the Queen's Westminsters at Buckingham Palace after the Kaiser's inspection. The unit mustered 790 of its 1,100 members for the parade. *(Courtesy of The Times and the 4th Royal Green Jackets)*.

5. The Army tries automobilism. On the initiative of the Automobile Association, whose members provided 300 cars, the War Office provided a battalion for a mobilisation exercise involving transportation from the Crystal Palace to Hastings, 1909. *(Courtesy of the AA)*.

6. The London Scottish marching down from Ludgate Hill in the Lord Mayor's Show before the First World War.

7. The Artists Rifles march past HM King George V.

8. Buglers of the 3rd Queen Victoria's Rifles practise in Richmond Park.

9. No pollution or refuelling problems; a company of the Hampshires training in 1914.

10. These territorials, part of a parade of thousands reviewed by Lord Kitchener, march off at ease after a parade on Epsom Downs. Note the long Lee Enfield rifles.

11. The Westmoreland and Cumberland Yeomanry make light work of this hedge.

12. Territorials digging trenches on Hampstead Heath at the start of the First World War.

13. The Maxim gun section of the Northumberland Hussars.

14. These AA patrolmen parade in front of their head office before marching off to war. Nearly 500 of them followed the lead of their secretary, Stenson Cooke. *(Courtesy of the AA)*.

15. 'Charge!' Territorials of the Gloucestershire Regiment. Note the curved brass shoulder titles which included the letter T welded to the battalion number and regimental title.

16. After the shoot, the boiling water. These Yeomen are going through the old standard practice of pouring boiling water down their rifle barrels after firing on the range.

Cloak with socks in pocket, wrapped into a roll 26in wide and tied in front of saddle
Food
Mess tin on off side of cloak
Neck strap and head rope around animal's neck
Nosebag, containing brush, comb, rubber and sponge, suspended from near side front of saddle
Heel rope, rolled and strapped on saddle
Farrier's toolbag on off side of saddle
Picketing pegs and rope, in saddle cover on back of saddle

Additionally, officers and some NCOs had swords and scabbards, maps and mapcases; one man in each section carried a mallet.

TO FRANCE

The regular Army divisions went speedily to their field positions with the BEF, though the despatch of two of the six infantry divisions was held back as a precaution pending full turn-out of the Territorials. Every detail for the mobilisation of the regular Army and its deployment in France had been prepared. 'From the King to the printer, everyone knew what he had to do.'[3] Territorial units were given guard duties, fulfilling their legal role.

While the regulars were undergoing the grim sequence of the first British shot to be fired, the first British soldier to be killed in action, the first VC to be awarded in the continental conflict, individual Territorials volunteered to serve beyond their commitment and their offer to fight overseas was quickly accepted. In that first month the War Department asked units whether they would volunteer as a whole to go overseas. In fact five units as well as some individuals had already volunteered before the war to do so (it was known as imperial service[4]) in the event of hostilities. The first to volunteer were the Diehards, the 7th Battalion of the Middlesex Regiment. The others were all Royal Fusiliers: the 1st, 2nd, 3rd and 4th (City of London) battalions of the London Regiment, who were all in 1 London Infantry Brigade. (This is known as a solid brigade, composed of four battalions of the same regiment). The first unit of 2 London Infantry Brigade to volunteer was the 5th (City of London) Battalion of the London Regiment (the London Rifle Brigade); its fellow members of the brigade, the 6th, 7th and 8th (Post Office Rifles) battalions, followed suit within two weeks.

For a unit to be recognised as volunteering as a whole, the individuals accepting overseas commitment had to reach 75 per cent of its strength. Where the 75 per cent was achieved, the War Office promised, members so voting would continue to serve with their comrades. Members of a unit which volunteered as a whole but who themselves preferred to remain in the United Kingdom (which they were legally – and morally – entitled to do: they had taken on a voluntary commitment and it would have been inequitable to increase it unilaterally) were usually posted to the embryo second-line battalions of their units, as had happened in the case of the Sherwood Rangers (see page 70). The CO of the London Scottish was apparently scrupulous about insisting that no pressure should be put on Territorials to volunteer. Men were interviewed separately and privately before being asked to decide on serving overseas.

Because of the alacrity with which Territorials volunteered, by the time the war was a few weeks old, TF units were steaming to overseas stations to release regulars for the front. An example is provided by those early volunteers, the Diehards and the Royal Fusiliers. On 4 September, exactly a month into the war, the 7th Middlesex sailed for Gibraltar, and the same day the 1st, 2nd, 3rd and 4th Londons began their embarkation for Malta. These garrisons were all near home, but distant stations too would soon see Territorials replacing regulars. Little more than a week later, the East Lancashire Division was on its way to Egypt and trying to accustom itself to its new numerical title, the 42nd, granted because it was the first TF division to sail from the United Kingdom for overseas; 42 was the lowest, and so the most senior, number allocated to TF divisions.

TERRITORIAL DIVISIONS OF THE FIRST WORLD WAR

Unlike regular divisions, the original Territorial Force divisions were un-numbered but were identified by a regional title. For example, Northumbrian, Wessex, Lowland, Welsh or Home Counties. Numbering came with the war and seniority was based upon the date of a division's departure for service overseas. The 26 Territorial divisions of the First World War were:

42nd (East Lancashire)
43rd (Wessex)
44th (Home Counties)
45th (2nd Wessex)
46th (North Midland)
47th (2nd London)
48th (South Midland)
49th (West Riding)
50th (Northumbrian)
51st (Highland)
52nd (Lowland)
53rd (Welsh)
54th (East Anglian)
55th (West Lancashire)
56th (1st London)
57th (2nd West Lancashire)
58th (2/1st London)
59th (2nd North Midland)
60th (2/2nd London)
61st (2nd South Midland)
62nd (2nd West Riding)
65th (2nd Lowland)
66th (2nd East Lancashire)
67th (2nd Home Counties)
69th (2nd East Anglian)
74th (Yeomanry)

The 74th was formed in Egypt after it became apparent that Yeomanry could be better employed as infantry; usually two Yeomanry regiments amalgamated to form an infantry battalion in the division. The 74th's formation sign, a broken spur, symbolised the dismounted role. The substantial body of replacement garrison troops needed for India were found by the 43rd (Wessex), the 44th (Home Counties) and the 45th (2nd Wessex) divisions, and they were all on the high seas before autumn was over. Other Terriers who volunteered for foreign service went straight into the BEF with their battalions.

The first Territorials to get to France were the London Scottish, on 16 September. They were followed by the 1st Battalion of the HAC, who landed two days later, and the 5th Battalion of the Border Regiment, who arrived on 26 October. But the first Territorials to engage the enemy were a troop of the Queen's Own Oxfordshire Hussars, who were patrolling on 5 October not far from Ypres, when they surprised a cyclist unit of the Germans' IV Cavalry Corps in the Mont des Cats area. The Oxfordshire Hussars were not, however, the first part-time cavalry troops to be in action against the Germans; that honour is held by A and C squadrons of the North Irish Horse and B Squadron of the South Irish Horse, who, as part of the Cavalry Special Reserve, had gone to France when the war was two weeks old and engaged the enemy on 24 August. It was not destined to be a hit-and-run war, however; no one at that stage would have thought it possible that by the time it ended, millions would have been killed, many millions of lives ruined by injury, disease, revolution and destitution, monarchies overthrown, empires shattered and maps redrawn.

THE LONDON SCOTTISH PAY THE TOLL

The London Scottish were not only the first unit to arrive in the theatre but also the first into full-scale battle. This action was at Messines on 31 October 1914, a date that must go down in history as that upon which Haldane's Territorials endured their baptism of fire. The battalion suffered no fewer than 640 casualties, revealed at a sad roll-call after the stand down, leading to the writing of many sorrowful letters by the officers to men's next of kin.

The London Scots' first day in the line, on 30 October, at what would come to be known as Sanctuary Wood, had been quiet and resulted in no casualties. But on the next day they were rushed to the Messines area. There they had to defend the Messines Wytschaete spur under heavy attack. It turned out to be a grim Hallowe'en for the Territorials when they discovered they had to stand up to the German offensive with single-shot rifles. They had been issued with short Lee Enfield rifles on 14 September, the day before they left Britain and had not had a chance to fire them. The weapons were the Mark I converted to accept Mark VII ammunition. It was not until they were facing the enemy that the men discovered that the magazine spring was too weak and the front stop clips were the wrong shape for the Mark VII round. The enemy attacked in waves, bands playing and the troops singing the national anthem. The London Scottish found themselves in hand to hand fighting and having to make a desperate counter charge to save themselves from being outflanked. When they had caught up their wounded and withdrawn, a roll call was taken; only 150 answered their names. The Territorials' baptism of fire had resulted in the battalion losing 394 killed, missing or taken prisoner.[5]

THE NURSES

The nursing services had been well prepared by the start of the war; there were 46,791 women VAD members, 40,018 from the British Red Cross Society and 6,773 from the St John Ambulance Brigade. Although, like the TF, the VADs had been envisaged as an organisation to serve the home defence forces, in common with the volunteering Territorials they were soon overseas. Some of them had volunteered for the Balkans in 1912. In 1914, others were in France before the first Territorials, setting up their units in Belgium and Brittany. A number of the detachments in Belgium were captured when the Germans advanced to the capital.

While the London Scottish were enduring their ordeal, a London group of VADs had established a wheeled rest station at Boulogne. It comprised two coaches and three wagons. Incredibly, about 1,000 wounded troops had been fed and cared for in 24 hours.

INTO THE TRENCHES

1st Battalion HAC got to France on 18 September, came under fire and learned what it was like to see casualties among their drill-night comrades on 13 November while digging trenches in the Les Lobes area. On 21 November they went into the front line for the first time. They did not fight immediately as a unit but, as was the practice to give the TF experience, were attached company by company to regular battalions in the 3rd Division. It was not until 9 December that the descendants of London's Hopefull Infantrie occupied a battalion position at the front, at Spanbroek Molen. It was a dreadful winter and the trenches were inadequate in both defence and drainage.

In 72 hours, the battalion suffered 262 casualties, most of them through the weather. The misery brought on by the cold, snow, rain and shallow, water-filled trenches was something that stayed with those members of the BEF for the rest of their lives. Eric Kennington, the artist who depicted two world wars, was a sergeant in the Kensington Regiment and painted a memorable picture, *The Kensingtons at Laventie.* The finished work is painted on a large sheet of glass but he drew the preliminary sketches of his comrades from life while recovering from frostbite. He has left us a legacy of witness of those times; his haunting, darkened faces tell us better than any words of the hardships and suffering of the troops.

THE HOME FRONT

Back at home, where the Yeomanry units of the Welsh Border Mounted Brigade had been given 20 miles of coastline near Great Yarmouth to defend, the Territorials had also experienced their first taste of enemy fire – but from a much safer distance. On 3 November, ships of the German Navy appeared off Great Yarmouth and fired a 20-minute bombardment, all the rounds falling short except one and even that caused little more than a splash on the shoreline. Nevertheless, as the first enemy projectile to land on British soil since the Napoleonic wars, it had its significance. More serious were the attacks on 16 December in which German warships bombarded the coast of north Yorkshire and Durham, the targets being Scarborough, Whitby and, further north, Hartlepool and West Hartlepool. At the two Hartlepools, Territorials of the Durham Garrison Artillery engaged the enemy in a duel so terrifying that the sound of the guns could be heard in Weardale at the other side of the county.[6]

On 19 January Great Yarmouth figured again as a milestone by sharing with King's Lynn the experience of being the victims of the first bombing raid by zeppelins. Again it was in the sector defended by the Welsh Border Mounted Brigade.

On Christmas Eve, a new dimension entered the war with the dropping by a German aeroplane of a bomb on Dover. It was the first plane to bomb England.

PRIVATE ARMOURED CARS

The Duke of Westminster, a Yeomanry officer who had seen service in South Africa, had been intrigued by the sight there of an armoured train. He was convinced that the principle could be applied to road vehicles and that now that there was a European war, it was time to put his theory into practice. With ducal grandeur, he began a series of experiments with Rolls-Royce engineers in the first few months of the war. By the end of the year, he had 13 armour-protected motor cars – all created at his own expense. On New Year's Day, outside Beccles, he commanded the cars successfully against his old regiment the Cheshire Yeomanry in what is thought to have been the first exercise of armoured vehicles against horses. He commanded the same vehicles at the second battle of Ypres.

A FRONT-LINE SANDHURST

Meanwhile, in the British Expeditionary Force, a unique honour befell the 28th Battalion of the London Regiment(Artists' Rifles), who were made an officer training unit in September 1914. They became a Sandhurst in the field, producing officers under fire in the trenches. The story is best told by Field Marshal Sir John French, commander in chief of the British Army there:

> I established the battalion as a Training Corps for officers in the field. The cadets pass through a course which includes some thoroughly practical training, as all cadets do a turn of 48 hours in the trenches and afterwards write a report on what they see and notice. They also visit an observation post of a battery or group of batteries and spend some hours there. A commandant has been appointed, and he arranges and supervises the work, sets schemes for practice, administers the school, delivers lectures and reports on the candidates. The cadets are instructed in all branches of military training suitable for platoon commanders. Machine-gun tactics, a knowledge of which is so necessary for all junior officers, is a special feature of the course of instruction. When first started, the school was able to turn out officers at the rate of seventy-five per month. This has since been increased to one hundred. Reports received from Divisional and Army Corps Commanders on officers who have been trained at the school are most satisfactory.

By the end of that year 1,517 former Artists had been commissioned. Of the total, 447 were posted to regular Guards or infantry battalions, 410 to TA battalions, 53 to the Special Reserve and 324 to Kitchener's new armies. The rest went to artillery, sapper, transport or miscellaneous units. The commandant had a long record of instruction, having taught at Sandhurst, and in India. He had been director of military studies at Cambridge University before rejoining the Army on the outbreak of war. On mobilisation the Artists were 650 strong and had to stop recruiting after a week. Although the unit had been earmarked for training corps status in the September, it went to France and fought in the first battle of Ypres. The 7th Division was short of officers as a result of casualties so about 50 Artists were given pips to place on their privates' uniforms and put in charge of platoons in action throughout the division. Another 50 were also made instant officers but were given tuition in the battalion before being posted to other units. After this, French made the Artists an officer training unit in the field. A second battalion was formed in Britain to send it drafts, and eventually a third battalion was established.

TRIBUTES

A tribute to the Territorials in action by the first November was paid by Major General Sir Frederick Maurice:

> It is difficult for those who saw only the trenches of the later years of the war to envisage the conditions of those days, when our parapets were dissolving under the steady rain, when communication trenches were nothing but water channels, when we had few sand bags, few guns, few shells, no trench mortars and few hand grenades; when 'trench feet' thinned our ranks more than the enemy's fire. It was in these conditions that the first Territorial battalions reached the front. Their arrival meant for the least thinking regular a day or two less in the trenches, a night or two more in a warm billet. That was enough. No more questions were asked as to whether the Territorials were fit to fight the Germans. From that beginning the Territorials went on winning the confidence of the Army and of the Nation, till at the end their divisions were ranked by friend and foe alike as peers of the best.[7]

Another senior officer, Lieutenant General Sir William Marshall, recalled later how, when he was commanding the 1st Sherwood Foresters:

> People who were in the trenches generally wanted to get out, whilst those who were out wanted to get in; in the latter category I include the Northamptonshire Yeomanry, who begged so hard of the Divisional Commander to be allowed to have a turn in the trenches that eventually one squadron was sent down to me to put into 'A' lines, and I posted the squadron to the left section, which was looked upon as the easiest and safest. To my surprise the squadron was accompanied by the Colonel (Wickham) and the Adjutant (Lowther) . . . Nothing I could say, however, would deter Wickham from going into the trenches that night, as he stoutly maintained that his duty was to be with his men.[8]

'SCHOTLANT FOR EFFER'

Territorials revealed themselves as more forthcoming than regulars in describing their experiences. For example, *The Times* of 12 November 1914 published letters from three members of the London Scottish. One of them, penned by a private soldier and dated 6 November, told those at home:

> Well, we've had a dig at the Germans, and on the whole seem to have made a good job of it. The whole thing came very suddenly – we moved up one afternoon in motor buses, and passed the night in deserted cottages near the firing line. We roused out at 4 am and spent the morning wandering about from wood to wood, being followed by aeroplanes, beastly things. Finally, we entered a village, and a spy in a windmill gave them the range and we had our first shells, horrible, 'coal boxes' and then shrapnel. We lost five men wounded there; then the battalion attacked up a valley and we had to lie in a gutter about 2ft. deep along a road with poplars...Then we had to advance across a field about a quarter mile under fire and get into a deserted trench – there we stopped till dark, still being shelled. At dusk we made another trench, and seven of us went into it. There we had a fine time – moonlight and Germans only 200 yards off. We could spot them through the glasses and made very good practice: some crept down a hedge to 20 yards, but we did them in. You could hear them all talking, and twice they came on in force, but we beat them off and they left any amount on the ground. Finally, at 12.45, they came on five or six deep, singing their national anthem and walking quite slowly. Not liking German music, we gave them rapid fire, but they were too many. At last the cavalry had to hop it on both sides of us and we ran like hares for our main trench; there we were 32, and had the Germans in front, left, and rear five or six deep. There were thousands of them, all creeping up, and bullets everywhere. We all thought it was UP. I even took off my overcoat so as to be freer for the bayonet, as we knew what prisoners get and didn't want to be done in cold blood. Then they lit a farm, and the black smoke from the wet thatch blew across our front, and between us they were only 50 yards away, still creeping, so we dashed out to the right and all got through except six. Then we got separated, and nine of us, including our lieutenant, had to wander round, with one shot through the back, looking for the regiment or British troops. We kept running into shell fire and rifle fire, but finally got to a village and found some officers at 4.45, very tired; there we reported, and we went to join a cavalry regiment about two miles off. We had only had one biscuit and jam since the previous breakfast. Well, for breakfast we had to attack the same village that we had been driven out of the day before. It was most exciting, shells and bullets everywhere.
>
> Then we got mixed up with the Germans and got the order to clear the houses with the bayonet. That was great sport: no shells and only scrapping in a decent sort of way. We took four prisoners and scuppered all the rest of them about 200; then we were just examining the slain for pistols and other handy souvenirs when the shrapnel started again all among us . . . One bullet turned my bonnet round on my head and I sat down in the mud, and I got one

through my kilt, but I don't think I shall be shot after that, as you can't get much closer. At last the French arrived in force and we were sent back for a rest. I am longing for another dig at them; it is the finest excitement going, and the things you see and hear make you absolutely merciless. Fancy, they came behind one of our trenches in kilts and said, 'Schotlant for effer and London Schottish', but a volley put an end to that . . .

FOOTBALL AT LOOS

The 18th (London Irish) Battalion of the London Regiment distinguished themselves at the battle of Loos. At dawn on 25 September 1915, the bombardment finished, British engineers turned on the gas which swirled over the German lines and into the throats of the 22nd Silesian Regiment opposite. At 06.30 the order to go up and over was shouted. Platoon by platoon, half a minute between each, the London Irish thrust themselves over the top and formed into lines before charging into the enemy fire. Some of the men had a football and were determined to score a goal by kicking it into the German trenches. A wounded survivor recalls in *The Weekly Dispatch* that day:

> One set of our men – keen footballers – made a strange resolution; it was to take a football along with them. The platoon officer discovered this and ordered the football to be sent back – which of course was carried out. But the old members of the London Irish Football Club were not to be done out of the greatest game of their lives – the last to some of them, poor fellows – and just before Major Beresford gave the signal the leather turned up again mysteriously.
>
> Suddenly the officer in command gave the signal, 'Over you go, lads'. With that the whole line sprang up as one man, some with a prayer, not a few making the sign of the Cross. But the footballers, they chucked the ball over and went after it just as cool as if on the field, passing it from one to the other, though the bullets were flying thick as hail, crying, 'On the ball, London Irish', just as they might have done at Forest Hill. I believe that they actually kicked it right into the enemy's trench with the cry, 'Goal!' though not before some of them had been picked off on the way.
>
> There wasn't four hundred yards between the trenches, and we had to get across the open – a manoeuvre we started just as on parade. All lined up, bayonets fixed, rifles at the slope. Once our fellows got going it was hard to get them to stop, with the result that some of them rushed clean into one of our own gas waves and dropped in it just before it had time to get over the enemy's trench.
>
> The barbed wire had been broken into smithereens by our shells so that we could get right through – but we could see that it had been terrible stuff,

and we all felt we should not have had a ghost of a chance of getting through had it not been for an unlimited supply of shells expended on it. When we reached the German trench, which we did under a cloud of smoke, we found nothing but a pack of beings dazed with terror. In a jiffy we were over their parapet and the real work began; a kind of madness comes over you as you stab with your bayonet and hear the shriek of the poor devil suddenly cease as the steel goes through him and you know he's 'gone West'. The beggars did not show much fight, most having retired into their second line of trenches when we began to occupy their first to make it our new line of attack. That meant clearing out even the smallest nook or corner that was large enough to hold a man.

This fell to the bombers. Every bomber is a hero, I think, for he has to rush on fully exposed, laden with enough stuff to send him to 'kingdom come' if a chance shot or a stumble sets him off.

Some of the sights were awful in the hand to hand struggle – for, of course, that is the worst part. Major Beresford was badly wounded. Captain and Adjutant Hamilton, though shot through the knee just after leaving our trench, was discovered still limping on at the second German trench and had to be placed under arrest to prevent his going on till he bled to death.

They got the worst of it, though, when it came to cold steel, which they can't stand and they ran like hares. So having left a number of our men in the first trench, we went on to the second, and then the third, after which other regiments came up to our relief and together we took Loos. It wasn't really our job at all to take Loos, but we were swept on by the enthusiasm, I suppose, and all day long we were at it, clearing house after house, or rather what was left of the houses – stabbing and shooting and bombing till one felt ready to drop dead oneself. We wiped the 22nd Silesian Regiment right out, but it was horrible to work on with the cries of the wounded all round.[9]

When it was all over, the adjutant who had been restrained, Captain A P Hamilton, was awarded the MC. An American serving in another British regiment gives an outsider's account of the London Irish:

By all rights the entire regiment should have been wiped out, as the odds were against them, and they were running right into a death-trap. The fact that they went at it in such a devil-may-care way as to joke and play with footballs in the very face of certain death broke the Germans' nerve and they gave way with practically no resistance at all. Instead of the regiment being wiped out, as it should have been, the men took the trenches with losses of under a hundred. It was wonderful.[10]

The human cost of the war by the spring of 1915 can be glimpsed by a situation report sent to the brigade commander by the 1st London Rifle Brigade, dated 8.25pm 2 May:

> Situation quieter. Fear casualties very heavy, will report later. All supports now in trench. Improbable that we can hold length of trench without assistance. Men have had no sleep for seven nights. This, with the incessant shelling, has told on them. Germans are entrenching nearer to us, opposite to our centre. No 3 Company, which is there, hopes that it did good execution on them. Can you send any Very lights?[11]

Later that night, Corporal G G Boston, leading three men, crawled to within 50 yards of the German trenches and succeeded in wiring the whole of the company front. He won the DCM.

The action had started on the previous day with a heavy bombardment by the enemy. Everyone except the sentries took cover. At 5.20pm the Germans released poison gas and a heavy cloud of it appeared on the left opposite the Royal Irish and 3 and 4 companies of the LRB. The respirators, the first of their type to be issued, were rudimentary, merely strips of cloth soaked in chemical. When the chemical was exhausted, the official advice ran, the cloth must be soaked in urine. The gas resulted in no more than a handful of casualties, and these staggered away for treatment at dusk. The Germans set up a machine gun near their gas cylinders and riflemen started a ground attack against the LRB position. By early evening, the Londoners were exhausted, having been shelled initially, subjected to the retching caused by the gas and fighting off the attack all afternoon. For the chores of the evening, the ration and ammunition replenishment, the services of the East Lancashires were obtained. The rear party of two platoons of X Company of the 4th Yorks, from whom the LRB had taken over the position, helped to evacuate the wounded. The final casualty, a man wounded in the thigh at daybreak, was bumpingly wheeled away on a bicycle.

BLIZZARD OVER GALLIPOLI

The fiasco that was the Dardanelles campaign usually conjures up images of intense heat, rocks, shortage of water and gunshot wound casualties, but there was another aspect of that massive miscalculation. When autumn arrived to find the Allies still without room to manoeuvre, sickness rivalled wounds in the casualty lists. The campaign had started with a naval bombardment in February 1915, followed by minor raids by the Royal Marines, but the first major landing did not take place until 25 April. By the time that the campaign ended in early January 1916, British Commonwealth casualties in the fighting had reached 117,549, of whom 28,200 were killed; sickness claimed a further 96,683 many of which were fatal. The total was 214,232.

On 17 November 1915 rain of tropical intensity fell for two hours after a frightening thunderstorm. Mule tracks and footpaths were swept away and trenches were flooded. The pattern was to be repeated for weeks. Mud, soaking clothes and frost are usually associated in British minds with France and Flanders, but it was far worse for the Allied troops fighting on the Gallipoli peninsula. These included the Territorial formations the 42(East Lancashire) Division – plus their attached Yeomen turned infantry of the South Eastern Mounted Infantry Brigade, comprising the Royal East Kent and West Kent Yeomanry regiments and the Sussex Yeomanry – and the 52(Lowland) Division. It was worse because there was no room on the beach head to provide hot baths, warm billets, dry clothes and a change of diet – all of which were usually available to the soldiers of the Western front when they came out of the line. It was worse too because, at Gallipoli, you were never out of range of enemy fire. You were pulled out of the trenches when your turn came but there was nowhere to go for respite. A rest camp provided a rest in name only; there were no places that were warm, dry, comforting, entertaining and offering a change from life in the line. On top of this, there were always tasks to be done, such as carrying supplies from the beach.

A member of the 2/2nd Battalion of the London Regiment, Private T J Underwood, describes the misery of 26 November:

> I was just snatching a sleep on a ledge in the support trenches when it started to rain – rain such as I have never seen before. In a minute I was swept off the ledge and lay in a foot of water, the lightning meanwhile, flashing about incessantly, making the intervals of blackness like ink. I began to think that the Turks were letting a dam loose, as the water was steadily rising.[12]

It was not the Turks but nature doing its worst. The enemy almost became neutrals, having no thoughts of fighting as they sheltered from the weather's onslaught. The storm heightened the effect of the tide, washing away bivouacs on the beach. In Gully ravine an unstoppable torrent twisted its way downwards carrying men, mules, crates of supplies and hay bales into the sea. The rainstorm turned into sleet and developed into a blizzard. The cold was almost indescribable, so intense that it turned oil into solid blocks. The water jackets of the Vickers-Maxim machine guns froze and then their locks jammed, as did the soldiers' rifle bolts. In one fraught period there were only 30 working rifles in the whole of the 2/2nd Londons. The battalion was trapped in trenches in which the water froze around the men's feet, as they clutched weapons that would not work.

The whole of 2 Brigade's front was similarly affected. To the dismay of the brigade machine gun officer only one gun would work. It belonged to Lance Corporal G E Griffiths, of the Second to Nondons, and it worked because his officer, Second Lieutenant D L Child, had searched until he located a tin of glycerine. He put it in the cooling system and smeared the lock, and kept the water from freezing by firing bursts long enough to heat it. The blizzard raged for three days, causing about 6,000 deaths. Some 10,000 casualties were evacuated from the peninsula as a result of the storm. Captain Bateman describes how men of the 2/2nd Londons were kept alive:

> The men's joints were so stiff from the cold that they had to be lifted on to the fire step and lifted off again when their turn of duty was over. Some were so far gone that in order to keep their blood moving, they were pushed about from one man to another like human tennis balls, and it was only the rum served in the mornings that kept them alive at all.[13]

The storm of 26 November, filling the trenches at Suvla and Anzac with water, presented the men of the East Lancashire Division with the problem of sheltering in them and being drowned or huddling on top and being exposed – fortunately the enemy too had his problems of survival and there was no shooting. The next day brought more rain and this was followed by a frost so severe that men were frozen to death at their posts. The cold was of a ferocity that, to survive, men were constantly foraging for wood to make fires, to the extent of breaking crates of tinned food from dumps, leaving the food and taking the crates. Even the butts of rifles of comrades who would never fire another round were used as fuel.

The Second to Nondons were relieved on 1 December by the naval Drake Battalion and the 2/4th Londons and went to their comfortless rest camp. There was danger everywhere. No sooner had the blizzard abated than the Turks increased their barrages, triumphantly demonstrating the arrival of massive supplies of ammunition from Germany, made possible by Bulgaria's joining in the war and opening the Danube route. As for the Allied troops, the storm through the Gully had not only washed away supplies and mules, it left fresh deposits of mud several feet deep through this vital communications artery for the East Lancashires. After 10 days, the Second to Nondons were back in the line, where, moving from sector to sector, they stayed for 18 days. Members of the battalion who were serving on the Western front by the next winter made the point that Flanders had nothing that could compare with that blizzard at Gallipoli.

The battalion spent Christmas in the line, were relieved on Boxing Day and were among the last to be evacuated in January. The final days on the peninsula were an eerie experience. Stores that had cost much in toil and suffering and which could not be evacuated, were dumped on the beach in great piles and soaked in paraffin ready to be burned. On the last afternoon, the usually thronged ravines and tracks between the beach and the trenches were empty. People were packed into the front line – in some places of the East Lancashire divisional front only 15 yards from the enemy. When the early night fell, the weather, so cruel in past weeks, turned friend: the sky was ink. Silently the troops filed out of the front line and support trenches, leaving a few fixed rifles to fire at the burning down of candles tied with weighted string to triggers. Slowly they moved to the beach, leaving tiny parties of sappers and medicals. The sappers' task was to close gaps in the defences; the medicals, in groups of one doctor and four orderlies, crept along helping the stragglers and the recently wounded. How long would it be before the enemy realized he was facing empty trenches? 'If ever man knew terror I knew it that night', admitted one of the officers[14] of this first Territorial division to go abroad and by now a battle hardened veteran.

The troops climbed into lighters, some of them crammed with 400 souls that shuttled them to transport ships; still the Turks failed to appreciate what was happening. The sapper parties set fuses, hurried into the last lighters and, as they sailed away, watched the supply dumps exploding; fires illuminated the beach and shoreline. The enemy realized he had been cheated and started shelling. But it was too late. The only successful thing about the Gallipoli campaign, the evacuation, had been accomplished.

Long before the troops pulled out, the padres had put in long, dangerous hours in the line comforting the wounded and administering the last rites. The Reverend E T Kerby, a chaplain of the 42nd Division, alone conducted the burial services of nearly 1,000 of the Manchester Regiment's fallen.

Despite the casualties and the hardships, the British troops apparently regarded the Turks as a brave and sporting adversary who respected the Red Cross and treated wounded prisoners with humanity. The Red Cross flag at the 42nd's advanced dressing station at Y Beach was in full view of the enemy for three months and it was never shelled. 'When the field ambulance of the South East Mounted Brigade took over in December, the Union Jack was hoisted in addition to the Red Cross flag. The change was made at midnight, and promptly at dawn the Turks opened fire. The first two shells were short; then came three "overs", and the sixth and last brought down the flagpole'.[15]

In another incident, the Turks threw an inert bomb from their trenches into the lines of the Sussex Yeomanry. Attached to it was a message: 'Goodbye, Sussex Yeomanry. Sorry you can't stay, but we'll meet again on the Canal'.[16]

DAN TO BEERSHEBA

The action did indeed shift to the Near East. The Territorial divisions taking part there included the 42nd (East Lancashire), two brigades of the 46th (North Midland), detached temporarily in early 1916, the 52nd (Lowland), the 53rd (Welsh), the 54th (East Anglian), the 60th (2/2nd London) and the 74th (Yeomanry). As part of Allenby's army they would engage the Turks successfully in the desert, fight through the Holy Land and go on to conquer Jerusalem, following in the steps of those other troops from England eight centuries earlier. They would eventually control not only Biblical Palestine, from Dan to Beersheba, but far beyond.

There are many tributes about the way the commanders in this campaign conducted their warfare. It was also notable for what is usually regarded as the last cavalry charge of the British Army. The author does not want to be drawn into controversy about whether this action was in fact the Army's last horsed charge, or indeed about the definition of what constitutes such an action (for instance, is a charge of colonial troops led by British officers a British Army charge? And how many horsemen must take part for it to be a 'cavalry charge'; will a troop do?). But there is no doubt that the action on 8 November 1917 near Huj, south east of Gaza, where the Turks had had a headquarters, was an outstanding feat of arms, and probably the last full-scale cavalry charge by a British unit. The action, which consisted of a series of three charges, the first against foot soldiers, the main thrust against guns, then a scattering operation against recovering troops, was conducted by 170 Territorials of the Warwickshire Yeomanry and the Worcestershire Yeomanry and the main element involved their galloping straight up to the muzzles of nine field guns, which with three 5.9in howitzers, had earlier been registered on the division's infantry. During the charge, which was over about a mile and a half of terrain that dropped, rose into a mound, then sloped upward to the ridge held by the enemy guns, the Yeomen were also under fire from three machine guns and rifles. The Yeomen were led by Lieutenant Colonel H A Gray-Cheape, of the Warwickshire, who was awarded an immediate bar to his DSO. The action, which killed 35 of the 170 Yeomen and wounded many others, and cost the lives of about 100 chargers, is best described by Major General J S M Shea, commander of the 60th Division, in a report dated 9 November to GHQ via General Chauvel, commanding the Desert Mounted Corps. Shea said:

> I beg to report that yesterday, after my Division had taken the high ground N. of Montaret-el-Baght, I was scouting ahead in an armoured car. I saw many Turks with guns marching N.E. across my front. It was impossible for my Infantry to catch them. Some cavalry came up on my right (about a mile

away) which turned out to be ten Troops of Worcester and Warwick Yeomanry. Judging that immediate action was necessary, I went and ordered Lieut.-Col. Cheape to gallop, what appeared to me, to be the hostile flank guard. I judged the distance at 2,500 yards. This gallop was at once carried out with the result that some twelve guns and three machine guns were captured and the gunners (German and Austrian) were all killed or wounded at their guns. I visited the scene of action shortly afterwards and can testify to the complete demoralization of the enemy flank guard. The gallop, which was carried out in the face of heavy gun, machine gun and rifle fire, was executed with the greatest gallantry and élan and was worthy of the very best traditions of the British Cavalry.

I very much regret to hear that the Yeomanry lost some 25 per cent. but they completely broke the hostile resistance and enabled my Division to push on to Huj. Lieut.-Col. Cheape led the gallop with the greatest personal gallantry and with conspicuous judgment. I recommend him strongly for immediate reward, and would venture to commend such names as he may forward to your most earnest consideration.[17]

In December, the British entered Jerusalem. The large war cemeteries at Ramleh and Mount Scopus indicate the cost but it was small compared to the prices being paid on the Western front. Many of the Territorials, having played their part in Allenby's campaign, now found their divisions switched to take part in that main show.

7

Digging In: The Somme 1916

By all the glories of the day and the cool evening's benison,
By the last sunset touch that lay upon the hills when day was done,
By beauty lavishly outpoured and blessings carelessly received,
By all the days that I have lived make me a soldier, Lord.

LIEUTENANT NOEL HODGSON, MC,
9TH BN OF THE DEVONSHIRE REGIMENT,
from *Before Action*, written two days before he fell, aged 23,
at Mansel Copse on the first day of the Somme.

The aims of the British Army's greatest, deadliest and worst battle were stated by General Sir Douglas Haig, commander in chief, as:

1. To relieve the pressure on Verdun.
2. To assist our Allies in the other theatres of war by stopping any further transfer of German troops from the Western front.
3. To wear down the strength of the forces opposed to us.[1]

The first battle of the Somme started at 7.30am on 1 July 1916 and before the long, beautiful summer day was over, the British Army had suffered 57,470 casualties, nearly 20,000 of them fatal. No other single day would prove as devastating but by the time that the series of battles known as the Somme ended in November, its toll had become more than 1¼ million casualties, some 630,000 of them from the ranks of the Allies. The Allies' gains had been microscopic. By and large, Haig had achieved his aims: Verdun had been saved, the enemy had been ground down and we have it on impeccable authority that the Germans were worn out by the sustained ferocity of the offensive.[2] But the cost had been beyond belief. 'Ask anyone who was on the Somme whether we should ever have another war' was a remark often heard by the author in childhood.[3]

While the principal thrust had been the responsibility of the Fourth Army, with 13 divisions, and the French Sixth Army, with five divisions, to the south, there were subsidiary attacks by the Fifth Army, north of the Fourth, and at the extreme north, by the Third Army on both sides of the Gommecourt salient, with the aim of diverting the enemy's resources. Two Territorial divisions, the 46th and the 56th, of VII Corps, were on the start line of the diversionary attack, the 46th's task was the northern edge of the salient and the 56th's was the southern side. The VII Corps front line was some 700 yards from the enemy trenches, so the commander, using initiative and intelligence (and no doubt smiled on by the fortune that favours the bold), redrew it by establishing a new front line under the cover of night in no man's land, leaving his forces 250–300 yards on average to advance across open ground in the attack. The digging of this advanced trench system fell to 167 Brigade of the 56th Division.

Once the summer darkness had fallen on 25 May, the men of the brigade slithered out and spent the night indicating with twine the line of the new trench. The next night was one of Herculean labours as about 300 men of the brigade silently dug the trench. It was completed by 2½ hours past midnight. Major C H Dudley Ward describes the scene of the secret trench held by posts from the covering parties and reinforced with Lewis gunners. 'They had rations, water, and shovels to improve their positions, and were in telephone communication with the old trench, and all the working parties had filed away as silently as they had come'[4]. The next night a similar number reinforced the trench and dug support lines and two other communication trenches. Ward again:

> The 56th Division had then started its career with the astounding feat of having in the space of 48 hours constructed and wired a new system of trenches, comprising 2,900 yards of fire trench and 1,500 yards of communication trenches in No Man's Land and within 250 yards of the enemy. Casualties were eight killed and 55 wounded.[5]

It must not be assumed from Ward's words that the units were newcomers to the field; only the division was starting its career in the forward area, having been formed in France on 6 February 1916. The infantry units were all first-line TF battalions and by now battle hardened.

In spite of their Herculean efforts, the diggers of 167 Brigade were not finished yet. As the attack would be made by 168 and 169 Brigades, who would therefore need rest and time for preparation, the responsibility for the security of the entire divisional front was given to 167 Brigade from 24 to 26 June. The digging of this Territorial formation had almost certainly saved thousands of lives by shortening the distance which the attacking brigades would have to cover.

On 1 July, the daylight artillery barrage that had continued for five days was resumed at 6.25am, building up to its peak during 7.15 and 7.25. Smoke was discharged, and into the swirling dust clouds the burdened troops went over the top . . .

FIRST DEPLOYMENT OF TANKS

Two and a half months into the offensive, the British were heartened by the battle debut of their secret weapon, the tank. The very name, now so universally accepted, was a security cover, meant to imply storage tanks rather than a fighting vehicle. But their use was premature, patchy and ill-thought-out and the machines were mechanically unreliable; the gains were not followed through and were therefore illusory. An old Militia-descended unit made a milestone when, moving over their start line at 5.30 on the morning of 15 September, near Delville Wood, they became the first infantry of any army to go into action with tanks. The men comprised two companies of the 6th Battalion of the King's Own Yorkshire Light Infantry. A County Durham man who went into action in a tank that day had two overwhelming memories: the secrecy that had cloaked their vehicles' approach to the line and the problems of fuelling the engine when moving through shellholes – an aspect that had presumably been overlooked in training – and much practical engineering had to be employed to solve it.[6] One of the few tanks that achieved their objectives was the subject of a combat message that deserves to rank with Nelson's 'England expects . . .' signal at Trafalgar. A Royal Flying Corps aviator reported: 'Tank seen in main street Flers going on with large numbers of troops following it.'[7]

With the benefit of a decade of hindsight, Lloyd George could declare on the deployment of the first tanks in battle: 'So the great secret was sold for the battered ruin of a little hamlet on the Somme'.[8] But Lloyd George was one of the men who could have prevented the committal of armies in such a way that British Empire and French soldiers died in their tens of thousands. Perhaps the pithiest comment on the offensive came from F Scott Fitzgerald, who in his novel *Tender is the Night* has one of his characters say:

> See that little stream. We could walk to it in two minutes. It took the British a whole month to walk to it – a whole empire walking very slowly, dying in front and pushing forward behind. And another empire walked very slowly backwards a few inches a day, leaving the dead like a million bloody rugs.

Among the many Territorial units that fought on the Somme was the 4th Battalion Royal Welsh Fusiliers who gained three battle honours there for their tenacity at Albert, Morval and Le Transloy.

8

1918: Hurricane of Steel and Victory

In Flanders fields the poppies blow
Between the crosses, row on row,
That mark our place; and in the sky
The larks, still bravely singing, fly
Scarce heard amid the guns below.

LIEUTENANT COLONEL JOHN MCCRAE,
CANADIAN AMC,
from *In Flanders Fields*, 1915

Although the fighting went on until November, the year 1918 had to be the last of the war. The Germans knew that they must finish the struggle before the Americans could establish themselves in strength in the field. Turkey was retreating, Baghdad and Jerusalem had fallen in 1917; Austria-Hungary was wavering; the families of the Fatherland were questioning the endless lists of casualties, and the emergence of a new order in Russia was turning some Germans' thoughts to a new system for the Fatherland too – and martial law had been declared in Berlin.

To necessity was added opportunity: with Russia out of the war more than a million German troops and some 3,000 guns could be redeployed on the Western front, which added to the existing forces fighting them, meant that the Allies would be far outnumbered. These were the reasons for the Germans' last and most violent offensive of the war.

The years of fighting had taken their toll on both Britain and France and although Britain had been augmenting its forces with conscripted troops since early 1916, the Army had had to change its brigade make-up. From February 1918 the practice in France was for brigades to have three instead of four battalions. An example of the change is provided by the 74th Division (the old broken spur badged cavalry formation). It consequently shed the 24th Battalion of the Royal Welsh Fusiliers (Denbighshire Yeomanry Regiment), the 12th Battalion of the Royal Scots Fusiliers (Ayrshire and Lanarkshire

Yeomanry Regiments) and the 12th Battalion of the Norfolk Regiment (Norfolk Yeomanry Regiment). These three battalions became part of the 31st Division.

In another Territorial division, the 56th, the GOC decided that the reduction could most fairly be carried out by each brigade's losing the highest numbered of those battalions listed for possible disbandment. Thus 167 Brigade lost the 1/3rd Londons, 168 Brigade lost the 1/12th Londons and 169 Brigade lost the Queen Victoria's Rifles. It was a sad time for men who had fought together for so long to have their unit consigned to the history book and to be posted to other battalions. The 58th Division was similarly depleted, losing from 173 Brigade the 2/1st Londons, from 174 Brigade the 2/5th Londons, and from 175 Brigade the 2/11th Londons.

A sadly stretched and battle weary BEF now braced itself for what was to prove one of its greatest trials but also the beginning of the end for the enemy.

LUDENDORFF'S MARCH OFFENSIVE

General Erich Ludendorff, who with his chief Field Marshal von Hindenburg directed the German war effort, decided that the only way to win in a Europe tired of war was to drive the British right off the battlefield and into the Channel.[1] He correctly appreciated that the British had their strongest forces protecting the area of the Channel ports, their lifeline, and decided to attack where they were weakest, to the south. The Allies knew that a great offensive would start with the spring. What was not known was the timing and location.

Haig, under pressure from his political masters and the French, had reluctantly agreed to take over an extra 30 miles of the front from the French. This meant that Britain's Fifth Army, commanded by General Sir Hubert Gough, now had a 42-mile front extending from Gouzeaucourt south to Barisis, in the St Gobain forest. Among the formations under his command was the 58th Division, whose units, transferred from Flanders, found themselves on a front far removed from the north's flat, treeless moonscape of craters, destroyed towns and evil mud saturated with persistent poison gases. Now they were in an area that had escaped devastation; this was beautiful, wooded, undulating *France profonde.*

Some dates of the war will long be remembered in the British Army, those of the retreat from Mons, the landings at the Gallipoli peninsula, and the first day of the Somme. Now a new date was to swell the list, 21 March 1918. Intelligence gained on the 20th and confirmed that night by a patrol of the 18th Division had established that the morrow was to be the day, and, urgently, the message was passed along the front: 'Stand by for attack'.

For the men in the British trenches, it was an eerie time waiting for the dawn, the scents of spring rising from the gentle countryside. The occasional far-off rattle of a sentry's machine gun or the tactile plop of a Very light bursting its radiance into the sky seemed only to emphasise the stillness.

Instead of making their intentions known by a protracted artillery barrage lasting for days, the German commander in this sector, von Hutier, decided on surprise, storm troops then wave after wave of infantrymen. The attack on 21 March, mainly on a front stretching from Arras south to La Fère, was preceded by a ferocious artillery pounding, but one of only two hours' duration. It started at 04.50 and men of the 2/2nd Londons described it as a period of continuous explosions, with columns of earth hurled high into the sky and orange flames everywhere. On average, every ten yards of the Fifth Army's front was raked by an enemy field gun. On the front of Britain's Third Army, on Gough's left, 153 Brigade of one of the great Territorial divisions, the 51st(Highland), lost virtually all its troops in the forward area – killed, buried or taken prisoner. The impact on the British front line of 6,473 guns and 3,532 mortars was devastating. As the barrage died away, the great mass of German infantrymen, each man carrying a week's supply of food and ammunition, his blankets and a spare pair of boots, surged forward behind a strong screen of well-trained storm troopers, skirmishing their way towards the stunned British, woefully thin on the ground but grimly determined to sell their lives dearly.

The British were relying on a strong front line system coupled, in some sectors, with the water barriers of the Oise canal and surrounding swamplands. But it had been an unusually dry winter and the Germans found little difficulty in crossing the water, in some places with boat bridges and, in others with planks. The British were hampered by a thick dawn mist (the morning mists would be a remembered feature of the first three days of the offensive). Once the Germans had broken through the British lines by weight of numbers – in some places they had a four to one advantage in manpower – they were impossible to hold. There was no defence in depth (such as the Germans had enjoyed against the British offensive on the Somme of 1916). The early result of this German last offensive was the retreat of the Fifth Army. To the north, the Third Army, commanded by General Sir Julian Byng, withdrew at its extremity to maintain alignment with the Fifth.

Haig issued an exhortation to the troops:

Special order of the Day
by Field-Marshal Sir Douglas Haig
K.T., G.C.B., G.C.V.O., K.C.I.E.
C.-in-C., British Armies in France

To all ranks of the British Army in France and Flanders.

We are again at a crisis in the war. The enemy has collected on this front every available Division, and is aiming at the destruction of the British Army. We have already inflicted on his army in the course of the last two days very heavy loss, and the French are sending troops as quickly as possible to our support. I feel that everyone in the Army, fully realising how much depends on the exertions and steadfastness of each one of us, will do his utmost to prevent the enemy from attaining his object.

D. Haig, F.M,
C.-in-C.,
British Armies in France

General Headquarters
23rd March 1918

Only a lack of cavalry or armoured cars and the magnificent response of the exhausted British divisions to Haig's exhortation, had prevented complete breakthrough by the Germans who, by now, were as exhausted as their opponents. By 26 March, a combination of that exhaustion and the effects of their earlier successes had gone to the heads of the German divisions opposite the Fifth Army and their discipline had deteriorated so far that many units became more interested in rape and pillage and the lure of strong drink than in the fight. Rawlinson, who had taken over from Gough the command of what now became the Fourth Army, stopped the enemy just nine miles short of Amiens. On 5 April, after 16 days of some of the most bitter fighting of the war, Ludendorff's '*Kaiserschlacht*' was over. It had cost the British 178,000 casualties, of whom 70,000 were prisoners. The French losses were some 77,000 and the enemy had lost roughly as many men as the two Allies together.

The enemy's success against the Fifth Army had caused a change of plan. Instead of turning to the north, his axis pressed west with the new aim of taking Amiens and controlling the rail system to Paris. Although they had made progress at a speed unknown in the warfare of the past 3½ years, the Germans were able to consolidate their gains in the next two weeks. Turning their ambitions to Flanders, they attacked the British again on 8 April, on the La Bassée–Armentières front, nearly as far north as Ypres. By now the Germans had taken nearly 88,000 prisoners and more than 1,000 guns.

Seven weeks later, and to the south, it was the turn of France to suffer the most menacing attack of all. Challenging the French Sixth Army, the Germans captured more than 40,000 prisoners and about 400 guns. The result of the German offensive was that they had dented the Allied front line with three enormous salients, all of which were blunt and therefore easier to defend. The two largest, each about 35 miles deep from the start line, were to the south; they formed prehensile arms, one reaching within 35 miles of the northern suburbs of Paris, the other ending about 32 miles east of the capital. This must be regarded as the high point of the war for the Germans. It is just possible that victory could have been theirs, with troops so near to the capital and the British and French armies having suffered so many casualties over four years, only to be driven further back than when they started. Hundreds of thousands of Parisians fled in panic. The northernmost salient was 15 miles deep. In some sectors the British found themselves defending places in which previously they had taken their ease as safe rest areas far behind the line.

Meanwhile the Americans were establishing their formations much more rapidly than Ludendorff had thought possible. When the Germans sought to exploit their gains in the southernmost salient on 15 July the untried Americans fighting alongside the French proved themselves worthy comrades in the three-day attack and these two Allies immediately counterattacked on the fourth day, winning this second battle of the Marne.

To the north the Empire forces of Britain, Canada and Australia were preparing for their counterstroke. It came at 04.45 on 8 August, a misty morning. The aim was to relieve the pressure on Amiens and to push back that dangerous middle salient. Britain scraped together from tankodromes all over northern France, 604 tanks, using this mass to inflict upon the Germans what Ludendorff would describe as a 'black day' for the Fatherland.[2] Out of that vast total of tanks it was not expected that all would be mechanically able to engage but the operation, kept a secret and unheralded by the customary lengthy artillery barrage, was a complete success. The mist lasted for two hours and the tanks and infantry, effectively balanced, emerging from it were frightening foes. The day brought an eight-mile gain for the Empire and the great Hindenburg Line was broken.

The double blow meant that Germany would never go on the offensive again in the war. When the pursuit phase opened, those Contemptibles who had survived began to pass through towns and features with which they had been familiar four years earlier when the war was going to be over by Christmas. But now, far away in south west Europe, the war ended at the end of September for Bulgaria with Allied success in the Balkans campaign, which meant that her allies Germany and Turkey had lost their land link with each other.

By now the Germans were retreating too rapidly for the Allies to catch up with them: using railways, roads and bridges that they would destroy in their wake. It did not mean the danger for the troops was over, booby traps were left, some mines were detonated later by timers. A Territorial, Lance Corporal William H Coltman, DCM and bar, MM and bar, of the 6th Battalion of the North Staffordshires, gained his VC in early October (see Chapter 17 Soldiers Supreme).

THE COLLAPSE BEGINS

On October 31, Germany started making peace approaches. Turkey was out of the war with effect from noon on 1 November. By now Austria, too, was finished.

It was symbolic that the war's last deed of heroism to be rewarded by the VC should be by a Territorial. On 6 November Major Brett Cloutman, of the 59th Field Regiment, RE, who had started part-time soldiering in London University OTC and then joined the 12th County of London Regiment(Rangers), frustrated an attempt to blow up the Quartes bridge at Pont-sur-Sambre by swimming the river and, defying heavy fire, cutting the leads to the charges and swimming back to the British bank (see Chapter 17 Soldiers Supreme). It was no fault of his that the Germans later demolished the bridge by other means.

That day, 6 November, the 1st Battalion of the London Rifle Brigade had their last action. Montignies was the objective but they failed to take it. The battalion, depleted in strength, crossed the river Honelle on foot at 05.30 and started their assault up the slope on the far side. But the enemy was too well protected. Three hours later, the LRB were back where they had started, wet, exhausted and fewer. They were relieved by the 7th Middlesex at 21.00 and went into rest billets. The switch was operational but it was symbolic too that the 7th Diehards should still be fighting at the end of the war: they had been the first Territorial battalion to volunteer to serve overseas.

On 8 November, 125 Brigade, comprising the 5th, 7th and 8th battalions of the Lancashire Fusiliers, crossed the river Sambre at the point where Cloutman had won his VC. They went over by footbridge provided by the sappers and this added to the symbolism because the brigade was part of the 42nd Division, the old East Lancashire formation that had been the first TF division to go overseas. The next day a vehicle bridge was erected across the river, which helped the supply situation of the advancing troops. The 7th Lancashire Fusiliers were given responsibility for the brigade front with an outpost line 1,000 yards east of the Maubeuge to Avesnes road. In the evening, patrols of the battalion penetrated Ferrière and Le Trieux, more than 3,000 yards in front of the outposts, and captured three trains packed with munitions as well as a motor lorry and machine guns. But by now the question of supplies or no supplies was of only academic interest to the Fatherland, which was collapsing and that day the Kaiser, who in August 1914 had promised his troops leaving for the Western front that they would be home before the leaves had fallen from the trees, abdicated. *Waffenstillstand*, the courageous first and final enemy begged. Suddenly, all along the British front early on the 11th day of that 11th month pencils were scribbling on to grubby message pads the incredible order from GHQ:

Hostilities will cease from 11 a.m. to-day. Troops will stand fast on line reached at that hour. Defensive precautions will be maintained. There will be no intercourse of any description with the enemy.

ARMISTICE

It was all over but the cost of victory had been enormous. More than 908,000 of the Empire's servicemen had died; and among the fallen were no fewer than 129,806 of Britain's Territorials. As though the deaths by violence were not enough, a great influenza epidemic had swept westwards from the Far East in the closing months of the war. The troops in Mesopotamia were badly affected. By the time it had scourged France, the disease had killed more American troops than had the bullets and bombs.

Horses too had suffered in the fighting. An example can be provided by an incident that befell the Sherwood Rangers Yeomanry. Having completed their service in the Balkans, they sailed from Salonika for Egypt in the transport ship *Cestria* under cover of night on 23 June 1917. The regiment, 556 strong and with 612 horses, shared the vessel with a field ambulance and a field troop of engineers. The total number of animals carried exceeded a thousand. Most of the Yeomanry were at stables at 09.30 the following day when a torpedo struck the ship. The explosion amidships burst part of the main deck and showered the rest of it with water and coal from the shattered bunkers. An escorting destroyer, HMS *Ribble*, manoeuvred alongside and took off most of the men; others left in boats and were picked up by another destroyer, HMS *Racoon*. All were off the stricken vessel by 10.15 with only one casualty, a subaltern slightly injured in the explosion. The *Racoon* towed the *Cestria* for more than four hours but it sank within six hours of Skyros, taking every horse and all the troops' equipment and baggage to the bottom. The only animals saved were the pet dogs Spanc, named after the river in Macedonia, of B Squadron, and Mickey, of C Squadron.

The 58th Division's memorial at Chipilly, near the Somme, is a reconstruction in stone of a Territorial saying goodbye to his stricken horse.

One of the first results of the end of the fighting was a symbolic victorious entry to that early battleground of the British Army, Mons, by General Sir H S Horne, commander of the First Army. Units were represented in the parade on 15 November by detachments of 80. It was a time for style as well as thankfulness and units had their colours brought from Britain. An example is provided by those of the 1/2nd Londons, presented by Edward VII at Windsor in 1909 at a parade of his infant Territorial battalions. The Second to Nondons' colours were carried out of sanctuary at Christchurch, Streatham Hill, south

London, and proudly borne through the streets of Mons. The Territorial Force had won its spurs.

WAR RECORD OF THE TERRITORIAL DIVISIONS

The service of the Territorial divisions in the First World War was as follows:

The 42nd was the first TF division to go overseas, sailing for Egypt and garrison duties on 9 September 1914. Later it served in the Dardanelles and, after the evacuation, it fought in Egypt including the Sinai desert. From early 1917 it served on the Western front.

The 43rd, the 44th and the 45th sailed for India respectively on 9 October, 19 October, and 12 December 1914 for internal security duties.

The 46th landed in France on 24 February 1915 and, apart from two of its brigades being detached in Egypt during early 1916, it fought continuously on the Western front.

The 47th arrived in France on 9 March 1915 and fought continuously on the Western front.

The 48th landed in France in the same month and served in that theatre until moved to Italy on 28 November 1917.

The 49th, the 50th and the 51st arrived in France respectively on 12, 16 and 30 April 1915 and fought continuously on the Western front.

The 52nd sailed for Egypt on 19 May 1915, fought in the Gallipoli landings and, after the evacuation, took part in the Egypt and Palestine campaign. After victory in that theatre it moved to the Western front.

The 53rd and the 54th sailed for Gallipoli on 17 and 20 July 1915 respectively. After the evacuation, they fought in the Egypt and Palestine campaign.

The 55th and the 56th were formed in France on 3 January and 6 February 1916 respectively and fought continuously on the Western front.

The 57th and the 58th landed in France on 6 February and 20 January 1917 respectively and served continuously on the Western front.

The 59th, after service in Ireland in 1916, landed in France on 21 February 1917 and then served continuously on the Western front.

The 60th arrived in France on 21 June 1916. It served in Macedonia and Salonika early in the following year and later that summer fought in Palestine.

The 61st, the 62nd and the 66th landed in France on 21 May 1916, 3 January 1917 and 26 February 1917 respectively and fought continuously on the Western front.

The 65th, the 67th and the 69th served in the United Kingdom on home defence duties.

The 74th was formed in Egypt on 3 March 1915. After the end of the Egypt and Palestine campaign it moved to France on 1 May 1918.

FIRST WORLD WAR FIRSTS

First TF unit to volunteer for overseas service – 7th Middlesex (volunteered before war).

First TF brigade to volunteer for overseas service – 1 London Infantry Brigade (comprising 1st, 2nd, 3rd and 4th(City of London) battalions of London Regiment(Royal Fusiliers)) (volunteered before war).

First TF division to go overseas – East Lancashire sailed midnight 9 Sept 1914; redesignated 42nd (lowest available number for TF) thus senior Territorial division.

First part-time cavalry to engage enemy – North Irish Horse(SR) and squadron of South Irish Horse(SR), 24 Aug 1914.

First Territorial unit to land in France – London Scottish 16 Sept 1914.

First Territorials to engage enemy – Oxfordshire Hussars clashing briefly with German cyclists on 5 Oct 1914.

First Territorials in battle – London Scottish on 31 Oct 1914.

First double VC – Lieut Colonel Arthur Martin-Leake, RAMC, Territorial, who had won his first VC in South African War, gained bar between 29 Oct and 8 Nov 1914.

First Territorial division to fight in France – 46th(North Midland) arrived in theatre on 24 Feb 1915.

First (and only) double VC wholly of First World War – Captain Noel Chavasse, RAMC, Territorial, attached 1/10th King's (Liverpool) Regiment(Liverpool Scottish), who had won his first VC on 9 Aug 1916, gained bar between 31 Jul and 2 Aug 1917, posthumously. As he also had MC he must be counted Britain's most decorated soldier of war.

Most decorated junior rank of war – Lance Corporal William Coltman, VC, DCM and bar, MM and bar, North Staffordshire Regiment, Territorial stretcher-bearer, won VC between 3 and 4 Oct 1918.

Last VC of war – won by Major Brett Cloutman, MC, RE, Territorial, on 6 Nov 1918.

9

Between the Wars

This house will in no circumstances fight for its king and country.
OXFORD UNION MOTION CARRIED ON 9 FEBRUARY 1933

Guns will make us powerful. Butter will only make us fat.
HERMANN GOERING SPEAKING ON GERMAN WIRELESS IN MID-1936

The Territorials had proved themselves in the field, never the less there was a period of doubt about the government's intentions in 1919 after the disembodiment of the first-line units in May when the part-time soldiers found their regimental family reduced to a tiny office staff. Territorials were represented at the peace festivities, the major celebrations being held in London and Paris. London troops had their own march through the capital on 5 July. After nearly a year of uncertainty, in March 1920 the part-time force was formed again, this time as the Territorial Army. One difference between the TA and the TF was that members of the new force had to be prepared to serve overseas as required.

Britain was exhausted economically and in manpower but as an imperial nation there were traditional low-intensity tasks that the regular Army had still to perform. For full-scale continental warfare of the future, the character of armies would have to change. The tank was a war winner; complete mechanisation of supply was now essential and communications were so important that they must be made a corps in their own right. The aeroplane, despite its cool reception by military planners in the early days of powered flight, had forced itself into the armoury as an indispensible element of warfare, and defence against it would have to be provided, as much for protecting civilian populations from the heavy bomber as for soldiers from the strafing fighter. The horse, for general purposes of supply and for fighting, was finished, though another generation would pass before Britain's last cavalry operation took place; this, as we shall find, was fought by Territorials in the Levant, and there would be isolated instances of the horse being used for reconnaissance in the Italian mountains in the Second World War. But substantial use would be made of mule transport in the same war in terrain unsuitable for other methods, for instance in the Horn of Africa, the Levant, Italy and the Far East.

RE-ROLING THE YEOMANRY

The number of cavalry regiments had to be cut. Fifty-six Yeomanry regiments had been used in the war, two, the Welsh Horse and a second regiment of Lovat's Scouts, were creations of the war. The Welsh Horse, the Lincolnshire Yeomanry and King Edward's Horse were disbanded. Of the remaining 53 only the senior 14 were allowed to retain their horses. The remaining 39 were mechanised or re-roled; eight became armoured car companies of the Royal Tank Corps; some went into the Royal Corps of Signals; and one became infantry. Half of the old Yeomanry, 27 regiments, converted to artillery, either field or medium.

Because of long established traditions, these new gunners were allowed to retain their badges and buttons, though under the overall tutelage of their new arm. For example, in the Surrey and Sussex Yeomanry Field Regiment the two Surrey batteries kept their cap badge, Queen Mary's cypher, and the two Sussex batteries wore the Sussex badge. In the Commonwealth war cemetery at El Alamein lie members of the regiment, the two badges carved into each of their gravestones. Another unit, the City of London Yeomanry (Rough Riders) wore the RA cap badge but Rough Rider collar dogs, RHA ball buttons and on parade carried swords instead of rifles. The Rough Riders' side cap of purple and green was retained for suitable occasions and it was worn with the old Rough Riders' spur badge. In blues, RHA basic uniform was adopted with busby lines and shoulder chain. Gorget patches were worn on the collar beneath Rough Riders' collar dogs. In service dress members wore a Y above the brass RHA shoulder title.

These mixed items of dress were typical of the TA between the wars and the War Office looked on the practice indulgently while inserting its official caveat 'provided that no expense to the public is incurred'. Bandmasters, for instance, held the rank but received sergeants' pay. They were allowed a bandmaster's frock coat and in service dress they could wear a warrant officer class I's khaki in officer's quality material 'provided that. . . .' (*Territorial Army Regulations* 1936 paras 541 and 546).

All ranks were allowed to wear blue patrols (para 547) at their own expense. In the City of London Yeomanry it was customary for all ranks to wear officer's quality 'blues' (the cost was about £8 in 1938). No doubt many regulars would have shuddered at the eccentricities of dress affected by the Yeomanry but, as much of the expense fell on the regiments themselves, officialdom appears not to have gone out of its way to curb departure from regulations. Thus, in the

Rough Riders, staff sergeants and above were permitted to wear brown boots and leggings when in service dress. All NCOs and WOs wore the RHA cross-belt (although this had been abolished in the RHA in 1922) and they bought it themselves from Pipe & McGill. On promotion in 1940, Herbert Sawyer bought his from that establishment for three shillings and sixpence, equal in today's currency to 17½ pence. Although para 547 forbade it, the Rough Riders at guard mountings at annual camp in the 1930s insisted that the orderly WO, orderly sergeant, orderly bombardier and duty trumpeter all wore 'blues' with white gloves.

The Yeomanry regiments remaining horsed were: the Royal Wiltshire, Warwickshire, Yorkshire Hussars, Nottinghamshire(Sherwood Rangers), Staffordshire, Shropshire, Ayrshire, Cheshire, Yorkshire Dragoons, Leicestershire, North Somerset, Duke of Lancaster's Own, Lanarkshire, and Northumberland Hussars. At the time they were informed that they too would be mechanised or given a change of role. But, in the event, the conversion was slow and, in general did not take place until 1939, and even later in some instances. It sounds unbelievable today but these 14 regiments were equipped with swords, a weapon that, on the recommendations of the Yeomanry committee that deliberated after the South African War, had been discarded, officially at least, in favour of the rifle and bayonet.

A regiment that switched to the gunner role was the Royal Devon Yeomanry. (Today, despite further changes, their cap badge is still worn in the West Country. The Wessex Yeomanry, later the Royal Wessex Yeomanry, of which they are a squadron, were an infantry unit in the 1970s and early 1980s. They converted into an armoured reconnaissance unit in 1983).

In 1921 Britain was wallowing in an economic depression. *The Economist* described it as one of the worst depressions since the Industrial Revolution. The threatened mine and railway strikes of that year, against a background of disturbances and coming at a time of tension in Ireland, and while most of the regular Army was out of the country on occupation duties, resulted in the forming of a Defence Force. For political reasons it was deemed inadvisable to embody the TA. The strikes did not take place and the new force lasted for only a few months.

A splash of pageantry occurred on 26 February when Princess Mary, later awarded the title Princess Royal, presented all the second-line and third-line battalions of the London Regiment with King's colours on Horse Guards Parade. The colours of these war-winning but now phantom battalions were then handed over to church, city or borough authorities for safe keeping.

Politically there was little enthusiasm for spending the sums on the Army that with hindsight we can see were necessary. The cost of switching from horses to lorries, tanks and gun-towing vehicles was enormous for an economy crippled by war. In 1920, the bounty for a TA recruit, who had to sign a commitment for four years, was £4 and for a trained soldier, who had had four years of war service and was allowed to sign on for from one to three years, was £5. For the remaining mounted Yeomanry, the horse allowance was £5. The money did little to attract interest. The anti-aircraft arm was particularly heavily undersubscribed; batteries with an establishment of 150 men had to be content with 30. The TA generally, like the regular Army, would continue to be short of manpower through into the 1930s. But, on 22 July 1922, there was an impressive turn-out when the King reviewed the 47th(2nd London) and 56th(1st London) Divisions in Hyde Park.

THE WOMEN'S SERVICES

Two committees had considered the part played in the war by the Voluntary Aid Detachments (VADs); consequently the Army Council set up a new scheme in 1923. The original intention of the VAD organisation, was to supplement the medical part of the TF at home. Now the scheme was broadened to include all the armed forces in any part of the world once general mobilisation was declared. But besides this, VAD members would be invited to sign an undertaking in which they volunteered for their original role with the TA in the event of its call-out. If they did not do so they lost their VAD status (though remaining members of their own nursing organisations, the Red Cross Society, the St John Ambulance Brigade or the St Andrew's Ambulance Association). A list of VAD members appears regularly in Army orders.

In their short history, the VADs had put in a lot of service overseas. Some were serving in the Balkans fighting in 1912 and even after the First World War they were on duty in North Russia and were helping in the hospitals used by the British Army on the Rhine during the occupation

In 1924 the Supplementary Reserve was formed. Recruiting began in October for this ready supply of technical troops.

Call-out came unexpectedly for the TA in 1926 when the general strike threatened to bring Britain to a standstill. The embodied service lasted for 90 days. Members of the women's unpaid service, the FANY, drove cars and lorries for the Army and the police. This and their service during the First World War led the authorities to insert the corps into *The Army List* of the following year. The corps was 20 years old and in view of its record of free service to the ambulance section of the Army during the war, the insertion was belated recognition.

By now the VADs too were drawing closer to the Territorials. Besides their own camps they attended TA camps, doing duty with medical officers. As early as 1928 they were being instructed in the nursing of poison gas casualties. Some of their officers attended Army Anti-Gas School courses for

17. How to evacuate a wounded soldier using two rifles and two bicycles as an ambulance.

18. Officers of the 1st (City of London) Battalion of the London Regiment relax near Fleurbaix, Western front, August 1915. *(Archives of the 1st Londons)*.

19. Sergeant Hurcombe and Sergeant Sedgwick, both of the 2/19th Battalion the London Regiment, accept the surrender of Jerusalem in 1917.

20. Territorials in the victory parade pass through Trafalgar Square, 1919.

21. 'The grub's good, Mum!' Young drummers of the 8th Battalion Royal Fusiliers (TA) at camp in 1925. *(Archives of the Royal Fusiliers)*.

22. Illustrating the quantity of brassware worn by Territorials on their shoulder straps in the early 1930s. These men are being instructed on the Vickers gun.

23. The first Territorials entrusted with public duties. Members of the HAC take over the King's Guard from the Scots Guard for 24 hours, Buckingham Palace, 6 July 1938.

24. Members of 188 (Antrim) Heavy Battery, RA, and Antrim (Fortress) Company, RE, get down to essentials at Northern Ireland Territorials' first camp, at Grey Point, County Down, June 1938. *(Courtesy of Northern Ireland TA&VRA)*.

25. Winston Churchill, honorary colonel, inspects the battalion he commanded in the First World War, the 6th Royal Scots Fusiliers, at Colchester 1941. *(Courtesy of Lowland TA&VRA)*.

26. The 2/5th West Yorkshire Regiment march off after forming a guard of honour for Field Marshal Ironside at Swaffham, Norfolk, 1941. *(Lynn News)*.

27. Members of the anti-tank platoon of the 4th Welch Fusiliers receive orders for an attack in north-west Europe, April 1945. *(Courtesy of the RWF Museum)*.

28. Number 3 mortar team of the 2/7th Middlesex Regiment relax during security duties in Syria, May 1945. Later that month they came under fire in Damascus; the following winter in Palestine the Diehards became the last TA battalion on active service.

29. Field Marshal Montgomery inspects the 7th Royal Welch Fusiliers at Mulheim, Germany, 1946. *(Courtesy of the RWF Museum)*.

30. Signals platoon of the 4th Welch Regiment, winners of the 160(W) Infantry Brigade signals shield, at camp, 1954. *(Courtesy of the regiment)*.

31. The Lord Mayor of Liverpool, escorted by Major (later Lieutenant Colonel) A J Moore, inspecting the 5th King's Regiment after the city presented silver drums to the battalion, 1965. *(Courtesy of the King's and Manchester Regiments Association)*.

instructors. The VAD membership was split into two categories: mobile and immobile. The former, recruiting between the ages of 19 and 45, were to be called out for service anywhere in Britain or overseas; the latter, recruiting between 18 and 65, were expected for duty within reach of their homes.

TANKS COMMANDED BY RADIO

A glimpse of the tactics and weapons of the future was obtained in a demonstration on Salisbury Plain in 1927 by the Experimental Mobile Force. A battalion of medium tanks and one of light tanks and armoured cars, working with carrier-borne machine gunners, lorried artillery and lorried engineers, supported by aircraft, outmanoeuvred a traditional divisional formation comprising infantry and cavalry and supplied by horse-drawn vehicles. A number of foreign observers watched the demonstration; they included Germans, whose army was later to make such successful use of this new type of warfare.

It is not recorded how much, in those money-conscious times the demonstration cost, but Territorials suffered a blow in the March of that year when, to economise, the Army halted recruiting for the tiny air defence sector of the TA. To give his men the sort of training he considered necessary, the CO of one Territorial unit paid personally for his men's ammunition at camp. In spite of the fact that London had been bombed many times, the government seemed reluctant to commit funds to air defence. Equipment was ancient and the gunners were given little chance to practise their craft. A report in 1926 revealed that 'out of 2,935 rounds fired at a target on a known course at a known speed and at the best height for shooting, only two actual hits were obtained'. The RAF became responsible for the Air Defence of Great Britain, ground as well as air, but the Army units were under the command on the War Office for all non-operational matters.

Available funding meant that the RAF was faring better than the Army. The air defence exercises of 1931 proved to be failures. Air Chief Marshal Sir John Salmond reported:

> If there was an immediate declaration of war we could only man 27 per cent of the guns and 22 per cent of the searchlights out of the total authorised for A.D.G.B. [Air Defence of Great Britain], whereas 80 per cent of the number of squadrons required under the full air defence scheme [of the Romer committee, which had been set up to organise the administrative details for the Committee of Imperial Defence's anti-aircraft defence of Britain] have been completed or are now forming.[1]

As for ground warfare, in 1931 Salisbury Plain was the scene of the first full-scale armoured formation manoeuvring in response to commands issued by wireless. And as though to counter this display of technology, in that year and against the national trend, the Cheshire Yeomanry, still horsed, was not only fully recruited to its establishment of 273 other ranks, but there was a waiting list for recruits.[2]

The economic crisis, which reached its height in 1932, affected TA training along with every other type of public expenditure. To save money, all camps that year were cancelled. But members of the FANY, pursuing their independent way, held their own camp in Surrey during the summer and took part in manoeuvres with the regulars.

As if economic problems were not enough, internationally a series of sinister events occurred in 1933 that would affect the lives of hundreds of thousands of Territorials within six years. Hitler came to constitutional power in January, obtained the enabling statute giving him absolute power in March and withdrew Germany from the League of Nations in October. Japan too, in angry response to condemnation over its invasion of Manchuria, left the League that year.

For years Britain had been willing itself never to get into a situation in which it would have to fight another continental war.

This attitude was reflected by successive governments in the notorious 'Ten Year Rule' under which all defence expenditure was governed by an assumption that Britain would not become engaged in another major war for at least ten years. Under Winston Churchill's direction, when he was Chancellor of the Exchequer, this rule became self-perpetuating. The effect of it upon the TA needs no imagination. Not until Hitler marched into the Rhineland in the middle thirties were the politicians shaken out of their lethargy and a crash programme of rearmament begun – far too late, as the sorry events of 1940 were to show.

The peace movement had thrived among the intellectuals and there was an embarrassing debate in 1933 at the Oxford Union where the motion that 'this house will in no circumstances fight for its king and country' was carried. This occurred during the last month before Hitler gained absolute power in Germany; and seems certain to have given some encouragement to the dictators.

One valuable aspect of TA training in the 1930s was the requirement for the Yeomanry that newly joined subalterns should spend a month with a regular cavalry unit to familiarise themselves with Army procedures. This was a relic of the old Volunteer days when the Volunteer officer was allowed to spend a month with a regular or Militia unit to increase his experience.

A memorable. day for military historians dawned on 1 April 1934: Britain's first postwar Tank Brigade was formed. This, apart from Brigade HQ, comprised: 1st (Light) Tank Battalion, 2nd Tank Battalion, 3rd Tank Battalion, and 5th Tank Battalion.

It would be another five years before Britain established an armoured division – and even that was woefully ill-equipped. However, on the Continent, the Italians began to build up a tank force in the early Thirties and even used them against the Abyssinians when they invaded their country. Despite the prohibitions of the Versailles Treaty, which denied them a tank force, the Germans had long been working secretly with the Soviet Union to develop their own tank and, by the end of 1934, the first German tank battalion was formed. Although machines were very light and designed only for training purposes, the *Wehrmacht* despatched a tank unit to Spain to support General Franco's Fascist troops and to gain invaluable experience of cooperation with their new Stuka dive bombers. The result of their foresight would be seen all too clearly in Poland and France in 1939–40. One sign of the British realisation of the need to modernise their Army could be seen in the recruiting posters which heralded the arrival of a degree of mechanisation for the infantry, so that they would no longer have to footslog into action. At long last, the Army was becoming mechanised.

In 1934, the British Army in the United Kingdom consisted of:

Regular

13 regiments of cavalry
1 cavalry armoured car regiment
5 battalions of the Royal Tank Corps
117 batteries of artillery of all types including six anti-aircraft units for the Expeditionary Force
70 battalions of infantry

Territorial

16 regiments of cavalry (including scout units)
8 armoured car companies of the Royal Tank Corps
261 batteries of artillery (excluding AA and coast defence)
168 battalions of infantry

The imbalance is obvious as is the importance of the TA on mobilisation.

By the outbreak of war in 1939, whilst some progress had been made in the mechanisation of a number of cavalry regiments for use in the reconnaissance role, only the Royal Tank Corps (now the Royal Tank Regiment) had any tanks heavier than light and what they had were quite unfit for battle – although new vehicles were coming along and a number of Territorial infantry battalions were reforming as units of the RTR. In contrast, the Germans had six armoured divisions in being with the capability to increase this number to 12 – however, even their tanks were thinly armoured and lightly armed.

Despite their importance on mobilisation, the units of the TA were woefully undermanned and even more poorly equipped than the regular Army. Platoons represented companies on training and the lack of heavy weapons meant that flags were waved on exercises to represent anti-tank and mortar fire – small wonder that recruiting suffered. Anti-aircraft units, which would form the backbone of the air defence of the country were equipped with 3-inch guns from the First World War.

THE THREAT OF AIR ATTACK

Despite the deadening effect of his handling of the Ten Year Rule as Chancellor in the Twenties, there was one man who recognised the growing danger of the German threat and in particular the threat of the *Luftwaffe*'s bomber force. Though out of office, Winston Churchill was determined that his voice should be heard. On 28 November 1934, moving an amendment to the loyal address to King George V, he said: '. . . the strength of our national defences, and especially of our air defences, is no longer adequate to secure the peace, safety, and freedom of your Majesty's faithful subjects'. Pointing out that to urge the preparation of defence was not to assert the imminence of war, he added:

> On the contrary, if war were imminent, preparation for defence would be too late. I do not believe that war is imminent, and I do not believe that war is inevitable. But it seems very difficult to resist the conclusion that if we do not begin forthwith to put ourselves in a position of security it will soon be beyond our power to do so. What is the great new fact which has broken upon us in the past 18 months? Germany is rearming. That is the great new fact which rivets the attention of every country in Europe – indeed in the world – and which throws almost all other issues into the background. That mighty power, which only a few years ago within our own experience fought almost the whole world and almost conquered, is now equipping itself again – 70 millions of people – with the technical weapons of modern war, and at the same time is instilling into the hearts of its youth and manhood the most extreme patriotic, nationalistic and militaristic conceptions.
>
> According to what we hear and are told and what comes in from every quarter, though little is said about it in public, Germany has already a powerful, well equipped army with an excellent artillery and an immense reserve of well trained men. The German munition factories are working practically under war conditions, and war matériel is flowing out from them, and has been for the last 12 months certainly, in an ever broadening flow. Much of this is

> undoubtedly in violation of the treaties which were signed. Germany is rearming also to some extent at sea but what concerns us most of all is the rearmament of Germany in the air.

But few people in Britain wanted to think about the possibility of war, and this affected the outlook of politicians. In the Peace Ballot of 1935 about 11 million voted to support the League of Nations, for securing international agreement on outlawing war and for the banning of private armaments manufacture in Britain. Churchill continued with his warnings.

In 1936, the so-called 'Jarrow Crusade', a march made by thousands of unemployed workers from the north east, from County Durham to Westminster, brought home to many the devastating plight of British heavy industry. Ironically, it would be the warlike pressure of international events that would bring about the recovery those marchers had sought but it would be another three years before the shipyards and ancillary industries would be back working at full strength to counter a threat that had now become reality.

THE BOMBER WILL ALWAYS GET THROUGH

In the later years of the decade the civil war in Spain produced frightening newsreel footage showing the power of modern bombs. The Italian dictator Mussolini had earlier shown his ruthlessness and had no compunction about drenching with poison gas the lightly armed, barefooted native troops who tried to defend Abyssinia. The German air force was growing in strength. Poison gas occupied the thoughts of a large part of the population of Britain and was perceived as the ultimate weapon against civilian populations, now that it could be delivered by long-range bombers. Many thousands of people had relatives or acquaintances who had experienced the horror of a gas attack in the First World War: if it was a vesicant such as mustard gas or lewisite, the victims probably were blind or had scars on their chests or backs; if it was phosgene, they had a hopeless cough and difficulty with breathing. As the Prime Minister, Stanley Baldwin, had earlier remarked: 'The bomber will always get through, and it is very easy to understand that if you realise the area of space'.[3] This very thought was at the back of many people's minds now. The Home Office established a countrywide cadre of unpaid civilian volunteers, many of them war veterans, willing to be trained as gas instructors. In war their task would be to teach the hundreds of thousands of Air Raid Precautions wardens who would be needed.

As a ground defence against enemy bombers, an elaborate anti-aircraft organisation was in process of creation in the mid 1930s, largely through the acceptance of the recommendations of a committee chaired by Major General

Tompson (who died through overwork). In the main, the manpower came from TA infantry units, and the country owes a debt to those men who were retrained despite poor facilities and shortages of equipment and who would in the 1938 crisis and again in 1939 be the first to be embodied because of fears that Germany would bomb first and declare war later. This debt to the Territorial gunners and engineers, barely acknowledged at the time, is probably forgotten now. The pilot scheme, in 1935, was the Southern Division, formed by transferring eight battalions from the 47th (2nd London) Division and the 56th (1st London) Division, both TA. The units were the 4th City of London (Royal Fusiliers), the 6th City of London (City of London Rifles), the 7th City of London (Post Office Rifles), the 11th London (Finsbury Rifles), the 19th London (St Pancras Rifles), the 20th London (Queen's Own), the 21st London (1st Surrey Rifles) and the 7th Battalion of the Essex Regiment. The depleted veteran infantry divisions were amalgamated to form the London Division. Their hived-off battalions became either RA, if equipped with guns, or RE, if given a searchlight role.

A second AA division, the Northern, followed within 18 months. Again the manpower came from infantry units, which meant that the depleted Haldane division, the 46th (North Midland), ceased to exist.

When the Southern was renamed the 1st AA Division, it had achieved 50 per cent of its establishment; the Northern, which became the 2nd AA Division, exceeded 45 per cent. In the light of the voluntary nature of their recruitment, these figures were creditable but, when allied to the chronic shortage of equipment which had dogged the TA throughout the post-war period, meant that the divisions were a long way short of being fit for war. By the end of 1937, there were only 180 AA guns and 800 searchlights to protect Britain. They were spread among the two AA divisions and two independent AA brigades. Territorials were manning the mark of 3-inch AA gun that some of them had used 20 years earlier in the First World War.

By 1938, Germany's adventurism had become obvious, there was public and press interest in defence and votes were at stake. Mr Leslie Hore-Belisha, Secretary of State for War, announced on 28 June that a corps of five AA divisions would be formed and grouped into the 1st AA Corps under the command of a lieutenant general. The divisional headquarters were: 1st (formerly the Southern), London; 2nd (formerly the Northern), Nottingham; 3rd, Edinburgh; 4th, Chester; 5th, Reading. By the early spring of 1939 the corps comprised about 80,000 Territorials. On 1 April it became Anti-Aircraft Command and gained two more divisions, on paper. The problems of recruiting and equipping the two new divisions were formidable, bearing in mind that the five original ones were not yet ready for active service. Divisional boundaries of responsibility had to be redrawn not only for the Army but to mesh in with the RAF's responsibilities.

A PROUD RESPONSIBILITY FOR THE TA

It was a tribute to the proved efficiency of the TA, Haldane's foresight coupled with the dedication, courage and sacrifice of his Territorials in action that the War Office had decided in 1935 to entrust the United Kingdom's ground defence against air attack to part-time soldiers. Funding, that bane of the 1930s, had clearly influenced the decision, for five divisions of Territorials came very much cheaper than five extra divisions of regulars. Despite their overall responsibility for the ADGB, the RAF were reluctant to see their own bids for money in the Defence Estimates, so badly needed for their urgent expansion, pared to meet the needs of a greatly enlarged ground-based defence system. Nevertheless, it had to be recognised that, if things went wrong, this was no mere dent in some overseas front line or loss of a tribal area in a corner of the far-flung Empire that was at stake but the very heartland of the nation. It is difficult to appreciate today the fear of air attack that prevailed throughout the country. The recent actions of Europe's new dictators left no doubts about their ruthlessness. Many thousands of ex-soldiers understood all too well the effects of high explosive and poison gas from their time in the trenches. The newsreels showing the bombing of defenceless Spanish cities in the civil war left no room for doubt about the growing power of modern aircraft. Furthermore, many of those aircraft were those of the very countries that now posed so great a threat to the peace of Europe. Nothing was more frightening than the prospect of bombers over Britain; the decision to place this vital defence into part-time hands was politically courageous.

Those defenders would have to be efficient and manning their posts even before a declaration of war. Gun and searchlight units would be needed on a vast scale, as well as a big training programme. In fact, the War Office did have another look at the decision to place the ground sector of air defence in TA hands. In early 1938 the government made more money available for defence and an Army sub-committee went into the question of whether the ground air defence should be in the hands of regulars, given to 'semi-regular' soldiers (envisaged as former regulars who would be given AA training and would then stay efficient by putting in two weeks' training every year), or simply transferred to the RAF. The sub-committee, under the chairmanship of General Viscount Gort, VC, decided that 50,000 regulars would be impossible to raise without impairing the efficiency of the other areas of the Army; semi-regulars, although at first sight attractive, were an unknown quantity; and the RAF handover was a non-starter. It had to be the Territorials.

The story of the weekend soldiers and air defence starts, oddly enough, in the late 19th century and at sea, well before there was such a thing as an air threat. The London Electrical Engineers and the Tyne Electrical Engineers were coastal searchlight units before the First World War and their original role was to illuminate enemy torpedo vessels so they could be destroyed. The zeppelin raids meant that these units had to learn a new role at the same time as they went into action against the raiders. When the Territorials were reconstituted after the war, four artillery AA brigades were raised (each brigade consisted of two batteries) and the London Electrical Engineers created two companies of searchlights. Just as the country was climbing out of the economic depression, it was becoming apparent that hopes placed in the League of Nations were illusory and that another European war was a possibility. In 1935 this tiny AA force, which had in the meantime seen its task grow to defend key naval installations, was expanded, as we have seen. Financially, there was no doubt that the Territorials were more attractive than regulars but it was not only the savings they represented that were so important to an impoverished nation but their wonderful spirit of service and comradeship which enabled them to tackle their vital new role with such enthusiasm and efficiency.

THE AA's PATROLMEN VOLUNTEER

In 1937, the Army held large-scale manoeuvres and 40 Automobile Association (AA) patrolmen helped to marshal the convoys of vehicles. Later, the AA informed its members and staff that in addition to their annual holidays, male staff would be given two weeks' paid leave if it were used for training in an essential service during a national emergency[4]. The following spring, the War Office announced that a supplementary reserve for the Corps of Military Police was being established from AA patrolmen. More than 900 patrolmen applied for the 500 posts.

The TA, and in particular the HAC, enhanced their prestige on 6 July 1938 when the oldest unit was chosen to find the guard for public duties and take post at Buckingham Palace. Peter Baker, 6ft 3in tall, was one of the many six-footers selected for that King's Guard. On drill nights, for over three months, they were given an intensive drill course in preparation for the 24-hour guard. The order was service dress with puttees and the Territorials took over from the Scots Guards, who were in their customary public duties dress of scarlet tunics and bearskins. It was the first time that Territorials had guarded the heart of the Empire. Baker recalls that it was a court night and many guests in glittering outfits were at the palace[5].

At the Munich crisis, the government took no chances: RAF stations and the rest of the Air Defence of Great Britain were ready in case the Germans raided Britain from the air. The RA's anti-aircraft guns and the RE's searchlight units were manned by Territorials who had been embodied and standing by. As we know, most of the units had been infantry and they retained a trace of the old name, such as 317th Company of the 36th (Middlesex) Regiment, RE. That unit had paraded at their smart new drill hall in Edgware Road, north London, in August 1938 when it was opened by no less a person than Mr Leslie Hore-Belisha, Secretary of State for War, whose picture seemed to be in almost every newsreel and newspaper during this period, opening drill halls, testing new equipment or talking about the merits of the new uniform, battle-dress (to be known by millions as BD), that was being introduced. No sooner had the Edgware lads got used to the premises than they were embodied to man their searchlights for three weeks.

This was a period when the nation owed much to the Territorials. It was by no means their finest hour, but the part-time soldiers quietly manning the ground defences of Britain against a possible attack by the most powerful air force in the world deserved a recognition they never received.

TERRIERS RESPOND

Events on the European mainland were awakening all but the most blinkered of the public to the need for defence, as we have noted, although TA recruiting was still faltering as late as 1937. But the Munich crisis of late September in the following year brought out the patriots. The sight of thousands of part-time soldiers manning the country's defences that autumn, while civilians wondered whether Baldwin was correct and that, if it came to war, enemy raiders could get through, provided an impressive boost for TA recruiting. The total number of recruits for 1938 was a massive 77,000. (This influx was three times the figure for 1935 and it exceeds by 12,000 the TA's scheduled establishment for 1 April 1944. It was a remarkable inrush, bearing in mind the much smaller population of 1938.)

The revelation to the public – and to regular troops – of the importance of the Territorials' role came in the last week of September 1938. The telegrams, telephone calls and key men (easily contactable troops, who lived near the drill hall or who had telephones, and who were each given a list of neighbouring Territorials to alert) had been sent out at 2.30pm on 23 September. The weather in the south east was atrocious, which delayed travel and deployment to isolated, sodden sites overnight. But by daybreak 30 searchlight battalions and 24 gunner regiments were standing to at their posts. They were all Territorials of the Air Defence of Great Britain.[6]

The government was aware of the sort of men with whom it was negotiating in Germany and it was determined not to be caught unprepared. It took this step of calling out the Territorials by proclamation even though the regular Army reservists (men who had served their time with the colours but who still had a commitment to be recalled if needed) had not been embodied. The naval reservists were called out later. Those Territorials manning the air defence posts achieved a 97 per cent turn-out. This was remarkable, considering how many of them there were, nearly 50,000 – and they were continuing to recruit rapidly. They stayed at their posts until stood down on 14 October, after being embodied for three weeks. They had been paid an embodiment gratuity of £5. The gratuity was, of course, for existing Territorials called out for a specific defence task. But such was the rush of recruits wanting to enlist and such was the need for them to join AA (within six months the number would increase by 30,000) that, by an administrative oversight, those joining the TA after the proclamation also received the £5. The government had made more money available for defence, but there were limits to its generosity. Those who were mistakenly paid the gratuity were made to repay it!

WOMEN VOLUNTEER

The aftermath of Munich brought a new type of soldier to the drill halls – female. The government had authorised a somewhat casual scheme to recruit women other than nurses into an auxiliary for the TA. It became law from 9 September 1938 and it was organised, like the rest of the TA, on a county association basis. While the associations were choosing county commandants, who in turn would appoint commanders for the new companies of the Auxiliary Territorial Service (ATS), as it was called, they were also tasked with accepting names of women who would eventually volunteer to join. But events in Germany overtook the leisurely approach. The TA associations and drill halls suddenly found themselves having to cope with thousands of applications for women wanting to play their part. The public announcement of the new force, for which women aged between 18 and 50 would be eligible, had been made on 27 September, Chamberlain waved his piece of paper on the 30th. The scheme was that the ATS companies, once formed, should be attached to a local TA unit.

One young woman, an officer after her five and a half day course at the Duke of York's Headquarters in Chelsea, later became director of the ATS. She was Leslie Whateley, who served as director from 1943 to 1946. Another young woman, who attended the course later in the year, became Colonel S Crawley. She remembers her days as a company assistant (junior officer) in the 13th (General Duties) County of London Company. Her unit was attached to a popular Mayfair drill hall, home of the Queen Victoria's Rifles. The battalion and the women's company soon established a *modus vivendi*. On drill nights the men taught them how to handle a rifle and instructed them in drill and bugling. The women sewed thousands of regimental black buttons on to greatcoats that had arrived with brass general service buttons. The women also helped in the canteen. 'We used to catch up on our paperwork on an evening when QVR were not training and the drill hall was hired out to the Women's League of Health and Beauty'.[7]

THE ONSET OF WAR

As 1939 progressed, it seemed that nearly everybody was assuming that Britain would soon be at war. The doubling of the establishment of the TA (a gesture that, in view of Britain's shortage of *matériel*, looked grander on paper and sounded far more impressive in Parliament and overseas than in fact it was), the first intake of the revived Militia and the increased volume of recruiting generally soon caused problems of supply. One youngster aged 17, Norman Sawyer, who joined the 2nd London Divisional Signals (with the signed permission of his father, as required by TA Regulations 1936, para 164) that spring was told by a storeman on being issued with a mixture of ancient items of equipment that all 'the new stuff is being diverted to the Militia'. There were shortages in all sorts of military equipment but the item most people remember was the greatcoat. The 2nd Queen's Westminster Rifles counted themselves fortunate in obtaining a consignment of London bus drivers' coats. The capital's bus drivers' cabs were open to the weather in those days, so the coats had to be warm.

Lord Killanin (later president of the International Olympic Committee, businessman, author and one of the most highly internationally decorated persons in the world apart from heads of state) recalls to the author that when he joined the Westminsters, recruits were being issued with only two articles of kit, civilian respirators and busmen's overcoats. A few First World War steel helmets were available for the guard. He has an endearing memory of Frank Lawton, the actor who had many leading film roles to his credit, being on sentry duty at Willesden Junction station and trying to look warlike while surrounded by children asking for his autograph. 'Frank remained unmoved by this recognition but I think he was highly embarrassed by the fact that his helmet was far too small for him and he looked quite ridiculous with his busman's overcoat.'

Killanin, a newspaper correspondent who had been a pacifist at university, joined the TA almost immediately after going to Downing Street for his paper to cover the return from Munich of Chamberlain and his famous piece of paper at the end of September 1938. Killanin was commissioned into the Queen's Westminster and Civil Service Rifles in the October. He was made assistant adjutant and a company OC of the 2nd Queen's Westminster Rifles, as it became on the doubling of the TA, and eventually the 12th King's Royal Rifle Corps. He gained early fame in the TA as the founder of the so-called

Killanin's Horse. This was potentially the most unmanageable (and, to a regular sergeant major, heart-breaking) group of recruits ever assembled in the TA. A number of professionals, such as newspapermen and actors, who wanted to become Territorials could not do so because they worked at night. Killanin shrewdly got in touch with every national newspaper office and every theatre in London asking for recruits who would be prepared to train in the afternoons.

The response was heavy and those volunteering for the afternoon training company included some names already famous through the cinema and the stage (for instance Frank Lawton and Hugh Williams) and others who would become distinguished after the war (Bill Deedes, later Lord Deedes, reporter, MP, government minister, columnist and editor of *The Daily Telegraph*, and the actors Nigel Patrick, Guy Middleton and Wallace Douglas). They all joined the Westminsters at 58 Buckingham Gate. Douglas was appearing as Joey in *Lot's Wife* at the Savoy theatre in the year he joined the TA. He was later commissioned into the KRRC and was one of those Green Jackets chosen to hold back the German forces around Calais so that the bulk of British troops could be evacuated at Dunkirk. This vital operation changed Douglas's life, because he was captured. During the five years he spent in a prison camp he staged entertainments for fellow prisoners and on his repatriation the experience he had gained gave him the confidence to switch from acting to directing.

Killanin remembers: 'I had two rows of men from the chorus of Ivor Novello's *The Dancing Years* and they drilled beautifully. As we marched at rifle pace we made rings around the Guardsmen at Wellington Barracks, which was the nearest parade ground to our headquarters. One day a rather pompous Irish Guards officer came up to me and asked: "Michael, have you inspected your men today?" I replied that I had not because we had nothing to inspect but he then said: "I think you should have. You have a damned fellow at Wellington Barracks wearing sandals!"'

Another young Territorial Green Jacket, Frank Cullen, later to be a sergeant major in the Royal Fusiliers, a veteran of the North African and Italian campaigns, and after being demobilised, a member of the security staff at *The Times*, well remembers his first dress for guard duty – his London busman's overcoat![8]

Many units had to make do with civilian overcoats for later recruits. In the City of London Yeomanry (Rough Riders), when the greatcoats ran out in certain sizes, a Burton's civilian overcoat was supplied to a gunner named Grant. There were two Grants in the unit and to distinguish them one was known (without racial overtones) as Jewish Grant, the other as Overcoat Grant. Incidentally, Overcoat was the first member of his troop to be wounded in action. During the Blitz, a near miss by a German bomb on the troop's gun site at Rochford RAF station toppled the predictor on top of him. Two other young recruits, Ken Pegden and Freddie Brazier, who joined the Rough Riders at the same time as Overcoat reckoned themselves lucky in being issued with khaki coats even though they were greatcoats MS (mounted services) and were ill-fitting.[9] One of the officers in the Rough Riders at this time was a Mr Grosvenor, later to become Duke of Westminster.

A south Londoner, Roger Blankley, remembers the severe shortages of kit that dampened enthusiasm when he joined the 48th Battalion of the RTR at Clapham. Many recruits wore overalls to go to camp in August 1939. Even into 1940, when his unit was accommodated in civilian billets at Sanderstead, Surrey, he received a 7s 6d grant to use his civilian overcoat.[10]

Peter Erwood, who joined the 65th Field Regiment, RA, in April 1939 at Lee Green, recalls how, when the TA establishment was doubled and he was transferred to the second line unit, the 118th Field Regiment, he and his comrades expected that they would be fully equipped within weeks. They did not even have rifles. He went to camp for a fortnight at the end of July and early August but it was not until 1940 that he actually fired a rifle and that was in action, aiming at a Junkers 87 dive bomber. Incredibly, he was subsequently charged by the quartermaster with using ammunition without authority. The charge was dismissed by the battery commander and the enthusiastic defender's record remained spotless.[11]

THE TA IN MARCH 1939

On 1 March 1939 the Territorial Army was about 212,000 strong, compared with its establishment of 228,989 and recruiting was rising. Before the Prime Minister's announcement in the House of Commons that the establishment of the TA was to be doubled the force was arranged into the following field formations:

42nd East Lancashire Division with headquarters in	Manchester
43rd Wessex Division	Salisbury
44th Home Counties Division	Woolwich
48th South Midland Division	Oxford
49th West Riding Division	York
50th Northumbrian Division	Darlington
51st Highland Division	Perth
52nd Lowland Division	Glasgow
53rd Welsh Division	Shrewsbury
54th East Anglian Division	Hertford
55th West Lancashire Division	Liverpool
The London Division	London
The Mobile Division	(no peacetime headquarters)

1st AA Division	Uxbridge
2nd AA Division	Hucknall
3rd AA Division	Edinburgh
4th AA Division	Chester
5th AA Division	Reading
5 Cavalry Brigade	York
6 Cavalry Brigade	Leicester

The 50th, the 55th and the London divisions were all motor divisions and therefore were not as large as the others.

The Mobile Division drew largely on London but also relied on units from widespread parts of Britain. For instance, its holding brigade, consisting of a machine gun battalion and two motor battalions, came wholly from the capital: the machine gunners were Princess Louise's Kensington Regiment and the other two battalions were the Rangers and the Tower Hamlets Rifles. Its cavalry armoured car regiment was provided by London, and its tank brigade was composed of reroled infantry battalions from Bristol, Leeds and London rebadged to the Royal Tank Regiment. Its cavalry light tank brigade came from Derby, Gloucester and Northamptonshire.

The remaining nine infantry divisions were each allocated a horsed Yeomanry regiment as divisional cavalry. It will be remembered that there were 14 Yeomanry regiments which were left with their horses in the postwar reformation of the TA. The 5th Cavalry Brigade (consisting of the Yorkshire Dragoons, the Nottinghamshire Yeomanry and the Yorkshire Hussars) and the 6th Cavalry Brigade (consisting of the Cheshire Yeomanry, the Staffordshire Yeomanry and the Warwickshire Yeomanry) took six of the Yeomanry regiments. One of the units that lost its horses, the Scottish Horse, became Yeomanry again.

The London Division had been formed from the amalgamation of the old 47th London Division and the old 56th London Division both of which had served in the First World War, but because of the need to remove constituent infantry units to be converted to form the emergent AA divisions, had become depleted. The old 47th's units formed the 1st AA Division. On the doubling of the establishment of the TA these famous divisions came back in their original form as the 2nd London Division and the 1st London Division respectively.

On 18 November 1940 their titles were changed again to the 47th (London) Division and the 56th (London) Division; this was to avoid confusion with the regular Army formations the 1st and 2nd divisions. The 46th (North Midland) and its First World War second line unit the 59th (2nd North Midland) had by now disappeared. The 59th went in the postwar reformation and the units of the 46th went to form the 2nd AA Division.

THE VADs DEPART

By the spring of 1939 the Army Council released the so-called immobile members of the Voluntary Aid Detachments, of whom there were by now nearly 30,000, from their Territorial obligation to allow them to staff the Civil Nursing Reserve that would be the mainstay of the Emergency Medical Service hospitals for the civilian population.

ENTER THE MILITIA

As we have seen, in April, always a significant month for Territorials, the establishment of the TA was almost doubled. Today we would probably call it cloning. In the infantry, for example, you might get the 5th and 6th battalions of a regiment expanded into four major units; their titles would be the 1/5th, the 2/5th, the 1/6th and the 2/6th. Some battalions retained the double title until the end of the war; others changed them into higher numbers, in which case the 2/5th might become the 7th and the 2/6th might become the 8th. (Later, as the war took its toll, a TA unit would be given the proud title of a regular battalion that had become a casualty. For instance, when the 1st Battalion of the Diehards was lost in the capitulation of Hongkong in 1941, the 2/8th Battalion was renumbered the 1st, not bad for a second line TA unit.)

The seriousness of the situation became apparent with the calling up of young men into the Militia for what was planned to be six months. They were issued with the new design of field uniform, battledress. It was worn in barracks and off duty with the khaki field service cap. Before the outbreak of hostilities in 1939 the War Office had provided those latter-day Militiamen with a natty walking-out kit of dark-blue sports jacket and grey trousers almost as wide as 'Oxford bags'. But the onrush of war stopped all such frivolity. The order of dress became battledress for the duration.

When Parliament authorised the formation of the Militia and pointed out that Territorials were exempt from conscription into it this led to a rush to join the TA. Peter Erwood, now of Lincolnshire, who joined a south-east London Territorial RA unit, remembers long queues at drill halls as men rushed to join the TA. But, as he pointed out to the author, the fact that the government was alarmed enough about German expansionism to introduce conscription had brought home to people that Britain must be prepared. 'I think the greater number joined from the sincere motive that it was high time that we started getting ready'. As for anyone of conscription age who was less sincere, 'it is a moot point which is the better bargain: six months full time service or four years part time'.[12]

As 1939 progressed, the AA divisions, growing more important daily, had been receiving press attention. The first 4.5-inch AA gun was emplaced in February and no doubt the government hoped that the Germans would read all about it in the newspapers and be duly impressed. The next month the Secretary of State for War announced that the AA would be nearly doubled and two more divisions would be added, bringing the total to seven. It would be called Anti-Aircraft Command. The change came on 1 April.

THE COUVERTURE

From the end of May the Couverture operation came into effect. Its aim was to give permanent blanket AA cover for the most vulnerable swathe of Britain. Briefly, 960 searchlights and as many guns as the country could assemble were to be emplaced throughout a tract 25 miles across and sweeping from Portsmouth along the south coast, fanning out to include Dover and London and climbing north to Newcastle upon Tyne. It looked good on the map but how was it to be manned? The answer was: by Territorials. But if the country was not at war how were these troops to be mobilised? The answer was: by staggering the manning, month by month, unit by unit, so that although the sites were manned continuously, the units would do no more than a month's service. The necessary legislation was rapidly passed. The Territorials in AA units, who had volunteered for two weeks' camp a year, now found this commitment doubled. It was a hard time for the TA, which was already being reorganised; and into that month's service had to be fitted a fortnight's camp training. There was a part to be played by the newly instituted Militia, too, but it was nowhere near as effective as the TA. The Militiamen had to be trained for three months in basic principles and then serve on a gunsite for the remaining three months of their full-time service, but events would overtake the planning.

In August 1939, with war 10 days away, some of the Territorials were already in uniform and at their gunsites again. Telegrams had gone to AA units on 24 August using the codeword: 'Plummer requires all posts filled immediately'.

Many AA Territorials, their families and their employers had by now just cause for complaint. Having completed summer camp in 1938, they had been embodied for three weeks in the Munich crisis, they had done their month's Couverture duties, and now here they were called out yet again. There was a feeling of patriotism in the air, people were conscious of the need to do their bit, but the government had hardly been fair. Many employers stood by their staff and, if not making up their Army pay to that of their civilian employment, at least kept their jobs open; others applied a harsher standard of commercial ethics. But incredible as it may seem to us today, the government did nothing to protect the employment of those Territorials called out for the 1938 crisis and for the Couverture in 1939. The Reinstatement in Civil Employment Act did not appear until 1944. General Sir Alan Brooke (later Field Marshal Lord Alanbrooke), commander in chief of AA Command, had been aware of the injustice, and a month before leaving the command he wrote to the director general of the Territorial Army on 28 June 1939, urging that something be done to relieve this unfairness. He said:

> I am uneasy about the financial treatment meted out to the troops of the AA Command on this year's embodiment. There is a sense of grievance arising, mainly, from the withholding of the Proficiency Grant and of certain other allowances, normally admissible, towards messing costs.
>
> Recent international events have enabled us to fill up our AA units very rapidly with the best elements of all classes of the population. These men, appreciating the urgency of pushing ahead with AA training and organisation, have accepted the sacrifice of most of the leisure-time and amenities which go to lighten the daily rounds and have put in an immense amount of voluntary unpaid work.
>
> In addition, they have accepted a normal peace liability and an abnormal war liability, both having an effect on their domestic budgets. The normal peace liability includes an annual camp of 15 days or 8 days. In accepting this they took stock of all the emoluments of all kinds available from Government sources, and of their employers' concession, with their eyes open. In accepting the financially more serious war liability, their general view is that, in war, everyone will have to 'do his bit', and that, as all will be in the same boat, a general financial upset will be inevitable.
>
> Now, what has actually happened?
>
> Under the pressure of a deteriorating international situation the Government rushed through legislation which enabled it to embody all the AA troops for the extended period of one month, in batches. This extended period serves two ends, firstly, increased peace-time security against sudden air attack, and secondly (but only incidentally), facilities for intensive training. In fact, however necessary these special measures may be, it cannot honestly be contended that there yet exists a state of war. In other words, the AA troops are being required to honour a liability for which they did not contract.
>
> Many men are seriously hit, both financially and in their domestic arrangements, by being called on to do a month. Those in skilled or semi-skilled occupations, normally earning from £3 to £5 a week, are badly out of pocket, since employers can hardly be expected to extend their existing concession in order to make good what the Government ought to provide. Household budgets, providing for hire purchase for houses, furniture, cars, etc., leave no margin for unexpected set-backs of this nature. In view of the very proper solicitude of the Government for the financial well-being of the conscripted militia-men, there is a strong feeling that the voluntary enlisted Territorial,

> upon whom an unexpected burden has fallen, should also receive generous treatment of his difficulties.[13]

Brooke's advocacy fell on deaf ears. The official sentiments of the time cannot be better described than in the words of the man who succeeded him on 28 July, General Sir Frederick Pile, an admirer of the Territorials serving under him, who later wrote:

> For these three months before the war everything was done for the Militiamen. If Territorial units had, by chance, been issued with beds, they must surrender them for the more comfortable housing of the conscript. The Territorial was lucky if he had a tent board to sleep on. The conscript was housed in warm barracks.[14]

WAR

The preliminary act of the greatest war in history started with a cold-blooded murder at the end of August. The Germans shot a concentration camp inmate, dressed the body in Polish uniform and placed it at a radio installation just inside the German border, so that they could claim that the unfortunate pawn had been a saboteur. This gave Hitler his excuse to march. At dawn on 1 September the *Wehrmacht* invaded Poland and started the war. Britain was prepared and later that day hundreds of thousands of children, hospital patients and other vulnerable groups started to arrive in country districts from areas deemed likely to be bombed from the air. These were the people or families of people who accepted the conditions of the official evacuation scheme, and about a million and a half were evacuated under it. About two million others were evacuated privately. Adjutants of TA units had documentation and accommodation ready for embodiment. Territorials were reporting to the drill halls throughout the day. By 2 September all TA units had been embodied, though it would take several more days before every individual reported. The following day Chamberlain, speaking at 11.15 from the cabinet room in a broadcast that millions of Sunday morning listeners would never forget, informed the people that Britain was once more at war with Germany.

At 11.27 there was an air raid warning. People in vulnerable areas were struck by fear. But it turned out to be a false alarm. In London, the sirens brought traffic to a standstill. The country's oldest TA unit, the HAC, now embodied, grabbed their respirators and took shelter in the trenches dug in their ancient greensward, the Artillery Ground.

10

Off to War Again

> *. . . we shall fight on the beaches, we shall fight on the landing grounds, we shall fight in the fields and in the streets; we shall never surrender.*
>
> WINSTON CHURCHILL, 4 JUNE 1940.

'Report 9RF'.

The adjutant of the 9th Battalion of the Royal Fusiliers evidently believed in economy with Government money. The telegrams were sent on 1 September 1939 to all members of the battalion. For one of them, Alf Knight (who would turn out to be one of the Balham drill hall's most faithful servants: he was still serving it in a civilian capacity as a permanent vehicle fitter in the 1980s), the first indication that he had been called to the colours came when he got home from work. 'My father was polishing my kit so it would be ready for me to go'. After donning his uniform and having a meal, Alf called at the public-house by the bridge at Balham station. It was full of like-minded Terriers having a last drink as civilians. Some had been there for a long time, he recalls, and many were in a happy mood as they navigated the 300 yards to the drill hall.[1]

The TA had been mobilised by royal proclamation on 24 August but there were variations in the call-out dates of individual units. Certain units were already standing by. The government, expecting an enemy air strike in advance of a declaration of war, had taken the precaution of calling out AA units in the Air Defence of Great Britain.

Units differed in their approach to the call-out. Compared with the situation today, far fewer private homes had telephones, so commanding officers set up a system of key men. There were in fact two types of key men: those who were administratively vital and who had already been called out in advance of their comrades, once the way was cleared by proclamation, and those who were easily contactable. Every man in the easily contactable group had been provided with a list of comrades in his neighbourhood and his task was to ensure that each was alerted on call-out.

'In my office on that Thursday 24 August, TA people were saying goodbye and leaving throughout the day as they got the call from their units', Herbert

Sawyer, of the City of London Yeomanry (Rough Riders), recalls. 'When I got home at 6pm my mother had the message for me; so after supper off I went, in uniform with all my kit. On arrival at the drill hall I was paid my mobilisation gratuity and told off by Second Lieutenant David Clowes for having a tunic pocket undone. We were told to not go too far away and to be ready to move after 10pm. So off we all went to a pub in Chiswell Street and ate (or rather drank) into our gratuities. We left around midnight in our vehicles, towing Bofors guns, not knowing where we were going – perhaps the driver did. We ignored red traffic lights and eventually arrived at Canewdon, Essex, in the small hours. We were in the Crouch estuary and we deployed our four guns to defend one of those new-fangled early-warning stations – all very secret.'[2]

In the same office as Sawyer, Douggie Caton was one of the first to be called out. His anti-aircraft unit telephoned him on the morning of 24 August ordering him to report immediately. His fiancée, Ellie Jones, who worked there, spent most of the day crying and saying she might never see him alive again. Ironically, she was seriously injured in an air raid, whereas he survived the war without scratch.[3]

Frank Lawton, film star and West End actor, marked his call-out to the 2nd Westminster Rifles with a luncheon at the Berkeley Hotel. 'We arrived back home from America and found his papers had arrived', his widow, the actress Evelyn Laye, recalls. 'Frank immediately said: "We must have a splendid lunch", and we did.'[4]

For the Reverend Eric Gethyn-Jones, rector of Dymock, Gloucestershire, and chaplain to the 5th Battalion of the Gloucestershire Regiment, the call was dramatic. When mobilisation was proclaimed he had reported at his drill hall but was told to stay with his parish for the time being as his call-out notification would have to arrive separately. At 11pm on Saturday 2 September he was talking on the telephone to his father when the operator interrupted the conversation to say she had an important telegram for Dymock Seven-0. It read: 'Prepare to join 144 (Gloucestershire and Worcestershire) Infantry Brigade. Instructions following. Commander Salisbury.' Canon Gethyn-Jones, who was made a MBE for gallantry in saving life when his unit's ship was sunk in the Normandy landings, became an honorary chaplain to the Queen. He is the author of a number of books. Throughout the war he kept a diary and published a book, *A Territorial Army Chaplain in Peace and War*, based upon it.[5]

Bruce Hobbs, 17-year-old winner of the Grand National on Battleship in 1938, was a peacetime Territorial for only a few minutes. He was sworn in by the adjutant at a Bath drill hall and received the King's shilling shortly before Chamberlain made his fateful speech on 3 September[6]. Hobbs's unit was the Bath Squadron of the North Somerset Yeomanry, with whom he went via France to Palestine as part of the 1st Cavalry Division. He would eventually serve, when commissioned, in the last phase of the last campaign in which

British troops would be in action with horses and his regiment, the Yorkshire Dragoons, would be the last Yeomanry to lose their horses. Hobbs later won the MC in Tunisia.

Embodiment on 1 September for Peter Erwood, 18-year-old clerk with the LNER at Ilford railway goods yard, upset the confident assertion by his boss, the goods agent: 'There's not going to be a bloody war, and you've had too much time off playing bloody soldiers already'. Gunner Erwood had been back only three weeks after his summer camp at Okehampton, Devon, with his unit the 118th Field Regiment, RA. After work he caught a train ('two five-car articulated units behind an N7 0-6-2T'), changed at Stratford ('an F4 2-4-2T') for North Woolwich, crossed the Thames in the Woolwich ferry and walked home. His call-out papers from his drill hall in Lee Green were waiting. 'So I put on such fragments of the King's uniform as I had been issued with, had a cup of tea, put some odds and ends into my sister's old Girl Guides kit-bag – I had not been issued with a kitbag – and went off to the wars'.[7]

For Peter Baker, one of the HAC men who had been selected for the King's Guard at Buckingham Palace the previous year, embodiment was an anti-climax. He reported to Armoury House on 1 September, found the gates locked and was told to come back the next day. On the Saturday he was put into the advance party and sent to Bulford Camp on Salisbury Plain.[8]

Four brothers reported for duty when the Cheshire Yeomanry was mobilised. The unit received its embodiment orders at 16.47 hours on 1 September and by the evening of the following day most members were with their squadrons. Among those reporting were George, Alf, Lionel and Fred Gander. George was a squadron quartermaster sergeant (and later became regimental quartermaster sergeant and a MBE); Alf had become a sergeant when he filled the vacancy created by his brother's promotion to SQMS (and he later made it a double when he filled the vacancy created by his brother's promotion from SQMS to RQMS). Lionel became a sergeant. A fifth brother, Dennis, also served in the regiment but he had left before the war to join the Royal Horse Guards.[9]

Miss A G Learmouth, who had joined the ATS in February 1939, was in a small group of women who had been attached to the King's Regiment but were switched to Mersey AA Defence. She was embodied on 1 September and reported to her new battery within an hour of Chamberlain's declaration of war. 'The last two girls arrived during the afternoon. Their fathers, being old soldiers, had made their daughters have something to eat before they left home.'[10] Miss Learmouth, who was commissioned, was subsequently made a MBE and gained her TD. Another Liverpool ATS girl, Sheila Heaney, who reported that day would later become Director of the Women's Royal Army Corps.

The Reverend Kenneth Oliver, chaplain to the HAC, reported to his unit in style, in a milk van on 3 September. He was alighting from his train at Holborn Viaduct station, in the City, when the first air raid warning of the war sounded. Most of the traffic had stopped and by the time he arrived at Moorgate, the only moving vehicle was a milk delivery van. The milkman gave him a lift to Armoury House but Oliver failed to make the impression he might otherwise have created – everybody was sheltering, clutching their respirators, in the trenches that had been dug in the HAC's sports ground. Oliver saw action in North Africa and went on to serve the HAC as chaplain for 50 years. He became a CBE and wrote a book on his experiences, *Chaplain at War*, (Angel Press Chichester 1989).[11]

Another Territorial who reported to the HAC was William (Ted) Pryke, a member since 1936. He was embodied on the Saturday, but after being given his embodiment gratuity of 10/- for turning up with his full kit, he was told that he would not be needed until Monday. He returned home and was in the country, driving to a public house for luncheon, on the Sunday when the sirens sounded. He thought: 'This is a funny place to have an air raid'.[12]

For members of the 64th (Queen's Own Royal Glasgow Yeomanry) Anti-Tank Regiment, RA, embodiment was gradual. They were at camp at Buddon when mobilisation was announced, so the preliminary stages of the procedures were carried out as a unit in good time for the actual embodiment on 1 September. They then went to their war role with the 15th (Scottish) Division.

Embodiment for most Territorials was an administrative affair, but for the 188th (Antrim) Heavy Battery, RA (TA) there was action. The 188th, together with its sister unit the Antrim Fortress Company RE (TA), were already manning the defences of Belfast Lough at Greypoint and Kilroot in the August. When a vessel tried to enter harbour without observing the recognition code, the 188th fired a warning shot across its bows. That was at about 08.00 hours on 3 September. The 188th wonders whether it was the first British unit to fire a shot in anger on that first day of the war.

The embodiment forms sent by TA units to all members stated:

Army Form E 635
(In pads of 50)

No. . . . .

Territorial Army
EMBODIMENT
Notice to join

No., Rank and Name ....
....Regt. or Corps

Whereas the Army Council, in pursuance of His Majesty's Proclamation, have directed that the.................................... be embodied on the.........day of Sept 39

You are hereby required to attend at....................................not later than 9 am o'clock that day. Should you not present yourself as ordered you will be liable to be proceeded against.

You should comply with the instructions contained in your Army Book 3 (Territorial Army Soldier's Pocket Book) regarding procedure on being called out for service, and disposal of your National Health Insurance Card and Unemployment Book.

If married you should complete the statement of family particulars in the pocket book before you leave home and bring that book with you ready to be handed in when you report for duty.

....Adjutant

....

Date ....

The notice was usually overwritten with an item or two of individual unit advice such as 'You should bring with you sufficient food for the day of joining' and 'Packs will be worn'.

DEPLOYMENT IN FRANCE

Within five weeks of Britain's declaration of war the expeditionary force sent to France totalled 158,000 men and 25,000 vehicles, it was under the command of General Viscount Gort, VC. His two corps commanders were Lieutenant General Sir John Dill and Lieutenant General Alan Brooke.

Many Territorials were still wearing service dress, the uniform of the First World War. The steel helmet was unchanged from that of the earlier conflict and small arms were largely the same, the Lee Enfield .303 rifle, which was used in abundance (though the later mark IV with the cheaper, short spike bayonet was increasingly being produced), and the mechanically reliable but inaccurate .38 revolver. The .303 Bren light machine gun was a step forward in the armament of the infantry, offering efficiency combined with lightness. The Vickers .303 medium machine gun, which had been used with devastating effect in the static battlelines of the First World War, was widely employed. Despite its disadvantages of weight, water-cooling, the awkward separation of tripod, unwieldy gun and ammunition belts whenever movement by foot was necessary, the intricacy of its mechanism (there were 16 moving parts in the lock alone) and the high profile of the firer sitting on level ground, the Vickers would prove a reliable servant for many years to come.

Tanks were a disappointment. The bulk of those in the BEF were light tanks in the divisional cavalry regiments. Armed with a medium and a heavy machine gun and with woefully thin armour, they were fit only for reconnaissance purposes though, inevitably, they would be involved in fighting for which they were not designed. Several of these divisional regiments were from the Yeomanry. As for the medium or cruiser tanks, these were also thinly armoured and sadly undergunned with a 2-pounder high velocity gun. They were pitifully few in number, as were the much more heavily protected but equally ill-armed infantry tanks whose weight restricted their speed to no more than a fast run. These last were at least proof against most German anti-tank weapons and the two battalions of 'I' tanks(as they were called) would fight an historic battle at Arras with the 50th Division, known to all by its 'TT' (Tyne and Tees) divisional sign.

On 1 September the Home Office decreed that all buildings had to be blacked out, which in some public buildings, notably colleges and churches, led to a wealth of imaginative and unwieldy constructions of cardboard and lath to cover windows many feet tall; as time went by the blackout screens in colleges tended to be covered in graffiti. Street lights were extinguished and traffic lights were masked to allow only a modest cross to indicate stop or go. Railway stations were blacked out and thereby was inaugurated the system of loudspeaker announcements; road vehicles had running boards and wings outlined in white paint; headlamps were masked allowing the beam to shine down from three slits. White rings were painted around roadside trees. White paint was in demand too for kerbstones and for the sandbags that protected the windows of military, police and Air Raid Precautions posts. Although a 20 mph speed limit was imposed during darkness, the number of road deaths rocketed. Magistrates punished speed offenders with fines varying from ten shillings to £20 according to the commission area of the bench; this was at a time when a recruit's pay was two shillings a day. In camps the guard commander was responsible for enforcing the blackout.

INFANTRYMEN LEARN NEW SKILLS

One factor that distinguished the British Army of the Second World War from that of 1918 was the far smaller number of infantry battalions put into the field, another was the switching of battalions (in the main these were TA but in the case of a new mini-arm of service, infantry support, regular battalions too) into different roles. Tanks, reconnaissance vehicles, anti-aircraft guns, searchlights, anti-tank guns and the 4.2in mortar and the Vickers .303 medium machine gun were among the new equipment that the erstwhile Territorial infantrymen had to master. The country could not wait for direct recruitment to undertake these specialised tasks, so the job fell to the men of the line.

Former Yeomanry regiments too had to switch roles: mechanisation for some, an artillery role in field, anti-tank or anti-aircraft specialities for others, and signals or searchlights for others. For the gunners, the artillery brigade had been replaced by the 24-gun field regiment, comprising two batteries; each battery now had three troops and each troop had four guns. Within the infantry battalion itself there had been changes. It was much smaller and it contained specialised elements. For instance, instead of comprising 1,008 men formed into eight rifle companies and supported internally by only two Vickers .303 medium machine guns, it would have only four rifle companies, each with three platoons and each platoon having three sections. Each section had its own support element with the admirably portable .303 Bren gun. The battalion had its own anti-tank rifles and 2-inch and 3-inch mortars. The large headquarter company would contain specialist groups: a pioneer platoon, a Bren carrier platoon and a signal section.

Even the way in which the Army paraded had changed. Troops now marched in threes. Gone were the days of marching in fours, or if the road were narrow, in twos ('Form fours!' and 'Reform two deep!', were commands no longer heard).

Once the government had hardened to the conclusion that preparation for war was inevitable, the enlargement of the RAF began and it was followed by that of the Army. In May 1937 the Royal Tank Corps reestablished two of its wartime battalions, the 7th and the 8th. The following year six more tank battalions were added, the manpower coming from six Territorial infantry battalions. Thus the 40th Battalion of the RTR was formed from the 7th Battalion of the King's Regiment, based at Bootle, Lancashire. The others were:

41st RTC from the 10th Battalion of the Manchester Regiment (Oldham)
42nd RTC from the 7th(23rd London) Battalion of the Surrey Regiment (Battersea)
43rd RTC from the 6th Battalion of the Royal Northumberland Fusiliers (Newcastle upon Tyne)
44th RTC from the 6th Battalion of the Gloucestershire Regiment (Bristol)
45th RTC from the 7th Battalion of the West Yorkshire Regiment (Leeds)

With the doubling of the TA establishment in April 1939, these six too were doubled. In the same month the name of the Royal Tank Corps was changed to the Royal Tank Regiment(RTR), making it one of the largest regiments in the Army; the 'Corps' became the Royal Armoured Corps(RAC) to embrace the mechanised cavalry regiments as well as the old RTC. The new TA battalions of the RTR were:

46th (Liverpool Welsh) Battalion RTR
47th (Oldham) Battalion RTR
48th Battalion RTR, based at Clapham
49th Battalion RTR, based at Newcastle
50th Battalion RTR, based at Bristol
51st Battalion RTR, based at Leeds.

The RAC now consisted of all the original tank and armoured car units of the RTR (eight regular and 12 TA battalions), the 18 former cavalry regiments now mechanised, and the eight mechanised Yeomanry regiments; 46 major units in all. There was also a training depot. Recruits there would wear a common cap badge until trained and posted to a regiment within the corps, whereupon they would wear the regimental badge and other distinctions of dress.

For the former Territorial infantrymen this meant considerable training as tank crews were handling highly technical, dangerous and expensive hardware. It took a year to train a regular tank soldier, which would be shortened in wartime to six months (including 14 days' leave). The Britain of those days was far removed from the Britain of today as far as the internal combustion engine was concerned; you had to be comfortably situated to run a car, railways played a dominant role in passenger and freight transport, and in cities there were trams as well as buses, which all meant that there were fewer road vehicle drivers available. Consequently, intensive training cadres had to be established, first in lorry handling and maintenance then in driving tracked vehicles. The Territorials in the RAC had to learn to drive, to operate the tank's main armament, usually a two-pounder at that time, later a six-pounder or a 75mm and its machine guns, to operate the wireless set, to carry out basic maintenance on vehicle, guns and set, to become proficient with the pistol and sub machine gun, and to master Morse code (12 words a minute was the trade test minimum for the operator; 8 words a minute for the gunner), map reading and tactics. Tank drill and dismounted drill had to be learned. Pistol drill was strange to infantrymen and probably they marvelled at the enormous cloud of blanco dust that arose when an enthusiastic body of men carried out the movement requiring hands to be slapped on the holster prior to withdrawing the weapon.

Most drill halls were located in busy cities unsuitable for tanks. Examples of these were the 42nd RTR at Battersea, whose drill hall was on St John's Hill, immediately opposite the main entrance to Clapham Junction railway station, or the 43rd in Newcastle. Tactics, enemy recognition and trade training took place in the drill halls but the driving and tactical training could be done only periodically on suitable training areas.

Britain went to war with only two tank divisions of which one was in Egypt and they were incomplete; 11 training regiments were established in country districts by the RAC. The long training of tankmen was complicated by the fact that it had to be undertaken in overlapping tranches of semi-competence so that if necessary they would be able to crew tanks in action at various stages even though their skills were limited. Three training regiments, the 54th (with tanks), the 59th (armoured cars) and the 61st (tanks) were located near the tiny market town of Barnard Castle, County Durham, on the boundary with the North Riding. The town was also host to the Infantry Battle School. Another RAC tank training regiment was located at Catterick, a few miles away, in north Yorkshire. Eventually, when industrial production became effective and American munitions were forthcoming, each of those training regiments became an impressive complex: everything was on a big scale – millions of pounds' worth of vehicles, with a taste for millions of gallons of fuel and millions of rounds of ammunition and millions of spare parts for vehicles, guns and radios. Many years after hostilities, mile after mile of the drystone walls of the roadside bore testimony to the presence of training tanks; it seemed that hardly a stretch of a dozen feet managed to survive the war without having to be rebuilt.

An inevitable corollary of the growth of armoured units was the need to develop an adequate anti-tank capability. It was therefore decided that every division should have a divisional anti-tank regiment – a role to which a number of TA infantry battalions and Yeomanry regiments were converted. The .5-inch Boyes anti-tank rifle with which the infantryman was equipped imparted a horrendous kick to the firer but would penetrate only the lightest German armour – it was soon found to be of more use against buildings.

Another new role for some regiments was infantry support. Five regiments were grouped into a miniature arm. They were the Royal Northumberland Fusiliers, the Cheshire Regiment, the Middlesex Regiment, the Manchester Regiment and Princess Louise's Kensington Regiment, one of the last of the old rifle Volunteer units to preserve its suburban tang. Using Vickers .303 machine guns, 4.2in mortars and Oerlikon 20mm AA cannon, their role was to provide close support for the infantry. All the battalions of these regiments, TA as well as regular, other than those TA units reroled to armour or AA, were given the support role. It was a disjunctive life in the field as the battalion was rarely together in one place. The system of operation was that an infantry division was allocated one support battalion and on active service this battalion was fragmented so as to be attached to the division's brigades. For example, a machine gun company would go to a brigade and a platoon of the mortars would accompany them. In certain theatres the enemy air threat was insufficient to justify an AA defence, so some support battalions did not have Oerlikons.

For a TA battalion that had trained together, it was dispiriting to be split into minor units in action, and this was especially so for the mortar platoons, who were necessarily hived not only from battalion but from company. Regimentally it was difficult to qualify for unit battle honours. The war would show however that grateful brigadiers would not be slow to recommend MCs for commanders of companies that provided effective support leading to a successful operation, though honours for other ranks were rare. The author recalls seeing in the troopship SS *Chitral* a captain from the Cheshire Regiment who had won three MCs.

DRESS

Although many TA units in 1939 were still wearing service dress (and would start the war and go on active service in that order of dress), the public were beginning to notice the appearance of troops, and most notably the much publicised Militia, in an unfamiliar and unsoldierly uniform. It was khaki, certainly, but was more like a boilersuit than a military uniform. Baggy and anonymous, it had no brassware or other adornment. Only two buttons, those holding down the shoulder straps, showed and these were made of horn or Bakelite. The large map pocket on the thigh spread over the crease in the trouser leg and as the material was of double thickness it was difficult to press and aesthetically unsatisfactory. Battledress was not liked. But a manufacturer of the uniform, who described himself in a letter to *The Times* as a practical tailor of more than 40 years' experience, described BD, as it became known, as 'practical and suitable for its purpose, ie work and fighting . . . the buttons are concealed, and not only afford protection from snipers but they do not get in the way of any movement and they are a boon to the private, as they do not require any polishing'.

That tailor was right. Once people got used to it, BD was not so bad. Of course it had to be house trained, and in the process dreadful things were done to it. For instance, some issues were made of cloth that had been treated to make it to some extent blister gas resistant; this put a whitish bloom on the material. Troops were not going to have any of that untidy nonsense when there were girls to be impressed at the Palais or Odeon after duty. So out came the scrubbing brushes and the protective layer was washed away.

The early anonymity of battledress was in marked contrast to the uniform of the 1930s when soldiers had more brass on their shoulders than a brigadier wearing Guards pips. A typical soldier would have the curving shoulder title giving his regiment. Above it he might have a subsidiary title such as City of London or Cinque Ports; above that might be an emblem such as a grenade or a bugle; then a battalion numeral; and above it all would be a T for Territorial. About battledress the regiments too had their own views and soon put a stop to the anonymity: a lanyard here, a flash there, a square of tartan somewhere else.

Originally unit shoulder titles were in drab cloth with black initials – a refinement was to pad them with cotton wool to give a slightly rounded effect. Later in the war there came the colourful arm-of-service flashes about two inches long and worn on the upper arm: scarlet and yellow for the RAC, scarlet and blue for the artillery, reversed for the engineers, scarlet for the infantry, maroon for the medicals, green for the dentals, blue and white for the signallers, bright green for the intelligence men, blue and yellow for the RASC, scarlet, yellow and blue for the REME, and so on. In 1943 there arrived coloured shoulder titles, in most instances unabbreviated and in the livery of the arm of service: scarlet letters on yellow for the RAC, white letters on scarlet for the infantry, and so on.

In 1944 wound stripes and war service chevrons made their reappearance. Both had been used in the First World War. In each conflict, after a few years of hostilities, the authorities decided that war service and wounds should be made patent on uniform.

All these items were additional to corps and divisional signs, badges of rank, medal ribbons, trade and skill at arms badges, parachutist and pilots wings, and traditional regimental emblems such as the Royal Welch Fusiliers' black flash, worn at the back neckband and the tank arm badge of the Royal Tank Regiment – worn four fingers' width down from the right shoulder. Some TA battalions had distinctive flashes, for instance the 8th Royal Fusiliers had a square of cloth, the top half red, the lower half blue; the 9th Battalion had the square divided diagonally in the same colours.

So it was that battledress, which had started the war as the dullest and most anonymous uniform ever inflicted upon the Army, became the most colourful and informative.

At this time, the standard issue hat for the Army was the khaki fore-and-aft side hat,worn by all except the horsed regiments, the Guards and the Royal Military Police – all of whom wore peaked caps (the RMP and VP police wearing red and mid-blue cap covers respectively). The standard headdress for the RAC was the black beret, formerly peculiar to the RTR alone. The field service cap, to give the side hat its official designation, was also worn in corps and regimental colours by all ranks in battledress but off duty, and often on duty by officers. These coloured caps were bought at the individual's own expense but without the surrender of precious clothing coupons.

RANKS AND DRESS OF THE ATS

In the ATS it was decided in 1940 that although auxiliaries, as non-commissioned ranks were designated, should have the same system of ranks as the generality of the Army, from private to warrant officer class I, officers' ranks should be different. These were:

ATS	Army
Second subaltern	second lieutenant
Subaltern	lieutenant
Junior commander	captain
Senior commander	major
Chief commander	lieutenant colonel
Controller	colonel
Senior controller	brigadier
Chief controller	major general

The official issue of clothing and equipment made to every non-commissioned member of the ATS was:

2 tunics	1 pair shoelaces
2 skirts	2 pairs titles
1 greatcoat	3 pairs panties
1 cap	2 pairs pyjamas
3 pairs shoes (or 2 pairs and boots)	1 sanitary belt
1 pair canvas shoes	3 vests
1 jersey woollen	1 kit bag
1 anti-gas cape	1 linen bag
1 anti-gas wallet	1 sling bag
2 pairs gas detectors sleeve	2 towels
1 respirator	3 pairs knickers
1 steel helmet	1 pair gloves knitted
6 eye shields	4 pairs stockings
2 containers ointment anti-gas	1 table knife
1 field dressing	1 fork
3 brassieres	1 spoon
2 belts corset	1 drinking mug enamel
1 lanyard	1 brush button
1 button stick	1 brush shoe
4 shirts	1 cap badge
8 collars	1 set identity discs
3 ties	2 oz cotton waste
2 studs	

Besides the official issues members of the ATS received something not available to men soldiers – 10 clothing coupons a year to enable them to buy such items as handkerchiefs and slippers. When off duty they were allowed to wear the field service cap, the fore-and-aft, in corps colours, basically dark brown picked out in leaf green and hazel.

GLASWEGIANS' ANTI-TANK ROLE

When it was decided that the Royal Artillery should supply an anti-tank regiment for every infantry division an old Yeomanry outfit, the 101st(Queen's Own Royal Glasgow Yeomanry) Field Brigade, was among those reroled. In November 1938 it became the 54th(Queen's Own Royal Glasgow Yeomanry) Anti-Tank Regiment, establishment was a regimental HQ and four batteries. It will be remembered that an artillery brigade consisted of two batteries, so in the new role two extra batteries would have to be found. They came from the 312th(5th City of Glasgow) Battery, RA, based at Govan, and B Company of the 9th Argyll and Sutherland Highlanders, of Kirkintilloch. The batteries took seniority as the 213rd, 214th, 215th and 216th(Queen's Own Royal Glasgow Yeomanry) Anti-Tank Batteries, RA.

When the TA establishment doubled the 54th formed its second line unit, the 64th(Queen's Own Royal Glasgow Yeomanry) Anti-Tank Regiment, RA, consisting besides the regimental HQ of 253rd, 254th, 255th and 256th Anti-Tank Batteries, RA. Recruiting was strong enough to provide the new unit with an inflow of volunteers, stiffened by trained members of the 54th. It was an interesting camp that year for both units, the 54th learned to handle the new two-pounder anti-tank gun at Trawsfynydd in July. The 64th, in camp at Buddon the following month, found its training schedule interrupted by mobilisation and it went through the first stages. Embodiment occurred on 1 September: the 54th took post with the 52nd(Lowland) Division, and the 64th went to the 15th(Scottish) Division.

Three Territorial divisions went to France as part of the British Expeditionary Force(BEF). For many people there was a feeling of *déjà vu*: a BEF, deployed in northern France, some of the uniforms and rifles were the same pattern as those used by that other BEF a generation earlier; the steel helmets were the same and the Vickers machine gun was there with its familiar tripod; again there were the trenches; as in the case of that earlier war the first winter was bitterly cold. Pioneer battalions were formed to dig trenches. Some British units served in France's static defence system the Maginot line (and were issued with the 'They shall not pass' badges recalling the stand at Verdun of the First World War). But the methods of that war were long outdated. Britain was about to pay the price for tardy mechanisation and lack of sufficient funding for the Army.

THE 1ST CAVALRY DIVISION

The 1st Cavalry Division took up position in Palestine between early January and the middle of February 1940. It was an enormous undertaking to get them there and with hindsight it was an unfortunate decision in view of the mechanisation that was vital if Britain was to win the war. Few Yeomen who took part in the snowbound journey across France to Marseilles in that desperately cold first winter of the war will forget it. Regiments moved to Dunkirk by boat train and, once there, transferred the horses to boxcars with accommodation for eight horses and from two to four men to look after them. It was so cold that the horses' urine froze on the floor of the cars. Water for the animals froze; the food froze. Some regiments reached their destination in two days, others took longer. The North Somerset Yeomanry had to endure the trucks for four days.

Every regiment had a story to tell of that journey. After a halt at a country station, the train carrying A and B squadrons of the Cheshire Yeomanry was just getting into its sluggish stride when a squadron leader noticed that one of his horses was galloping alongside it. The driver refused to stop and apparently did so only after being shown a revolver by one of the officers. In the train transporting C Squadron, a huge horse kicked a hole in the rear of the boxcar in which it was travelling and its leg became trapped in the aperture. When the train halted at a station the major commanding the train climbed on to a buffer and tried to free the horse's leg. It would not move, but the train did and no one apparently realised that the OC was not inside it. Desperately clinging to the horse's leg and the ice-cold buffer, he went through nightmarish agony for half an hour until the train made an unscheduled halt and he could force his frozen limbs to scramble down.

In Marseilles the division embarked for Palestine and landed in Haifa, where the brigades divided and entrained for their locations. The North Somerset Yeomanry loaded their horses on to flat railcars, with no sides, and made the short journey south to the Jewish town of Hadera. After that they went inland to the Arab town of Jenin.

The military planners must have regarded Palestine as traditional cavalry country in view of First World War triumphs there (though few of the troops who fought over that terrain in more recent years, the Israeli army, the Arab Legion of Jordan or the Egyptian army would necessarily agree with that view). Never the less the troops were there and their task was to safeguard the League of Nations mandate in Palestine and Transjordan as well as being a reserve for the protection of the Suez canal and the far-off oilfields of Britain's other area of influence, Iran and Iraq and the Persian Gulf generally.

ORDER OF BATTLE 1ST CAVALRY DIVISION

The order of battle of the 1st Cavalry Division was:

1st Cavalry Division
Divisional signals, Middlesex Yeomanry

4 Cavalry Brigade
Household Cavalry
Royal Wiltshire Yeomanry
North Somerset Yeomanry
104th RHA(Essex Yeomanry)

5 Cavalry Brigade
Yorkshire Hussars
Sherwood Rangers
Yorkshire Dragoons
107th RHA(South Nottinghamshire Hussars)

6 Cavalry Brigade
Warwickshire Yeomanry
Staffordshire Yeomanry
Cheshire Yeomanry
106th RHA(Lancashire Yeomanry)

In Europe the *Wehrmacht* in its own good time ended the phoney phase of the war.

Among Territorial units who were soon in action were the 4th and 5th battalions of the Royal West Kent Regiment. They had been posted to the BEF in April and joined with their comrades of the 1st Battalion to form a brigade consisting entirely of Royal West Kents. The next month two more of their TA battalions, the 6th and 7th were in action in France. The three brigaded battalions took part in the fighting withdrawal along the Hazebrouck canal.

Once the agonising decision had been made to quit the field, leaving behind all heavy equipment, the men of the BEF were ordered to withdraw to Dunkirk. With the perimeter getting rapidly smaller it became a time of quiet heroism. Chosen regiments knew that they would be staying at their posts while the rest of the expeditionary force escaped to Britain. Among a formation of riflemen tasked with this lonely defence were the Vics, Queen Victoria's Rifles, descendant of an early Volunteer corps. For four days they helped to hold the port of Calais and kept the Germans from bursting through and destroying the embarking army, but for the defenders the cost was enormous. About 100 miles south west of Dunkirk, at St-Valéry-en-Caux, the Territorial division, the 51st(Highland), was surrounded at cobra speed and in spite of a courageous stand against overwhelming numbers was captured.

Of all the TA formations that went to France, none had a more devastating experience than the three second line divisions (12th(Eastern), 23rd(Northumbrian) and 46th(North Midland and West Riding)) who were sent, virtually unarmed, to provide labour for the vast network of camps, supply dumps, marshalling yards and airfields which formed the base area. It had been assumed that French civil labour would be available to provide the muscle-power for all these important logistic organisations – but the planners had failed to appreciate the effects of national mobilisation in a country where conscription ruled and where almost every able-bodied man had a reserve commitment in the event of war.

As a desperate measure, the War Office decided to send the infantry and engineer units of these three divisions to France to meet this need for labour. The battalions were quite untrained and were woefully short of even light weapons – some had only 3 Bren guns and 5 Boyes anti-tank rifles against an establishment of 55 Brens and 22 Boyes rifles, few soldiers had fired these weapons anyway. There were no Bren carriers and no 3-inch mortars. Communications were equally sketchy and staffs had no experience of handling brigades, let alone divisions, in the field.

The battalions were sent piecemeal to their various tasks. As the Germans began to sweep through France and Belgium and there were ominous signs of a French collapse, the three TA divisions were committed in desperation to the battle. The story of that tragedy is lucidly told in the second chapter of Michael Glover's *The Fight for the Channel Ports 1940: A Study in Confusion* (Leo Cooper 1985). Nobody who seeks to study the contribution of the TA to the Second World War should fail to read that chapter. It tells a story of great courage in an aura of utter chaos – 12th Division lost six of its nine battalions in one day amidst a welter of order and counter order, facing the oncoming Panzer divisions with nothing more than their rifles. The other divisions suffered a similar fate.

The ignominious retreat of the BEF was part of a pattern of humiliation that would characterise Britain's early years of the war: it had started in Norway, now France and it would soon be repeated in the Channel Islands, after which would come Greece, Crete, the Western Desert (after one magnificent victory), Hongkong, Singapore, Malaya and Burma. But strangely the Britons, forced back to their island *sans* weapons, *sans* vehicles and *sans* comrades of famous regiments and formations, could never bring themselves to think of defeat. Indeed, so determined was Winston Churchill that the British should not desert the French in their hour of need that a second, and much smaller, force was sent back to France under Lieutenant General Sir Alan Brooke after the evacuation had taken place.

This force set off from England and landed due south of Jersey at St Malo on 13 June as the nucleus of a proposed fight-back. Territorials of the 52nd (Lowland) Division moved deeper into France to the Le Mans area. But France's leaders had lost the will to fight and the 7/9th Royal Scots and the 4th and 5th battalions of the King's Own Scottish Borderers comprising 155 Brigade scarcely had time to get used to their locations when, two days later they were ordered to fall back on Cherbourg for evacuation. Equipment and, later, vehicles had to be abandoned. On 18 June, a fortnight after the last troops had left Dunkirk, the 5th KOSB became the last formed infantry unit of the miniature expeditionary force to leave France when they were evacuated from Cherbourg in the SS *Manxman*. Small isolated groups of troops were still in Normandy and most of them managed to get back to Britain – with many a tale for evenings in the Naafi – by commandeering fishing boats and other craft. For instance, Sergeant Selkirk, of A Company of the 5th KOSB, leading a party of evaders, slid a small boat from the beach at Dielette into the sea and escaped. A few hours into the Channel they discovered the boat was leaking; a Dutch cargo vessel came into view but ignored their hailing, whereupon Selkirk dowsed a pair of trousers in petrol, set them alight and waved the flaming clothing above his head. The ship picked them up and took them to Dover.[13]

One of the TA formations evacuated from France was the 44th(Home Counties) Division. Among the divisional RASC units were the 507th Ammunition Company, whose drill hall was at Maidstone, Kent; the 508th Petrol Company, from Sutton, Surrey; and the 509th Supply Column, based at Croydon. Back in Britain they were reorganised into composite companies each containing men with their specialist skills in handling ammunition, fuel and general supplies. The old numbers were retained and 507 went to 131 Brigade, 508 to 132 Brigade and 509 to 133 Brigade. They would live to fight another day – and win.

Apart from the humiliation of the BEF's rapid retreat and its effect on the Empire and Britain's standing in the eyes of the United States and the rest of the free world, the short campaign cost the expeditionary force 68,111 casualties, 63,879 vehicles and 2,472 guns (far more than Churchill admitted to in Parliament at the time) as well as the loss of millions of gallons of fuel and millions of tons of coal used to transport the force to its field positions, only to have to carry it expensively back again. But a tribute was paid during this period. 'The English soldier has always shown himself to be a fighter of high value. Certainly the Territorial divisions are inferior to the regular troops in training, but where morale is concerned they are their equal'. The tribute came not from a British propagandist but from IV Corps of the German Sixth Army.[14]

The BEF withdrew into what has been called Fortress Britain and waited with the rest of the Home Army and the whole British people to meet the threatened German invasion.

Anything that would make life difficult for the invaders was done: town name signs, direction posts, railway station names were removed. The Automobile Association and the Royal Automobile Club removed their signs. Invasion never came but the Battle of Britain and the Blitz did.

During the Blitz, householders could save their homes from destruction by fire if they acted quickly enough against the incendiary bombs. An evocation of those frantic days is seen in a manufacturer's advertisement in *The Daily Telegraph* among other newspapers:

The Belling Bomb Snuffer
For incendiary bombs only
12s. 6d.

No house or building can afford to be without at least one of these simple appliances for controlling incendiary bombs. Any man or woman can use it without any previous training or practice. Simply pick it up on the end of a pole or a broom handle (hook supplied) and drop it over the bomb. The contents of dry sand will then be immediately released on the bomb and smother it. Any fires the bomb may have started can then be confidently dealt with in accordance with your local ARP instructions.

Belling & Co. Ltd., Bridge Works, Enfield, Middlesex.

BATTLE OF BRITAIN

Every autumn we celebrate the Battle of Britain and the celebrations are always based on the RAF. No one doubts the value of the air arm's overwhelming contribution to victory and the bravery of the fighter pilots and of those ground crews who operated under attack. But that is no reason why the contribution made by the AA crews, nearly all of them Territorials, should be forgotten. Perhaps Air Chief Marshal Sir Hugh Dowding, commander in chief of Fighter Command, a dour fighter for his pilots, paid the AA teams the finest compliment when during the battle he appealed to the government to let him have more AA guns and searchlights for his stations. They were needed of course for the moments of the fighters' greatest vulnerability – at take-off and landing.

There are various versions of the exact start of the Battle of Britain, some German leaders doubted even the existence of such a battle, as opposed to a series of heavy raids growing in intensity during the summer and autumn of 1940. But we can accept Churchill's authority on the matter. The first phase, directed against ports and shipping, lasted four weeks. It started on the night of 9–10 July with attacks on the Thames estuary and on East Anglia, the latter objectives being mainly airfields. At dawn there were violent raids on Bristol, Portsmouth and Southampton, followed by attacks on Cardiff, Falmouth and Portland and on a convoy in the Strait of Dover. The AA made only one kill that first day, a Junkers 88 brought down at Cardiff but the defenders, tracking without radar, were hampered by low cloud. The most ferocious raid was that suffered by the convoy but the guns failed to score as the enemy was out of range. The gunners made up for it next day by bringing down three bombers at Portland and one at Portsmouth. Guns at Dover, Newcastle upon Tyne and Portland shot down three bombers on 13 July, followed the next day by another kill by the Portland batteries. On 15 July the Dover guns brought down a Junkers 87.

A young London railway clerk who had volunteered for a Territorial RA regiment in April 1939, Peter Erwood, would later describe conditions at Dover, where he served on a gunsite, as reminiscent of the First World War. The harbour there was a prime target, and we can catch a glimpse of the ferocity of the action with the statistic that of the 26 raiders confirmed as shot down by AA over Britain in the month of the first phase of the battle, 13 were downed at Dover. As General Sir Frederick Pile, GOC-in-C of AA Command, pointed out, the port was the first defended area in Britain where the war establishments of the batteries had to be doubled to keep them in action day and night.[15]

While maintaining his attacks on some ports as Portsmouth, and shipping in the channel and off the Isle of Wight, the enemy switched his main forces to target airfields in the next phase of the battle, opening on 12 August. Starting with the Kent aerodromes of Hawkinge, Lympne and Manston, the raiders attacked most of the RAF stations of the south east over the next few days. On that first day, Portsmouth gunners destroyed six ME 109s, machine gunners at a searchlight unit at the Isle of Wight brought down another, a bomber fell to gunners in one of the station raids and another was severely damaged.

In the course of the Battle of Britain the AA gunners shot down a total of 357 enemy aircraft, 145 of them during September[16] when the battle was at its height and the enemy finally realised he could not win it.

LAST OF THE CAVALRY

The European war spilled over into Palestine on 16 July when Italian bombers blew up four of the tanks at Haifa refinery, where oil from Iran and Iraq was processed. On the 24th, the bombers returned and killed 46 Arabs when a bomb exploded on a mosque.

Units of the 1st Cavalry division were gradually being mechanised or converted to artillery, signals or searchlight units. Two squadrons of the Royal

Wiltshire Yeomanry, for instance, became searchlight units (in a few months' time, at Tobruk, as was befitting the senior Yeomanry regiment, these squadrons shared with the RHA regiments the privilege of being the first units in the cavalry division to take part in battle operations). But an historic event occurred on 6 December near Nathanya, on the coast, when 6 Cavalry Brigade was visited by Lieutenant General P Neame, VC, the new General Officer Commanding in Chief Palestine and Transjordan, during an exercise. When it was over, the brigadier announced to his COs that they would all take part in brigade drill with orders relayed by trumpet. The regiments did so, with drawn swords, wheeling and turning, cantering and trotting to the trumpet. It was the last time that a British brigade of cavalry drilled as a whole.

An even more significant milestone was achieved by the Territorials in the following year, in the Syrian campaign and the Yeomanry regiments became the last units of the British Army to fight on horseback. The North Somerset Yeomanry took over from the Cheshire Yeomanry the task of guarding Ras en Naqqura, the headland frontier position between Palestine and Lebanon, which has one of the most breath-taking views in the world. The Cheshire moved two miles along the mountain range to the magnificently sited Hanita, one of the earlier Zionist settlements, that had been founded around an ancient Jewish village. This was the start line for the move into Lebanon and Syria against the Vichy French forces and the Cheshire were flank guard for 21 Infantry brigade. At 05.00 hours on 8 June 1941 the Cheshire moved across the frontier, with swords, cap badges and stirrup irons blackened. The campaign was expected to be over in five days; it lasted for five weeks and the honour of being the last to fight with horses fell to the Cheshire Yeomanry.

At the end of the campaign, the Yorkshire Dragoons, who would later become the last Yeomanry regiment to part with their mounts, were near Soueida. Lieutenant Bruce Hobbs (the rider and later trainer) recalls it as 'very rough country'. His troop arrived at the allotted position, unstrapped their Hotchkiss machine gun from the pack horse, and sheltered their horses behind rocks. 'We exchanged a lot of shots with the enemy, they were French colonial troops, very tall soldiers.'[17]

It was not long after this that the French capitulated. The campaign had produced some vigorous fighting and two VCs. A victory parade was held in Beirut on 16 July.

THE HORSE'S BURDEN

In that campaign, the mounted soldier carried a haversack, a respirator and a bandolier of 90 rounds. In addition, he wore a steel helmet. His horse carried:

Saddle
Rifle in rifle-bucket; mess tin attached
Saddle wallets containing rations
Sword and scabbard (1908 pattern, designed for thrusting rather than slashing)
One blanket each for horse and soldier
Soldier's personal kit and spare clothing
Shoe case with two spare shoes and nails
Greatcoat on front saddle arch
Grooming kit
Two ground pegs, rope and shackles
Ground sheet on rear arch
Hay net
Two feed bags
Canvas water bucket
Tea can

Apart from the weight of the rider and his clothing, this load added up to about seven stone.

11

Soldiering On: 1941–44

We are but warriors for the working day;
Our gayness and our gilt are all besmirch'd
With rainy marching in the painful field.
WILLIAM SHAKESPEARE, KING HARRY
IN *Henry V*, 4.4

'The Auxiliary Territorial Service has proved so valuable to the Army in replacement of men that the government have decided to increase its numbers greatly and to enlarge the range of duties which it performs.' That was how Mr H D R Margesson, Secretary of State for War, introduced his speech in the House of Commons on 10 April 1941 in which he announced that the ATS would be declared members of the armed forces and be accorded full military status. A Defence regulation of 25 April 1941 implementing the decision decreed that medical women serving with the RAMC, women of the Queen Alexandra's Imperial Military Nursing Service and its reserves, the TA Nursing Service and the ATS were members of the armed forces. The Army Act, with certain modifications, applied to the ATS from 1 July that year.

The ATS had indeed come a long way. At the start of the war there had been five trades available for its members: those of drivers, cooks, storewomen, clerks and orderlies. By 1941 the number of trades open to women exceeded a hundred, and every job done by a woman in all those trades released a man for active service in the battle area.

Chief Controller Dame Helen Gwynne-Vaughan, a biologist of Birkbeck College, London University, who had been a leading pioneer of the WAACs of the First World War and who had been recalled to form the ATS, retired as director of the ATS on 21 July 1941 and was succeeded by Chief Controller Jean Knox. In the middle of the war, there was a further change and from 1943 to April 1946 the director was Dame Leslie Whateley.

The women's service made a significant contribution to AA Command. The war cabinet had agreed that the command needed 280,000 troops, though it is doubtful whether it ever had such a number on strength. In many ways, the command was the Cinderella of the armed forces and the Cinders of the command was the searchlight section. In September 1941, the Army demanded that AA must part with 50,000 men, who would be transferred to field expeditionary units, 30,000 of these troops must come from the searchlights.

Women, and later the Home Guard, proved effective at making good the losses caused by the transfer of men crews. A problem with the latter was that they were men with civilian jobs, some of them important to the war effort. They were not allowed to do more than 48 hours' duty every four weeks without the written permission of their employers. In many instances the situation was like today's Territorials reporting to their centres, but instead of putting in a few hours' training they would have to engage the enemy overhead and then go home to do their daytime civilian jobs.

An early experiment with women crewing had yielded indifferent results, but AA Command decided that in view of the manpower losses that it would suffer, women replacements were vital. The result was the formation of the pioneer unit, the 93rd Searchlight Regiment. It was commanded by a man and the officers commanding batteries too were male but the adjutant was a woman and all the troops were led by women. Perhaps the women crews of the command have never been given the credit they deserve. There they were, posted to small sites that were often in lonely places, sometimes only a dozen strong, poorly armed and going on sentry duty with pick helves. For reasons of contemporary delicacy, they were not allowed firearms. Indeed, often the male soldiers had not had the benefit of small arms – simply because the command had had to forgo them for field troops. It is well known that at one stage the Home Guard had been armed only with pikes, but it is not usually realised that in some areas the wartime Army at such sites had nothing better than pikes, bayonets welded to steel pipes. For protection against enemy saboteurs, or opportunist criminals with other intentions, these small groups of women had to rely on their pick helves. What was kept from the press and the politicians of the day was that initially each of these sites had a resident man soldier. His task was to start the generator, a job needing more strength than could be summoned by the average woman, at least until the luxury of self-starters could be supplied.[1] Apparently the male was scrupulously selected for his isolated job; no doubt the authorities were apprehensive about cartoonists and comedians getting wind of the situation of 12 girls and a man. (Query: did those lone squaddies dare to divulge their unit's composition to their wives or girl friends?)

There was a different type of problem for some searchlight crews in urban sites. Massed searchlights in an area told the enemy where important installations were located. At certain times for tactical security reasons, searchlight crews would be ordered not to expose. When this happened, crews were sometimes vilified by local civilians who heard enemy bombers and wanted to know why the lights were not searching.

The GOC-in-C of the command, General Sir Frederick Pile, paid a moving tribute to his women soldiers: 'The girls lived like men, fought their lights like men, and, alas, some of them died like men. Unarmed, they often showed great personal bravery. They earned decorations and they deserved more . . . they were grand.'[2]

Little seemed to go right for the Commonwealth in 1941. To be sure, there were successes against the Italians, initially in North Africa and in the Horn of Africa, resulting in the capture of Italians by many tens of thousands, to the delight of British cinema audiences watching the newsreels. But apart from the liberation of the Abyssinians and the restoration of the emperor, Britain had little to be happy about in the year as a whole.

At home, the intensity of air raids increased; a new type of air raid shelter, the Morrison (named after Herbert Morrison, the Home Secretary), was issued to those in vulnerable areas and even in areas that were far from the coast or armaments complexes. It was a small, indoor shelter and could fit under a dining table; it was in fact a strong cage in which the householder lay.

The VADs and their component organisations, the Red Cross Society, the Order of St John and St Andrew's Ambulance Service opposed the Army Council when the latter in May 1942, proposed to incorporate the VADs into the ATS. Looking back from today it seems to have been an incredibly insensitive proposal by a desk man overcome with the totality of war. The VADs of course, enjoyed the traditional protection conferred by the usages of the Geneva Convention of 22 August 1864 (as confirmed on 27 July 1929) that those engaged in caring for the wounded and sick in time of war should be treated as citizens of neutral countries. Altogether apart from this, the Order of St John had been treating the sick and wounded since the Crusaders captured Jerusalem. The Army Council retreated: the VADs could retain their identity as detachments and their members could stay in the uniforms and within the rules of their separate organisations. But the appointments of commandant and assistant commandant were abolished and VAD warrant officers were appointed to help matrons in supervising private matters affecting members of the VADs. Ungraciously, the Army Council removed the privilege under which VADs of agreed length of service could be promoted to Grade I, which offered benefits of officer status, including first-class rail travel when in uniform and accommodation scales and board and washing allowances based on those of the Queen Alexandra's Imperial Military Nursing Service. Instead, they were confined to the status of ATS nursing orderly. The Royal Navy and the RAF, perhaps more appreciative of the VADs' services, left the privileges untouched.

DESERT VICTORY

In the autumn of 1942, the Allies began their ascent to victory. Britain led the way with the brilliant battles of Alam Halfa and El Alamein, in which Territorials played a big part. The Sherwood Rangers, already chalking up the actions that would lead to Lieutenant General Sir Brian Horrocks's describing them nearly three years later as the most battle hardened of all the armoured regiments, suffered severe casualties. One of the Rangers' officers, the war poet Keith Douglas (who was later killed in north west Europe), found himself in double trouble – with friend and foe. When the regiment was in Palestine he had been appointed command camouflage officer with the result that when his regiment was ordered to the desert Douglas had to stay behind. When Britain's offensive began, he decided that the Levant was no longer any place for him: he should be with his regiment. Off he set, without benefit of authority or valid movement order, and made it to the regiment in the desert. Apparently, when he established contact, the fighting was so intense that none of his old-time comrades thought to inquire what he was doing there.

Douglas took charge of a tank and, through the toll of casualties, by nightfall found himself commanding a squadron. Later the CO contacted him on the radio and ordered him to get the squadron into formation and to keep it together. Douglas replied: 'My squadron now consists of my own tank and one other'.[3]

In one day's action at Galal station, appropriately enough on Guy Fawkes Day, the Rangers took about 300 prisoners, destroyed 22 Italian tanks, four German tanks, two 75mm guns and an assault gun and captured many vehicles and their supplies. Montgomery congratulated them on their 'magnificent victory'.

When the paperwork caught up with Douglas and the unit he was in trouble. Apparently it was only the CO's spirited intervention on his behalf, pointing out the value of Douglas's contribution to the Rangers' achievements that saved the poet from the serious charge of being absent without leave from his post in Palestine.

The 7th Black Watch, in the 51st(Highland) Division, were heavily engaged at close quarters in the El Alamein fighting. Casualties were so severe that the CO, a solicitor, Lieutenant Colonel James Oliver, formed survivors into two companies, attacked again and won their objective. He was awarded the DSO.

Another officer who fought with the 51st(Highland) Division in the battle was the war poet Major John Jarmain, a teacher in civil life but now a gunner. Jarmain, who was killed in north west Europe, wrote of the desert:

For with a greater than armies we contended
– The desert – and that too we overcame:
And the desert will live in us when war is ended
Though we forget, we shall not be the same.

Churchill, speaking at the Mansion House in London on 10 November 1942, the eve of Armistice Day, caught the historic trend: 'This is not the end. It is not even the beginning of the end. But it is perhaps the end of the beginning'.

It was a good beginning. The war rolled west, the flat desert was left behind and the battlefield moved to the mountains of French North Africa,

The danger posed by German advances in south east Russia meant that troops had to protect the oilfields of Iran and Iraq. The garrison in the area was named Paiforce (Persia and Iraq Force) and the Territorials of the 56th (London) Division found themselves part of it. But once the enemy was stopped, the division was ordered to join the Eighth Army and combine with the First Army in pushing the Axis troops out of Africa. This involved an approach march of about 3,000 miles from Kirkuk to Enfidaville. They set off on 28 March 1943 on the route Baghdad, Mafraq (in what is now Jordan), Tulkarem (in central Palestine), then through the Sinai desert to the Suez canal, Gizeh (location of the pyramids of Cheops and Chephron and the Sphinx, where the 8th and 9th battalions of the Royal Fusiliers encountered sandstorms of such ferocity that some of their vehicles were brought to a standstill and a few motor cycles had to be abandoned).

The division pressed on to Mersa Matruh, where, despite the debris of war, they were able to enjoy the sight of miles of spring flowers, with poppies in overwhelming abundance. After 28 days of travel, the Territorials arrived at Enfidaville, to find themselves able to have only two weeks of preparation before making an attack. The moment of crossing the start line is best recalled in the words of Sergeant Johnny Myall, of the 9th Battalion of the Royal Fusiliers:

> We advanced out of the olive groves completely into the open and I have never seen the battalion so grand. They advanced in their section formations just as if it was a manoeuvre . . . There were shells dropping among them right from the start. I have always been proud of my battalion and knew they would uphold themselves in action, but they towered miles above even my expectations . . . When we topped the ridge, there was a vast open plain in front of us with not a scrap of cover, and beyond this the hills – mountains you might call them – which were the enemy's positions. I gave up all hope then, because I thought we'd never be able to cross this and survive, but on they pressed completely undaunted. Now we were actually in view and the fire increased tremendously – shells, mortar bombs, bullets, everything he had.[4]

Myall was indeed proud of his battalion. His medals, including campaign stars, Coronation Medal and TEM with three bars are today in the history room of his old drill hall.

THE MEDITERRANEAN

By 12 May, the fighting in Africa was over. After much hard, and often costly, fighting, the enemy had surrendered in his thousands and the First and Eighth Armies, together with their American allies, had joined hands. The victory prepared the way for Allied forces to invade first Pantellaria, the stepping stone to Sicily, then Sicily itself followed by the Italian mainland. Pantellaria, which held an Italian communications complex, had a garrison of 15,000 Italians and some Germans. The invading troops included the Territorials of the 2/7th Battalion of the Middlesex Regiment, infantry support unit of the 1st British Infantry Division. Fortunately the garrison surrendered and the only British casualty was a soldier bitten by a donkey.

Men of the 56th(1st London) Division sailing from North Africa to invade Sicily dyed their sun-bleached khaki drill uniforms with coffee to darken them for the forthcoming battleground. It is not known whether any members of the 8th and 9th Royal Fusiliers making this improvisation thought of their ancestor unit, the 2/2nd Londons, who in their own day of sailing from North Africa to invade Europe at the Gallipoli peninsula, had gaily thrown overboard their khaki drill pith helmets when their CO told them they would not be worn at Gallipoli (see chapter 18 Anecdotes).

At the beginning of December, the 8th and 9th battalions of the Royal Fusiliers of 167 Brigade found themselves tasked with capturing Monte Camino, a German-held massif about 3,000ft high dominating the southern approach to the Liri valley. They crossed the start line near Clemente and attacked the mountain. Each man was wearing a leather jerkin over his battledress, and besides his rifle, bayonet and steel helmet, carried a groundsheet cape, 100 rounds, grenades, 48 hours' rations, a blanket and spade or entrenching tool and spare underwear and socks. The attackers were constantly 'stonked' by enemy mortar fire from the monastery at the summit occupied by the Germans. The 9th's medical officer was killed early in the ascent and casualties had to be carried down a donkey track for seven hours from the regimental aid post to the nearest vehicle point. The track was the only supply route and it was constantly mortared. The regimental history tells of the cries of the 're-wounded'. This officialese obscures the terror of the situation. What it conceals is the hopelessness felt by wounded men borne in agony on stretchers down a mountainside under mortar attack and on slippery terrain; their impotence becoming overwhelming when the stretcher bearers were killed and the wounded men, helpless, in continuous rain on that grim slope and far from succour, were hit yet again by the shells. The Fusiliers gained their objective at the summit and on the next day the 2/5th Battalion of the Queen's Royal Regiment, in 169 Brigade, forced the Germans in the monastery to surrender. The attack had cost the 8th Battalion 18 killed and 117 wounded. The 9th suffered 14 killed, 48 wounded and five missing.

Back at home, Britain's AA defences had downed 81 enemy aircraft in that year, 1943. This brought the gunners' total of confirmed enemy planes blown out of the home skies to 750 since the start of the war.

KOHIMA

In the Far East, the 4th Battalion of the Royal West Kent Regiment were to win undying fame in 1944 in their historic defence of Kohima. Here, after 16 days intense fighting, which had left the remnants of the shattered battalion facing the Japanese across the width of what had earlier been the tennis court of the local Resident's house, they were relieved in the nick of time by airlifted troops of the 2nd Division. Their stand, rated by many as one of the greatest in the proud annals of the British infantry, earned the battalion the unique battle honour 'Defence of Kohima'. During the battle, a 30-year-old son of the county, Lance Corporal John Harman, won a posthumous Victoria Cross for his charge against a Japanese strongpoint in which he killed five men before losing his own life. On the previous day he had made a similar lone charge to destroy a machine-gun post. By the time help arrived, the battalion had suffered 200 casualties.

12
Unconditional Surrender

At the going down of the sun and in the morning
We will remember them.
LAURENCE BINYON, FROM *Poems for the Fallen*

The 6th Battalion of the Green Howards landing on D-day found themselves on beaches reminiscent of those in their own recruiting area on the Yorkshire littoral from Redcar to Whitby. Of all the tens of thousands of British Commonwealth troops who took part in that biggest sea invasion in history only one received a VC. He was Company Sergeant Major Stanley Hollis, of that battalion, who had joined the TA in 1939. He neutralised two enormous pillboxes, taking 26 prisoners from one of them alone. Wherever the fighting was heaviest, he appeared, displaying the utmost gallantry, the citation noted:

. . . it was through him that his company reached its objectives.

Among the many gunners landing in Normandy on that day were the 86th Field Regiment (Hertfordshire Yeomanry) with their 25-pounder self-propelled guns. The CO, Lieutenant Colonel George Fanshawe (later a major general) had to wade ashore through about 300 yards of waist-deep water after his landing craft grounded. Another Yeomanry unit, the Sherwood Rangers, fighting on yet another battlefield of their war, had been among the early invaders.

A TA unit that landed on D + 1 were the 4th County of London Yeomanry (Sharpshooters); a week later they were to be severely tested in the fighting around Villers Bocage. Here, despite about 100 casualties and the loss of 26 tanks as well as their regimental headquarters, the Sharpshooters fought all day and cleared the village by nightfall. Today Villers Bocage has a street named *rue Sharpshooters* in celebration of Yeomen's bravery.

The 43 (Wessex) Division, an all-Territorial formation, landed in Normandy and on 27 June impressed Montgomery with its first battle, at the Haut du Bosq, outside Caen. The 5th Battalion of the Duke of Cornwall's Light Infantry, whose six-pounder anti-tank guns were locked in a traffic jam, were confronted by a *Waffen SS* battalion supported by two troops of Panthers. This meant that the battalion had to rely on its PIAT (projector infantry anti-tank) teams with their hand-held weapons. They worked their way forward to get within range. In the meantime the CO and a crew freed a six-pounder, enabling them to knock out two tanks before the CO was killed. The PIAT teams destroyed four more. When the action ended, the enemy had lost more than a company; DCLI casualties, killed and wounded, totalled 20.

FIGHTING THE FLYING BOMB

At home, AA Command, which had been expecting to relocate thousands of guns to the continent (and the Far East) as the liberation army advanced against the Germans, encountered an unexpected snag: Hitler's first secret weapon, the doodle-bug, or flying bomb. The AA Command had already shot down 83 enemy planes in 1944 and now the gunners became highly skilled in combating this new menace. Out of a possible 387 targets over the United Kingdom, they brought down 237, a success rate of 61.2 per cent. Weather and darkness did not deter the new weapon and some of the establishments of the AA batteries had to be increased by more than 100 per cent to provide 24-hour cover.

As so many AA teams were Territorials it will be worth our while spending some time on the subject. Typical of the unfair treatment, in the author's view, accorded to those AA defenders compared with the recognition bestowed on their fellow defenders in the RAF was the award of a bar to the DSO of a pilot who had shot down a number of flying bombs. In the week that the award was announced, the pilot's CO was dining in the mess of an AA battery on the south coast and a fellow guest was an AA brigadier. This battery had shot down far more flying bombs than that pilot, so his CO casually inquired of the brigadier whether the battery commander would receive a DSO or MC. When told neither would be forthcoming, he supposed the battery commander and leading members of his teams would be awarded mentions. When informed that they would not be so honoured, the RAF officer pointed out that on the previous day Fighter Command had awarded mentions to four people in ground crews who had maintained fighters in operations to combat doodle-bugs.

General Sir Frederick Pile, Commander-in-Chief of AA Command, pointed out that he had no uncertainty about which deed required more firmness – 'to stand on a gun-site and fire at a directly approaching flying-bomb with the knowledge that, if you hit it, you will bring it down either on to or near your own site, or to fly an aircraft at a suitable distance behind the bomb and shoot it down.'[1] He observed that if the mentions were for qualities other than courage he could not believe that AA teams, in the front line as they were, could be regarded as less deserving than RAF ground crews working far from the battle.

We may cite this distinguished general, recipient of a DSO and an MC in the First World War, as authority for the extraordinary statistic that throughout the Second World War the only officer in his command to be mentioned in despatches was himself – and his award came not from his superiors at the War Office but from the Air Ministry, which evidently appreciated the work done by AA teams at air stations. 'It is preposterous to suppose that there was nobody else during those six years who was worthy of that honour,'[2] he notes. The subject of a campaign medal for those defenders who had served in the Battle of Britain, the Blitz and the operations against the flying bombs was raised in the Commons. Pile had wanted more recognition for his troops who in every sense of the phrase were in the front line, and he had often raised the subject with Churchill. So when, in November 1944, Pile was at Chequers and the Prime Minister congratulated him on 'a first class victory' on the south coast, he seized his chance and asked his host about the possibility of a specific medal, the Prime Minister said the RAF was being difficult in demanding one for all ground crews. At this point, Pile remembers, Anthony Eden interrupted with another matter and the opportunity was lost.

TERRIERS ACROSS THE RHINE

During the fighting on the Rhine, the GOC of the 51st(Highland) Division was killed by a mortar bomb and command of the division was taken over temporarily by a Scots solicitor, Brigadier James Oliver, commander of 154 Brigade, a Terrier for 19 years. Oliver was a highly experienced soldier who had led 152 Brigade, also in the 51st Division, in the Sicily campaign and had commanded 154 Brigade since January 1944. Earlier, as CO of the 7th Battalion of the Black Watch, he had won DSOs at El Alamein and in Tunisia.

Among the forces of 4 Armoured Brigade that were in the fighting that established the Rhine crossing at Xanten was one of the Territorial units that had been converted from infantry in 1938, the 44th RTR. Their drill hall was in Bristol and they had been the 6th Battalion of the Gloucestershire Regiment. As soon as their Duplex Drive (DD) Sherman tanks in line flotation were across the river, shortly after 8.00am on 24 March, they used their guns in support of the bridgehead. A painting by Terence Cuneo commemorates the action. It shows a Sherman climbing up the bank.

The 44th RTR, which had already fought with distinction in Italy, was only one of the many TA armoured regiments that emerged from the war with a magnificent fighting record. The strength of their Old Comrades Associations to this day is a clear indication of the spirit of comradeship and pride which these former Terriers all shared. By 1944, with many months, and even years, of fighting experience to their credit, they ranked amongst the finest units in the RAC.

The first troops to cross the land border into Germany were reconnaissance vehicles of the Sherwood Rangers. The Rangers found themselves at the Siegfried Line.

IT WAS ALL OVER

The German armies of the north surrendered to Montgomery at 6.25pm on 4 May, and Britain recognised 8 May as the official celebration of the ending of the European conflict.

Euphoria at the victory obscured the job still to be done in that worst of theatres, the Far East, where prisoners were treated with a sadism belonging to earlier ages. Among the Territorials serving there were the 4th and 9th battalions of the Border Regiment. The Allies had turned the tide against the Japanese and were winning by conventional means when the *Enola Gay* dropped its payload and warfare entered the atomic age. Japan surrendered unconditionally on 14 August. In Britain 15 August was decreed the official day of victory over Japan.

It was all over. The cost to British Commonwealth land forces was: United Kingdom 144,079; Canada 37,476; India 24,338; Australia 23,365; New Zealand 10,033; South Africa 6,840; colonies 6,877. For the Commonwealth, the total of 253,008 was overwhelmingly lighter than that of the First World War. We may note that the total of British soldiers killed was not much greater than the number of Territorials alone who fell in 1914–18. That being said, we must never forget the very high cost to the other two services, the Merchant Navy and, for the first time, the citizens on the home front. The cost to the enemy was incalculable but certainly not less than eight million killed.

As an example of one TA unit's sacrifice in the Second World War we may cite the Sherwood Rangers, who suffered 250 deaths in five years. Of the full strength regiment that went overseas in 1940 only 125 original members were still in it at the end of the war. These Nottinghamshire men, after reporting to their drill hall on embodiment, and undertaking guard tasks, had travelled with their horses by rail the length of France in the icy first winter of the war, had gone to Palestine on security duties, had become a motor battalion, had been in action in Crete, had become artillery and fought at Tobruk, had converted to tanks and gained honour at El Alamein, had fought in French North Africa, had gone ashore on D-day, and had taken the war into Germany. Haldane would have been proud of them.

The Territorials had done their duty. It was not all in spectacular action.

Sometimes they had boring things to do, such as guard duties. They secured pipelines in Paiforce and some of them served in places that they described as the sinkhole of the universe. They sweated in India, where your rail warrant could take you a clear 2,000 miles from cantonment to cantonment, sometimes with bare feet sticking out of the train window. In Britain, Territorials shot the raiders, piloted or pilotless, out of the sky. They cleared North Africa of a confident, competent enemy. They forced that enemy yard by yard up the spine of Italy. They fought across the broad farmyard face of Normandy. Last and toughest of all they saw it through in South East Asia, where they came under attack from germs, insects and animals, some of them humanoid.

This is an appropriate point at which to record the achievements of women and the Home Guard in defending Britain. By the end of the war in Europe the United Kingdom had roughly the same number of heavy AA guns as it had at the end of 1940, yet in 1945 they were being operated with 60 per cent fewer male soldiers. The shortfall had been made good by women and the Home Guard.

At about the time that the war in Europe was ending, huge rolls of green and yellow ribbon began to appear in quartermasters' stores. In the rush to join the TA from the time of the Munich crisis and more spectacularly from the period when the establishment was doubled, many recruits had become Territorials on the same day – some drill halls had queues waiting to get inside. The result was that among those who had survived many had qualified simultaneously for long service awards, as wartime service counted double.

A NEW SUIT FOR A NEW LIFE

By now thoughts were turning to home life. An advertisement in the national press addressed, not altogether flatteringly, to service women, was headlined 'Civilian sylph'. It went on: 'Yourself – and nearly a million other Service selves – will soon be civilians again, and anxious to be sylphs. We are making as many Utility Berleis as we possibly can, and if you keep some coupons in reserve you may be fortunate enough to get a belt and a couple of Unda-lift brassières' (*The Daily Telegraph* 7 August).

Soon it was time for demobilisation. Territorials, like conscripts, had been given a release number. This was officially called an age and service group. The group (or number) was determined by two factors: age and length of war and postwar service. The lower your number, the earlier was your release. A man who had been called up at, say, 47 on the same day as a youth of 18 would have a lower number so he would be released before his companion.

Being 'demobbed' was a complicated business – far more so than being called up. Leaving the Army was like leaving the womb. In the Army food, clothing, accommodation and medical and dental treatment were all arranged for you; meal times, sleeping times, sports times and free time were all allocated. Being released into a world of shortages was unsettling.

There had been discharges throughout the war, for medical reasons or, for example, on the ground that the person was needed for work of national importance; for members of the ATS pregnancy was an additional exit route. All these individual discharges had been processed by the regimental depots. But now, with millions to be released at around the same time, a different system was needed. The government was prepared for the rush. As early as 16 October 1944, it had announced that, as from that date, people being discharged would benefit from new arrangements. There would be no distinction between officers and men in the standards of civilian clothing issued. The old austerity suits would no longer be supplied; they would be replaced by clothing of superior quality.

The system under which a serviceman could claim a cash grant of £2 15s 9d (in today's coinage £2.79) instead of a civilian suit would end. Today that figure hardly seems sufficient for a suit but then it was more than enough; a tailoring company was so confident of its ability to continue producing a three-piece suit at this sort of price that in the 1930s it had named itself the Fifty Shilling Tailors; it delivered the goods and expanded into a national chain. Until the military clothing and dispersal units capable of processing millions of servicefolk into civilians could be established, individuals continued to be released through their regimental or equivalent depots though with the better quality material and a higher scale of issue. What happened to all the stocks of inferior clothing? They were shipped to the continent for the relief of the millions of refugees there.

Demobilisation started on 18 June 1945. Between then and the end of 1946 a total of 2,450,286 servicefolk had been demobbed (2,273,357 men and 176,929 women).

Each demobbed service person received a civilian outfit and a cardboard box in which to carry it, three weeks' pay, at least 56 days' paid leave, a travel warrant home and money for a meal on what would in most cases be his last journey in uniform. He also received (but not in cash) his entitlement to 'post-war credits', a modest capital sum that had accrued to him depending on his pay, rank and length of service. In most instances the statutory 56 days' paid leave was extended by a provision entitling him to an extra day's paid leave for each month served overseas – so five years abroad would more than double the 56 days. He was also entitled to a 'further education and training grant' if his studies or training had been interrupted. The grant paid tuition fees and, in the case of university studies, gave him £200 a year until the end of his course. Finally he had the right to return to the service within six months.

By the time the waves of demobilisation started, the government had set up 12 clothing and dispersal centres, one located in Olympia, the London exhibition centre. Clothing centres were like huge outfitters' stores overflowing with goods and set up in warehouses. The only difference was that the customer was not only right, he chose his clothing and he paid for nothing – nor did he have to surrender coupons. After this day in Aladdin's cave, his brand-new ration book would give him access to further clothing in civilian shops but he would have to pay for it.

The government had stated that there were about 100 different patterns of suitings from which to choose, but no demobbed serviceman would accept that he had a choice of anything like that figure. There was a marked revival in the civilian clothing industry and many tailoring firms, including some specialising in high-quality products, had been brought into the scheme. The quality suits were not allowed to bear a manufacturers' label, only a code – meaningless to anyone unconnected with procurement. But, as the lawyers say, *res ipsa loquitur*, and such products as Daks, made by Simpson's of Piccadilly, spoke for themselves. The result was that by the autumn of 1945 a thriving black market had developed in these quality products. Excellent suits in some centres were concealed by certain staff at point of service, and palms crossed with silver would produce, for example, a superior outfit instead of one from the Fifty Shilling Tailors. The erring civilians went to prison and troops to the 'glasshouse' (you were still subject to military discipline even as you strolled fancifully through the give-away emporium). Herbert Sawyer, a RA captain formerly of the Rough Riders, who had served in Burma, after which he was in Germany, remembers:

> I was called to an assembly camp at Munster. It took a couple of days to assemble a sizable party, then we entrained for Cuxhaven, whence we embarked for Hull. Customs were thorough. A customs officer charged me a fiver for my German typewriter, which had cost me many cigarettes. We went by train to York, reporting to No 2 Combined Military Clothing and Dispersal Unit. Here a loudspeaker was constantly booming out, exhorting us to stay on. We were documented and briefed on how to register for a civilian identity card, ration book, clothing coupons etc., after which we proceeded to a large sort of warehouse to receive our demob clothes. The issue was of hat (or cap), a suit (or sports jacket and trousers), overcoat (or raincoat), a shirt with two collars, studs, cufflinks, a tie, one pair of shoes and two pairs of socks.
>
> The exposure of the racket in quality suits had made front-page news and when I went through the centre in April 1947 (I had voluntarily deferred my demob for a year), a bemedalled 27-year-old captain among the downy cheeked youths by then being demobbed, something akin to panic broke out.

> The staff must have thought I had been planted by the War Office. The master tailor was sent for and I was given the VIP treatment. Needless to say I was not given a Simpson or similarly superior suit. But the tailor chose for me a reasonably good suit and assured me that a grand gentleman like me was sure to have his own tailor, who for a few bob would alter it to perfection – which is in fact what happened. We were given our travel warrants, leave ration coupons and six shillings (30p) pocket money and sent to York station carrying our demob outfits in cardboard boxes. Although my warrant had provided me with a first class ticket I had to stand most of the way to London, the train being so crowded. The bloody-minded chief steward refused to open the dining cars until Peterborough – so I started to learn what being a civilian was all about.[3]

The chaplain of the 43rd Reconnaissance Regiment(the Gloucestershire Regiment), the Reverend Eric Gethyn-Jones, and soon to resume the cure of his parishioners as rector of Dymock, was waiting for a suit in Hereford Military Clothing and Dispersal Unit. He observed two tall private soldiers in front of him were being given a lot of attention and detailed measuring by the civilian outfitter. When the padre's turn came, the outfitter put down his tape measure and shouted to an orderly on a ladder at the stacked clothing shelves: 'Short and podgy!' The orderly slung down a suit, the padre tried it on and it fitted perfectly.[4]

Peter Erwood, by now a captain in the RA, had been serving in India after the end of the war in Europe. He returned in the SS *Duchess of Richmond*, docking at Liverpool and proceeding by troop train to Reading for his last night in the Army. The next day, 29 April 1946, seven years to the day since he had queued to join a RA field regiment as a Territorial, he was demobbed at Arborfield. 'My suit was the chalk stripe variety but I never wore it, and I gave it away around about 1952 to a young lad who was working for me at the time. I don't think he wore it either. It was pretty terrible.'[5]

Bruce Hobbs, by now a decorated officer in the Yorkshire Dragoons, did not even get a demob suit. He had fractured his spine in a riding accident, had broken a wrist in 1940, had been blown up at Anzio and had then been on sick leave until his discharge. Though he failed to get a suit, he did get to Buckingham Palace where the King presented him with the Military Cross that he had won in Tunisia.

13

Peace for Some

The tumult and the shouting dies;
The Captains and the Kings depart:
Still stands Thine ancient sacrifice,
An humble and a contrite heart.
Lord God of Hosts, be with us yet,
Lest we forget, lest we forget.
RUDYARD KIPLING, *Recessional*, 1897

The euphoria after victory over Japan did not last long. Apart from the absence of battle and casualties, peace did not come up to the expectations of most of the British people. Returning Territorials found that rationing became worse: bread, never rationed during hostilities, could be bought only by courtesy of the coupon. There were children who had never seen an orange or a banana, let alone a pineapple. Tea would remain rationed until 1952 and it was not until 1954 that sweets and the last of the foodstuffs would be ration-free. Even then, restrictions in certain commodities, for instance, newsprint, continued. There were power cuts.

Service people's jobs were protected on demobilisation and for full-time students there were further education and training grants that were not ungenerous. For instance, a university undergraduate would receive rather more than £200 a year, a third of which was payable at the start of each term. In addition, his fees were paid in full, and he was given a refund of any fees that he may have paid in the year in which he was called up and had therefore been unable to complete his examination.

The Territorials returned to a Britain that still had an enormous colonial empire to administer, as well as enemy lands to occupy, so conscription continued. The realities of the cost of the war were becoming apparent. At the time of victory in Europe, Britain had 5,090,000 people serving in the armed forces or their auxiliaries, it was a fearful burden on top of all the military *matériel* that had had to be produced and the corresponding loss in productive commercial capacity. Export markets had been lost and the nation's overseas investment portfolio spent. Taxation continued at high levels, and the money you were left with could not necessarily be spent how you wished. You could not take a holiday in a hard-currency area. Holidays in the rest of the world, apart from the sterling area, were subject to a currency ceiling. Cars were difficult to come by and many other British goods were kept off the home market to give priority to exports. It was gloomy enough for Britons, but of all the Europeans touched by war they were the luckiest. The continent was awash with refugees.

The establishment of the United Nations Organisation seemed a bright spot in an exhausted world. But it could not do anything to stop fresh fighting. No sooner had Japan surrendered than the British forces were struggling to contain emergencies in South East Asia and Palestine. For a time there was a more sinister threat when the Soviet Union showed its unacceptable hand in Iran. But even before these crises, a Territorial contingent became the first British troops outside the Far East to be fired on after VE Day. They were C Company and a platoon of D Company of the 2/7th Battalion of the Middlesex Regiment. They had been on internal security duties in the Lebanon and Syria. Fighting had broken out between the Syrians and the French over the interpretation of France's pledge to withdraw from the League of Nations mandated territories of Lebanon and Syria when the war in Europe was over. The Syrians insisted on a more literal interpretation of that promise than France was prepared to give.

The Diehards had their Bren gun carriers and Carden Loyd carriers strapped on flat rail cars ready to rejoin their battalion in Palestine. But the fighting had taken a fierce turn and the Syrians captured five railway stations down the line from Damascus, which meant that the Diehards could not move from Qadem, a suburban station. On May 29 and 30 the French shelled Damascus from the Djebel Druze and bombed it with a few aircraft, killing about 500 people, as it emerged later. The station at which the Territorials were trapped for three days was part of a complex of railway workshops in which the Syrians were fabricating do-it-yourself armoured cars by bolting steel plates on to lorries. The French sought to discourage them by dropping bombs on the works from time to time, and on one occasion *tiffin* was ruined when a troop of French armoured cars machine gunned the Diehards, assuming them to be Syrian troops. It was a noisy, exciting three days but probably none of them wrote home about it, as it was small beer for a unit that had engaged the massed German divisions at Anzio.

By the end of three days, supplies were running out; after sending out patrols for food, without success, the company rolled the carriers from the cars, mounted and cocked every Vickers gun, and, helmeted heads down, made a midnight dash from the position and clear out of Damascus. They rumbled along to the Golan Heights without encountering opposition and made the steep descent into Palestine, laagering for the night south of Rosh Pinna. An early morning bathing session in the Sea of Galilee was followed by an engine-boiling climb up the Horns of Hattin, a feature with twin peaks. The situation made at least one of the group ponder the fate of those other volunteer soldiers, many from England, on 4 July 1187 when Saladin destroyed a Crusader army on the Horns. What would those Crusaders have given for the fire power of the Diehards? The carriers threshed on to rejoin the battalion in a tented camp at Gedera, south of Tel Aviv. For tracked vehicles without REME support it had been quite a journey.[1]

THE HOLY LAND

Palestine, that bittersweet land, familiar to us all from our Sunday school days, was the last theatre of operations in which a Territorial major unit was on operations. During the last deadly years of the mandate, which ended in May 1948 (though for purposes of official recognition on 30 June),[2] the country's integrity was in the hands of regular units. But earlier, the 2/7th Middlesex had undertaken security duties with the police in Jerusalem, the exonym for the Hebrews' Yerushalayim, later known to the Romans when they rebuilt it as Aelia Capitolina, and for the Arabs it is El Quds (the Holy One). A patrol would go through the Zion Gate into the Old City and along the Street of Sorrows. It would keep the peace at Judaism's most sacred location, the Wailing Wall, the edifice formed by the lower courses of stonework of Herod's great Temple rising up to Temple Mount, the plateau containing Islam's third most sacred place, the Dome of the Rock, as well as the El Aqsar Mosque, the fuse in an explosive city. The Diehards patrolled down Julian's Way, where later a terrorist attack would kill 93 people at the British headquarters in the King David hotel . . . out to the Hill of Evil Counsel . . . around and down to the Kedron Valley . . . past Absalom's Pillar . . . and up to the other side . . . past the Garden of Gethsemane . . . on up the Mount of Olives and along to Mount Scopus, where lie 60 Territorials of the 2/4th Battalion of the Queen's Royal Regiment, Allenby's soldiers from Croydon, who had marched to war from their Mitcham Road drill hall and who fell in 1917 in the fighting for the city in which their Saviour was killed. The Diehards would swing around to their left, down into the Wadi el Joz (Walnut Valley) and to the Damascus Gate and the Old City, then on again to their tents outside Allenby Barracks.

The postwar emergency started on 27 September in terms of official recognition[2] (though there had been murders, gun-running and arms thefts for years before then). The Middlesex, now based in tents between Binyamina and Zikhron Ya'aqov, took part in hill patrols against Irgun Zvai Leumi and Stern Gang terrorists. In November, the police called for help at a large kibbutz, Giv'at Hayyim, they wanted to search for arms. The *mukhtar* (mayor) refused to permit a search and on the perimeter about 1,500 settlers were brandishing cudgels and throwing stones at the police. By now large groups from other kibbutzim were converging there. The Diehards and the 2nd Battalion of the Royal Scots cordoned the kibbutz and dug in through the night while about 2,500 settlers inside reinforced their defences.

The kibbutzniks were warned just after dawn that they had until 10.30 to let in the police. When the deadline arrived three platoons of police behind a selfpropelled gun breached the outer barricade and, followed by members of 6 Air Landing Brigade, were preparing to enter when about 500 demonstrators armed with sticks and lengths of piping arrived from another kibbutz to stop them. Six times a Diehard company commander warned them to halt, and when the crowd still pressed on he ordered a marksman to fire at the leader. At this, settlers with firearms started shooting from the flanks, enabling about 50 to burst through the cordon. The British returned fire and contained the reinforcement crowd as well as the 2,500 inside the kibbutz. Four settlers were killed and 12 wounded. The British had no casualties.[3]

Palestine was a symbolic setting for a TA unit's last operation: a tiny country of contrasts from the Biblical ambience of Jerusalem and the modern sophistication of Tel Aviv to the simplicity of a Bedou encampment in the Negev; from the Dead Sea, where the temperature reached 130°F in the shade, to Jerusalem, 4,000ft higher, where the magazines of weapons were covered with superficial rust when you came off night patrol. The battalion arrived on 17 December at the General Base Depot, Cairo, where it was disbanded. The men had been together for what seemed a lifetime, in fact it was since TA camp of 1939. In between had been the defence of Britain, North Africa, the invasion of Pantellaria, the invasion of Sicily, the invasion of Italy, the Anzio beach-head landing, the mountains of Italy, security duties in Syria during which they burned drug-producing crops, and finally Palestine. Now they were not even to go home as a unit. The older Diehards went back by troopship, the younger ones, not yet qualified for release, were posted all over the Middle East, some to headquarters and one to the staff of the town major of Cairo; some went into Army education and the largest group became crew members of the troopship *Empire Battleaxe*. What a camp it had been.

We have now reached what was virtually the end of the Territorials' magnificent contribution during the Second World War and its immediate aftermath. It is not always recognised that once a Territorial unit had been on active service in a theatre of war for a matter of very few months, it became virtually indistinguishable from its regular counterpart – except that the magic of the spirit which is unique to a Territorial regiment or battalion gave it a special ingredient to its morale. Like most regular units, those of the TA adjusted quickly to the challenge of battle. The trivia and pomposities of peace were pushed into the background and a new set of values took over, based upon all that is best in the British Army's fighting tradition, a tradition which their forebears had done much to enhance, as we have seen. The discipline of duty, loyalty to the regiment and of reason, together with the courage born of that discipline and of comradeship, rather than any sort of 'gung ho' spirit, became the norm. A realisation pervaded all that a job had to be done and that sloppiness and inefficiency in the execution of one's duty could, at best, only lead to the frustration and discomfort of others and, at worst, might be paid for in their blood, breeding a new professionalism in Terrier and regular soldier alike. All too often one hears a man with a fine wartime record who says apologetically, 'Of course, I was only a wartime soldier' – what finer qualification as a soldier could he have? That he had given his time and service voluntarily to the country by joining the TA before that war broke out merely adds to his stature.

Britain can never repay the debt that her citizens owe to the men and women of the Territorial Army. It is a matter for regret that the scale of that debt is not always acknowledged in high places and that, at times, particularly in the early days of the nation's crisis, the Territorials were treated as less than equals by those with whom they were committed to a common cause.

11 TERRITORIAL DIVISIONS

The TA was reconstituted on 1 January 1947 officially; recruiting did not start until 1 May. It is a wonder that anybody rejoined. Even though Britain's armed forces and their auxiliaries had shed about 3,800,000 people since the war, there were still 1,292,000 serving. Some young Terriers had had nearly seven years of full-time service, much of it in battle and discomfort. They had careers to resume and home to rediscover. Why families allowed their menfolk to rejoin after being away for so long is a mystery. Perhaps the men were too steeped in making their own decisions to be dissuaded. But not only did they rejoin, many officers and senior NCOs came well down in rank to do so. Many wartime ranks were local, acting or temporary. War substantive was the highest achievable. Captains volunteering as subalterns were commonplace. In one unit two brothers, both majors and both with MCs and one of whom had served as a lieutenant colonel for a time rejoined as subalterns. It was reminiscent of 1920 when officers of field rank became private soldiers to form tent parties for the Territorials' first postwar camps.

The defence plan in 1947 was for a TA of nine infantry divisions and two armoured divisions. The 25 Yeomanry regiments were formed into armoured brigades. The individual commitment was 15 days' camp plus 30 hours' obligatory out-of-camp training. But to qualify for the £12 tax-free bounty a further 30 hours' training and a range course had to be completed. New recruiting was slow, so it was a TA small in numbers but massive in skills. Comradeship was in evidence and the social life was important in an austere Britain short of everything but war experience and war surplus stores. The nation, having put millions under arms in two successive generations, was tiring of things military. Yet there were commitments to fulfil and conscription continued.

An example of a unit that built up more quickly than most was 51(Ulster) AA Brigade(TA), which was established in 1947 with headquarters at Palace Barracks, Holywood. By 1948 its units were:

60th Heavy AA Regiment, RA, a regular unit
245th(Belfast) (Mixed) Heavy AA Regiment, RA(TA)
246th(Derry) (Mixed) Heavy AA Regiment, RA(TA)
247th(Ulster) Light AA/Searchlight Regiment, RA(TA)
248th(Ulster) Light AA Regiment, RA(TA)
502nd(Mixed) Heavy AA Regiment, RA(TA)
51st(Mixed) AA Fire Command Tp, RA(TA)
51st(Ulster) AA Independent(Mixed) Signal Sqn, R Sigs(TA)
931st(Ulster) Coy, RASC(AA) (Mixed) (TA)
53rd AA Workshop Coy Stores Section, RAOC(TA)
53rd AA Workshop Coy, REME(Ulster) (TA)

An example of another type of TA brigade formed in 1947 is 23 Independent Armoured Brigade. It consisted of:

Staffordshire Yeomanry
Cheshire Yeomanry
40th RTR
41st RTR
267th Field Regiment, RA
23rd Signals Squadron, R Sigs
1st Battalion of the Liverpool Scottish
23rd Field Ambulance, RAMC
23rd Ordnance Field Park, RAOC
Detachment of Armoured Workshops, REME
Detachment of Provost Company, RMP

NATIONAL SERVICEMEN REPORT

In 1950 a unique factor entered the Territorial scene: national servicemen reported to drill halls. After two years with the Army they had to serve three and a half years with the TA to finish their commitment. It smacked of the old Militia and was not liked by the old hands (or by the involunteers). But it had one great advantage: units were brought up to strength. For the first time since before the war, there were realistic numbers attending camps. Until the arrival of the national service intake a typical major unit would have been able to manage only about 120 at camp, 1 in 5 of them being officers. As the numbers of national servicemen increased we get a picture of well filled drill halls in the 1950s. One unit's records show 567 other ranks and 32 officers in 1952. Their composition was interesting: of the other ranks only 128 were original (that is true TA) volunteers, 89 were national service volunteers (men originally posted in as conscripts but who later volunteered) and 350 national servicemen (who were there because they were legally bound to be there). Of the officers 25 were volunteers, 5 were national service volunteers and 2 were national service officers. The TA as a whole numbered 198,500 at the end of 1952 and two thirds of them were national servicemen.

Compulsory TA service certainly fulfilled its creators' aims. It provided a young trained reserve for the country's needs during the cold war. In strictly TA terms it kept units at strength. But magnificent though it was, it was not volunteer soldiering. It also brought unheard-of consequences. Much unpleasantness was caused by having to deal with determined non-attenders. Eccentric and memorable medical certificates were produced showing cause why Private Snooks was not able to attend camp. The national serviceman's commitment was light: 60 days to be completed in his three and a half years' TA service; this comprised a 15-day camp plus five other days a year. If he wished, he could count four one-hour training periods for each day missed. If he liked the TA he could change his status to volunteer. (It is instructive to compare this 60-day commitment over three and a half years with the much more onerous annual programme in the TA of the 1990s: 15-day camp, 12 individual days, no substitution of drill night periods, regardless of how many have been amassed, for a single training day, and far more proficiency tests to be passed each year).

In the 1950s, units had to discipline those national servicemen who failed to complete their training. Courts martial were convened, some of the recalcitrants were punished by COs and there was also provision to have the matter dealt with in magistrates' courts. In a country trying to forget the war and all its compulsions and restrictions, it must have reflected adversely on the TA to have its members fined or placed in military detention for not going to camp, but it was the law. A way of avoiding publicity was to have a persistent offender posted to a regular unit for a short period. This could be done on the signature of the general officer commanding.

In the early 1950s, training majors were instituted to help COs, with training and in some RAC units extra regulars had to be put on the strength to deal with the technical problems of the vehicles. An armoured or armoured car regiment would have 30 regulars on its books.

Training of a different kind was undertaken in the spring of 1953, for the coronation of Queen Elizabeth II on 2 June 1953. Territorial major units were represented by one officer and three other ranks in the procession and one officer and 17 other ranks on street-lining duties. Best uniforms and medals had to be worn. The task was far more onerous than it might seem, as can be gathered from the parade instructions circulated to units in February. Street-lining troops were informed that they would be on duty from 10.00 hours until 17.00. No liquid refreshment would be countenanced, but haversack rations could be carried. They would have to stand at attention continuously for 45 minutes while the procession went past. The parade route was 13 miles long and the marching contingents, with rifles at the slope and bayonets fixed, could not have any refreshment.

The middle 1950s, with national servicemen at drill halls, continued to be well recruited. In Northern Ireland alone, the TA's strength was more than 7,000 by 1954.

Today it is easy to forget how perilous the 1950s were. In the early years of the decade, the fighting in Korea was threatening to spread. The Home Guard was reconstituted and there was a selective recall of Z reservists (these were wartime soldiers who were automatically placed on the reserve after demobilisation). The emergency in Malaya, which neatly enough had started in mid-1948, just as that in Palestine had concluded, continued through to the end of the 1950s. The Mau Mau terrorism of Kenya which began in October 1952, continued until November 1956, all of which overlapped with the constant armed challenges to the British presence in the Canal Zone of Egypt, culminating in late 1956 with the short Near East campaign over the Suez canal. The June of that year also saw the start of terrorism in Cyprus. The Suez fiasco was hardly over when fighting broke out in the Arabian Peninsula. The extent to which the Army was extended can be seen in the statistic that troops qualified for six British campaign medals or clasps to the General Service Medal during the 10 years.

REORGANISATION

The pace of development in aeroplane capabilities and in weaponry forced change in Britain's defences against attacking aircraft by the middle 1950s. In December 1954, the Government announced that Anti-Aircraft Command would be disbanded. This meant massive reductions in ground defences. In 1955, the five Territorial regiments in 51(Ulster) AA Brigade(TA) were merged into the 245th(Ulster) Light AA Regiment(TA). This was typical of the scale of the amalgamations throughout the United Kingdom as that once mighty command disappeared.

The TA was reorganised in 1956 to produce, in the words of its director, 'a reserve capable of dealing with any eventuality because it is impossible to predict with certainty the form that a future war might take'. A recruiting campaign began. To attract TA and Army Emergency Reserve (AER) officers a new bounty of £20 a year, tax-free, was paid if they signed on for extra training and agreed to serve overseas in advance of mobilisation, if necessary. After three years the bounty became £25. Extra evening training without the overseas commitment was rewarded with £7 a year for the first three years, after which it became £15. Women were offered lower rates.

On reorganisation, the TA became a force of 10 infantry divisions, only two of which, the 43rd(Wessex) and the 53rd(Welsh), were maintained at full strength and given a NATO role. This meant that these two had tanks, medium guns and mobilisation equipment. The remaining eight divisions, along with the AER, had a home defence task; this included close cooperation with the civil defence organisation. Six armoured regiments were earmarked for the two NATO divisions. Inevitably the reorganisation brought amalgamations. Only 11 Yeomanry regiments retained their individual identities. The Yorkshire Hussars, the Yorkshire Dragoons and the East Riding Yeomanry merged into the Queen's Own Yorkshire Yeomanry. The Warwickshire Yeomanry and the Worcestershire Yeomanry became the Queen's Own Warwickshire and Worcestershire Yeomanry. The North Somerset Yeomanry and the 44th Royal Tank Regiment amalgamated into the North Somerset and Bristol Yeomanry. The 40th RTR and the 41st RTR merged to become the 40/41st RTR. The Ayrshire Yeomanry became a second line delivery unit and the Westminster Dragoons and the Sherwood Rangers were retained as armoured regiments for the Army's strategic reserve.

In a reversal of the wartime role changes, three TA Royal Tank regiments and the Rough Riders were converted into infantry, a considerable saving for the Army Estimates but a shock for their members. By now the Rough Riders were used to change in their comparatively short existence, and in this they typify the volunteer spirit. Raised as part of the Imperial Yeomanry for the South African War, they became the City of London Yeomanry in 1902. In the Gallipoli campaign of the next war they fought as infantry, were back on horseback for the Palestine campaign in which among other engagements they fought in the battle of Gaza, and they became infantry once more in France in 1918. In 1921 they became a regiment of the RHA. In common with so many other units, they became light AA during the war; after it ended they became an armoured regiment; now they were to be infantry again. *Plus ça change. . .*

One of the regiments that rode out the reorganisations was the North Irish Horse. It was originally intended that the NIH would lose its Daimler armoured cars and convert to a light reconnaissance role but the plan was changed and the regiment retained its armoured cars.

A resumption of IRA activity in Northern Ireland resulted in a half-finished drill hall in Enniskillen being severely damaged in December 1956 and a few weeks later a nearly completed drill hall at Dungannon was wrecked. From then on, Territorials voluntarily found permanent armed guards to patrol their halls, imposing a strain on their spare time.

GOLDEN JUBILEE

The celebrations for the TA's golden jubilee occupied much of 1958. It was now a well-recruited force that made full use of the available manpower and put on a good show. The national celebrations started in Northern Ireland with a review on 10 May by Queen Elizabeth the Queen Mother of 3,000 troops, both men and women, in No 1 dress at the Royal Navy air station at Sydenham, Belfast. In the evening, she attended a reception at the Ulster Hall, Belfast. On 21 June, there were thanksgiving services in Westminster Abbey and Westminster Cathedral, followed the next day by a review of 8,000 troops, including contingents from Wales, Scotland and Northern Ireland, by the Queen in Hyde Park. On 5 July, the Queen reviewed 3,000 troops in Edinburgh. Besides these national celebrations each county association organised its own festivities. Typical was that for the West in which a commemorative thanksgiving service was held in Bristol Cathedral, at which a wartime chaplain, the Reverend Eric Gethyn-Jones (see page 122) preached the sermon.

The HAC, which in 1938 had been the first TA unit to protect Buckingham Palace, was again honoured 20 years later by being asked to find the guard there as part of the jubilee celebrations. It was a 24-hour guard, William (Ted) Pryke, a member of the HAC since 1936, who had been commissioned in the Duke of Cornwall's Light Infantry shortly after the outbreak of the war and after the end of hostilities resigned his commission and rejoined the HAC as a private, was on that guard. He recalls: 'We all felt it was a distinct honour. People volunteered to do the intensive drill course. And after it, the members of the guard were chosen.'

Officers and senior NCOs were on the course and if they were among the chosen, they removed the pips and stripes from their battledress and took their place in the ranks for their day and a night of public duties. They took over from the Welsh Guards, and as they were short of a drummer, the Guards lent them one. By the end of the 24 hours, he was a bewildered man. The guard, whatever they were in the HAC, had all been officers in the war, and had ordered smoked salmon and champagne from a leading caterer, 'and as the drummer lay back on his bunk sipping his champagne he was obviously thinking what an extraordinary thing the TA was'. Worse confusion was to fol-

32. The Cambrian March competition team of the 4th Royal Regiment of Wales, 1974. *(Courtesy of the regiment)*.

33. A WRAC contingent marching across Westminster Bridge to a reception for London's TA units at County Hall in 1979. *(© Crown copyright 1992/MOD reproduced with the permission of the controller HMSO).*

34. Members of the Royal Wessex Yeomanry arriving at Harrisburg airport, Pennsylvania, in July 1981 for training with the Maryland Army National Guard. *(© Crown copyright 1992/MOD reproduced with the permission of the controller HMSO).*

35. The combined pipe bands of D Company of the 4th(V) Battalion, Royal Irish Rangers and of the London Scottish on Horse Guards Parade, 1981. *(© Crown copyright 1992/MOD reproduced with the permission of the controller HMSO).*

36. Part of the test for the Courage Trophy, the major skills contest for Territorials in Greater London, held at Pirbright. Watching are Major General (later Sir) Christopher Airy and Colonel and Alderman Sir Greville Spratt. *(Courtesy of The Times)*.

37. Another part of the course proves no obstacle to these cadets from London University OTC in March 1988. The undergraduates usually finish high in the women's section of the competition. *(Courtesy of The Times)*.

38. A subaltern giving radio instruction to WRAC members of the 6/7th (V) Battalion of the Queen's Regiment on Salisbury Plain in 1989. *(6/7th Queen's)*.

39. Territorials were among the members of the auxiliary forces abseiling down the atrium of Lloyd's headquarters in the City. The demonstration, held during an open day organised for Lloyd's Volunteer Reserve Forces Fund, was in aid of the Star and Garter Home. The 238 foot descent established a world record for an indoor abseil. *(Courtesy of Lloyd's)*.

40. Number 2 on the .50 Browning machine gun is Fusilier Dave Allen, of C (City of London) Company of the 8th Queen's Fusiliers, practising on the range at Gibraltar, November 1990. *(The Author).*

low. In the morning the drummer went to the bathroom to run a bath for the officer of the guard but found it full of other members of the guard and when the officer arrived he was told to queue like everybody else.

On 18 July 1959, the first Territorial unit to perform public duties at the Tower of London, the 8th Battalion of the Royal Fusiliers, took over the Royal and Spur Guard from the 1st Battalion of the Grenadier Guards for 24 hours to commemorate the centenary of the founding of the TA Fusiliers' ancestor unit, the Working Men's College Corps. It was a symbolic gesture for a large part of the TA as many of today's units date from Volunteer rifle units formed in 1859.

The late 1950s formed an era labelled by the press, sacrificing accuracy in the interest of a good headline, as 'never had it so good', seizing on a chance remark by Harold Macmillan, the prime minister. Top of the Pops was Elvis Presley's 'Jailhouse Rock' and Britain was poised to start swinging. Inflation (which at the time of writing in 1990 is more than 10.9 per cent and set to rise) was hardly noticable. There was little unemployment. Our society was not as violent as it is today. We seemed a less strident nation.

CONTRACTION

National service would soon be discontinued, and to prepare for it the contraction of 1960–61 resulted in the amalgamation of units in London and Middlesex as follows:

263rd(6th London) Lt Regt (minus two batteries) merged with 291st(4th London) Fd Regt, 298th(Surrey Yeomanry Queen Mary's) Fd Regt and 381st(East Surrey) Lt Regt to become a field regiment.

264th(7th London) Fd Regt merged with 290th Fd Regt(City of London), 452nd HAA Regt and 353rd(London) Med Regt (minus a battery) to become a field regiment.

265th LAA Regt merged with 458th(Kent) LAA Regt (minus a battery) and 570th LAA Regt to become a light AA regiment.

289th Para Lt Regt merged with 880th Locating Bty to become a parachute light regiment.

297th(East Kent Yeomanry) Lt AA Regt merged with 3/4th County of London Yeomanry(Sharpshooters) to become a RAC regiment.

Berkshire Yeomanry Battery of 299th (Royal Buckinghamshire Yeomanry and Queen's Own Oxfordshire Hussars) Fd Regt merged with Westminster Dragoons (2nd County of London Yeomanry) to become a RAC regiment.

304th (Essex Yeomanry RHA) Fd Regt merged with a battery of 517th LAA Regt (5th Essex) and a battery of 353rd (London) Med Regt to become a field regiment.

459th (Essex Regt) HAA Regt merged with 512nd LAA Regt and 517th LAA Regt (5th Essex) (minus a battery) to become a light AA regiment.

624th LAA Regt (9th Bn the Royal Fusiliers) (City of London Regt) merged with 8th Bn the Royal Fusiliers to become the City of London Bn of the Royal Fusiliers.

873rd (Middlesex) Movement Lt Bty became 873rd Movement Lt Sqn RE.

5th Bn the Queen's Royal Regt (West Surrey) merged with 6th Bn the Queen's Royal Regt (West Surrey) and 565th LAA Regt to become a battalion of the Queen's.

6th Bn the East Surrey Regt merged with 23rd London Regt to become a battalion of the Queen's.

7th Bn the Middlesex Regt merged with 8th Bn the Middlesex Regt and 571st LAA Regt (formerly the 9th Middlesex) to become a battalion of the Middlesex.

Queen Victoria's Rifles, the King's Royal Rifle Corps, merged with the Queen's Westminsters, KRRC, to become a battalion of the 2nd Green Jackets, KRRC.

City of London Yeomanry (Rough Riders) merged with the Inns of Court Regt to become a RAC regiment.

TAER INSTITUTED

Most of the last intake of national servicemen were demobilised in 1963 but because of overseas commitments, some were retained until early 1964. These commitments were subjecting the Army to pressure so, on 2 April 1962, a scheme was started to provide some of the manpower from the TA. That day John Profumo, Secretary of State for War, accompanied by the Duke of Norfolk, chairman of the Council of TA Associations, enrolled the first of the Territorials who had volunteered to accept a rapid call-out commitment to serve anywhere in the world for six months. It was called the Territorial Army Emergency Reserve, quickly dubbed 'the Ever Readies'. The establishment was 15,000; volunteers wore on their battledress shoulder a green flash having in yellow the letters 'TAER'. They received an annual bounty that seemed enormous: £150 taxable (compare this with the £1 per year paid to the Militiamen at the turn of the century for an overseas commitment). Ever Readies also received the ordinary bounty of £15 and pay provided they fulfilled the TA training requirements. On call-out, they would receive £50 tax free and they would be remunerated at the relevant Army rate plus overseas allowances for the six months of their commitment.

A state of emergency in the Arabian Peninsula resulted in call-out warning orders in April 1965 to 175 of the Ever Readies. The main contingent were reinforcements for the Royal Sussex in Aden. Smaller numbers of such volunteers were needed from RA, RE, Intelligence and REME Territorials. Not everybody served; by the next month 14 of those warned had appealed, largely on the ground that their employers had objected to losing their services at short notice. The appeals were studied personally by Fred Mulley, the Army minister. But most of the Ever Readies responded to the call. One who did so was Sergeant Bert Bedford, of the Queen's, who served in the operations and returned with a bright new GSM to go with his TEM. He later transferred to C(City of London) Company of 5th(V) Battalion of the Royal Regiment of Fusiliers. He was still serving, although now at Headquarter Company of the 8th Battalion of the Queen's Fusiliers, until the middle of 1989. Some of the Ever Readies gave their lives in action. 'Money for old rope' was the comment of one officer in 1964 in discussing that £150 bounty.

14

A New Kind of Reserve

The greatest commander is he whose intuition most nearly happens.
T E LAWRENCE, *The Science of Guerilla Warfare*, 1929

The Territorial and Army Volunteer Reserve came into existence on 1 April 1967 but preparations to end the TA had been in hand before the turn of the year. Early 1967 saw the disappearance of TA divisions and of TA armoured and infantry brigades (the only survivor was 44 Para Brigade). These disbandments meant the dismantling of headquarters, the sad sale of mess properties. ('Come on somebody, the dining table's got to go to a good home; I know it's big but somebody must be able to use it' . . . 'Did we really have all that many fish knives?' . . . 'And all those brandy glasses?' . . . 'The property member never did get around to fixing that leg on the writing table' . . . 'No you can't have that painting, it's only on loan to us')[1]. So the Territorials said goodbye to famous fighting formations that had served the country well in two world wars.

Headquarters, unlike regiments and corps, cannot easily parade on Remembrance Sunday, Cambrai Day, St David's Day, St Patrick's Day and similar commemorative occasions. But one mess at least refused to disappear. By a resolution made on the edge of Dartmoor on the penultimate day of the last camp, the officers of HQ 47 Infantry Brigade voted to form themselves into a dining club and meet at least once a year. And so they have. Now known as the Fire Escape club, they meet in a West End club every spring. They dined as usual this year.

At about the time that the part-timers were undergoing their spasm, the regular Army too was under the attack of change. The Ministry of Defence seemed intent on amalgamating just about every regiment in its field of fire. Other arms were targets too. Although these mergers were of regular units, their Territorial battalions would eventually be affected by them.

The first wave of amalgamations had washed over the Army in the late 1950s. The 1960s saw not only more amalgamations but amalgamations of amalgamations.

The four new organisations that formed the new reserve, the T&AVR, owed their existence to the Reserve Forces Act, which became law in August 1966. Members of Categories I and II were known for administrative purposes as the Volunteers; Category III comprised the Territorials. Category IV consisted of miscellaneous units, chiefly university OTCs. Categories I and II had an establishment of about 50,800, set in the Statement on the Defence Estimates 1966–67. The statement estimated that by 1969–70 Categories I and II would save Britain about £20 million a year compared with the old TA and the AER. Category III, whose role would be primarily to help the police to maintain law and order and to give support to the civil authorities in time of general war, would be limited to 23,000 members. These Territorials would be organised into 87 units, with an average of three units in each civil defence sub-region. Not more than £3 million a year would be spent on it.

Categories I and II were favoured with the best of training, equipment and uniforms, the former being the equivalent of the old TA Emergency Reserve, the latter being an upgraded but much smaller TA. Later the two were merged. Better weapons were forthcoming, COs were mainly regulars, and more suitable uniforms were issued: combat kit and service dress. The commitment was more stringent but the money was better: there were two bounties. One, a tax-free £20, was for completing commitments; the other, a taxable £60, was recompense for the call-out liability. Parliamentary approval for call-out was not required.

The Territorials soon found that they were the T&AVR's poor relations: no bounty, camp limited to eight days, out-of-camp training limited to four days and no more than 18 drill nights. Members had to continue to make do with the ancient battledress for field and parade. It was a dreary outlook and many good men were lost. Without a bounty, many members simply could not afford to attend camp. Worse was to follow when, after a year, the funding for category III units was discontinued. In the spirit of the old TA, many soldiered on without pay but after a further year, they were reduced to eight-man cadres. By 1974 the cadres were abolished.

The ending of the TA had meant that regiments lost the bulk of their remaining Second World War veterans. No longer did units have those stalwarts with three or even four bars on their TDs and TEMs. One or two individuals managed to slip through the files, fool the computer or perform whatever sleight of hand was necessary to stay in uniform. After all, part of the art of being a good Territorial is to know how and when to beat the regulations – not in arrogance but in advocacy. The departure of those war-experienced veterans was a milestone. It would be foolhardy to claim a record in matters Territorial, but the length of service of a member of the Cheshire Yeomanry, Regimental Quartermaster Sergeant George E Gander, MBE, deserves notice. When he retired from the TA on 31 March 1967 he had served continuously for 46 years. When you know that six years of this was war service you begin to realise the awesome number of training days recorded on his documents. He was one of five brothers to join the regiment, so some sort of double record was probably established.

The 1970s were a decade of a new phenomenon: a number of T&AVR units were commanded by officers who had never served in the Army either as wartime soldiers or as national servicemen.

WOMEN IN COMMAND

In 1979 a Conservative government came into office and the 1980s were a decade of expansion and a rebirth of some traditional Territorial features, such as the return of some Territorial units to county regimental names borne by regular regiments. One untraditional feature, however, was the appointment of women officers as commanders of mixed operational major units, which might be thought appropriate as Britain now had its first woman Prime Minister. In March 1982 Lieutenant Colonel Jean Blackwood became commanding officer of the 37th Signals Regiment, whose headquarters are in Bristol, and the first woman to command a mixed TA unit. Ten days later, on 1 April, Colonel Kathleen Clarke became the second to assume command of a mixed unit, but the first to reach the rank of colonel, when she took over as CO of the 201st(Northern) General Hospital, RAMC(V) at Fenham Barracks, Newcastle upon Tyne. Lieutenant Colonel Blackwood, who was made an OBE and contributed to the Sharp report on the status of women in the TA, retired in 1987 but three years later she returned as Colonel WRAC(TA).

It is not strictly accurate to say that 1982 was the first time that women Territorials had been in command of mixed major units. An officer of the Auxiliary Territorial Service commanded a British leave camp in Beirut, capital of the Lebanon, towards the end of and shortly after the Second World War. Leave camps in overseas locations played a vital part during the war and the postwar emergencies when servicemen thousands of miles away from home, perhaps lonely and debilitated, needed a rest from explosions, hardships and shortages of food and sleep. The Beirut leave unit was a tented camp sited near the beach. Security was essential and it was provided by a platoon of volunteers found by battalions in Palestine who mounted guard for a week at a time.

The early 1980s saw the Yeomanry regiments who had been formed out of cadres in 1971, the Royal Wessex, the Queen's Own Mercian, the Queen's Own, and the Duke of Lancaster's Own, and given an infantry role returned to the RAC. They are now all operating in the reconnaissance role.

A centenary of service was celebrated in June 1987 by the 220th(1st Home Counties) Field Ambulance, RAMC(V). An edition of 150 commemorative medals was struck and the pieces were presented to members of the unit.

In 1988 some traditional county regimental titles were given to TA regional units. For instance, the 1st Battalion of the Mercian Volunteers became the 3rd(V) Battalion of the Staffordshire Regiment and the 2nd Battalion of the Mercians became the 3rd(V) Battalion of the Cheshire Regiment.

TERRITORIALS WITH REGULAR UNITS

The punch in today's rapidly deployed TA consists in advanced weaponry, better equipment generally and a closer relationship with the regular Army. This propinquity gets increasingly intimate: methods of payment, including tax and national insurance deductions, uniforms (service dress, combat kit and protective clothing), identity cards, transport and rations have all become identical. Relief postings of Territorials have added to the process. A Territorial doctor spends three months in the Gambia looking after the health of the 2nd Battalion of the Coldstream on exercise there . . . another TA doctor goes to Hongkong . . . TA signallers serve in Cyprus on United Nations duties . . . a RCT port regiment unloads ammunition during a beachloading exercise in northern France, live ammunition for NATO use . . . a TA unit takes over duties in Gibraltar . . . Yorkshire Volunteers spend three weeks in the Falklands . . . TA public information officers go all over the world with regular formations, from Hongkong, to Belize, to the United States, to Berlin, to Cyprus. It is heady stuff and whatever the regular thinks of it all, the Territorial values the system that gives him such opportunity. Simultaneously he achieves an interesting camp, has a real job to do and experiences pride that someone in the MoD has confidence that a part-timer can be trusted at that moment to perform a regular's job.

The so-called One Army concept, although modern in practice is about 60 years old in precept. The phrase 'we are in the one Army' was around in the early 1930s. But one curious aspect of this drawing together of the regulars and the Territorials is that the more that ministers and senior generals refer to the concept the further apart the two forces are placed in *The Army List*. In the days of the old TA the names of TA officers appeared with their parent regular regiments. Then after the formation of administrative divisions, the Scottish, the Queen's, the King's, the Prince of Wales's, and the Light, the Territorial officers were placed in a group, still under their battalions and regiments, but in battalion blocks after every regular officer in the division, thus the regular regiments were separated from their part-time siblings. Today TA officers are placed together much further back in the book, after the regular officers. In view of the official emphasis that is placed on integration it is illogical that this estrangement should have been ordained in the official list.

However, integration there certainly is. Effectively it is as though Britain's small Army is one gigantic regiment, of which the TA is the second battalion. If war or similar emergency should loom then this second battalion can be in position early enough and powerful enough to defend effectively. This must be a forward step in these cynical times when, as happened in the Falklands, foreign troops can invade and British fleets, brigades and squadrons unleash massive firepower on the invader, inflict and suffer grievous loss and take thousands of prisoners – all without a declaration of war.

The modern TA has demonstrably justified the disruption to the old system. It must have fulfilled its creators' expectations. After initial uncertainties, anomalies and some disappointments, professionalism has become paramount. 'Lighthearted but efficient' was an epithet coined two generations ago by a brigadier of the regular Army when he described one of his part-time units. Today light-heartedness may not be so apparent but efficiency there is in most units, particularly in the specialist units. The non-specialist areas have problems in high turnover with its consequent disruption of training schedules. About 30 per cent of recruits leave in their first year (see Chapter 20 The Way Ahead). An increase of even 2 per cent in retentions would be a considerable stabilising factor.

One problem is that some senior ranks and officers, particularly commanding officers, are putting in hours that leave little time for any other activity outside their civilian jobs. To give two examples from opposite ends of the scale: one senior major known to the author was made a MBE for his military service in 1985, but it so happened that his civilian company was going through a lean time, and the award, which was reported in the local press with the implication that he had put in much service to the TA, was used as an excuse to choose him as one of the directors who should be made redundant on the ground that he had considerable outside commitments. A young man who completed his commissioning course with the gruelling two weeks at Sandhurst in 1988 had allowed some of his civilian work to accumulate. He was presented with an ultimatum by his employers: chose between your job and the TA. So he had to resign immediately after being commissioned. Perhaps the Ministry of Defence was wiser than many Territorials gave it credit for when in the 1960s it wanted to have all major units commanded by regular officers. Happily the burden of most Territorials does not seem to equate with that of a brigadier general of the Maryland Army National Guard, who in 1981 at Fort Indiantown Gap, Pennsylvania, told the author he had to communicate with his wife by scribbling notes on top of the refrigerator. 'Yes, sir, I have a lot of travelling to do, 380 miles from doorstep to flagpole'.

EXPANSION AND HSF

In June 1981 Parliament was informed of good news for the TA. Its permitted strength would rise from 70,000 to 86,000 eventually. The regular Army formations in Germany were to be reorganised into three armoured divisions. A British infantry division would be formed, mainly of TA units. Although based in Britain its emergency role would be to reinforce I(BR) Corps. Independent units' permitted man training days would increase from a yearly average of 38 to 42.

The following March Mr John Nott, Secretary of State for Defence, gave more details of the infantry division. It would include two brigades mainly made up of Territorials. Logistic support would be supplied by TA units in Scotland and northern England. He emphasised the government's appreciation of the TA's importance by announcing that 12 new centres would be started during the year and new units would be raised. These included six RE squadrons for home defence and an extra company each for the Royal Irish Rangers, the 51st Highland Volunteers and the Royal Regiment of Wales. Three Yeomanry regiments would be reroled to provide improved reconnaissance in home defence. He noted that the issue of Milan anti-tank weapons and Clansman radios was going well. The eight-tonne truck issues had started recently. He promised that the new series of small arms for the 1980s and of LAW, the anti-armour weapon would be issued early to TA units with a BAOR role. Mr Nott also announced an imaginative adjunct to the TA: a pilot scheme for a Home Service Force. It would make use of older men with service experience, particularly those who could not afford the time to put in the full TA commitment. Its role would be the defence of key installations in Britain. The scheme, consisting of four companies, was set up in the following autumn. It comprised units in East Scotland, East Anglia, the Midlands, and Berkshire. The pilot cost less than £500,000 and proved extremely successful, so it was expanded into a full force covering many parts of the country. It did not have its own cap badge; it was part of the TA and its units were badged according to the administrating parent units of their areas. (During the nine years of its existence the HSF recruited far more successfully than did the TA as a whole. When HSF recruiting was discontinued at the end of 1991 as part of the defence cutbacks the latest available figures showed that the force stood at 3,297, including 50 women (the establishment was 4,596). The force was absorbed into the TA's Group A in 1992, provision being made for members who wished to continue serving to be allowed to do so).

Much as its members were fond of the TA that ended in 1967, it is unlikely that anybody who served in both that and its successor would want to go back. Old hands may sigh for vanished regiments and Territorial divisions, but what has taken their place is more valuable. The Territorial today is a peacetime part of the Army. If an emergency arises he will be required to join a formation that consists of mixed regular and TA units, probably in an international force. A lot is expected of him, and it can be seen as a privilege that he should be so regarded. For the taxpayer he should be a welcome sight, costing only a fraction of the expense of a regular soldier.

The TA is generally held by its professional assessors to be efficient. This efficiency should remind the part timers that they owe a great deal to the associations, the regular instructors and adjutants and the administrative staff at their TA centres. There are sometimes grumbles about the constant updating of documents and quartermaster sergeants who get uneasy when too much kit is taken out of the stores, always on the defence against some feared sudden inspection and a feeling that if the worst happens they cannot put Army pressure on part-time soldiers. But it is the associations, regulars and administrative staff who keep the machine going. The high turnover rate puts considerable pressure on clerical and stores staff who have the task of processing civilians into military and back to civilians. If mobilisation is ordered, they are the first who will be blamed from below and above whenever a unit fails to report on time, fully equipped and at strength. Everybody must sympathise with the Welsh Guards sergeant who, having had a brief encounter with one TA unit, commented incredulously: 'That . . . lot, they don't even obey . . . orders!'

Discipline is a subtle thing in the TA, subtle but effective.

THE TA TODAY

The Territorial Army has at the time of writing 67,812 members. This figure is based on returns available in the autumn and relating to 1 March 1993. The establishment for the period is 68,195. By now separate statistics for women are not published and the HSF had been disbanded. Under present plans the establishment will drop to 65,000 by 1 April 1994 and to 63,500 by 1995.

The government need not wait for a declaration of war before embodying the Territorials for full-time service. They can be put into the field for warlike operations to enable the country to be prepared against an aggressor. The TA is not an army (technically two or more corps) that will proceed as a whole to active service. It is an army in terms of administration from which brigade formations, major units, independent squadrons or companies, or individual soldiers will be slotted into regular Army operational formations for the field when required. In this today's TA is far removed from Haldane's TF with its 14 Territorial divisions and 14 Territorial cavalry brigades. As an organisation the TA of today can be sliced in a number of ways. For instance, into groups A and B. There was previously a group C but it was abolished in 1992 and its members were able to transfer to group A.

THE GROUPS

Group A consists of the vast majority of the force. These troops are legally liable to be sent anywhere in the world on embodiment. They receive the highest bounty (which now is £775 for a person of three years' standing) and have the most demanding training commitment. The underlying recruiting trend has been slightly downwards in the past year. For recruits the age limits are fairly flexible but the minimum is 17½ years for units other than bands, for whom it is 17. For recruits, most teeth units have an upper limit of 32, or 35 if he has previous experience in the armed forces. But since 1967 the Ministry of Defence, although in broad terms insisting on a younger reserve than that provided by the old TA, has adopted the sensible and economic approach of not rejecting any fit and suitable person who has qualifications that the TA can use. For those already serving inside the TA, the ministry is not too pedantic about retirement ages providing the persons concerned are fit enough to pass their tests and fulfil a need. Intelligence personnel are a case in point, where certain experts can be retained until the age of 65.

Group B consists mainly of some specialist pools and university officers' training corps. Pool members too can be sent anywhere in the world.

Group C consisted of the Home Service Force, older (but usually far more experienced) troops who, as the name implies, were legally bound to serve only in the United Kingdom and surrounding islands. They had a higher upper age limit for recruits, 50, and for the retirement of serving troops, 60. The reason for the high entry ceiling was that the group required recruits to have served at least two years in the regular or auxiliary forces or have been a member of the Ministry of Defence police for a similar period. Their training was less demanding in time, six training days was the minimum requirement, usually completed in three weekends, and reflecting this they received a smaller bounty. Camp, which was not compulsory, was for eight days. Their main war or warlike role was the guarding of key installations. The HSF, besides being the smallest, was the most recently formed group in the TA. It dated from 1982 when it started with four experimental companies. Finally, it had 3,277 troops in 47 companies in widespread locations. Its underlying recruiting trend was slightly upwards for the last year (in which it attracted about 500 newcomers). In 1992 the HSF was abolished but its members were allowed to transfer to group A on their previous terms of service.

Group A troops can themselves be divided into two parts: those who have or whose unit has a NATO role, and those who have or whose unit has a role in the defence of the United Kingdom. About 72 per cent of TA units have a NATO role. But the fact that an individual is allocated to an immediate place in the defence of the United Kingdom does not mean that he will not be sent overseas later; if the exigencies of war demand it he can be sent abroad.

INDEPENDENT UNITS AND SPECIALIST UNITS

Another way of dividing the TA is into independent units and specialist units. Specialist units used to be described as sponsored units. Seventy-five per cent of all Territorials are in an independent unit.

An independent unit, which is what all Territorial units consisted of from Haldane's day, 1 April 1908, until 31 March 1967, is a recognisable operational group under command. A member of an independent unit is a member of a team. An independent unit trains as a whole, is under command of a formation, is embodied as a whole and fights as a whole, usually as a battalion or equivalent force, though there are some independent squadrons, batteries and companies. A few examples of the many independent major units are the HAC, the battalions of the 52nd Highland Volunteers, the recently formed London Regiment, the 3rd Battalion of the Royal Welch Fusiliers, the 10th(V) Battalion of the Parachute Regiment, and the 151st Support Regiment(V) of the RLC. An example of an independent minor unit is the 135th Field Surrey Squadron, RE(V), at Ewell. In other words, these units form the bulk of the TA, and have their own TA centres and a programme of weekly two-hour training periods throughout the year besides annual camp and weekend training. Though most independent units' mid-weekly training periods are at squadron, battery or company level, there are many that train in detachments as small as a troop or platoon in their own centre. This is in the traditional mould of the public's perception of a Territorial, locally recruited, locally trained and, if necessary, going on operations as an identifiable unit. A member of an independent unit must complete the full training requirement of two weeks' (15 days) camp and 12 training days (usually taken as six weekends). But a recruit must attend for 16 training days in his first complete training year to gain initial competence.

A Territorial who has completed his full annual camp (or attended a 15-day instructional course in lieu) and has done 12 training days outside camp must also achieve efficiency in basic military skills. All Territorials are tested annually in these skills. The compulsory tests include firing his personal weapon, usually the rifle, and passing his British Army fitness test, which is a run; and he must gain passes from a number of other tests: first aid, chemical warfare defence (which used to be known as passive air defence), map reading and fieldcraft. The fitness test is modified for older men. Once he has satisfied all these requirements, a Territorial of three years' standing will receive a tax-free bounty. A member of an independent unit will have the opportunity and be encouraged to attend the weekly two-hour training sessions, which used to be known as drill nights. They are not compulsory but these evenings give a unit cohesion, character and *esprit de corps*. This is enhanced by the social half-hour in the mess or junior ranks' club after the evening's training.

The continuity and feeling of family are important; without them a part-time soldier is in the position of a member of a specialist unit – an individual training on a limited number of occasions. Such isolation was one of the reasons for the Militia's ineffectiveness as was identified by the Norfolk commission in 1904. At the weekly sessions of today's independent TA unit the officers and sergeants will usually have dinner before or supper after the two-hour period. They pay for the meal themselves and the rest of the unit can use the junior ranks' club after the training is over. If a unit is taking part in a competition, regimental, district, Army wide or NATO wide, its team cannot hope for success unless the members train more frequently than the minima laid down for bounty qualification.

SPECIALIST UNITS

The specialist units are at central volunteer headquarters (CV HQ) or TA headquarters at 19 locations throughout Britain.

A specialist unit consists of a central volunteer headquarters or a TA headquarters into which from time to time a number of individual Territorials report. They may, for the sake of convenience, train as a group, or merely as a part of a group, but they will not fight as a group. When wanted on operations they will be sent where they are needed, as individuals. Typically, though not necessarily, these troops will be in a corps, such as the RLC, the RAMC or the REME. To some extent they have taken the place of the old Army Emergency Reserve, which was a force separate from the pre-1967 TA. Members of sponsored (or specialist) units have no TA centre; their training base is, for example, at Central Volunteer HQ at Grantham, Lincolnshire, for RLC members, or at the Central Volunteer HQ Royal Engineers, at Blackwater, Camberley, Surrey for those who are sappers. Members of specialist units must complete their annual 15-day camp plus four training days and pass their tests to qualify for the bounty. Some units, however, insist on six training days.

SPECIALIST POOLS

Another type of unit is the specialist pool. As the name implies, these troops are highly trained in civilian life and their reason for being in the pool is that they can be called out for service at short notice without further training. An example is the pool of engineers practising in a number of branches of the discipline, civil, electrical, geological or mechanical, whose skills the Army might want to use urgently. Another example is the TA Pool of Information Officers, known as TAPIOs, many of whose members are journalists in civilian life, who could go to their field positions without further training. Members retain the cap badge of their regiment or corps. Membership of pools is usually small. At the start of the T&AVR on 1 April 1967 this latter pool (or as it was called then, the Pool of T&AVR Observer Officers) consisted of two men. In the 1970s the strength grew to one for each military district, except Northern Ireland, and members were known as TAPROs. The pool was enlarged, Northern Ireland was included, and it now has a strength of 56. The huge increment was largely driven by the ministry's experience of the role of public relations in the Falklands fighting. Members of the pool were early volunteers for the Gulf when the crisis developed and they served there.

Another example of a small pool is the Army Air Corps TA Pool of Pilots, though this has developed and since 1986 it has added an independent unit, 666 Squadron(V), of the AAC.

The Royal Artillery is responsible for operating two pools, both of them large. They are the All Arms Watchkeepers and Liaison Officers Pool(V), at Woolwich, and the RA Specialist Pool(V), who train at the School of Artillery, Larkhill, Salisbury Plain, or with Royal Navy units. The Woolwich pool consists of officers, including women, of the rank of captain to lieutenant colonel in various regiments or corps, as the name implies, who will go to any number of formations on mobilisation but who train together. This training may include ground liaison work for aircraft cooperation, staff duties or watchkeeping. The other pool is the RA Specialist Pool and this caters for all ranks of gunners and offers training in artillery intelligence analysis, artillery meteorological systems, air defence systems, naval gunnery liaison, and for officers field artillery. Although they are both pools in name, they are in fact central volunteer headquarters. The character of such a headquarters is that it has hundreds of members, is in a settled location and offers training *ab initio*. The essence of a pool is that its numbers are small, it has no buildings dedicated to it, and its members need no 'trade' training, merely refresher courses or courses that will give them training in branches of the Army other than their own. The TAPIOs, for instance, although posted individually to specific working headquarters, at a district, for example, and although administered, usually, though not necessarily by their own regiment, have no pool headquarters, other than HQ United Kingdom Land Forces. Consequently they train peripatetically – a weekend with a signals unit at Catterick, with a tank unit on Salisbury Plain, at Hythe, Bulford or at Winterbourne Gunner, the chemical warfare establishment.

MALE AND FEMALE

A more traditional way of dividing the TA is into men and women. Today the TA has more than 9,000 women. But many units are mixed and it is important to bear in mind that the gender distinction in the allocation of tasks becomes more blurred every year.

British Army is not yet at the stage reached by that of the United States, Canada, the Netherlands and Norway in sex equality. Less than a decade ago it seemed strange to British Territorials on exchange exercise with the Maryland Army National Guard to see women going on early morning runs in the same squads as men. Today Dutch women soldiers flourish on ceremonial duties. Apparently United States troops deployed in Saudi Arabia shared the same squad tents whether they be men or women. It is a far cry from the Second World War when young armed sentries at base camps crept shyly into the out-of-bounds quarters of the ATS to wake early-duty women cooks.

Hospitals have been mixed units for generations, but transport and catering followed in the First World War, and signals, searchlight and other AA duty as well as special operations followed in the next war. In 1939 women of the ATS were allowed to work at only five trades but well before the war ended they were working skilfully at more than a hundred, and many of the women were in fighting units such as the AA batteries. They did not actually operate the guns, one reason being that some of the shells were too heavy for women to lift, but they did every other job, range-finding, predicting, operating the searchlights and driving and maintenance. Every such task they performed released a man for the sort of combat that could get hand-to-hand in its closeness. The women of those AA units, so much admired in the days when Britain was being raided on consecutive nights for weeks on end, would no doubt be astonished to learn that in 1988 a lieutenant of the WRAC became a bomb disposal officer of the 101st(London) Engineer Regiment(Explosive Ordnance Disposal), RE(V). In the postwar era legal services are among corps that have become mixed. Nowadays many infantry units too have women serving in them, usually as assistant adjutants or in the orderly room. This mixed membership takes place in the bands too – a typical TA band being allowed to have up to six women in it. And women now drill with rifles.

RECOGNISABLY TERRITORIAL AND QUASI REGULAR

There is yet another way of dividing the TA. This consists of units that are recognisable immediately as Territorial by their cap badge and stable belt contrasted with those that share a cap badge and other distinctive features of uniform with their parent regular regiment or corps. Those that are uniquely TA are: the HAC and the Royal Monmouthshire Royal Engineers(Militia), the 52nd Lowland Volunteers, the old Yorkshire Volunteers, the Wessex Regiment(Rifle Volunteers) and the 51st Highland Volunteers. To this category must be added all the Yeomanry regiments: the Royal Yeomanry, the Royal

Wessex Yeomanry, the Queen's Own Mercian Yeomanry, the Queen's Own Yeomanry and the Duke of Lancaster's Own Yeomanry. Additionally all university OTCs are in this category, having their own cap badges (in somewhat illogical contrast to the youth organisations, the CCFs and ACFs, which have regular Army cap badges and stable belts).

Those who share a cap badge and other distinctive features of uniform with their regular counterparts include: the Royal Artillery, many of the TA battalions of infantry regiments, the Parachute Regiment, the Special Air Service and all the Corps (with the notable exception of the Royal Monmouthshire Royal Engineers(Militia) – see above).

REMUNERATION

Pay is relatively good and there is now no distinction between male and female salaries. Under scales operative up to 1 April 1994, a recruit today starts at £20.34 (taxable) for a full day's training. His pay will subsequently rise in various bands. A second lieutenant receives £35.98p a day. Travel to duty is reimbursed. All ranks receive a tax-free £3.25 allowance for attending a training period (drill night) and in addition are credited with a quarter-day's pay, taxed. All Territorials of three years' standing who qualify as efficient receive a tax-free £775 annual bounty. Those with one year's or two years' training receive less.

TERRITORIAL BANDS

The TA has only a fraction of the number of bands that it could once muster. Before mechanisation nearly every major unit had its own band, and some had two. The Queen's Westminsters, for instance, paraded both their bands when the unit was inspected by the Kaiser in 1891. Today the TA has 24 full bands, and besides these there are numerous pipe bands, bugle bands and corps of drums. Irish units have five pipe bands plus bugles and corps of drums. There are many pipe bands in Scotland and the London Scottish have had a pipe band continuously since the raising of their ancestor Volunteer unit. TA bands are hard-working, in demand and very much part of their communities.

Regular army bands are to be reduced from 63 to 29 by April 1995, Archie Hamilton, Minister for the Armed Forces announced on 16 March 1993. But the number of TA bands and bandsmen will not to be reduced, the government has said.

Members of corps of drums are fighting troops first, drummers second. They are trained in their unit's usual weapons. The pipers' traditional role is in the defence platoon of HQ. Musicians of full bands have a war role as combat medical orderlies. During the Gulf operations, regular Army bands were deployed in field hospitals. TA musicians must obtain their regimental medical certificate; every third camp must consist of two weeks' training with a military general hospital. Most conductors are warrant officers in rank and they are termed bandmasters. They too must qualify medically. A higher grade of band, a staff band but not necessarily bearing this title, is in the charge of a commissioned officer termed a director of music. Usually he is a captain or major. Some TA bands have women musicians. TA musicians are required to rehearse regularly. The minimum joining age is 17 and retirement is at 55 after many years of a more tolerant attitude by the authorities. Regulations for TA bands were tightened in the late 1980s when they were transferred from Group B to Group A. They now have a 15-day camp instead of eight days.

A SMALLER TA FOR THE REST OF THE 1990s

On 10 December 1991, Mr Tom King, Secretary of State for Defence, outlined the government's proposals for restructuring Britain's reserves for the 1990s. The TA would be reduced to about 63,500, he announced. (At that date it had an establishment of 90,068 with an actual recruited strength of 73,800, including the Home Service Force, according to the returns available at the end of December but relating to 30 September). He added that the HSF, whose members had more flexible age and medical standards, would be 'absorbed within the mainstream TA and its members given the opportunity to transfer initially on their present terms of service'. This means that the HSF moved from group C to group A. It is to be hoped that good use will continue to be made of these veterans as the HSF proved extraordinarily successful since it was set up as a pilot scheme of four companies in September 1982. Returns at the end of 1991 showed that it was recruited at 3,297, including 50 women. Over its final years the HSF has registered a consistent rise in strength compared with the TA as a whole which has been declining slightly. The reduction of the TA to 63,500 will come into effect by April 1995. Although the minister had some welcome news about new weapons and equipment to be issued to its members, for the most part the proposals were in line with the depressing policy of optimistically slicing away a large part of the nation's reserves in the interests of saving perhaps £40 million–£50 million a year. With the regular Army drastically reduced, it would have made sense for the government to expand the TA. The world is in a state of flux: western Europe is joining together as never before; in eastern Europe, nations are disentangling themselves from federal groupings and becoming smaller and more nationalistic (there has been ruthless fighting in two parts of the continent). With the former Soviet Union disintegrated and leaving powerful nuclear and chemical weapons to sell in exchange for foreign currency, with the survival of sinister tyrants in other parts of the world and an easier access to nuclear capability for small nations, we live on an unstable planet.

The minister said that a cut of about 18 per cent would be made in the TA's infantry strength, but he pledged that more volunteers would be needed for the Royal Engineers, the Royal Signals, the Intelligence Corps and the Army Air Corps. The infantry would have only 36 battalions, compared with 41 at the date of the announcement. (These will, with one exception, be of three rifle companies instead of four. The exception is the London Regiment, formed in 1993, welcome return of an honoured title from Haldane's day. The Londons comprise a Headquarters company plus rifle companies designated: B(Queen's Regiment), C(City of London Fusiliers), A(London Scottish) and D(London Irish Rifles). The Londons, as in 1908, have no common cap badge; instead the four companies wear the badge and uniforms of their parent regiments. B, called Queen's Regiment, is badged to the Princess of Wales's Royal Regiment.) The 15th Battalion of the Parachute Regiment would amalgamate with the 4th Battalion, the merged unit to have its headquarters and one company based in Glasgow. There would still be five Yeomanry regiments, but they would be reorganised (one of them would be responsible for reconnaissance in NATO's new Rapid Reaction Corps).

Two artillery air defence regiments would merge and some engineer and signals units would be reorganised for expanded roles. Medical units will be reorganised into smaller, selfcontained ones (but the overall size of the RAMC would be subjected to further scrutiny as part of a wider review of defence medical services). A second AAC squadron would be formed.

Three air defence regiments would be equipped with the Starstreak surface-to-air missile when it entered service. Two regiments would be equipped with 155mm FH70 towed howitzers for the first time. Engineer units would assume more responsibility for airfield damage repair and support of the RAF Harrier force and there would be a widening of other engineering roles. Finally, some signals units would have Ptarmigan communications systems for national defence deployment as well as in the Rapid Reaction Corps.

Inevitably the 1990s constituted a period of flux for the Army. The Adjutant General's Corps was formed in 1992 from an amalgamation of the Corps of Royal Military Police, the Military Provost Staff Corps, the Royal Army Pay Corps, The Royal Army Educational Corps, the Army Legal Corps, the staff clerks' branch of the Royal Army Ordnance Corps plus clerks from other arms, and the Women's Royal Army Corps members not assigned to individual regiments or corps. Many battalions were phased out or put into suspended animation. More sadly, regiments were ordered to merge. Two of the more poignant amalgamations announced were those affecting Britain's senior regular infantry regiment, the Royal Scots (scheduled to merge with the King's Own Scottish Borderers) and the senior English infantry regiment, the

Queen's, which merged with the Royal Hampshires to form the Princess of Wales's Royal Regiment (Queen's and Royal Hampshires). The Cheshire Regiment was scheduled to amalgamate with the Staffordshires, but the ministry dropped this merger and that planned for the Royal Scots and the KOSB.

In 1992 the Royal Irish Rangers amalgamated with the Ulster Defence Regiment to form the Royal Irish Regiment, the British Army's biggest infantry regiment. The Women's Royal Army Corps was disbanded and so too was the Home Service Force of the TA. The next year saw the formation of the Royal Logistic Corps, from the Royal Corps of Transport, the Royal Army Ordnance Corps, the Army Catering Corps, the Postal and Courier Service of the Royal Engineers and the Royal Pioneer Corps.

The Gloucestershire Regiment and the Duke of Edinburgh's Royal Regiment(Berkshire and Wiltshire) are scheduled for amalgamation in 1994, as are the Queen's Own Highlanders and the Gordon Highlanders. The Gurkha regiments are to amalgamate into the Royal Gurkha Rifles in 1995. The 2nd battalions of the Grenadier, Coldstream and Scots Guards will go into suspended animation, and the Life Guards and the Blues and Royals will merge but maintain their individual cap badges. The RAC will drop from 19 to 11 regiments by 1995.

The pressure for contraction was applied to the TA but the government kept emphasising that no Territorial who wished to remain in service would be forced to leave, though he might have to change his cap badge, and even his war role. To this extent the sweeping changes were kind to the TA, and the hurricane that blew over the army as a whole was only a breeze for the Territorial. Although the government was determined to diminish the TA along with the reductions in size of the regular Army it was in the meantime studying ways of increasing the role of the reserves and obtaining access to this trained body of servicefolk in the event of an emergency well short of general war. This centred on the attractions of the Ever Ready concept.

The result was that a Ministry of Defence open government document, published in March 1992, envisaged a wider and swifter use of the reserve forces of all three services. The document, *The Future of Britain's Reserve Forces*, was the outcome of a study ordered by Mr Tom King, Secretary of State for Defence, in the wake of *Options for Change in Defence*. The report's authors, of necessity seeking to provide manpower in the post-*Options* climate, go back a generation to the problems that faced the Army when conscription ended. The consequence is a recommendation that all three services should have Ever Ready reservists. Ever Readies would be divided into two categories, Type A and Type B, and members of each could be either regular reservists (those ex-regulars who have completed their time with the colours) or volunteer reservists (Territorials or their equivalent in the other services). Type A would provide immediate reinforcement for the regular order of battle. In the main they would be individuals, but there would also be a few highly specialised units. All would be essential to the regular order of battle. Type B would be used as pool reinforcements, specialist or non-specialist, to be employed as individuals or in sub-units. They would serve either in the line or as United Kingdom replacements for regulars deployed in the operational zone.

A novel aspect of the report is that the Type B Ever Ready is envisaged additionally as a resource for providing military aid to the civil community (MACC) in the event of a major natural or industrial disaster. [This would bring Type B Territorials, incidentally, into a similar role as the United States National Guard in its state mission, as opposed to its federal mission (war role).]

The report makes a nod of acknowledgement to the sort of world in which we now live with its proposal that the ministry should consider using volunteer reserves of all three services as United Nations peace-keeping observers. Further, the Type A Ever Ready is seen as a resource for limited active deployments such as evacuations or UN humanitarian operations.

In the author's opinion both these roles, the MACC and the overseas tasks would make a good deal of sense. In January 1993, for instance, Territorials performed valuable work during the serious floods at Perth. Just before hurricane-force winds made flooding inevitable, Territorials of the 225th (Highland) Field Ambulance, RAMC (V), of Dundee, were called out to ferry relief supplies, including blankets to drivers trapped by snowdrifts at Forfar. When Perth was inundated the permanent staff at the unit worked all night to transport boats there from Dundee. For seven days a vital generator was manned by Territorials.

In view of the demands on the regular Army the government had been over-enthusiastic in making its manpower reductions and regimental amalgamations. The cuts were clearly wrong. Sure enough, 3 February 1993 witnessed an embarrassing 'As you were!' with the reinstatement of four infantry regiments that had been ordered to merge into two. The plan to amalgamate the Royal Scots with the King's Own Scottish Borderers and the Cheshires with the Staffords was cancelled. The government granted the reprieve six days before the House of Commons Defence Select Committee recommended that all infantry battalion reductions should be cancelled. The committee noted that the MoD 'assured us that the Army would retain the capability to deploy on the scale of Operation Granby in the future. But everything in the past three years leads us to the bleak conclusion that the proposed rundown goes too far, and that . . . even minor contingencies are imposing an unacceptable strain on the Army'.

It added: 'If the Government does not soon recognise the very real possibility that the additional commitments in Northern Ireland and Bosnia could continue into the medium and long term, or be replaced, or even augmented by other commitments elsewhere, it risks finding that it no longer has the forces available to fulfil commitments that it needs or wishes to fulfil.' The report concluded: 'In the light of the chronic overstretch being experienced by the Army, which shows no sign of abating, we recommend that the Government cancel all amalgamations or disbandments of United Kingdom infantry battalions currently planned'.

As far as the TA is concerned, the latest statistics, which refer to 1 March 1993, the total of men and women Territorials was 67,812 at that date, compared with an establishment of 68,195. By now there were no separate figures for women, and the Home Service Force had lost its separate identity. The TA's establishment will drop to 65,000 on 1 April 1994 and to 63,500 on 1 April 1995. Of course, it is possible that even the lowest figure could be further reduced if the Treasury pressure on public expenditure is maintained.

15
TA&VRAs, the Administrative Providers

Good order is the foundation of all good things.
EDMUND BURKE,
Reflections on the Revolution in France (1790)

'Is the caretaker a cripple? Look at the moss growing out of the first-floor guttering.' It is 08.00 hours and the secretary of a Territorial, Auxiliary and Volunteer Reserve Association is making his first inspection of a TA centre in his area. The secretary, although addressed according to his military rank, is in plain clothes and is a civilian. He is addressing the unit's permanent staff administrative officer.

'Well, gentlemen, what are your feelings on this? The ministry has suggested that a way in which young, short-service officers who have completed their Army service can be attracted to the TA is to give them a £1,000 bounty after their first year.' . . . 'Dreadful thought! Nothing could be more divisive in a volunteer organisation: first-class members and second-class members. It would mean those who had served for years would be treated less favourably than people who became instant Terriers. Once there is discrimination in bounties there will be discrimination in other matters. I hope every member in this room tonight votes emphatically against it.' It is six o'clock in an evening of the mid-1980s and the recruiting and publicity committee are in session.

It is no exaggeration to say that most Territorials and regulars complete their service careers without being aware of the role and value of the Territorial, Auxiliary and Volunteer Reserve Associations. TA&VRAs provide essential administrative support for the TA and complement its operational function. The most obvious areas of responsibility of the associations are the provision of accommodation for independent TA units, for Royal Naval Reserve, Royal Marines Reserve and Royal Auxiliary Air Force units as may be required, for Combined Cadet Force units, for Army Cadet Force units and for Air Training Corps units. They also give advice to the Sea Cadet Corps in matters of common interest to other cadet forces. Associations are responsible for building and maintaining the accommodation they provide. They also have a recruiting, public relations and welfare role.

There are 14 TA&VRAs, each established under its own scheme as outlined by act of Parliament. Together they cover all geographical parts of the country; each is self-governing. They are designated: Highland, Lowlands of Scotland, North of England, Yorkshire and Humberside, North West of England and Isle of Man, Wales, West Midlands, East Midlands, Western Wessex, Eastern Wessex, East Anglia, Greater London, South East, and Northern Ireland.

To disseminate relevant information to the associations, to represent them as an entity in negotiations with government or other organisations and to act as a liaison body there is the Council of TA&VRAs. The council is the collective voice and ears of the associations, but it is in no sense a governing or disciplinary body. Each association is autonomous, administers its own funds, makes its own contracts, appoints its own staff and specialists, decides on its own recruiting and publicity campaigns and so on, covering the whole field of its responsibilities individually.

Each association represents the civilian catchment area of the units within its jurisdiction and is responsible for their administrative support. An association's geographical area must not be confused with a military district; the latter is an operational concept of responsibility, commanded by the regular Army, which is responsible for every aspect of all regular troops and for the training, safety and operational deployment of all Territorials in the district. For example, the district is responsible for determining the security alert state of a TA centre and for seeing that the troops observe the appropriate standing orders. If conditions are such that security considerations demand changes in the fabric of the buildings, these changes will become the responsibility of the association.

The associations were formed as Territorial Force Associations on a county basis in Haldane's organisation of the TF. There were 93 of them originally and none in Ireland or the Isle of Man. Later the total increased to 104, but over the years the number has been reduced progressively to 84, to 59 and finally to the present 14 on a regional basis. In spite of their long record of service, the outlook for the associations looked bleak in the mid-1960s. At the outset of the protracted negotiations between the Ministry of Defence and the associations' council, leading to the 1967 change from the old TA to the much smaller Territorial and Army Volunteer Reserve, the ministry made no secret of the fact that it wanted to disband the associations. With near-invincible ignorance the ministry claimed that they were wasteful and inefficient. But the council pointed out that the associations (whose members gave their time and the value of their experience free) were far less wasteful than would be the alternative, an enlarged staff at military district headquarters. A compromise was found under which the ministry accepted the retention of the associations but insisted on decreasing their number: it was agreed that there should be only 23 of them but that their geographical scope would be extended to take in the territory covered by their predecessors. The ministry then changed its mind and unilaterally cut the total of associations to the 14 that we have today. Despite the shock of this setback, the council's negotiators, led by Bernard Marmaduke Fitzalan Howard, 16th Duke of Norfolk, himself a former Territorial, and Hugh Tyler, a former regular brigadier who proved a determined negotiating secretary, felt that it would be unwise to strive further for the agreement to be honoured. Both men had worked long hours over many months in the interest of the TA.

Proof of the wisdom of this approach was forthcoming nearly a quarter of a century later. An internal Ministry of Defence study under the chairmanship of Major General P I Chiswell into the relationship between the TA&VRAs and the regular services was made and in 1988 the committee's report confirmed the value of the associations.

THE ORGANISATION

The council, whose ancestor was the Federated Association of Territorial Force Associations (perhaps a more self-explanatory title) founded in 1910, has today upwards of 200 members. The patron is Colonel Viscount Ridley: the president is Lord Younger of Prestwick: the chairman is General Sir John Akehurst. There are five vice chairmen. All these appointments are part-time.

A full-time secretariat, whose senior officers are customarily retired regular service officers, is now located at the Duke of York's Headquarters in Chelsea. The present incumbents are: secretary, Major General W A Evans: deputy secretary, Brigadier T S Sneyd; and there is a secretary of the staff pension plan, and secretarial support.

Unlike the associations, the council is not a statutory organisation. Besides the officers already listed, it consists of the president, vice presidents, chairman, vice chairmen and secretary of each of the 14 associations. The president of each association is a lord lieutenant of a county within the association's area, and the vice presidents are the lord lieutenants of the other counties in the relevant region. In Scotland the Highland association's vice presidents traditionally include the lord provosts of Aberdeen and of Dundee and the Lowland association's vice presidents customarily include the lord provosts of Edinburgh and of Glasgow. The Scottish associations, which cover a wide area, usually have more vice presidents than any of the other associations and most of them are members of the Queen's Body Guard for Scotland. Among the vice presidents of the North West of England and Isle of Man association is the lieutenant governor of the Isle of Man. Within the Greater London association there is a sub-association for the City of London, with the lord mayor as its president. The sub-association is not a corporate body but with parent delegation it enjoys some independence.

Each association has a chairman and he has vice chairmen representing each of the services. The association also has a full-time secretariat consisting of a secretary and a deputy secretary and sometimes an assistant secretary. The secretary is a retired officer, usually a brigadier, a colonel or a lieutenant colonel or their equivalents in the other services. To provide continuing liaison between the associations there is a committee of their secretaries and this meets usually three or four times a year. The City sub-association has its own secretary, a retired major. All the associations, as well as the council, have their own supporting clerical staffs. The associations also have surveyors, valuers and similar specialists with whom they have a contractual relationship from time to time for specific tasks. Some have, for instance, their own publicity consultants. The associations' staffs are not Civil servants, though their conditions of employment are based on those of the Civil service.

The membership of each association reflects the TA and the community of the region from whose citizenry come the recruits. When you attend a meeting of an association you are in discussion with serving Territorials, retired Territorials, retired regulars, the lord lieutenant, deputy lieutenants, local government councillors, educationalists, employers' representatives, trade union representatives and regular officers who are for the time being in command of TA units. Greater London has a member who is a well known show business broadcaster and can thus give advice on his speciality. An association meeting can assemble a formidable body of military, commercial and regional knowledge.

Most TA centres are maintained by the relevant association. Most are in the ownership of the secretary of state for defence for the time being and are entrusted to the care of an association. Some associations are responsible also for training areas and ranges. This means that each association is a considerable land agent, whether in the countryside or in a city. Some TA units own their own centres, for instance the HAC own Armoury House, near Finsbury Square. In the case of two other famous London units, the Inns of Court and City Yeomanry and the 4th(V) Battalion of the Royal Green Jackets, the centres – in Stone Buildings, Lincoln's Inn, and in Davies Street, in the heart of Mayfair – are leased from respectively the benchers of Lincoln's Inn and the Duke of Westminster's Grosvenor Estates. But in general, when you see a TA centre you see a piece of real estate that is under the care and responsibility of a TA&VRA.

If a unit based in such a centre wants to have changes in the fabric of its buildings it will have to persuade the association to undertake them. Similarly, if an association wants to modernise the premises or wishes to remove an eye-sore or a danger, then the unit will have to reorder its life to accommodate the disturbance. In the case of a substantial refurbishment or rebuilding, the unit might have to move out completely until the work is completed. If the unit wants to establish, say, a museum or even a modest history room, then the alterations will be subject to the association's approval. The associations' surveyors regularly inspect the TA centres and, in particular, they are interested in the miniature ranges for safety and the armoury for security.

The council is not a landowner or land agent. Its offices are located in the Duke of York's Headquarters, Chelsea, in buildings managed by the Greater London association. This substantial, impressive and valuable site, with its classical main building in front of a large open space in an attractive part of the capital, was once the home of the Duke of York's Royal Military School and was purchased in 1908 specifically to house the TF's secretariat.

Besides maintaining TA centres an association is responsible for furnishing, heating and lighting them. Desks, tables, chairs for lectures rooms, chairs for messes, carpets, curtains and other furniture are provided. Accommodation is also provided for caretakers. The caretakers, Ministry of Defence employees, will usually be appointed after consultation with the resident unit because a retired son of the regiment may wish to be considered for the post and such a person is more likely to have a mutual interest in looking after the needs of his regimental comrades. Naturally most units have acquired their own cherished property over the years: silver, pictures, furniture, medals, china, cutlery, books and archive material; such property is distinct from that of the association but there is a system of transferring this to the association's care if the unit so wishes.

The associations hold open days to increase public awareness of the part-time armed forces. They also host annual conferences for the COs of units in their areas. As most COs are regular officers such conferences provide a valuable opportunity to compare notes on the ways of running a TA unit and to listen to the counsel of TA&VRA members who may have commanded units in the past. Committees – for instance, general purposes, financial, or recruiting and publicity – meet regularly and the whole association may meet to deal with a specific issue.

The latest available statistic for the TA's strength is that it totalled 67,812 men and women on 1 March 1993, compared with the establishment of 68,195. Of course the establishment has dropped because of the cuts in the wake of *Options for Change*. But before the *Options* distortions the overall strength was 75,425 on 30 September 1990. It had been on a plateau for most of the year. This figure included 9,179 women and 3,277 members of the Home Service Force, with the strength of the women's section and the HSF rising slowly relative to that of the TA as a whole. These numbers were achieved towards an overall establishment of 90,344, including one of 4,953 for the HSF. The total strength of 75,425 compared with the strength of 47,589 in the T&AVR at the end of March 1970. This means that in slightly more than 20 years the TA increased its strength by some 28,000 men and women.

When an annual recruit wastage of about 30 per cent is borne in mind, it will be realised that the increase implies a tremendous recruiting effort. Most of the credit for this must go to the associations, with the caveat that units themselves help whenever a satisfied soldier persuades a friend to join. But, of course, for every satisfied soldier there must be a lot of dissatisfied ones, otherwise that 30 per cent fall-off rate would not be there, and the associations cannot be blamed for dissatisfied soldiers. In Northern Ireland recruiting per head of eligible population is almost double that of the rest of the United Kingdom.

RESPONSIBILITIES OF THE ASSOCIATIONS

Detailed analysis of the associations' finances and locations of their units and buildings is precluded by considerations of space but an indication of their importance may be gained by the examples below.

The Highland TA&VRA administers 21 TA units, a Royal Marines Reserve detachment, a Royal Auxiliary Air Force unit and seven Army Cadet Force units scattered over 17,210 square miles – a larger geographical area than of any other association. It is responsible for 63 TA properties (61 from 1994), 88 Army Cadet Force properties, eight Combined Cadet Force properties and eight ranges. In the last financial year, up to the time of writing, it handled a total of about just under £6 million. This included: new buildings and maintenance about £4 million; heating, lighting and caretakers, administration, establishment funds and similar matters; £1,750,000 recruiting about £70,000.

The TA&VRA for Eastern Wessex, which administers units in Berkshire, Buckinghamshire, Dorset, Hampshire, the Isle of Wight and Oxfordshire, and elements in the Channel Islands, is responsible for 29 TA centres and two ranges or training areas. Its property interests also include a Royal Marines Reserve centre and a Royal Naval Reserve centre. Additionally it administers 102 separate Army Cadet Force centres and 85 separate Air Training Corps properties. For 1993–94 the association received a works project grant of £2,590,000 and a property maintenance grant of £1,385,000.

The TA&VRA for Northern Ireland administers 13 TA units and two Army Cadet Force county groups. It is responsible for 16 TA centres. At the time of writing, the association receives grants totalling about £3,300,000. Of this some £2,600,000 goes towards new buildings, maintenance of property and works services. Rather more than £50,000 is allocated for recruiting and publicity.

16

Civilian Support

There is but one task for all –
One life for each to give.
What stands if Freedom fall?
Who dies if England live?
RUDYARD KIPLING,
For All We Have and Are

When the BEF was being evacuated at Dunkirk, the court of the Worshipful Company of Paviors reacted quickly: they bought 185 lbs of khaki wool and asked the ladies of the company's liverymen to start knitting. The result was a supply of comforts: gloves, Balaclava helmets, pullovers and scarves for the artillerymen of the Paviors' adopted TA unit. The Paviors had begun their association with 53 Medium Brigade, RA, a decade earlier. On the outbreak of war, realising that there would be hardship among some of the families of the mobilised Terriers, the liverymen started a subscription fund for the regiment (as it became in 1938, following the artillery's change in nomenclature). The fund reached £500 and grants were made from it throughout the war.

That help is typical of the support that the reserve forces have received from the City livery companies. When London was blitzed, Territorials' families bombed out of their homes received help from their adoptive livery companies. The companies understood the situation well: many of their halls were destroyed in air raids; some have never been replaced.

The capital's Territorials are lucky to have such long-established and influential institutions take an interest in their welfare. The companies, whose generic title derives from the fact that in the 14th century their members began to wear a distinctive livery according to their craft or trade, were founded in medieval times. Their role embraced trading standards offices, technical training schools, trade unions or professional organisations, welfare institutions for members and the provision of almshouses. On formal occasions, it is customary to insert the prefix 'the Worshipful' to the names of the companies, though many of them have a much longer full title. For instance the Drapers' full title is the Master and Wardens and Bretheren and Sisters of the Guild or

Fraternity of the Blessed Mary The Virgin of The Mystery of Drapers of The City of London. General educational institutions too have benefitted from the companies, for example, Mercers' School, the several Merchant Taylors' schools and Goldsmiths' College. From at least the days of Elizabeth I the companies have shown their appreciation of the role of auxiliary forces by making grants of money or supplies to the part-time soldiers ready to take on a commitment for the defence of London. The City's first Volunteer unit, the London Rifle Brigade, for instance, found itself hideously in debt after adding an annexe to its headquarters in Bunhill Row in 1895. Its ability to pay the mounting interest on the debt was reduced when recruiting fell off after the South African War. The City wards and the livery companies came to the rescue and donated £1,960. So strong are the bonds between some companies and their adopted units that part of the livery's insignia is still worn on their military uniform.

Another City institution, nowhere near as old as the bulk of the companies but of worldwide fame, is Lloyd's, and this too gives support to the part-time services. The Lloyd's Volunteer Forces Fund shows its appreciation of the work put in by reservists within the Lloyd's community by donating inscribed tankards to them when they have completed recruit training. The fund revives an earlier benefaction, the Lloyd's Volunteer Patriotic Fund, started by Sir Brook Watson in the early 19th century. In May 1990, Lloyd's put its main building at the disposal of the part-time services to enable an abseiling display to be staged in aid of the Royal Star and Garter Home for disabled ex-servicemen, and recruiting stands are often to be seen in Lloyd's premises.

To return to the livery companies; in the archives of the Painter-Stainers Company is a record of £2 11s 6d paid to the train band quartered in Painters' Hall in 1697. Even earlier, mention is made of an instruction of the lord mayor that powder and shot for the train band should be maintained in the hall.

Although most of the older companies have connections with part-time soldiering that, intermittently, go back centuries, the concept of support in the modern sense is comparatively new and has usually manifested itself in wartime. This was seen in the South African War, the First World War and the Second World War. But with peacetime restructuring and the disappearance of units, the link between some liveries and the forces was broken. In December 1952, during the Korean War, Earl Alexander, Minister of Defence, spoke of the need for the volunteer forces to be linked with the companies and suggested that the coming coronation year would be an auspicious time. The lord mayor of the day wrote to the masters of all companies recalling the Elizabethan period when they were associated with auxiliary defence bodies. He emphasised the importance of having City institutions re-establish links with the reserve forces and he urged companies that did not have such an association to consider the matter. The result was that the great postwar adoptive relationships were formed. Today 42 livery companies are associated with reserve force units in Greater London. Some companies support more than one unit. Others, although not associated with the reserves, provide support for regular forces; in this category are the Engineers Company and the Mercers Company. Other companies are affiliated to Naval or Royal Marines reservists and are thus outside the strict confines of this book, but by way of example they are mentioned briefly. The Fishmongers Company supports the London Division of the Royal Naval Reserve. The Master Mariners Company, too, supports the London Division as well as the Royal Marines Reserve (City of London). The Coopers Company supports the London Division of the RNR, and the Stationers Company supports the Royal Marines Reserves.

Outside London the Cutlers Company of Hallamshire supports the TA in a number of ways without having an individual affiliation (see page 205).

The pages which follow reflect the massive and generous support given to Territorial and other Volunteer units of the services over the years and to the present day by the City livery companies and other national organisations.

The Society of Apothecaries of London adopted the 167th (City of London) Field Ambulance, RAMC, in 1954. The society made regular grants to the unit until it was absorbed into the 217th (London) General Hospital, RAMC in 1967. The Apothecaries then decided to support 217 General Hospital and the relationship continues. Regular visits are paid to the unit and the hospital provides escorts at the Master's Day service. Officers attend Apothecaries' dinners and a number of COs of the unit have been admitted as members of the society. In 1967 the unit obtained Ministry of Defence permission to wear the society's crest on the shoulder when in service dress. The device, a rhinoceros with an extra horn, is known as 'Percy'.

The Armourers & Braziers Company affiliated to the City of London Yeomanry (Rough Riders) in 1938, made grants throughout the war and continued the association when the Rough Riders were amalgamated with the Inns of Court. Following further changes in the TA, the combined regiment was reduced to the Inns of Court and City Yeomanry Squadron of the Yeomanry. The Armourers' Bowl, presented to the regiment many years ago, is still competed for annually in inter-troop events. The OC is invited to dinner each year in Armourers' Hall and the squadron invites the master to an annual guest night. The master and clerk and their ladies go to the Rough Riders Association's annual remembrance service.

The Bakers Company has sponsored the London University Officers Training Corps since 1 October 1979 and regularly visits the cadets at camp. Two representatives of the contingent are guests at the Bakers' court dinners in April, July and October. Occasionally the whole unit is given a buffet supper in Bakers' Hall. The CO and wife are invited to the annual ladies dinner and the CO is guest at the company's election dinner in the Mansion House, at which the contingent finds a guard of honour for the lord mayor. The Bakers have donated trophies, a small-bore target rifle and a leather-bound photograph album. The master, clerk and senior members, with their wives, attend the contingent's annual dinner and cocktail party. A direct link with the past is provided by the Frankland Moore cup, presented by a past master of the Bakers and which is awarded at the annual shooting competition between the naval, military and air force sections of the cadets. The cup was originally won by Moore's grandfather, who joined the Queen's Westminster Rifle Volunteers in the 1870s.

The Carmen's Company is in close association with the Royal Logistic Corps, though mainly with the regular Army element of the corps. Never-the-less the Carmen give active support to 151(Greater London) Support Regiment, the capital's biggest TA unit.

The Clothworkers Company adopted the London Rifle Brigade shortly before the Second World War. The company's choice of unit was influenced by its clerk, Major W F Pothecary, who had won the DCM while serving in the LRB during the First World War before being commissioned into the Hampshires. Pothecary was unusual in that after serving as clerk from 1933 to 1950 he became master in 1952, an extraordinary jump in seniority. In 1950, when the LRB amalgamated with the 2nd Battalion of the Rangers to become the London Rifle Brigade Rangers, the Clothworkers continued the association and the relationship today exists with one of the successor units, C Company of the 4th(V) Battalion of the Royal Green Jackets. A guard of honour at Clothworkers' dinners is found by C Company. The Clothworkers and their charitable arm, the Clothworkers' Foundation, have been generous benefactors. In 1987–88 the foundation donated £15,000 to the Royal Green Jackets Museum appeal and in 1988 it gave £10,000 to the regiment. Earlier benefactions by the Clothworkers include £100 in 1958 towards the unit's centenary celebrations and £300 towards a weekend training centre at Bisley (the Salters Company gave a similar amount). By 1979 the Clothworkers' donations to their unit had totalled £1,731.

All ranks of C(City of London Fusiliers) Company, the London Regiment and their ladies look forward to the social highlight of their year, a six-course dinner provided by the Cordwainers Company after camp. All guests are presented to the master and senior wardens. After the meal the OC reports on the Fusiliers' progress and presents the master with a beret, badge and hackle. There are farewell drinks and the guests leave at a late hour. The master wears his beret when he watches them training and when in April he and the clerk dine at the Fusiliers' TA centre and he presents inscribed tankards to the best trained man and the best recruit. Times are less formal now but in the

1950s, 1960s, 1970s and 1980s the officers donned service dress and the master and clerk wore dinner jackets for the occasion, during which the visitors competed against a Fusilier team on the indoor range, firing .22 match rifles donated by the Cordwainers. They have presented pieces of silver to the unit and have made grants to the cadet company that shares the centre; one of the grants was used to buy a minibus. Officers are invited to two livery dinners each year and for the Fusiliers no important occasion is complete without the Cordwainers' presence. Such occasions have included the reopening of the Fusiliers' museum at HM Tower of London, the opening of the history room at the TA centre, a series of events for the parent regiment's 300th anniversary celebrations in 1985, and the reopening of the centre at St John's Hill, Battersea, as headquarters of the 8th Queen's Fusiliers. The Cordwainers' relationship started in 1953 when they adopted the 624th(Royal Fusiliers) Light AA Regiment, RA. When the unit was disbanded, the adoptive link was maintained with the City of London Battalion of the Royal Fusiliers. It continued in 1967 with the Fusiliers Volunteers, which later became C(City of London) Company of the 5th Battalion of the Royal Regiment of Fusiliers, which in turn became C(City of London) Company of the Queen's Fusiliers; in 1993 it became C(City of London Fusiliers) Company of the London Regiment. It is to the Cordwainers' credit that, despite so many changes of title, role, size or location they have remained steadfast in their support, whereas a lesser adoptive company might have lost interest through bewilderment. In 1991 the master, Mr Michael Uren, handed over a Transit Crew-bus to C Company as a personal gift to help the unit transport members to a new outstation in Kent.

The Cutlers Company have two adopted units, B(the Queen's) Company of the now reborn London Regiment, and the 221st(Surrey) Field Ambulance, RAMC, and the master and clerk visit them at camp and in their centres. The 6/7th link dates from 1973, with the Cutlers providing a sword for annual award to the best platoon; they also make grants to the unit. In return the Queen's provide a guard of honour at the Cutlers' Boar's Head feast. The Cutlers present awards to 221; its honorary colonel attends the Surgical Award dinner in Cutlers' Hall and the OC is invited to livery dinners.

The Distillers Company adopted the London Scottish in 1970 and the CO and his wife are invited annually to the ladies' banquet. Two pipers play during the loving cup ceremony, after which their health is drunk by the master.

The Drapers Company began an association with the 71st(Yeomanry) Signals Regiment in 1982, the City link being through the Inns of Court and City of London Yeomanry Squadron and the regimental band. The Drapers donate several hundreds of pounds a year to the CO's educational fund. The CO is a guest at livery dinners and on occasion all the officers and their ladies are invited to dinners. The master and clerk attend the officers' club annual dinner and the annual cocktail party.

The Founders Company adopted the London Irish Rifles in 1938 when they were a battalion and the link continues with the London Irish Company of the London Regiment. The relationship was particularly cherished by the London Irish during the war when the Founders gave generous support to families bombed out of their homes while the menfolk were on active service. The OC is invited to dinners and from time to time the Irish pipers play at Founders' functions. 'We appreciate our association', their clerk says.

The Glovers Company adopted the 21st Special Air Service Regiment(TA) (The Artists Rifles) many years ago and provides the unit with gymnasium equipment, canoes and other items developing physical fitness.

The Goldsmiths Company is affiliated to B Company of the 4th Battalion of the Royal Green Jackets and makes grants from time to time for the unit to buy ceremonial accoutrements. The Goldsmiths put their hall at the disposal of the battalion in rotation with the other livery companies affiliated to the battalion for the Green Jackets' annual dinner. The Territorials provide buglers or guards of honour at appropriate Goldsmith functions.

The Haberdashers Company supports a number of units. In 1983 it became affiliated to the Queen's Regiment; the association covered the regular as well as part-time elements, adding up to six major units, including the London Regiment. In eight months, the master and clerk visited the 1st, 3rd, 5th and 6/7th battalions of the Queen's (which included a trip to Cyprus). Sporting and social hospitality are exchanged between liverymen and units which are now in the Princess of Wales's Royal Regiment. The Haberdashers also support HQ Company of the 4th Royal Green Jackets, the link being maintained through the adoption of Queen Victoria's Rifles before the Second World War. Other beneficiaries of the Haberdashers connection are HMS Brave, a type-22 frigate, the Frimley and Camberley Army cadets and the cadet units of a number of schools. The Haberdashers' clerk, Captain M E Barrow, RN, sees the affiliations 'as being one of the few ways to educate City people about the services, and similarly to let servicemen know something of what goes on in the City.'

The Horners Company became affiliated during 1988 with the 73rd Ordnance Company(V), RAOC, with headquarters at Romford and its two sub-units at Gillingham and Colchester. The Horners visited the 73rd in Germany in 1990 and have attended mess dinners and an open day. The Horners, whose craftsmen members traditionally made objects of horn, have turned to plastics as their raw material, and this provided a link with the 73rd: plastics are made from oil and the unit, now renamed 124th Petroleum Squadron, RLC, as a result of reorgansiation, is a petroleum supply squadron. The unit has provided a guard of honour for the liverymen's annual banquet and the Horners have presented objects of horn as trophies and for mess adornment. The liverymen have also given the unit a microwave oven. The

Horners adopted the 51st London Anti-Aircraft Regiment RA(TA) in 1939 but the association lapsed with the cuts in air defence units after the war.

The Ironmongers Company affiliated with A(Highwood) Company of the 8th Queen's Fusiliers(City of London) at an inaugural supper at the TA centre in Flodden Road, Camberwell, attended by the master, wardens and clerk. Officers and senior NCOs were invited to a reciprocal inaugural supper in Ironmongers' Hall in 1990. Since the 1993 amalgamation the livery company has donated the Ironmongers Highwood Shield to the London Regiment for inter-company competition. The Ironmongers also support the City of London and North East Sector of the Army Cadet Force.

The Leathersellers Company supported the 6/7th Battalion of the Queen's Regiment, of Horsham, Sussex, in a relationship that started in 1930. In May of that year, the Leathersellers decided that the 20th Battalion of the London Regiment(the Queen's Own) was 'worthy of the Company's interest and support by reason of the existence in the battalion of a company set apart for old boys from local schools and in view also of the facilities afforded to boys from Colfe's School for rifle practice on the battalion's miniature rifle range at Holly Hedge House (Blackheath)'. The Leathersellers made an immediate grant of £20 to the battalion, which later became a searchlight unit, 34th(the Queen's Own Royal West Kent) AA Battalion, RE(TA). In 1938, its Christmas party, attended by 458 children, was helped by the company, which donated £35-6s-1d for each child to be given a present. In March 1939, the company presented the officers' mess with a framed print of Leathersellers' Hall and St Helen's Church. By now the company was making an annual £100 grant to the battalion. But hard times were coming, investments were hit and the Leathersellers were bombed out of their hall. The minutes of a court held in Merchant Taylors' Hall on 30 July 1941 note sadly that the 'grant be suspended for the present'. After the postwar reformation of the TA and more changes, the Leathersellers allowed their hall, magnificently rebuilt in the shape of a cube, to be used for an officers' mess dinner in 1954 by the 569th(the Queen's Own) (M) Light AA/SL Regiment, RA. In 1980, the Leathersellers made a £500 grant to 6/7th Queen's towards expenses which would be incurred the following year when new colours were presented by the Duchess of Norfolk, Lord Lieutenant of West Sussex. The company has also made grants to the ACF to enable cadets to take part in the Nijmegen March.

The Merchant Taylors Company is affiliated to the Royal Yeomanry and to the newly reborn London Regiment; in the latter instance their support extends to the whole battalion, and they have presented a large silver cup for contest among all companies of the unit. Merchant Taylor interest in the welfare of the TA is of long standing. They adopted the Territorials of the old Royal Fusiliers and the relationship has endured through many changes and amalgamations to the unit of today.

The Painter-Stainers Company's links with its adopted unit, the Intelligence and Security Group, are so strong that the crest of the company's arms, a phoenix, were approved as a shoulder badge on the unit's No 1 dress. The Territorials find a guard of honour twice a year for company banquets, and the master attends a training weekend at which he presents the Master's Cup to the winning company, which is known as the Master's Company for the year. At a time when war was inevitable, the Painters adopted the 33rd (St Pancras) AA Brigade, at a court on 6 May 1939. The company made an immediate gift of £25 to the unit and the master was subsequently entertained in the officers' mess. In September 1953 the Painters adopted the 168th Armoured Workshop, REME, and the master and wardens attended the opening of the unit's new headquarters, presenting an engraved silver cup and a shield, both bearing the company's arms, to mark the occasion. A decade later, the unit became part of another REME workshop which itself had already been adopted by the Turners Company. In early 1964 the Painters were approached by the Army Photographic Interpretation Section, Intelligence Corps (TA) asking whether they would consider adoption; so having been assured that the section would not be disbanded, the Painters adopted it. In 1967 it became a company of the only TA Intelligence unit, covering all aspects of intelligence, the other companies being of interrogators and counter intelligence, with a port security platoon in Belfast. The Painters adopted the broader unit, the present Intelligence and Security Group (V), with headquarters in Handel Street, Bloomsbury, and outstations in Edinburgh and Birmingham. A past master of the company, Noel Sissons, became the first honorary colonel of the group on 1 April 1967. He was succeeded by another Painter, John Nicholson, in 1970.

The Paviors Company is associated with two TA units, the 6/7th Battalion of the Princess of Wales's Royal Regiment and the 131st Independent Commando Squadron, RE. The Paviors adopted 53 Medium Brigade, RA, in 1930 and gave generous help in comforts and support for bombed-out families of the unit. Following changes in the TA, the situation in 1966 was that the Paviors were associated with Q (53rd London) Battery of the 254th (City of London) Regiment, RA; R (Surrey) Battery of the 265th LAA Regiment, RA; and the 101st (London) Corps, RE. More changes followed and by 1971 the Paviors' units were C (London and Kent) Battery, RA, and the 6th Battalion of the Queen's, which then became the 6/7th Queen's. The Paviors make general grants to their units and help towards specific projects, for instance, enabling unit participation in the Nijmegen March. Both 131 Commando Squadron and D Company find guards of honour for the Paviors' Ladies' Banquet. Reciprocal hospitality and visits by the master to camp and TA centres are regular occurrences. The Paviors treasure a silver rose bowl presented by R (Surrey) Battery and a silver loving cup presented by the 254th (City of London) Regiment.

The Saddlers Company support 100 (Yeomanry) Field Regiment, RA (V) and

D Company of the 6/7th Battalion the PWRR (ex-Queen's). This support can be traced back to the years before the TA was born. In 1894 the Saddlers began a programme of help for the 3rd City of London Rifle Volunteers. When the TA was formed, the regiment became the 7th (City of London) Battalion of the London Regiment, and in 1937 the Saddlers adopted it. The previous year the unit became the 32nd(7th City of London) AA Battalion, RE(TA), with headquarters at Grove Park. In 1941 it was transferred to the RA. On 1 May 1947 it became the 567th Light AA Regiment, RA(7th City of London) (TA). Reorganisation in 1955 resulted in the unit becoming RHQ and P(7th City of London) Battery of the 265th Light AA Regiment, RA(TA). In 1961 they became RHQ and Q(London) Battery, six years later, RHQ and Q Battery became RHQ and HQ Battery of the 100th Medium Regiment, RA and the rest became C(London and Kent Artillery) Battery, RA on a cadre basis. In 1975 the 6th and 7th battalions of the Queen's amalgamated to form the 6/7th with its headquarters at Horsham, Sussex. Meanwhile, C(London and Kent) Battery, at Camberwell, amalgamated with D(Surrey Yeomanry) Battery, at Sutton, Surrey, and HQ Company, at Wandsworth, to form D Company of the 6/7th Battalion of the Queen's. After operating from the three centres they came together at Farringdon House, Stonecot Hill, Sutton. The Saddlers and their two units are closely involved in each other's social functions.

The Skinners Company has supported the 39th(City of London) Signal Regiment since 1954; for many years the troops wore the company's lynx badge on both arms until 1966, when it was replaced by the City's sword emblem. The Skinners furnished and redecorated the junior ranks' club at headquarters and each squadron now has a Lynx club. For more than 30 years the unit has found the Skinner's Guard for the liverymen's Corpus Christi Day church service. Each year the master presents a pewter tankard to the best trained soldier of the Royal Signals and a silver powder compact for the best trained woman junior rank. The unit makes an annual visit to the Skinners' open day.

The Spectacle Makers Company took on the role of advocate in the 1960s to try to persuade the Ministry of Defence to retain a small, independent mobile medical unit in the City to maintain the tradition dating from 1883 when the ancestor unit of the 167th Field Ambulance, RAMC, was raised at Guildhall. The company made a grant to the 140th Field Ambulance, RAMC, in 1943, but it was on 20 October 1953 that it formally adopted the 168th Field Ambulance. In the adoption document, the Spectacle Makers resolved to present a gift of silver plate to the officers' mess, 'the article to be of a practical kind that can be used in the mess and at camp'; to make an annual five guineas donation to a prize fund; to encourage regular visits by the master and wardens to the headquarters in Farringdon Road and at camp; and to present a trophy for annual competition. The following year a series of prints of the City was presented to decorate the headquarters and in March 1955 a silver challenge shield was donated for competition. Later 168 Field Ambulance became 167 and the link between liverymen and Territorials continued with many social exchanges. The Spectacle Makers' advocacy was rewarded with partial success in that they learned in October 1966 that 167 would be absorbed into a new reserve hospital, the 217th (London) General Hospital, RAMC, and it was suggested that a detachment of the unit might be formed by 167 and titled the City of London Detachment of the 217th (London) General Hospital. In 1969 the Spectacle Makers were officially informed that, in the reorganisation, 167 had become part of the 217th (London) General Hospital. The company subsequently agreed to adopt the City detachment of the hospital and the liverymen made a further grant. At the end of 1984, the Spectacle Makers were told the detachment had been disbanded; the livery then made a grant for the refurbishing of the silver so it could be displayed in the RAMC Museum in good condition. In 1985 the silver challenge shield was returned to the company.

The Chartered Surveyors Company, founded in 1977, lost little time in associating with a unit. They adopted the 135th Independent Topographical Squadron, RE (V) two years later. 'The relationship is a good one', says the clerk. The squadron provides a guard of honour at the Surveyors' ladies banquet and the master attends squadron functions. Members of the company are frequent visitors at the unit's headquarters at Ewell, Surrey. The Surveyors provide the Endeavour award, an inscribed plate for the Territorial who has achieved most for the unit during the year, and they donate an engraved pewter tankard for the winner to keep. The presentation is made after the Remembrance service. The master visits the 135th Field Survey Squadron, as it is now named, at camp.

The oldest TA unit, the Honourable Artillery Company, is affiliated to one of the younger livery companies, the Chartered Accountants. Other affiliations include:

Basketmakers	289th Commando Battery, RA;
Butchers	No 1 MHU;
Dyers	10th Parachute Regiment;
Fan Makers	217th Field Squadron (EOD) RE;
Glaziers	36th Signal Regiment, R Sigs;
Grocers	Support Company, 4th RGJ;
Guild of Freemen	253rd Provost Company, AGC;
Innholders	31st Signal Regiment, R Sigs;
Lightmongers	220th Field Squadron (EOD) RE;
Salters	SW Sector ACF;
Tobacco Pipe Makers	HQ Company, 8th Queen's Fusiliers.

The lord mayor of London, as president of the City sub-association of the Greater London TA&VRA, takes an interest in all the City's TA units, but one unit in particular has strong mayoral links. This is the 39th (City of London) Signal Regiment (V). Every year the lord mayor visits the 39th at their headquarters in Worship Street. The practice started in 1958, the TA's 50th jubilee year. At the visit the lord mayor inspects a guard, watches training, visits the junior ranks and the sergeants and dines with the officers.

British Rail is supportive of the TA and not only gives leave to Territorials to attend camp, but augments their military pay for the period so they are not out of pocket. In 1989 BR named a high-speed locomotive after the 275th Railway Squadron, RCT (V), now RLC (V), a unit composed of railway workers. Earlier that year, BR gave the unit a long-distance restaurant car as a lecture and recreation room. The Territorials train with their regular counterparts in the 79th Railway squadron, RLC in Germany.

Another group of Territorials who train on the railways in Germany are members of the 335th BAOR Ambulance Train of the RAMC (V). They live in Germany and many of them, nurses in the unit, are married to British soldiers.

An organisation whose practical support for the TA goes back to the First World War is the Automobile Association. The first secretary of the AA, which is three years older than the TA, was Sir Stenson Cooke. He was a sergeant instructor in the cadets, was a Volunteer private in the London Rifle Brigade, was commissioned into the Essex Regiment in the 1908 Territorials, and was twice mentioned in despatches in the Essex during the First World War. The AA was responsible for transporting a war-ready battalion, 1,000-strong from London to Hastings and back in 1909. (see Chapter 5 The New Force)

Thousands of the Association's patrolmen have been part-time soldiers. In 1914 and 1915, an AA appeal led to 100 motor ambulances being donated to France. The AA uniform was based on that of the Army and after the Second World War it bought surplus battledress uniforms and issued them to patrols until civilian manufacturers could supply the traditional tunics, breeches and leather gaiters again. The AA smoothed the path of peacetime military manoeuvres and wartime troop movements with its patrols; its embodied men and their signposting were used to help get the BEF quickly into deployment positions in France in 1939 and to bring the force safely back again when hundreds of thousands of troops under attack were converging on Dunkirk. In 1937 the AA gave its men two weeks' paid leave to encourage them to join volunteer services. The result was an influx of patrolmen into part-time soldiering. When the Army established a reserve of Royal Corps of Military Police more than 900 patrolmen applied for the 500 posts. A former director general of the AA, Olaf Lambert, was honorary colonel of the redcap detachment. Support today includes leave to encourage its staff to become Territorials.

The Company of Cutlers in Hallamshire, although it has not formally adopted a TA unit, supports the services, asks employers to look favourably on their workers who give their time to the TA and other auxiliary forces and gives an annual dinner for the forces. The company has made grants to the Sheffield Artillery Volunteers, which became the Hallamshires, which in turn became a TA unit of the York and Lancaster Regiment. The Cutlers are affiliated to HMS *Sheffield*, just as they were affiliated to the previous *Sheffield* (dubbed 'the Shiny Sheff' because of stainless steel fittings donated by the Cutlers), which was sunk in the Falklands.

London Transport is another large undertaking that helps the Territorial by giving him time off work to complete camp.

The Midland Bank too allows its staff to attend camp without deduction of salary, and this has fostered a strong Territorial brotherhood among Midland staff of several generations. The Midland Bank Territorial Army Association met last year as usual in the In and Out Club, where it has gathered for dinner every year since 1949. Guest speakers have included some of Britain's most famous military leaders.

The Post Office has long been a supporter of the auxiliary forces. Its workers were among the early Volunteers, dating from 1867 in the form of a large body of special constables during the Fenian scares, and many senior staff – the so-called major staff – had earlier joined Civil Service corps. A large group of postal workers earned a place in the history of part-time soldiering when they became the first Volunteers on active service. This was in Egypt as postal and courier troops; it won them the battle honour 'Egypt, 1882'. The Post Office Rifles were embodied for service in the First World War, many of its workers fought in TA units in the Second World War and today's Post Office and its former communications arm, now British Telecom, give staff paid leave to attend camp.

In November 1990, after Iraq's invasion of Kuwait and the deployment of a multi-national force, the Ministry of Defence appealed for Territorials, particularly medical personnel, to volunteer for the Gulf. At the time of the appeal there was no legislation to protect such volunteers' security of civil employment, and British Telecom made its public-spirited offer. It announced on 7 December that any staff who were Territorials volunteering for full-time emergency service would be reinstated in their jobs. Furthermore, during their time in uniform, British Telecom would augment their Army pay to equal their basic civil wages.

17

Soldiers Supreme

The deed is everything, not the glory.
JOHANN WOLFGANG VON GOETHE,
Hochgebirg (1832)

Since the institution of the Victoria Cross in 1856 and the retrospection of its scope to include conspicuous heroism performed from 1854, only 1,351 people (including the Unknown Warrior of the United States) have won the decoration. There have also been three awards of a bar to the cross, that is, the recipient has won it twice. But down the years, from 1854 to the publication of this book, in the grand total of 1,354 awards (to 1,334 servicemen of the British Commonwealth and Empire, five civilians and 15 foreigners) there have been scores of Territorial recipients. Of the three people who have won Britain's premier decoration twice, two were Territorials: Surgeon Captain (later Lieutenant Colonel) Arthur Martin-Leake and Captain Noel Godfrey Chavasse. Two of Britain's most decorated junior ranks of the First World War were Territorials: Lance Corporal William Coltman, VC, DCM and bar, MM and bar, of the 1/6th Battalion of the North Staffordshire Regiment, who gained his VC about five weeks before the Armistice, and Private Henry Tandey, VC, DCM, MM, of the 5th Battalion of the Duke of Wellington's(West Riding) Regiment, who won the award at Marcoing, in France, on 28 September 1918. Tandey later became a sergeant.

Martin-Leake won his VC while serving with the South African Constabulary at Vlakfontein on 8 February 1902 for tending casualties about 100 yards from the enemy. He was severely wounded. He gained the bar for rescuing many casualties lying helpless and in pain in front of the German trenches near Zonnebeke, in Belgium, between 29 October and 8 November 1914. He was mentioned in despatches in both conflicts. In civil life he was administrative medical officer for the Bengal-Nagpur Railway. He was still giving public service in the Second World War, in an Air Raid Precautions unit.

Chavasse, medical officer of the 1/10th Battalion(the Liverpool Scottish) of the King's(Liverpool) Regiment, won his first VC at Guillemont, in France, on 9–10 August 1916 for dressing wounds under fire all day and searching no man's land for casualties at night. In the morning he and a stretcher-bearer carried a casualty 500 yards under heavy bombardment to safety. During the second night, he assembled 20 volunteers and rescued three casualties from their shellhole refuge 36 yards from the enemy. The citation says that in two days he saved 20 lives besides treating routine casualties. Chavasse was awarded the bar to his VC for tending casualties, although wounded himself, in no man's land at Wieltje between 31 July and 2 August 1917. He died on 4 August. With two VCs and an MC, he must be considered the Empire's most decorated serviceman of the war. A Liverpool TA centre of the 208th (Merseyside) General Hospital is named after him. Earlier, another drill-hall had borne his name. In 1990 Chavasse's medals and the group of his twin, Dr Christopher Chavasse, who became an Anglican bishop like their father, were handed over by Christopher's nephew John to the Imperial War Museum on permanent loan on behalf of St Peter's College, Oxford. Christopher too was a Territorial and his group includes campaign medals, the OBE, the MC, the TD and the French Croix de Guerre.

Many wounded men had cause to be grateful to Lance Corporal Coltman, a stretcher-bearer who gained his VC at Mannequin Hill, in France, on 3–4 October 1918. His earlier DCM and bar and MM and bar recognised valour over a long period during which he brought succour to many stricken comrades. In 1990, a new TA centre of the 3rd(V) Battalion of the Staffordshire Regiment was named after him at Burton-on-Trent.

The only VC to be awarded among the many feats of courage on D-day went to a Territorial, Company Sergeant Major Stanley Hollis, of the Green Howards, who, in the words of the citation, displayed 'the utmost gallantry' in the course of a 'magnificent day's work' after landing on the beach at La Rivière. By putting a number of enemy machine gun posts out of action, he saved the lives of many members of his battalion. After the war, Hollis became a licensee and renamed his public-house after his regiment.

He became a well-known 'guest artist' on battlefield tours run by the Army Staff College and so familiar to scores of officer students.

A list of awards to Territorials and other part-time troops is not easy to compile. Awards when gazetted give the recipient's unit at the time of the deed. An award to a member of a TA battalion is not necessarily an award to a Territorial soldier. Tiny groups of regulars have always featured in the key posts of TA units; again, in war, conscripts were often posted to TA units. The author recognises that the names that follow form an imperfect list; some courageous Territorials may have been omitted where it was not possible to establish that given recipients were at some stage of their careers part-time soldiers. The author has included two recipients who had OTC service but who did not join TF units until the war.

The recipients who follow are given in order of the date of the deed that brought supreme recognition. They include men who, while not Territorials in name, served in part-time forces that adumbrated the TA. After the VCs is a section on winners of the George Cross.

THE CRIMEAN WAR

Captain Robert James Lindsay (later Loyd-Lindsay) won one of the first VCs to be gazetted for his courage at the Alma on 20 September and Inkermann on 5 November, 1854, while in the Scots Fusilier Guards. Later he farmed, entered politics and joined the Volunteers, serving as colonel of the Royal Berkshire Volunteers for 35 years from 1860 and of the HAC from 1866 to 1881. Lindsay was Berkshire's MP for 20 years, serving as financial secretary to the War Office. A Red Cross pioneer, he visited Paris as chairman of the English Red Cross Society during the siege in October 1870. He was created Lord Wantage. He was appointed a KCB and a chevalier of the Legion of Honour.

THE ZULU WAR

Private Alfred Henry Hook (who was later promoted sergeant) gained his VC with the 2nd Battalion of the 24th Regiment of Foot at the battle of Rorke's Drift, in Zululand, on 22–23 January 1879. While in South Africa, he lost contact with his wife; he later found she had presumed him dead and had gone through a form of marriage with another man. Hook, a Gloucestershire farm labourer, had served in the county Militia before joining the Army. On discharge, he settled in London, obtained a job at the British Museum and joined the West Middlesex Volunteers, who became the 1st Volunteer Battalion of the Royal Fusiliers while he was serving. Members of C (City of London Fusiliers) Company of the London Regiment, direct descendant of Hook's Volunteer battalion, can today see a copy of his VC and an account of his deed in the history room at their TA centre, Fusilier House, Balham, south London.

THE BURMA EXPEDITION

Surgeon John Crimmin gained his VC in the Lwekaw area of Burma on New Year's Day 1889. He became a colonel, a CB and a CIE and gained his Volunteer Decoration.

THE SOUTH AFRICAN WAR

Lieutenant Alexis Charles Doxat won his VC at Zeerust on 20 October 1900 with the 3rd Battalion of the Imperial Yeomanry. He had twice retired from part-time soldiering – from the Loyal Suffolk Hussars Yeomanry Cavalry in 1890 and from the 7th Battalion of the Rifle Brigade in 1896. He later became a major in the First World War.

THE FIRST WORLD WAR

Private Jacob Rivers won his posthumous award at Neuve Chapelle, in France, on 12 March 1915 with the 5th Battalion of the Sherwood Foresters.

Second Lieutenant Geoffrey Woolley gained his VC at Hill 60, in Belgium, on 20–21 April 1915 with the 9th(County of London) Battalion of the London Regiment(Queen Victoria's Rifles, KRRC). He also won the MC. Later he became vicar of Monk Sherborne Hampshire. He was a chaplain to the forces in the Second World War and was made an OBE.

Lance Corporal Leonard James Keyworth won his VC at Givenchy, in France, on 25–26 May 1915 with the 1/24th(County of London) Battalion of the London Regiment(the Queen's).

Lieutenant William Thomas Forshaw gained his award at the Vineyard, Gallipoli, between 7 and 9 August 1915 while in the 1/9th Battalion of the Manchester Regiment. He became a major. Forshaw was one of the Territorials who had volunteered to serve overseas before the war.

Private David Lauder gained his VC at Cape Helles on 13 August 1915 with the 1/4th Battalion of the Royal Scots Fusiliers. During an enemy attack he threw a grenade but it rolled back among his comrades in the trench. Lauder put his foot on it. His foot was blown off but no one else was seriously injured. Serbia awarded him its Silver Medal for Bravery.

Trooper Frederick William Owen Potts won his award on Hill 70, at Gallipoli, on 21 August 1915 with the 1/1st Battalion of the Berkshire Yeomanry.

Corporal Alfred Alexander Burt gained his award at Cuinchy, in France, on 27 September 1915 with the 1st Battalion of the Hertfordshire Regiment. His quick thinking saved many lives when a *minenwerfer* landed in their trench. He could have taken cover in a traverse but chose to run to the bomb and disarm it by twisting out the fuse and hurling it from the trench. He was 20 and not yet of an age to vote. He became a sergeant.

Captain Geoffrey Vickers won his VC at the Hohenzollern Redoubt, in France, on 14 October 1915 with the 1/7th(Robin Hood's) Battalion of the Sherwood Foresters. His other decorations included the United States Medal of Freedom, and the Belgian Croix de Guerre. In the next war, he was a colonel at the Ministry of Economic Warfare. He was knighted and became legal adviser to the National Coal Board.

Second Lieutenant Alfred Victor Smith gained his posthumous award at Cape Helles on 23 December 1915 with the 1/5th Battalion of the East Lancashire Regiment. A grenade he was about to throw slipped to the ground. Shouting a warning to his comrades, he scrambled out of the trench, but noticing that they were unable to get clear in time he jumped back and lay on the grenade. He was killed but his comrades were saved.

Private Arthur Herbert Procter won his VC in the Ficheux area of France on 4 June 1916 with the 1/5th Battalion of the King's(Liverpool) Regiment. He returned to his job as a provisions salesman, was later ordained and in the next war was a RAF chaplain.

Sergeant John Erskine gained his award at Givenchy, in France, on 22 June 1916 with the 5th Battalion of the Cameronians. He died less than a year later at Arras.

Private James Hutchinson won his VC near Ficheux, in France, on 28 June 1916 with the 2/5th Battalion of the Lancashire Fusiliers.

Captain John Leslie Green, RAMC, gained his posthumous award at Fonquevillers, in France, on 1 July 1916 while MO of the 1/5th Battalion of the Sherwood Foresters.

Second Lieutenant Gabriel George Coury won his award near Arrow Head Copse, in France, on 8 August 1916 with the 1/4th Battalion of the South Lancashire Regiment. Before he was commissioned he had been in the 6th Battalion of the King's(Liverpool) Regiment. Later he joined the RFC. In the Second World War he was a captain in the RASC.

Lance Corporal Harold Mugford gained his award at Monchy-le-Preux, in France, on 11 April 1917 with the 8th Squadron of the Machine Gun Corps.

Lieutenant Reginald Graham won his VC on 22 April 1917 at Istabulat, in Mesopotamia, in command of a machine gun section. He had been commissioned into the 9th Battalion of the Argyll and Sutherland Highlanders and was attached to the 136th Company of the Machine Gun Corps. He was born into a wealthy Glasgow and East India merchant family and became third baronet in 1936. In the next war, still in the Argylls, he was a lieutenant colonel on the staff and was made an OBE. Norway made him a member of the Order of the King Haakon VII Liberty Cross.

Company Sergeant Major Edward Brooks gained his VC at Fayet, St Quentin, on 28 April 1917 with the 2/4th Battalion of the Oxfordshire and Buckinghamshire Light Infantry.

Second Lieutenant Reginald Leonard Haine, of the 1st Battalion of the HAC, won his award near Gavrelle, not far from Arras, on 28–29 April 1917. He was promoted captain and won the MC and bar. In the next war he was a lieutenant colonel in the Home Guard.

Captain Albert Ball, of the 7th(Robin Hood's) Battalion of the Sherwood Foresters, won his VC for daring between June 1916 and May 1917 as a RFC pilot. In his short life (he was still a minor when he died, aged 20, on 7 May 1917) he became one of Britain's most decorated men, gaining the DSO, two bars and the MC. France appointed him a chevalier of the Legion of Honour and Russia made him a member of the Order of St George.

Second Lieutenant John Craig gained his award in Egypt on 5 June 1917 with the 1/5th Battalion of the Royal Scots Fusiliers. Craig had served in France with the 6th Battalion of the Cameron Highlanders before fighting with the RSF in Egypt. By 1918 he was an instructor with the RFC. Later he attended Edinburgh University and Trinity College, Cambridge. Serving with the RAF in the Second World War, he became a wing commander.

Lieutenant Colonel Bertram Best-Dunkley won his VC at Wieltje, in Belgium, on 31 July 1917 with the 2/5th Battalion of the Lancashire Fusiliers. He died five days later.

Private George McIntosh gained his award at Ypres on 31 July 1917 with the 1/6th Battalion of the Gordon Highlanders. In the Second World War he was a RAF flight sergeant.

Sergeant Alexander Edwards won his VC near Ypres on 31 July 1917 with the 1/6th Battalion of the Seaforth Highlanders. He fell at Arras in 1918.

Private William Butler gained his VC near Lempire, in France, on 6 August 1917 with the 17th Battalion of the West Yorkshire Regiment.

Corporal Fred Greaves won his award at Poelcapelle, in Belgium, on 4 October 1917 with the Sherwood Foresters. He became a sergeant.

Corporal Arthur Hutt won his VC at Terrier Farm, near Poelcapelle, in Belgium, on 4 October 1917 with the 1/7th Battalion of the Royal Warwickshire Regiment. He was promoted sergeant.

Lieutenant Colonel Arthur Borton gained his award at Sheria, in Palestine, on 7 November 1917 with the 2/22nd(County of London) Battalion of the London Regiment(the Queen's). He had won the DSO in Gallipoli in 1915. Borton was made a CMG in 1918 and was mentioned in despatches, Egypt made him a member of the Order of the Nile and North Russia appointed him a member of the Order of Vladimir.

Second Lieutenant Stanley Henry Parry Boughey won his VC at El Burf, in Judaea, on 1 December 1917 with the 1/4th Battalion of the Royal Scots Fusiliers. He died three days later.

Corporal Charles William Train gained his award at Ain Karem, traditional birthplace of St John the Baptist, in the battle for Jerusalem on 8 December 1917 with the 2/14th Battalion of the London Regiment(the London Scottish). He became a sergeant.

Private Harold Whitfield won his VC at Burj El Lisaneh, in Egypt, on 10 March 1918 with the 10th Battalion of the King's Shropshire Light Infantry (formerly the Shropshire Yeomanry). He was promoted sergeant.

Second Lieutenant John Schofield gained his posthumous award at Givenchy, in France, on 9 April 1918 with the 2/5th Battalion of the Lancashire Fusiliers. His VC was presented to the Lancashire Fusiliers museum at Bury by his niece in 1989.

Private Robert Edward Cruickshank won his VC east of the river Jordan (an area later named Transjordan) on 1 May 1918 with the 2/14th Battalion of the London Regiment(the London Scottish). He was later Commissioned and rose to rank of major.

Lance Sergeant Edward Smith gained his award near Serre, in France, on 21–23 August 1918 with the 1/5th Battalion of the Lancashire Fusiliers. Earlier he had won the DCM. He was killed in action in 1940 when serving with the 2nd Battalion as a lieutenant.

Lieutenant Colonel Richard West, of the North Irish Horse and the North Somerset Yeomanry, won his posthumous VC while serving with F (or 6th) Battalion of the Tank Corps. The citation recalled valour at Courcelles and Vaulx Vraucourt, in France, between 21 August and 2 September 1918. He had earlier won the DSO and bar and the MC.

Private Jack Harvey gained his VC near Péronne, on the Somme, on 2 September 1918 with the 1/22nd Battalion of the London Regiment(the Queen's). He was promoted corporal.

Private Samuel Needham won his award at Kefr Kasim, in Palestine, on 10–11 September 1918 with the 1/5th Battalion of the Bedfordshire Regiment. He died at El Qantara, in the canal zone of Egypt, a week before the Armistice.

Lance Corporal Alfred Wilcox gained his VC in the Laventie area of France on 12 September 1918 with the 2/4th Battalion of the Oxfordshire and Buckinghamshire Light Infantry.

Corporal David Hunter won his VC at Moeuvres, in France, on 18 September 1918 with the 1/5th Highland Light Infantry. He became a sergeant.

Sergeant William Herbert Waring gained his award at Ronssoy, in France, on 18 September 1918 with the 2/5th Battalion of the Royal Welsh Fusiliers. Waring, who also had the MM, died less than three weeks later.

Second Lieutenant Frank Edward Young gained his posthumous VC at Havrincourt, in France, on 18 September 1918 with the 1st Battalion of the Hertfordshire Regiment.

Second Lieutenant William Allison White won his VC at Gouzeaucourt, in France, on 18 September 1918 with the 3rd Battalion of the Machine Gun Corps. He became a captain and gained his TD.

Lieutenant John Barrett gained his award at Partruet, in France, on 24 September 1918 with the 1/5th Leicestershire Regiment. He was presented with a £330 cheque as 'Paddington's second VC'. Barrett commanded the

5th Battalion of the Leicesters from 1937 to 1939 and gained his TD. He was a surgeon in civil life.

Lieutenant Donald John Dean won his VC near Lens, in France, on 24–26 September 1918 with the 8th Battalion of the Royal West Kent Regiment. He was mentioned in despatches. Dean became CO of the 4th Battalion of the Buffs in 1936. In the next war he was a colonel in the Pioneer Corps and was mentioned in despatches twice. He was made an OBE, gained his TD and Denmark appointed him a commander of the Order of the Dannebrog.

Sergeant Louis McGuffie gained his posthumous award in the Wyteshaete area of Belgium on 28 September 1918 with the 1/5th Battalion of the King's Own Scottish Borderers.

Sergeant William Henry Johnson won his VC at Ramicourt, in France, on 3 October 1918 with the 1/5th Battalion of the Sherwood Foresters.

Corporal James McPhie gained his posthumous award at the Canal de la Sensée, near Aubencheul-au-Bac, in France, on 14 October 1918 with the 416th(Edinburgh) Field Company, RE.

Lieutenant Colonel Harry Greenwood, who had served in the South African War and had been a Terrier since the formation of the TF, won his VC at Ovillers, in France, on 23–24 October 1918 while commanding the 9th Battalion of the King's Own Yorkshire Light Infantry. He also won the DSO and bar and the MC and was mentioned in despatches thrice. He was made an OBE in 1944. He was a businessman with interests in Africa.

Sergeant Thomas Caldwell gained his award in the Audenarde area of Belgium on 31 October 1918. He was in the 12th Battalion of the Royal Scots Fusiliers and later became a CSM.

Major Brett Cloutman, who had been in the London University OTC and the 12th Battalion of the London Regiment(Rangers) before being commissioned into the RE, won the last VC of the war. He swam the river under fire at Pont-sur-Sambre, in France, on 6 November to sever the wires of charges laid to destroy the Quartes bridge. Earlier he had won the MC. In the Second World War he was mentioned in despatches. He became a QC and was knighted.

THE SECOND WORLD WAR

Lieutenant Colonel Charles Newman, commissioned into the 4th Battalion of the Essex Regiment, gained his VC in the combined operations raid on St Nazaire on 27 March 1942. Newman, attached to 2 Commando, led the special service troops. Newman's honours included being made an OBE, appointed a chevalier of the Legion of Honour and awarded the Croix de Guerre by France and gaining his TD. In civil life he was an engineering and public works contractor.

Lieutenant Colonel Lorne Campbell of Airds, commanding the 7th Battalion of the Argyll and Sutherland Highlanders, won his award at Wadi Akarit, in Tunisia, on 6 April 1943. His other decorations include the DSO and bar and he was mentioned in despatches four times. He was appointed an OBE and gained his TD. The United States made him an officer of the Legion of Merit. He became a brigadier and is a past master of the Vintners Company.

Lieutenant Wilwood Alexander Sandys Clarke, of the 5th Battalion of the Loyal Regiment, gained his VC posthumously at Guiriat el Atach, in Tunisia, on St George's Day 1943.

Private George Mitchell won his award posthumously at Damiano, in Italy, on 23–24 January 1944 with the London Scottish.

Captain Richard Wakeford gained his VC in the Cassino area on 13 May 1944 with the 2/4th Battalion of the Hampshire Regiment. He was promoted major. He became a master in the Chancery Division of the High Court.

Captain David Auldjo Jamieson won his VC in Normandy on 7–8 August 1944 with the Royal Norfolk Regiment. Later he became a major. He is a businessman who served on the boards of several companies.

Lieutenant Tasker Watkins gained his VC near Martigny, in Normandy, on 6 August 1944 with the 1/5th Battalion of the Welch Regiment. He had joined the TA in the Duke of Cornwall's Light Infantry. He was later promoted major. He has had a long career as a judge and was advanced to the Court of Appeal as Lord Justice (Sir Tasker) Watkins, later becoming Deputy Lord Chief Justice.

Lieutenant Gerard Ross Norton, of the South Africa part-time infantry but serving in the 1/4th Battalion of the Hampshire Regiment, won his award at Monte Grindolfo, in Italy, on 31 August 1944. He was promoted captain. Earlier he had won the MM. He was a bank clerk until he retired in Southern Rhodesia.

Sergeant George Harold Eardley, of the 4th Battalion of the Cheshire Regiment, gained his VC at Overloon, in the Netherlands, on 16 October 1944. He had previously won the MM. Later he was a company sergeant major.

Fusilier Dennis Donnini won his award between the rivers Maas and Roer, in the Netherlands, on 18 January 1945 with the 4/5th Battalion of the Royal Scots Fusiliers. He was wounded twice that day, the second time fatally. This County Durham man with the Italian surname, fighting in a Scots regiment in the Netherlands, died aged 19; he would have had to wait nearly two years before being put on the voters' register.

Corporal Edward Thomas Chapman gained his VC in the Dortmund–Ems canal area of Germany on 2 April 1945 with the Monmouthshire Regiment. Earlier he had won the BEM.

THE GEORGE CROSSES

A small group of Territorials and a member of the Army Emergency Reserve were awarded Britain's second most senior honour, the George Cross. It was instituted by George VI in 1940 in response to the need to recognise gallantry other than in the face of the enemy and as an award available to civilians. The VC had been won by five civilians in Victoria's reign but the practice had been discontinued. The George Medal was instituted at the same time as the GC, to recognise less daring deeds. In 1971 living recipients of the Albert Medal or the Edward Medal (both for bravery other than in the face of the enemy) were invited to return the medal and accept the GC in its place. Similar substitution had applied to the Empire Gallantry Medal. Part-time soldiers who received the GC either *ab initio* or in substitution include:

Sergeant Sidney Williams, the 6th (City of London) Battalion of the London Regiment, the Cast Iron Sixth, who won the Albert Medal on 4 January 1918.

Lieutenant Bernard George Ellis, the 1/5th Battalion of the Buffs, who received the Albert Medal at Shahraban, in Mesopotamia, in 1918

Lieutenant Colonel Norman Baster, RAMC, who won the Edward Medal as a civilian doctor on 17 April 1936. He also gained his TD.

Lieutenant Bertram Archer, RE, who won the GC for bomb disposal at a Llandarcy refinery, near Swansea, on 2 September 1940. He later served in the 137th Bomb Disposal Regiment, RE (AER), retiring as a lieutenant colonel. He was made an OBE and gained his ERD.

Lieutenant Edward Reynolds, RE, who won the GC for duties with the 101st Bomb Disposal Section at Congresbury on 17 August and with the 102nd Bomb Disposal Section at Bristol on 3 September 1940. He had joined the TA in 1936.

Lance Bombardier Brian Spillett, of P Battery, the 289th Parachute Regiment, RA(TA), who won the GC posthumously as a civilian when he ran into a blazing house at Waltham Cross on 16 June 1965 to try to rescue the householder. By coincidence, 20 years later, Spillett's descendant unit, the 289th Commando Battery, RA(V), produced another peacetime hero Sergeant Barry Smith, a British Gas driving instructor, who won the GM for chasing two armed raiders. Despite being shot in the chest and twice in the groin, he held them until police arrived. Two years later bullet fragments were still emerging from his body.

18

Anecdotes

'Eyes right!' the sergeant said
As we passed the drill hall door.
And left it at that, so we marched cock-eyed
From three to half past four.
ARTHUR CONAN DOYLE, 1915

The part-time soldiers have left a rich anecdotage of humour in peace and war. Some of the anecdotes were distinctly not humorous at the time but most of them are worth sharing.

On the sands at Weston-super-Mare, the Bath Squadron of the North Somerset Yeomanry were getting used to their new horses in November 1939. Many of the Yeomen worked in offices and were far from proficient riders. A regular reservist squadron sergeant major accused one teenaged lance corporal, unpaid, of not being able to ride properly, saying he was riding 'too short'. It was the *faux pas* of all time. The lance corporal was Bruce Hobbs, who had been a professional jockey since he was 14 and who in 1938 had won the Grand National on Battleship only three months after his 17th birthday. Hobbs established two and perhaps three records that day: the youngest rider ever to win the National, his mount was the smallest to win the event, and he was probably the tallest rider to do so.

(Confirmed to the author in conversation with the trainer Bruce Hobbs, MC).

Lord Killanin, a journalist who recruited a company of the 2nd Battalion of the Queen's Westminsters (later the 12th Battalion of the King's Royal Rifle Corps) largely from Fleet Street journalists and actors in early 1939, was assistant adjutant at the time. He was telephoned urgently by the West End impresario Bronson Albury, who had discovered that the Westminsters had both Frank Lawton, the leading actor, and his understudy on sentry duty at the same time and the evening performance at his theatre could not proceed until one of them was released. Killanin obliged by adjusting the roster and the show went on.

(Told to the author by Lord Killanin).

Another officer in that company of the 2nd Queen's Westminsters, Bill Deedes, later an MP, minister, editor of *The Daily Telegraph*, who became Lord Deedes, had a similar experience. Deedes and about a dozen other journalists from the *Telegraph* had joined the unit. Shortly after the battalion was embodied, he received a plaintive telephone call from his editor, Arthur Watson, who was having problems in getting the newspaper produced. 'Ask the colonel if we can have a few subeditors back to help with the paper tonight'. Deedes obligingly passed on the request but received short shrift from the CO, Lieutenant Colonel Savile, who told him to tell Watson 'there's a war on'.

(Related to the author by Lord Deedes).

The recently graduated Teddy Taylor joined a Scots intelligence unit of the TA, where he became a corporal. His CO was a senior civil servant. Taylor resigned on being elected MP for the Cathcart division of Glasgow. Later he became a minister at the Scottish Office and moving into his department in St Andrew's House, he found that one of the senior civil servants directly under him was his former CO. 'It struck me that as the roles had changed, my clear duty was to start shouting at him. However, the Army discipline has a lasting effect and I must say that as a Government minister I felt just as terrified of him as I had done on the parade ground.'

(Told to the author by Sir Edward Taylor, MP (Conservative) for Southend East, and secretary of the European Reform Group).

Bernard Marmaduke, the Duke of Norfolk, was about to inspect a Territorial parade in his capacity as president of the Council of TA&VRAs. At that moment it began to rain heavily and an officer produced an umbrella which he opened and held over the duke's head. Norfolk waved it away and said grandly: 'There's nothing the troops like more than seeing silly old buggers like me getting wet'.

(Told to the author in 1965 by an officer present at the occasion).

On the second day of the Second World War the 48th Light AA Battery, a TA unit that had trained at Enfield, was sent to its war station. A member of the unit shot a swan and the battery cook served it for luncheon. Quartermaster Sergeant Arnold Goodman, who 'to my shame', as he commented later, had some of the bird, found it inedible. But most of those who persevered with the meal became ill with gastric poisoning. The swan had its revenge.

(Related to the author by Lord Goodman, CH, who described it as a 'most brutal episode').

During the fighting following the break-out from the Falaise Gap in August 1944, Trooper Youell, of the 43rd Reconnaissance Regiment, formed from the 5th Battalion of the Gloucestershire Regiment, went to attend to a call of nature at Conde. The mail having arrived, he took the opportunity to read his letters. Just as he was at his most exposed a group of German soldiers burst upon the scene and they insisted on surrendering to him. Could this be the most informal of all surrenders in history?

(Told by Canon Eric Gethyn-Jones, MBE, TD, in his book A Territorial Army Chaplin in Peace and War, *Gooday, East Wittering (1989)).*

The commander RA of the 55th Division was visiting one of his units, the 136th(1st West Lancashire) Field Regiment, RA(TA), in camp near Broxton, Cheshire, in 1939. His brigade major, although only a second lieutenant in the TA, lost no time in telling the gun position officer that the guns of the 347th Battery were badly sited: they could not possibly clear a hill to the front. The GPO pointed out that howitzers would have no difficulty in clearing the crest. The 136th, normally equipped with 25-pounders, had borrowed the howitzers from their fellow (first line) unit the 87th. The snooty brigade major replied: 'But you are equipped with 25-pounder field guns', and went on to give another battery the benefit of his experience. It was obvious he had thought all the 4.5in howitzers he saw that day were 25-pounder field guns. When they returned to camp the younger officers, offended equally by his military ignorance and his haughty manner, determined on revenge. That night in the mess tent the brigadier and his arrogant BM happened to be guests. After dinner, and just before the CO guided his senior officers and the brigadier to the anteroom tent for liqueurs, the subalterns formed an admiring ring around the BM asking questions, their object being to prevent him from going to the anteroom. As soon as the senior group were out of sight the officers grabbed him and carried him shoulder high into the countryside. They pulled off his trousers and underpants and poured beer over his lower parts while telling him what they would like to do to him with 4.5in howitzers and 25-pounders in a non-military capacity. Furious, wet, *sans* trousers and *sans* dignity, the BM ran off into the night shouting: 'This regiment will regret this!' That bumptious BM was Second Lieutenant Selwyn Lloyd, of the 149th Royal Horse Artillery, second line unit of the 106th(Lancashire Yeomanry) Regiment, RHA, later to become Secretary of State for Foreign Affairs, Chancellor of the Exchequer and Speaker of the House of Commons.

(Related by Major G W Robertson, MC, in The Rose and the Arrow – A History of 136th(1st West Lancashire) Field Regiment, RA(TA). *136th OCA, Liverpool (1986)).*

The officers' mess of the 24th Middlesex(Post Office Rifles) challenged the officers of the London Rifle Brigade to a match of tip-and-run, rounders and tug of war in 1905 and issued the invitation in French from *'Monsieur le Président du Sporting Vingt-Quatrième Mousquetaires (Postes et Télégraphie) à Messieurs les Officiers de la Brigade Chasse-Pots de Londres'.*

The LRB replied in Latin as follows:

'Primus in urbe' quae vocatur Legio Cohorti Mediorum Sexonum Vicesimae Quartae et omnibus ad quos hae praesentes litterae pervenerint – Salutem. Sciatis quod nos de speciali gratia et certa scientia nostra et mero motu, etc., etc., etc. Guadebimus suscipere (Anglice 'take on'*) ludibria ista quae vester magister ludorum proposuit – videlicet: Apicem et cursionem; Teretiores; et (si necesse fuerit) Tractionem de bello. Octeni octenis certentur. Spolia (scilicet poculum) victores suferant. Sciatis etiam quod de nostro exercitu nondum actum est. In cujus rei testimonium huic praesenti cartae nomina et sigilla affiximus apud castra Marivadiana (Seaford) nono die Augusti anno regis Eduardi septimi quinto, etc.*

(Told in The History of the London Rifle Brigade 1859–1919. *p 269. Constable, London (1921)).*

In the second decade of the 20th century, the president of the mess committee, the elected officer responsible for running the officers' mess of the Cheshire Yeomanry, was noted for his penny-pinching. His batman, Trooper C Thomas, complained that he was ordered, whenever the officer's bootlaces snapped, to repair them by stitching them together. But the mean PMC met his Waterloo from his opposite number in the sergeants' mess, the regimental sergeant major. Officers had protested at the poor quality of their mess beer, so the PMC, instead of pouring it down the drain, presented it to the sergeants' mess. Later he inquired of the RSM how the sergeants had liked the beer. The RSM replied: 'Just right'. Taken aback by the compliment, the officer asked the RSM what he meant by 'Just right'. The RSM replied: 'If it had been any worse we couldn't have drunk it; if it had been any better we wouldn't have got it.'

(Related by Lieutenant Colonel Sir Richard Verdin in The Cheshire (Earl of Chester's) Yeomanry, *published privately (1971)).*

A driver in the headquarter troops of 47 Infantry Brigade (TA) at the Duke of York's Headquarters, Chelsea, in the middle 1960s was a Ghanaian who had served in the Burma campaign with a West African unit. In civil life he was a journalist with an African news agency and was often dashing off to strange places - on one or two occasions in North Africa taking in his large car fellow TA men with him for the ride. He was fiercely against the Ghanaian government and it was rumoured that he was plotting against it. Came the day that a coup there was announced. He vanished, flew to Ghana and made ready to join the new government. But he had been misinformed. The coup had been carried out by another group of plotters, not his. The prevailing group, who consolidated power, put him on trial in humiliating circumstances. He had to endure the accusations while standing in the dock with a sub-machine gun jammed against his head. It was a show trial and pictures were published in the British press.

(The author, serving in the unit at the relevant period, knew the man).

When the war in Europe was nearing its end a German delegation consisting of an admiral and a general arrived at Montgomery's headquarters on 3 May to ask for peace terms. One of the two, General Kienzel, complained to Monty that before being escorted to the headquarters he had been searched and his wrist watch had been confiscated. A signal was sent to the infantry regiment responsible for the escort and back came the reply: 'This morning's bag 24 watches. Am sending back the biggest and flashiest in hope that it is the general's'. This proved indeed to be the general's timepiece and honour was satisfied.

(Told by T M Lindsay in Sherwood Rangers.
Burrup Mathieson, London (1952)).

The 1/2nd London Regiment were sailing from Egypt bound for the Gallipoli peninsula in 1915 when they were told by the CO that their pith sun helmets would not be worn in the new theatre of operations. This was followed by the order: 'Throw them overboard'. The troops witnessed the possibly unique sight of about 600 helmets bobbing in rough formation in the wake of the vessel.

(Related by Major W E Grey in The Second City of London Regiment(Royal Fusiliers) in the Great War (1914–19).
Regimental (1929)).

A cockney member of an Imperial Yeomanry unit in the South African War never lost an opportunity to express his poor opinion of the enemy's shooting. One day, while scouting he had just remarked that a Boer couldn't hit a target from 50 yards when there was a crack and he was felled by an enemy bullet fired from more than 1,000 yards. It turned out that he had been grazed on the temple. When he regained consciousness his first word was a contemptuous: 'Outer'.

(Related by J H Settle (arranger) in Anecdotes of Soldiers in Peace and War. *Methuen, London (1905)).*

In the Western Desert in 1942 the Yorkshire Dragoons, in their new role of motor battalion for the 1st Armoured Division, found themselves augmenting the division's apparent tank strength to deceive German reconnaissance aircraft by erecting tubular steel and canvas structures on their 30cwt trucks with stove pipes as guns. Gaps in the line of armour were thus filled with these fabricated 'Grant' tanks, which looked impressive on the ground. But they failed to deceive the enemy – a German plane swooped over them and among the fake tanks it dropped a fake bomb carved from a harmless piece of wood.

(Notorious in the regiment and confirmed to the author by Bruce Hobbs, MC, who was serving in it at the time).

In April 1946 Dame Leslie Whateley, director of the ATS from 1943 to 1946, was received by George VI on relinquishing her command and she was invited to have tea on the terrace at Buckingham Palace with the King, the Queen and the Princess Royal of the day. 'I was in the middle of a conversation with the King as to what colour should be chosen for the stockings of the permanent Service when there was a wild rush of fur and a corgi dashed along the terrace close on the tail of a large cat.' As the yelps increased in volume she wondered whether she would be failing in her military duty if she did not attempt to separate the pets or whether the correct etiquette was to continue her conversation with the monarch as though nothing was happening. Fortunately Princess Margaret appeared and separated the animals.

(Related by Dame Leslie Whateley, DBE, in her book As Thoughts Survive. *Hutchinson, London (1948)).*

During the fighting following the Argenta Gap and before the crossing of the river Po, in northern Italy, Territorials of X Company of the 9th Battalion of the Royal Fusiliers, preparing to take Bastia on 15 April 1945, found themselves held up by an unexpected obstacle, treacle. A large sugar factory had been bombed and the assault troops had run into the black, sticky mess. The company sergeant major fell into it and the crew of a Sherman tank of the 10th Hussars, supporting the company, were so amused at the spectacle that the driver failed to notice that he was heading for a huge bomb crater. The vehicle trundled into the crater which was filled with the viscous liquid and disappeared from the infantrymen's view. A Fusilier explained later: 'we were like flies extricating ourselves off flypaper'.

(From the records of the Royal Fusiliers and related by C Northcote Parkinson in Always a Fusilier, *Sampson Low, London (1949) He observed: 'How often is the historian privileged to record facts which no novelist would dare invent!').*

In December 1916 the 2nd Battalion of the London Rifle Brigade on Salisbury Plain was inundated with opportunities for courses for officers. The courses, it was ordered by brigade, had to be fully subscribed, which left few officers available for normal duty in the battalion. One Saturday, a lieutenant found that as well as commanding his own platoon he was commanding a company, was brigade musketry officer, battalion musketry officer, intelligence officer, transport officer and orderly officer. When a fire practice alarm was suddenly sounded and the brigadier general arrived to watch the unit's reaction, the lieutenant had some difficulty in deciding how he should report himself.

(Related in The History of the London Rifle Brigade 1859–1919, *p 269. Constable (London)).*

During the battle of El Alamein, British anti-tank gunners hit a Sherwood Rangers' tank with armour piercing shot in a confused period at Galal. Major M Laycock was wounded in the head but before being taken for treatment he grabbed one of the rounds and handed it back to the gunner who had fired it.

(Related by T M Lindsay in Sherwood Rangers. *Burrup Mathieson, London (1952)).*

In 1834 the Uxbridge Yeomanry were given the honour of escorting King William IV on a visit to Lord Westminster at Rickmansworth. The Yeomanry were entertained generously, perhaps too well, because on the return journey the officer leading the procession took the wrong road. The road they were travelling along became progressively narrower, then a track and finally ended at a gate into a ploughed field. The officer took the setback in his stride: he ordered the gate to be opened and stoically led the procession into the field and, carriages rolling and dipping among the furrows, made a complete circuit around the field until he arrived back at the gate and was able to get back on to the track and find the right road.

(Told by Major R Money Barnes in The Soldiers of London. *Seeley, London (1963)).*

While the 1/2nd Londons were training at Arques, near St Omer, in January 1915 the battalion's medical officer, Captain J. (Doc) McHoul, was issued with a charger so light in colour that it was almost white. He was constantly being warned by brother officers to do something about it as he would be a perfect target for snipers once the battalion moved to the front. One day he paraded on a purple horse. He had tried to change its colour with a safe dye from his dispensary and had used potassium permanganate. The MO experimented with other hues and, some time later, when the battalion was lined up ready to move the CO, Lieutenant Colonel Jim Attenborough, noticed that everybody on parade seemed to be chirping. He looked around and to his amazement saw Doc riding a horse the colour of a canary. Apparently the yellow horse brought amusement to the unit for months to come. A subaltern, Lieutenant E T Cooper, commemorated horse and rider in a poem that included the verse:

The rumour was he murmured 'cheep'
Instead of saying 'whoa',
And gave it groundsel in a heap
To make the beggar grow.

(Related by Major W E Grey in The 2nd City of London Regiment(Royal Fusiliers) in the Great War (1914–1919), *London (1929)).*

In January 1940, when Britain's 1st Cavalry Division was moving by train laboriously from Dunkirk to Marseilles, Corporal Harrison, of the Sherwood Rangers, discovered that his horse had developed colic. The horse, distinguished by a prominent wart on its nose, was a hunter owned by the Duke of Portland, who had allowed Harrison, his stud groom in civil life, to take into the Army. The animals were travelling in confined conditions, eight to a boxcar, so at the first opportunity Harrison took his hunter off the train. Finding himself in a small station miles from anywhere, he persuaded the station master to let him have the key to the waiting room and he locked the horse in there while he walked to the nearest town for brandy. On his return with several bottles he locked himself in the room with the horse and, defying indignant passengers who wanted to shelter from the cold, stayed there for several hours until both felt better. The problem now was how were they to catch up with the Rangers scores of miles away to the south? He remembered that the Duke of Gloucester, who was now liaison officer for the British and French armies, had visited the Duke of Portland at Welbeck Abbey shortly before the war and would remember the hunter. Harrison commandeered the station telephone and asked to be put through to the royal duke. He met with resistance from civil and military operators of two nations, staff officers and an aide but he persisted until unbelievably His Royal Highness was speaking at the other end of the line. 'You remember the horse with the wart on the nose when you visited Welbeck?' The duke remembered. Harrison explained the problem and not long afterwards a train arrived. Coupled to the back was an empty boxcar reserved for 'Wart Nose' and in attendance were three Indian Army veterinary officers.

(Told by T M Lindsay in his The History of the Sherwood Rangers in the 1939–45 War*).*

In the late 1880s, the Cheshire Yeomanry tried an experiment of bringing together pairs of independent troops to form squadrons. The adjutant, inspecting the squadron formed by the Tatton troop and the Tabley troop, noticed that they were seriously unbalanced, one having far more men than the other. He told the sergeant major to post some of the men from the larger troop into the smaller. 'Impossible', replied the sergeant major, 'One troop is Conservative and the other Liberal and they won't fight together'.

(Related by A B Armstrong, Supplementary Chapter 1, Verdin, op cit, p 551).

A snooty young subaltern joining the 5th battalion of the Lancashire Fusiliers on the Gallipoli peninsula was met at the battalion dump by the post corporal who was to be his guide into the line. An enemy shell whizzed overhead and the corporal remarked cheerfully: 'Not for us . . .' and as it exploded lower on the beach he added: 'Wrongly addressed'. The subaltern saw fit to rebuke the corporal for levity. As they neared the line they passed a mound from which came an unpleasant smell – probably from a dead mule. 'What's that terrible smell?' inquired the lieutenant. The corporal replied: 'That's where we bury our officers'.

(Told by Frederick P Gibbon, The 42nd(East Lancashire) Division 1914–1918. *Country Life, London (1920)).*

A company of the 2/7th Battalion of the Middlesex Regiment were celebrating Christmas Day in the line in Italy and considered themselves lucky to be having a peaceful time. A party of Ensa entertainers arrived and when shown D Company's 4.2in mortars, one of the attractive girls persuaded someone in authority to let them sign a bomb and fire it on to the enemy lines. (This signing of bombs was a wartime practice much in vogue by film actresses; it is believed that the fashion was set by Rita Hayworth, who while visiting United States Air Force bases signed blockbusters when the aircraft were bombing up ready to make a raid). The Diehards' mortar bomb exploded near to the Germans' position and they immediately and no doubt indignantly responded with a stonking of the Diehards' location.

(Related to the author when he was serving in the battalion by a participant on the mortar line).

It was Christmas Eve before the outbreak of the Second World War. After a Saturday on the South Coast the Artists Rifles' rugby team were waiting for a train to take them back to London. Because of the impending holiday, there was no food in the station buffet but a lot of beer. After a lengthy wait and a successful attempt to reduce the alcohol stock, the team were hungry by the time the train arrived, but all its refreshment car could offer was a plate of stale rock cakes. One Terrier's cake was so hard he could not even get his teeth into it. In famished disgust he hurled it through an open window as the train rattled along. When the team arrived at Waterloo they were confronted by a group of railwaymen and dozens of policemen interviewing everyone who left the carriages. A policeman explained that they were looking for the culprit who had 'thrown a half-brick at a porter' hitting him on the head as the train steamed through a station en route. The team fell silent and when asked their identities the first five gave their names in turn as Brown, Smith, Jones, Evans, and Williams. These were their genuine names but the police seemed to think the team were making them up. The next in line, Miles Partridge, replied 'Partridge' . . . and the man after him replied: 'Christmas' (his true name). This, on Christmas Eve, proved too much for the police. 'We're not going to get any sense out of this lot,' said an inspector. 'Tell them to push off and behave.'

(Related to the author by Christopher Partridge, the son of Miles (Ginger) Partridge, of the Artists, who was later commissioned into the Royal Berkshire Regiment and served in the Indian Army during the war).

On the subject of interesting names, the 5th(V) Battalion of the Royal Regiment of Fusiliers appeared in the late 1970s to be an unusually religious body. The CO was Lieutenant-Colonel Parsons, the adjutant was Captain Church,a platoon commander was Lieutenant Vickers and most impressive of all was the awesome Sergeant Apostell. It was said that at times, the padre, the Reverend Denis Spiller, wondered whether the battalion needed his cure.

(All the gentlemen were serving in the battalion when the author was a member).

When 'Kaiser Bill', Wilhelm II of Germany, visited Britain before the 1914-18 war he mentioned unexpectedly at the end of the state part of his visit that he would like to see a typical Volunteer regiment. This disconcerted the protocol organisers, and it is not known whether it was a serious attempt by the emperor to test the call-out time of a Volunteer unit. Nevertheless the honorary colonel of the Queen's Westminsters, the Duke of Westminster, volunteered his unit. The colonel commandant had 48 hours in which to get his men on parade. Notices were printed and flyposted in the area, and arrangements made for the men who wished to do so to sleep overnight at the drill hall, the Queen's Hall. This Mayfair unit managed to get on parade by 08.00 hours 730 of its 1,100 members, not bad in the days before mass telephones. The Kaiser inspected them and expressed his approval. He was not merely being polite: when he returned to Germany he sat for a portrait in oils, and presented it to the Westminsters as a token of his pleasure. It was hung in the officers' mess in Davis Street. On an adjacent wall in the place of honour was (and still is) a delightful Winterhalter portrait of the young Queen Victoria in a white satin gown. When the 1914–18 War started the officers removed the Kaiser's picture from its position where the Queen's portrait could 'see' this enemy, placed it behind an angle in another part of the mess, and turned the picture around so that it faced the wall. The portrait is now facing the proper way again and it was seen in October 1989 by a great grandson of the Kaiser, Prinz Nicholas von Preussen, when he visited the 4th Battalion of the Royal Green Jackets, the descendant unit of the Queen's Westminsters, to open the refurbished Fulham House, Putney, the TA centre for B Company, one of 4 RGJ's companies.

(Archive of 4 RGJ).

Oliver Woods, later to become an assistant editor of *The Times*, was serving in the Sharpshooters, the County of London Yeomanry, in the Western Desert when he proved his ability to wash his face without removing his Balaclava helmet. This gave rise to the term 'an Ollie wash' referring to a swift, cursory passing of the flannel over part of the face.

(Notorious in the regiment, told by Colonel Charles Pierce to the author, who knew both men).

That most distinguished of Terriers Sir Winston Churchill was wearing his uniform as honorary colonel of the 5th (Cinque Ports) Battalion of the Royal Sussex Regiment during a visit on 24 March 1945 to observe the crossing of the Rhine when he was nearly beheaded. He was sitting on a 'liberated' mattress tied on top of the turret of an armoured car while on his way to the position of a troop of the 3rd Division's signals regiment when the vehicle sped underneath an elevated field telephone wire. The wire whipped off his cap, grazing the top of the war leader's head. A despatch rider tailing the vehicle leant down, scooped up the cap and drawing level, held it out to Churchill, who thrust out his gold-topped cane and received the headgear. The great man, waving the cap aloft, smiled and observed: 'Better my hat than my head'.

(Recalled by Major-General Tony Tighe, who was commanding the troop at the time; also related in Tighe's obituary notice in The Daily Telegraph *in October 1989).*

The old comrades' association of the 4th Battalion of the Queen's Royal Regiment was conceived at a busy crossroads in Croydon in the early 1920s when a police constable on point duty held up a tram to allow traffic to pass in front of it. The constable, ex-Sergeant Harry Mann, recognised the driver as a battalion comrade of the First World War. They had a chat – no doubt to the consternation of other drivers – and there and then resolved to found an old comrades' branch in Croydon. Mann lived to be well over 90 and practically to the end of his days proved to be an energetic and faithful officer of the association. He died in 1989 and his memorial service in Croydon parish church showed the appreciation in which he was held by the younger generations of Territorials.

(The story of the tram inaugural chat was told by Mann in front of old comrades at a reunion luncheon in May 1987 at Croydon Parish Church Hall).

A private soldier in the Queen's, a south Londoner, trained seriously and hard. He had joined the TF in a spirit of patriotism, as did so many others of his generation. For a summer job he worked as a bugler in a cruise liner. It was a German ship and the year was 1914. Because of the impending outbreak of war the ship was redirected and berthed in the Fatherland. He spent the entire war as a civilian detainee in Rhuleben internment camp.

(Archive of the Queen's Regiment, researched by Major Peter Bateman, RRF).

The 2/7th Battalion of the Middlesex Regiment were invading Pantellaria, the Italian communications island halfway to Sicily, from North Africa. George, a shortish but sturdy cook, was first among a group of Diehards; he jumped from the landing craft into the sea, which was deeper than expected; he plummeted to the bottom and all that showed of him in the water was his steel helmet. One of the tall men to his rear involuntarily put a foot on to the helmet, using it as a stepping stone, and strode forward to where the water was shallower, thus getting less wet but adding to George's discomfiture.

(Notorious in the battalion when the author was serving in it).

19
Famous Part-Timers

But he'll remember, with advantages,
The feats he did that day.
KING HARRY IN SHAKESPEARE'S
Henry V, 4.4

Part-time soldiering attracted many people who were destined to become famous. An attempt has been made below to give an impression of the wealth of talent among part-time troops over the years. From the world of literature, Robert Burns, Sir Walter Scott, and Thomas Hughes, who wrote *Tom Brown's Schooldays*, were all amateur soldiers; so was Edward Gibbon, historian of the Roman Empire. In the world of art, Lord Leighton, Sir John Millais, Sir Edward Burne-Jones and G W Watts were Volunteers, all in the same unit, the Artists' Rifles. The founder of the Boys' Brigade, Sir William Smith, formed the organisation on the lines of his old corps the 1st Lanarkshire Volunteers. Lord Harding of Petherton, Britain's senior non-royal field marshal for many years and a former governor of Cyprus, started his military career as a 17-year-old in the Finsbury Rifles; well before it was over he had won three DSOs, an MC and been mentioned in despatches. Sir Ralph Hone, who straddled his three careers like a proconsul of ancient Rome, moving effortlessly between the law, the consular service and the Army, became a Territorial major general.

POLITICIANS AND LAWYERS

British prime ministers have been strongly represented among the nation's weekend soldiers. For the sake of completeness mention must be made of the younger Pitt and Palmerston. But as the former was colonel of the Cinque Ports Volunteers while in office and as the latter, although undoubtedly a recruit in the London Irish during the volunteering rush of 1859, was in his second term of office and in his 76th year, these outstanding political leaders' soldiering must be accepted with reservation. Palmerston had been running the country during the pressures of the Crimean War and the Indian Mutiny (and would continue to do so for six more years), he had been foreign secretary for more than 14 years and had been secretary at war in six governments. No doubt he wanted to set a good example for the Volunteer movement, though in 1859 his newly formed administration wanted their Volunteers on the cheap.

Stanley Baldwin was a genuine working part-time soldier, a lieutenant in the Worcestershire Artillery Volunteers. But he resigned because of the pressure of outside commitments.

Winston Churchill's service was long enough to earn him the TD. After early regular service in the 4th Hussars, he served as a major in the Queen's Own Oxfordshire Hussars and in 1916 commanded the 6th Battalion of the Royal Scots Fusiliers on the Western front.

Alec Douglas-Home, then known by his courtesy title of Lord Dunglass, was a major in the Lanarkshire Yeomanry in the 1930s. He contracted tuberculosis of the spine in 1938 and had the pain of lying on his back for two years with a plaster cast covering him from neck to ankles. As he explained to the author, this meant that he could not go on active service with his unit. His father the 13th earl was also a Territorial. The Queen made him a KG.

Edward Heath rose to command the 2nd Regiment of the HAC from 1947 to 1951. He then became master gunner within the Tower of London. He had served in the war as a major, was mentioned in despatches, was made a MBE in 1946 and gained his TD.

Margaret Thatcher's husband Denis was a wartime major in the RA, was appointed a MBE and gained his TD. In the dissolution honours of 1990 he was made a baronet, becoming at the threshold of the 21st century and at the start of John Major's classless Britain the first recipient of this hereditary dignity for several decades.

Among prime ministers' sons who were themselves ministers and who served in the TA were Gwilym, younger son of David Lloyd George, and Nicholas, son of Anthony Eden. Gwilym was home secretary and minister for Welsh affairs from 1954 to 1957. He later went to the Lords as Viscount Tenby. His younger son William, the third viscount, was a captain in the Royal Welch Fusiliers (TA). Nicholas Eden, second Earl of Avon on the death of his father, became a lord in waiting (a government whip) in the Lords; he was also spokesman there for the arts, the environment and transport. He joined the Queen Victoria's Rifles (TA) in 1953 and became a colonel T&AVR. He was vice-chairman of Greater London TA&VRA from 1976 to 1981.

Many ministers of the crown have been part-time soldiers, perhaps the most relevant being Churchill's son-in-law Duncan Sandys, Selwyn Lloyd and George Younger, all of whom held the defence portfolio as secretary of state. From an earlier age Hugh Arnold-Forster was secretary of state for war during the South African War and was the author of the memorable statement: 'We have got the whole organised Army out of the country, and the War Office is face to face with the problem of how to make an army to take its place'. That state of affairs, probably more than any other single factor, led to the formation of the TF. Arnold-Forster had been in the 2nd Volunteer Battalion of the Royal Fusiliers and his son was a member of its direct descendant, the 2nd Londons. The under secretary of state for war during the bleak early days of the South African War was George Wyndham, a troop leader in the Cheshire Yeomanry. In 1900 he became chief secretary for Ireland, which brought him a seat in the cabinet. He later commanded his regiment.

In more recent times, the second Lord Mancroft, Parliamentary secretary at the Ministry of Defence in 1957, was a Terrier who led his RA unit ashore on D-day, was made a MBE and got his TD. Sir John Stanley, minister of state, the Armed Forces from 1983 to 1987, gained his TD. Teddy (later Sir Edward) Taylor, Parliamentary under secretary of state at the Scottish Office from 1970 to 1971 and again in 1974, served as a TA corporal in the Intelligence Corps but he left on entering politics as MP for Cathcart. Later he became secretary of the European Reform Group.

Duncan Sandys, later Lord Duncan-Sandys, was well groomed for the defence portfolio. He had served in the British embassy in Berlin in the 1930s. He gained a TA commission in the RA in 1937 and the following year he co-founded the Air Raid Protection Institute, later renamed the Institute of Civil Defence. He served with the British expeditionary force in Norway in 1940. The following year, as a lieutenant colonel, he was invalided out because of motoring injuries received on duty. Churchill gave him office and he rose swiftly, his most important role being chairman of the war cabinet committee responsible for combating the flying bombs and rockets of the last year of the war.

Selwyn Lloyd, foreign secretary during the Suez crisis, joined the RA(TA) in June 1939 when he was a barrister. During the war he became a brigadier and served on the staff of the Second Army. He was leader of the Commons before becoming speaker. He became a life peer.

George Younger, who was with the Argyll and Sutherland Highlanders in the Korean War, served later as second in command of the regiment's 7th Battalion. He was made a life peer.

Anthony Barber, chancellor of the Exchequer in the Heath government, had an unusual Territorial career. After being evacuated from Dunkirk, he was seconded to the RAF, became a pilot and was a prisoner of war in Germany and Poland from 1942 to 1945. During his captivity he took a law degree with first class honours, by correspondence. He escaped, only to become a prisoner of the Russians for a time. He became Lord Barber.

Another wartime escaper and senior Conservative was Airey Neave, who joined the RA(TA) before the war. He was still serving in 1951, commanding

Intelligence School No 9(TA). Neave, MP for Abingdon for nearly 26 years, was murdered by a terrorist car bomb in the Commons in 1979 while opposition spokesman for Northern Ireland. It was the final episode in an adventurous life. Nearly 40 years earlier, he had been wounded in France and imprisoned by the Germans. He escaped in 1942 and joined MI9, the organisation responsible for helping Allied prisoners to escape. He wrote a book about the department, *Saturday Night at MI9*. Neave served the Nuremberg indictments on a number of Nazis, including Goering.

Another senior Conservative, Toby Low, MP for Blackpool North from 1945 to 1962, when he was made a peer as Lord Aldington, had a distinguished wartime career. He was commissioned into the RA(TA) in 1934 and saw action in the Greek, North African, Sicilian and Italian campaigns, serving as a highly decorated brigadier. He was a minister at the Board of Trade in the 1950s and was deputy chairman of the Conservative Party Organisation from 1959 to 1963. In 1989 he won the highest libel damages award known to English law, £1,500,000 in a case arising from a book by Count Nikolai Tolstoy.

Frederick Erroll, president of the Board of Trade from 1961 to 1963 and thereafter minister of power, was commissioned into the 4th County of London Yeomanry(Sharpshooters) in 1939. He was the minister responsible for issuing North Sea oil exploration licences, the results of which brought economic benefits for years ahead. He became Lord Erroll of Hale.

Dennis Vosper, minister of health in 1957, who ironically had to resign in the September of that year because of ill-health, joined the Cheshire Regiment(TA) in April 1939 and served fulltime from mobilisation until 1946. He was a company commander in the 5th Cheshires, a final training battalion in Anglesey for infantry support troops due to go overseas immediately. He was made a life peer as Lord Runcorn.

Ian Gow, MP (Conservative) for Eastbourne for many years until he was murdered by a car bomb outside his home in 1990, joined the TA after leaving the 15/19th Royal Hussars. He was minister for housing and construction from 1983 to 1985 when he became minister of state at the Treasury.

Lord Elwyn-Jones, lord high chancellor of Great Britain for five years from 1974 and subsequently a lord of appeal, served as Major Frederick Elwyn-Jones, RA(TA), during the war. He was a deputy judge advocate general and later was a member of the British War Crimes Executive at the Nuremberg War Crimes Tribunal.

Another senior lawyer and an adviser to Harold Wilson, prime minister in the 1960s and 1970s, Lord Goodman enlisted as Gunner Arnold Goodman in an AA unit in September 1939 ('Only just a Territorial', he told the author. 'I enjoyed rapid promotion. When I became a bombardier my mother was very proud; she never could understand the difference between a bombardier and a brigadier'). Like many Terriers of the period, Goodman played an important part in the ground defence of Britain against air attack. An attribute at one stage of his career, it was said, was that he was a first class quartermaster sergeant in those difficult days when everything was in short supply. Initially his unit was commanded by Mortimer Wheeler, the archaeologist (who was to find later fame as a television panellist). When the unit went overseas, Goodman tried to go with it but was refused on health grounds. Later most of its members became prisoners of the Japanese. He became a major. Goodman, solicitor, negotiator, arts administrator and Master of University College, Oxford, is one of the few Territorials to be a CH (by coincidence his old CO, Wheeler, was made one too). The others include Churchill, Selwyn Lloyd, Sandys and Elwyn Jones.

A wartime deputy speaker of the Commons from 1943 to 1945 and again from 1945 to 1951, James Milner was in the ASC(TF) and the Devonshire Regiment in the First World War. In the next war he was chairman of the fire committee and in charge of civil defence at the Houses of Parliament, a prime target of the Luftwaffe. He was made a peer as Lord Milner of Leeds.

A deputy speaker in both Houses of Parliament, Oscar Murton, received a TA commission in 1934. He served with the Royal Northumberland Fusiliers and as a lieutenant colonel on the staff during the war. He was made a life peer as Lord Murton of Lindisfarne.

A man who might have been a wartime prime minister, but for his peerage but who nevertheless held many top political posts, Edward Frederick Lindley Wood, was a long serving part-time soldier. He was a minister in both world wars and in between was Viceroy of India, responsible for the interests of about 319 million people. He commanded the Yorkshire Dragoons Yeomanry and later was honorary colonel for 25 years. He was created Lord Irwin in 1925, succeeded to his father's viscounty of Halifax and was later created first earl. He was secretary of state for war in 1935, but is best remembered as foreign secretary and wartime ambassador to the United States. There can have been no man in the whole history of the Volunteer movement who was so laden with national honours. A Knight of the Garter and a member of the Order of Merit, he was a Knight Grand Cross of the Star of India, Saint Michael and Saint George and of the Indian Empire, and a Privy Counsellor.

JUDGES

A name constantly before the public in the 1970s during the debate on devolution was that of Lord Kilbrandon. He joined the RA(TA) as an advocate and served throughout the war. As a senior judge first of Scotland then of the United Kingdom he was a member and later chairman of the Royal Commission on the Constitution.

A barrister who won the VC and then became a judge of the Court of Appeal, Lord Justice (Sir Tasker) Watkins was a Terrier in the Welch Regiment (vide chapter 17 Soldiers Supreme).

Another Court of Appeal judge, Lord Justice (Sir John) Stocker joined the TA just before the war and served with the Royal West Kent Regiment in the BEF, the Middle East and Italy. He was demobilised as a lieutenant colonel with the MC and TD.

A Terrier who joined an air defence unit was Stanley Rees, later Mr Justice Rees of the Family Division. He joined the 99th AA Regiment(the London Welsh), RA in 1939 before transferring to the judge advocate general's staff in Britain and later as a lieutenant colonel in Palestine.

Mr Justice (Sir Richard) Elwes was commissioned into the Northamptonshire Yeomanry in 1923 and by the autumn of 1939 was a staff captain with 69 Infantry Brigade in France. He later served as a lieutenant colonel at the War Office and was made an OBE. The United States awarded him the Bronze Star.

Another High Court judge who joined the TA before the war, Mr Justice (Sir Neville) Faulks, served at El Alamein. He was made a MBE and was twice mentioned in despatches.

A committed Terrier, serving the TA long after his uniformed days were over, was Mr Justice (Sir John) Willis. He joined the TA in 1938, was commissioned into the Royal Signals and served in France, India and Burma, where he was a GSO1 with the Fourteenth Army. After demobilisation he commanded the 1st Wessex Regiment. On retiring he became president of West Sussex TA&VRA. He was honorary colonel of the 37th Signals Regiment(Wessex and Welsh) for 10 years.

Another High Court judge, Mr Justice Macpherson, the Cluny Macpherson, otherwise Sir William Macpherson of Cluny, chief of the clan Macpherson, commanded the 21st Special Air Service Regiment(TA) from 1962 to 1965

One of England's greatest rugby players between the wars, the North-Easterner C D Aarvold, became a judge after TA and war service. He was capped for England 16 times and captained England seven times. He was made an OBE at the end of the war and gained his TD. He was an Old Bailey judge for 21 years and was knighted as Sir Carl while recorder of London.

THE CHURCH

Wartime listeners in Britain and the Middle East may remember the Radio Padre and his broadcasts. They were the voice and ministry of Ronald Selby Wright, later minister of the Canongate, the kirk of Holyroodhouse, and of Edinburgh Castle, chaplain to the Queen and entitled to the dignity of the Very

Reverend. He became chaplain to the 7/9th (Highland) Battalion of the Royal Scots (TA) in 1938, going with them to France in the BEF. Later he served in the Middle East and Italy. An author with dozens of titles to his credit, he published a series of wartime books aimed at servicemen; they included *Let's Ask the Padre* and *The Padre Presents*. He was mentioned in despatches and was made a CVO.

The Primate of Australia, Metropolitan of New South Wales and Archbishop of Sydney until he retired in 1966, the Most Reverend Hugh Gough, started his TA career as chaplain to the 4th Battalion of the Border Regiment. He was translated to a London parish and became chaplain to the 1st Battalion of the Rifle Brigade from 1939 until 1943. He was wounded in the desert and Tunisian campaigns, was deputy assistant chaplain general to X Corps in Italy, was mentioned in despatches and was made an OBE. He became a CMG in 1965.

The Bishop of Sodor and Man for 12 years to 1966, the Right Reverend Benjamin Pollard, was a Territorial of long standing. He was a chemistry research student at the Victoria University of Manchester (as it was then titled) before being ordained. For two years of the First World War he used his scientific knowledge in the Ministry of Munitions before serving as a chaplain to the forces. He was honorary chaplain to the forces (TA) for many years.

The Reverend Hugh William Clifford Frend, for 15 years professor of ecclesiastical history at Glasgow University and dean of divinity for three years to 1975, was commissioned into the Queen's Royal Regiment (TA) in 1947 after working in the Cabinet Office and the Foreign Office, serving in North Africa and Italy. He was in the TA for 20 years.

The Reverend John Kelman Sutherland Reid spent most of the war as a padre in the Parachute Regiment. He gained his TD in 1961 and was made a civil CBE in 1970. Before the war he was professor of philosophy at the Scottish Church College of Calcutta University for two years before taking up parochial duties in Edinburgh. For nine years he was professor of theology at Leeds followed by 16 years occupying chairs in the discipline at Aberdeen. He was honorary secretary of the joint committee on the new translation of the Bible for more than 30 years.

LORD MAYORS

Many lord mayors of London have been Terriers. Greville Spratt joined the HAC as a private in 1950 after military service in Palestine during the emergency and in other parts of the Middle East. At one time he was in the Arab Legion. He became regimental colonel of the HAC, and gained his TD and bar. On taking office as London's first citizen in 1987 he was made a GBE. He is chairman of the Greater London TA&VRA, president of the Federation of Old Comrades

Associations of the London Territorial and Auxiliary Units and became honorary colonel of the 8th Queen's Fusiliers and the London Regiment.

Alan Raymond Mais, of the Royal West Kents and the RE, who was a colonel when the war ended, was mentioned in despatches in three different theatres as well as being made an OBE and being appointed a member, first class, of the Order of the Patriotic War, of the Soviet Union in 1942. He earned a TD and an ERD. As lord mayor he was made a GBE. Later he became Lord Mais.

Denis Truscott, lord mayor in the 1950s, was one of the Terriers at their posts in the Munich crisis, manning a searchlight in the 33rd (St Pancras) AA. The following year he moved to a searchlight unit guarding Debden RAF station. After completing his active TA career, he was honorary colonel of the 290th Field Regiment (City of London), RA (TA). He was knighted in 1953 and became a GBE after his mayoral year.

Ronald Gardner-Thorpe, lord mayor 1980–81, was commissioned into the Hampshire Heavy Regiment, RA (TA) in 1938, was demobilised as a lieutenant colonel and earned three clasps to his TD. In the 1950s he commanded the 5th Battalion of the Buffs and retired as a colonel. He wrote a book *The City and The Buffs*. He was made a GBE on becoming lord mayor.

Ralph Perring was commissioned into the RA (TA) in 1938 but was invalided in 1940. He was knighted in 1960 and became a baronet in 1963 on completing his year as lord mayor of London. His father and son were Territorials.

A Fusilier who became lord mayor of London in 1993, the stockbroker Paul Newall was a company commander in the City of London Battalion of the Royal Fusiliers (TA) after national service in Egypt and the Sudan. When the battalion was disbanded in 1967 he was chosen as the first OC of C (City of London) Company of the Fusiliers Volunteers, which later became a company of the 5th (V) Battalion of the Royal Regiment of Fusiliers. He is a City lieutenant and was chairman of the City of London TA&VRA for five years.

GREAT LANDOWNERS AND THE TURF

Often described as Britain's richest man is Gerald Grosvenor, sixth Duke of Westminster, a lieutenant-colonel in the Queen's Own Yeomanry. In 1988 *Fortune* listed him the world's tenth richest person, estimating his wealth at $5,400 million. In being a part-time soldier he maintains a family tradition. His father the fifth duke and antecedent Grosvenors were members of the Cheshire Yeomanry. In 1898 three generations of Grosvenors were in the Cheshire Yeomanry: the honorary colonel the first duke (who had been CO for 12 years); his son Second Lieutenant Lord Belgrave; and the duke's grandson Captain Lord Arthur Grosvenor. Also in the unit was Belgrave's stepfather Captain George Wyndham, MP, under secretary of state for war at the time.

It is not everybody who can say that they had hit Hitler and lived to tell the tale but a TA man did just that. He is that great London landowner and stalwart of the Turf, Jockey Club member and veteran senior steward, John Osmael Scott-Ellis, Lord Howard de Walden. The incident occurred when Lord Howard de Walden was in Germany on a visit before Hitler came to power. His car accidentally struck an official at a demonstration. After he had apologised and the victim had walked away, a bystander informed Howard de Walden that the man was called Hitler and that he led a large political party. As John Scott Ellis, Lord Howard de Walden served in the Westminster Dragoons, as befits the landlord of something like 100 acres of London, and became a wartime major.

Another leading owner, Sir Harold Werner, baronet of Luton Hoo, was a long-serving Territorial. He was appointed GCVO.

Bruce Hobbs, the trainer and jockey, winner of the Grand National at the age of 17 on Battleship, has featured on several pages in this book. Joining the North Somerset Yeomanry only hours before the war was declared in 1939, he was commissioned into the Yorkshire Dragoons with whom he won an MC in Tunisia. He was badly wounded at Anzio (see Chapter 18).

A well-known figure of the Turf, as well as in the City of London, Dick Wilkins was a Territorial who served throughout the Second World War. He was a colourful stockjobber, building up Wedd Durlacher (now Barclays de Zoate Wedd). At one time, his firm featured in *The Guinness Book of Records* as having the biggest non-manufacturing turnover in the world. He lived in style – in a suite at the Savoy during the week and at his country home at weekends. He was a member of the Jockey Club and rode to victory in 1956. Wilkins had a collection of vintage cars and raced at Brooklands; he also raced power-boats. Larger than life, not only in his profession and spare-time pursuits but also literally, he had three wardrobes of different sizes to accommodate his figure which altered according to the fluctuations in his weight, from 16st to 20st. The Queen, the Duke of Edinburgh and the Prince of Wales were represented at Wilkins' memorial service in April, 1989; Queen Elizabeth the Queen Mother and Princess Margaret and her children attended and the Princess Royal, the Duchess of York, the Duke and Duchess of Kent and Princess Alexandra were represented.

BROADCASTING

The grandee of British broadcasting, John Reith, who gained a TA commission in 1910, served in the First World War initially in the Scottish Rifles then in the RE. In 1915 a bullet nearly ended his life. Passing through his face it left a deep scar from eye almost to ear. The scar, piercing eyes, beetling brows and 6ft 6in frame combined to make him awesome. The bullet that ended his active service caused him a different type of worry, he disclosed. In his delirium he was more concerned about the blood on his tunic and breeches, both new, and the breeches had to be tailored for his long legs. Subsequently he was given desk jobs, among them travelling to the United States to handle munitions contracts. His time there proved successful and led to the start of his course of honour in public life. In 1922 he was appointed general manager of the British Broadcasting Company Ltd. Reith was knighted and made a peer.

Encyclopaedic knowledge and an irrepressible personality that seemed tailor-made for television turned Mortimer Wheeler, one of the Commonwealth's leading archaeologists, into a cult figure in the 1950s when he appeared on the BBC panel game *Animal, Vegetable, Mineral?* He was a gunner major in the First World War, winning the MC and a mention in despatches. By 1939 he was a TA lieutenant colonel and ended the war as a brigadier. He was knighted in 1952. His many honours included being made a CH.

The architect of the new Coventry Cathedral, Basil Spence, served as a Terrier in the Second World War. He became an OBE in 1948, was knighted in 1960 and made a member of the OM two years later. His work included the British embassy chancery in Rome, the Household Cavalry barracks in Knightsbridge and Sussex University buildings.

NEWSPAPERMEN

A father-and-son team were the Maudes. The father, Colonel Alan Maude, CMG, DSO, TD, was a journalist at *The Times*, who had a distinguished war in the ASC. He wrote a book on the history of the 47th(2nd London) Division. The son, Angus, also a journalist and Terrier in the RASC in the next war, was captured while he was a major in the 56th(1st London) Division in North Africa. He became deputy chairman of the Conservative Party and later was paymaster general. He was knighted in 1983 and later became a peer.

Denis Hamilton, editor-in-chief of *The Times* and *The Sunday Times* from 1967 to 1981, started military life in the 11th Battalion of the Durham Light Infantry. He was second in command at 22. While acting CO of the 7th Battalion of the Duke of Wellington's Regiment in the Netherlands he was awarded an immediate DSO. He was knighted in 1976.

FILM STARS

Among a number of actors and film stars who were Terriers one of the earliest was Ronald Colman, Hollywood's epitome of the English gentleman. He joined the London Scottish when the TF was a year old. He left after four years but rejoined them on the outbreak of war. He was a private at the TF's baptism of fire at Messines. The action made his career because he was wounded in the ankle, invalided and took up acting. He starred in dozens of films and won an Oscar.

Frank Lawton joined the 2nd Queen's Westminsters after the Munich crisis. His war service gained him an American decoration, membership of the Legion of Merit.

An exact contemporary of Lawton on the West End stage, in films (they both appeared in *David Copperfield*) and in the TA was Hugh Williams. He too was in the 2nd Queen's Westminsters. During the war he served in the Devonshire Regiment.

Two other actors in the 2nd Queen's Westminsters were Nigel Patrick and Guy Middleton, both noted for men-about-town roles.

That veteran of stage and television William Fox was a young actor in the West End during the Munich crisis when he rushed by taxi to the Duke of York's Headquarters and joined the London Irish. At the outbreak of war he was playing a German officer on stage. He went into an arctic warfare battalion and later became a lieutenant colonel. When Britain gave the Soviet Union the symbolic Sword of Leningrad he was put in charge of it. After he handed it to Churchill, who was to present it to the evil Stalin, the sword slipped from its scabbard and fell to the floor. Nobody seemed to know the correct procedure, but a British officer picked it up and handed it to a Russian officer who passed it to Stalin. The incident went unreported in case it should be regarded as a bad augury.

Another veteran actor on the screen, radio and television, Maurice Denham, joined the TA before the Second World War. He was commissioned in the RA and modelled one of his scatter-brained radio characters on an officer of his acquaintance.

OTHER FIGURES OF NOTE

The wartime and immediate postwar director of the ATS, Leslie Whateley, was an early Territorial who served throughout the Second World War. She was made a CBE in 1943 and advanced to dame commander the year after the war. Her service brought recognition from the Allies: France made her a chevalier of the Legion of Honour and the United States appointed her a member of the Legion of Merit. She gained her TD in 1951. When the TA was reformed she was honorary colonel of the 688th Heavy AA Regiment, RA(TA) from 1948 to 1953. Later Dame Leslie served as administrator of voluntary services at Queen Mary's Hospital, Roehampton, for nine years.

To escape from Colditz and from one of the Spangenburg prisoner of war camps is no mean achievement. It was done by Peter David Storie-Pugh, a veterinary surgeon like his father and a lecturer at Cambridge for 29 years. Storie-Pugh served during the Second World War in the Royal West Kents and later commanded the 1st Battalion of the Cambridgeshire Regiment and the 1st Battalion of the Suffolk and Cambridgeshire Regiment. He won an MC early in the war and was made a MBE at the end. He became deputy commander of 161 Infantry Brigade and earned three clasps to his TD. He was also a civil CBE.

The formative influence on the Automobile Association, Stenson Cooke, its first secretary, was a Volunteer in the London Rifle Brigade. During the First World War he volunteered for the Army and persuaded about 500 of his AA colleagues to do so. He was in the forefront of steering the AA towards national voluntary service and gave the staff time off work for patriotic duties. He was knighted and received many foreign awards.

Garter principal king of arms is an impressive title, but one holder of it in the 1980s had an unofficial title that was almost as awe-inspiring: Col Col Col. It stood for Colonel Colin Cole, who after war service in the Coldstream joined the HAC and the 6th(V) Battalion of the Queen's Regiment. He became a lieutenant colonel in 1973 and in the 1980s was honorary colonel of the 6/7th Queen's. He was made a KCVO in 1983.

Older infantrymen will recall with (not unqualified) affection those two shoulder-held weapons of the Second World War, the PIAT (projector infantry anti-tank) and the Blacker Bombard. They were the inventions of Stewart Blacker, OBE, TD, who commanded the 58th(Sussex) Field Brigade, RA(TA). He was previously a regular officer, explorer and enthusiast of airborne operations – and took part in the flight over Everest in 1933. Blacker had qualified as a pilot in 1911 and as early as 1922, at Staff College, he was calling for the use of parachuting infantrymen.

When Southern Rhodesia declared independence, some residents in public posts resigned to distance themselves from the Smith government. One such was John Emerich Henry Lyon-Dalberg-Acton, third Lord Acton, the agriculturist; he gave up his job as chairman of Chibero Agricultural College. He had been a practical advocate of encouraging native smallholders. Acton, a Birmingham stockbroker, served in Italy as second in command of the Shropshire Yeomanry. After the destruction of Monte Cassino monastery General Sir Oliver Leese chose Acton, a Roman Catholic peer from the age of 16, patrician of Naples and Duke of Dalberg, to seek an audience of the Pope and apologise for the destruction of the monastery, explaining that the necessities of war made it inevitable. He had to point out that lives and perhaps Rome had thereby been saved. He was made a MBE. Acton emigrated to Southern Rhodesia, where he took up agriculture pursued business interests and became an influential figure. He was made a CMG in 1963.

After sailing before the mast in windjammers from the age of 15, thrice rounding the Horn in sail, Harry Edmonds joined the newly formed TF in the Royal Engineers in 1908, still only 17 but still in search of excitement. He led a full life. Some 80 years after joining his first ship, he was still piloting gliders and it was only with difficulty that he was dissuaded in his nineties from taking up hang gliding! He started to fly gliders when he was 75 and established a record when he was 80. Meanwhile, soon after he had given up the sea, he trained as an engineer, spending two years in New Zealand where he trained volunteers. He fought at Gallipoli and, now a Gunner, commanded a battery with distinction at Passchendaele. When his CO refused to recommend him for promotion, Edmonds demanded an inquiry, was sent back to England and incarcerated in the Tower for a night. He later served in Naval Intelligence.

A TA officer who looked after and brought Mussolini's pet dog to Britain after the Duce and his mistress had been killed, Reginald Houldsworth was a countryman happiest when on horseback and surrounded by dogs. In an obituary notice on 24 January 1989 *The Times* described him as 'one of the last of the old-fashioned county lairds'. CO of the Ayrshire Yeomanry from 1940 to 1942, then of the 4th Pack Mule Group from 1943 to 1945, he fought in Italy and was made an OBE. He was honorary colonel of the Ayrshire Yeomanry from 1960 to the disbandment of the old TA. He became fourth baronet in 1961.

William Smith, son of a soldier and a clerk by profession, was an NCO in the 1st Lanarkshire Volunteers when he began wondering why his Sunday school pupils at the College Church Mission Hall in Glasgow were never as enthusiastic about his lessons as were his Volunteer recruits. After prayer, he found the way ahead: he must found a brigade for boys on the lines of his Volunteer unit. The result was the Boys Brigade, founded in 1883, a quarter of a century before the Boy Scouts. By the time of the South African War, it was an international movement and Smith was knighted in 1909. The brigade's object, 'the advancement of Christ's Kingdom among Boys, and the promotion of habits of Reverence, Discipline, Self-Respect, and all that tends towards a true Christian Manliness' ('Obedience' was added when the brigade was 10 years old), seems to have made a deep impression on many of the brigade's old boys. Eleven of them gained VCs in the First World War and four gained the supreme honour in the next war.

20

The Way Ahead

I swear by Almighty God that I will be faithful and bear true allegiance to Her Majesty Queen Elizabeth II, Her Heirs and Successors and that I will as in duty bound honestly and faithfully defend Her Majesty, Her Heirs and Successors in Person, Crown and Dignity against all enemies and will observe and obey all orders of Her Majesty, Her Heirs and Successors and of the Generals and Officers set over me.

THE OATH OF ALLEGIANCE

What is the future of the TA? By the autumn of 1989 it was beginning to look a much safer world. By the end of the year it seemed that the satellite countries of the Eastern bloc were bent on outdoing each other in toppling the old system. As spring advanced it appeared that at last the Second World War was over for countries such as Czechoslovakia, Poland, Latvia, Estonia and Lithuania that had not known freedom for half a century. Then enter another menace: Iraq invaded Kuwait. But a by-product of this aggression was the most hopeful sign of the postwar era, the United Nations Organisation was working in the way it was intended to work, by sanctions bringing pressure on an aggressor nation. This was strengthened by the deployment in Saudi Arabia of a multi-national group of forces. Meanwhile in Paris, in late November, 34 nations signed a treaty pledging the biggest arms reductions in history. However the message remains obvious: we live in an unstable world.

The old East–West division of the cold war, on which two generations of soldiers have been tutored, is rapidly vanishing. What will probably replace it is the division between the mature nations and rogue outlaw dictatorships armed with weapons of mass destruction and having scant regard for international law, human rights or the opinion of anyone else. Nuclear capability cannot be undiscovered; progressively more nations will obtain it. Fanaticism too is something that will be with us for a long time. These two, fanaticism and nuclear capability, may well be united in some of the smaller nations that harbour ambitions over other countries.

The TA will not deter such ambitions but it can be brought to the pitch at which it can stand in for units of the regular Army; and those regulars can be despatched swiftly to smother incipient warfare, wherever it occurs. It is therefore in everybody's interest to have a large TA. As we saw in Chapter 14, at the time of Mr King's December 1991 announcement the TA's latest ascertainable returns showed its strength was 73,800, including the Home Service Force, compared with its establishment of 90,068. Thus, it was 81.9 per cent recruited (these figures relate to 30 September 1991). What can be done to improve recruiting? Perhaps not much. There seems to be little wrong in a system that can attract recruits the way the TA does. The problem is in retentions: 30 per cent of the recruits leave in their first year and 75 per cent of members leave within three years. This constant drain of strength is therefore the difficulty to be overcome. The bounty today is substantial, at the highest annual rate (after three years) it is currently £775 free of tax. The answer to retention problems might be to double the bounty at a stroke making it £1,550, but payable at this level only after four years (instead of the three required to reach today's £775). Thus, under my suggested system the recruit would receive a bounty of £200 after his first satisfactory year, £500 after his second, £900 after his third and £1,550 after his fourth year. The last tranche, an increase of £650, would surely be a great inducement for the man to stay on; and every man soldiering on for two extra years would slash that 30 per cent wastage enormously.

Britain's almost criminal military unpreparedness at the time of the South African War is well known. The good thing about that war was that it revealed the poor state of Britain's Army, particularly with regard to the lack of trained reserves for a sustained war, and this resulted in a significant improvement in time for the much bigger war that lay ahead. The regular Army was small but effective when we entered the First World War but when the casualties mounted to a scale never before experienced, the Territorials, volunteering beyond their home service commitment, stood in the front line until the new armies could be trained. By the start of the Second World War, Britain was again unprepared. It must surely make sense to have a large, cost-effective TA. Apart from fighting, elements of the TA could have a valuable civil defence role.

In olden days it was believed that there was healing power in the monarch's touch. Even as recently as Charles II's time, from which (albeit slightly inaccurately) the modern army is usually dated, we read that the king ritually touched 70,000 of his people in a year. Today there is still magic about royalty – as any charity organiser basking in royal patronage will confirm. Territorial recruiting would receive a fillip if one or two members of the royal family could be working members of the TA; not honorary colonels but company commanders, for example, even if they had to be shadowed by another officer in view of public commitments. In the 19th century, Prince Albert took a great deal of interest in the Volunteer movement, and his son Edward VII was a helpful supporter of the infant Territorial Force. It would be encouraging if one of their descendants could be a Territorial long enough to earn a bounty or two.

Internally there is much that can be improved. If, as a service, the TA is interested in fairness, should we take a look at the medal system? Officers with the TD, and before it the VD, put these initials after their names; why cannot the regulations give the other ranks the same privilege? Each is a volunteer, each has completed 12 years of satisfactory service and each has had this recognised with a medal. But there the equality ends. It would be hard to justify this divisive practice to another nation.

In his memoirs, Churchill related the story of the Whitehall cleaning lady who found in the street some top secret plans relating to the area of Allied operations. She handed them to the security authorities and her action came to Churchill's notice. In view of the lives that she might have saved by her action he recommended that she should be rewarded with a CBE, but the high priests of the system hit back with compelling reasons why she should not be given so senior an award, and he remained uncertain about whether she was ever honoured at all. Admittedly, he had a lot on his mind at that time and could not engage in a struggle against Whitehall incumbents, though if Churchill could not alter the system there was little prospect of anyone else doing so. But that was 50 years ago; today we live in a fairer, more questioning world. It was not until after the First World War that women were allowed to vote. It was not until well after the Second World and the Korean wars that people aged 18, old enough to be conscripted and to die in their country's uniform, were considered mature enough to vote. It was not until 1871 that purchase of commissions in the cavalry and infantry was abolished. Times have changed to give a fairer country – but we still live in a political system undemocratic enough to countenance membership of one of the legislative chambers to be inherited.

On the subject of our society, could the Army's public relations department stamp sharply on any official publicity material that eulogises Territorials as 'citizen soldiers'? This implies that regular troops are somehow not citizens. One for the chaplains and incumbents of regimental churches: can you campaign for the removal of the ponderous 'officers, noncommissioned officers and men of the regiment' so often seen on memorials? What is wrong with the simple 'members of the regiment'? A lot of churches, in the author's view, could benefit by the dictum above the entrance to the original Toc H club in Poperinghe: 'Abandon rank all ye who enter here'.

At present, broken service does not count towards a Territorial Efficiency Medal (TEM). This is a pity because it means that somebody who leaves after, say, 10 years cannot count this service towards his TEM if he should rejoin. Quite a lot of good Territorials leave, perhaps on marriage or with the arrival of a child, or perhaps for career reasons. In the meantime, most of the soldier's contemporary comrades have gone on to higher rank. It would be an encouragement if that rejoined man could hope for a medal within a reasonable time so that he can demonstrate to younger soldiers his seniority of service. This is a reform that would cost nothing and is in the author's opinion long overdue. It is churlish to refuse to credit a man with his previous service.

A long overdue reform was announced in 1993 by Mr John Major, the Prime Minister, when he declared that bravery and merit awards would no longer be made according to rank. At the time of writing there has been no tangible *sign* of the ending of the unattractive dichotomy by which the major's DSO is the sergeant's DCM and the captain's MC is the corporal's MM. But in the Birthday Honours of 1993 it became apparent that the BEM has been abolished and the number of people being made MBEs has been increased. So far the change has only made matters worse: existing MBEs feel affronted that the authorities have devalued their grade in the Order of the British Empire and existing holders of the BEM feel insulted that their medal is no longer being awarded, that it has somehow slipped off the roll of honour. There is nothing second class about the BEM, as many brave or meritorious deeds testify; the second-class element lay in the way in which it was bestowed. Instead of an invitation to Buckingham Palace to have it presented by the Queen it was pinned on by a lord lieutenant, general or similar worthy. This is yet another piece of wrongfootedness by the government. The BEM should return, should be available to officers and should be presented by Her Majesty Nevertheless, the news that rank should no longer govern the choice of bravery awards is welcome. Future generations of servicefolk, and indeed anyone who is interested in fair play, should be grateful to Mr Major for his reform.

Should the Army look at the question of rewarding long-serving Territorials with a pension? Contributions could be deducted from pay drafts. The United States Army National Guardsmen look askance at Territorials who say they will not receive a pension after, say, 20 or 25 years of commitment to serve the nation in battle overseas. Should we follow further along the lines of the National Guard and the PXs (post exchanges) and allow Territorials, the part-time section of the One Army that we hear so much about, to make more use of regular Army facilities? Why not give off-duty Territorials access to NAAFI shops and clubs?

Professionally, what sort of material support will the Territorial of the year 2000 be given? To be sure, the Ministry of Defence has kept its promise of the mid-1960s. Today the TA not only has better equipment than ever before but receives the same equipment as the regular Army. As far as the equipment of the future is concerned, electronics will be ubiquitous: minicomputers will be doing undreamt of tasks for the soldier, personal radios will have vast ranges. Radio-controlled aircraft will be in extensive use for observation, jamming, screening and as weapons delivery systems. The emerging science of artificial intelligence will be exploited. Robotics will have altered many aspects of the dangers to a soldier's life; it can hardly be hoped that robots will do the fighting but they could be useful for marking a path through a minefield.

Looking further ahead, what will it be like at the TA's centenary? It could be a safer world. Working techniques may be found to neutralise nuclear or germ-loaded bombs before they can explode. This must be the obvious way ahead, a network of sentinels of the sky, and this is where investment should not be begrudged. After all the answer to that double-edged weapon poison gas in the First World War was the respirator and the answer to the threat of poison gas in the Second World War was that troops and civilians were prepared for and protected from its effects as never before; consequently it was not used. Against bullets and shrapnel body armour of astonishing lightness and flexibility may be available. In military medicine seven-leagued strides will have been made. Poison gas was used in the Iraq–Iran War; dictators boast about their ability to produce and deploy it against enemies. Not every country has leaders as decent as those of Britain who rejected as dishonourable the suggestion in the Crimean War that the Russians holding out in Sebastopol should be overcome by poisonous sulphurous fumes. Perhaps we can develop ointments to smear on the body and protect it from harm: the phosphorus that sinks into the flesh, the deadly agents that enter the human system will all attack in vain. Plastic replacement hearts and other organs might become routine items in hospital stores.

No matter what great strides may be made in the technology of future war, and almost nothing is impossible, the question of cost must govern supply. Will it be possible to go on having common equipment between the regular and reserve armies? If not, what is the future role of the TA to be? As the Army continues to shrink, so does the *importance* of having well trained reserve forces increase. This simple fact virtually answers the question we have asked. But it means that new equipment, new tactical doctrine and new training must all take account of the fact that they must fall within the compass of the part-time Volunteer. For a part-time army that does not match its regular counterpart in performance and capabilities will be of little use. As war becomes more intense, as the power of modern weapons continues to increase, so must much of the research into new equipment seek to make the soldier's life on the battlefield easier, not more complex. This fundamental need is as real for the regular Army as the TA. The problems of adequate training in an urbanised society are as great for both. Much more will have to be done by simulation in training and thought needs to be given to the provision of simulation that can be shared – for the cost will be prodigious. These are the problems we should be tackling together today so that all know where they are heading in a common endeavour.

Whatever the world of the future brings, the Territorial will have to cope with more technical items of kit than did his predecessor in the great volunteering rush of 1859. But apart from requiring technical skills let us hope that Britain's leaders will perceive in the TA the same qualities as were discerned by that enthusiastic part-time soldier Thomas Hughes, novelist, lawyer, judge, hymnwriter, parliamentarian, and educationalist, who saw the Volunteer movement as 'the saviour of the home, the spreader of freedom and the solvent of class antagonisms'.

Appendix 1

MILITARY MILESTONES

1181	Assize of Arms
1285	Statute of Winchester confirms ancient obligation of free Englishmen to bear arms in defence of homeland.
1537	Henry VIII grants charter to Fraternite or Guylde of Saint George (HAC's ancestor and oldest of all documented TA units).
1577	Train band ancestor of Royal Monmouthshire Royal Engineers(Militia) founded; still the most senior TA unit in order of precedence and in unbroken service to Crown.
1588	Elizabeth I exhorts the militia at Tilbury in face of the threat from the Armada.
1663	Scotch Estates statute provides for Militia of 20,000 foot and 2,000 cavalry from Scotland.
1782	First Volunteer Statute.
1794	Volunteer associations regulated nationally; 28 true Yeomanry units formed.
1797	First battle honour for Yeomanry, 'Fishguard'; Provisional Cavalry Act and Militia Act but cavalry statute not needed as 65 Yeomanry regiments have by now been formed; Militia statute causes riots in Scotland.
1798	Armed associations formed for local defence.
1801	Peace of Amiens; preliminary articles signed.
1802	Definitive treaty signed.
1803	War restarts; three statutes passed to raise part-time forces; many Volunteer units founded, including Duke of Cumberland's Sharpshooters; Lloyd's Patriotic Fund opens to help wounded and dependants, later it encourages volunteers.
1804	Volunteers total 479,000.
1808	Local Militia Acts.
1811	Duke of York, C-in-C, describes Militia as 'never failing resource on every occasion of difficulty or danger'.
1815	Waterloo starts long era of peace; decline of part-time forces.

1828 Yeomanry partially disbanded and remodelled.
1837 Death of William IV.
1838 Further cuts in Yeomanry.
1846 Rail company tries to build station at Artillery Ground.
1848 Fears of invasion as Wellington privately discloses paucity of defences.
1852 Militia returns as voluntary force in response to threatened invasion.
1854 Crimean War; many Militiamen volunteer for overseas.
1856 War ends; Queen Victoria tells Militia of her appreciation of its 'conduct, zeal and spirit' on service in Britain, Ireland or Mediterranean; VC instituted, some awards retrospective.
1858 Militia embodied to replace regulars sent to India following mutiny.
1859 Renewed fear of French invasion leads to formation of Volunteer rifle corps throughout country in wave of civilian enthusiasm for defending Britain.
1860 Queen reviews 19,000 Volunteers in Hyde Park; jurisdiction of HAC passes from Home Office to War Office which tries to delete 'Honourable'.
1863 Volunteer Act sets higher standards: units to be inspected annually, trained men must attend minimum of nine drills in year; corps serving in formation with others must be commanded by general or field officer of regular Army.
1867 Militia Reserve formed as reserve for regular Army.
1870 Yeomanry regiments limited to eight troops; Westley–Richards carbines issued to them.
1871 Crown takes back control of auxiliary forces from lord lieutenants.
1871–81 Cardwell reforms reorganise the Army; seat of control moves from Horse Guards to Pall Mall; purchase of cavalry and infantry commisions abolished, flogging in peacetime abolished; 1881 last flogging and this year sees completion of localisation by introducing territorialisation of regiments and linked battalion system.
1873 Part-time forces move nearer to regulars with attachment to brigades.
1881 Militia becomes third and fourth battalions of regular regiments under Cardwell; Volunteers gradually become regiments' Volunteer battalions and most relinquish individuality of uniform to conform with parent regiment.
1882 First Volunteer troops serve in overseas theatre, individuals of Post Office Rifles in Egypt and Sudan win Volunteers' first battle honour, 'Egypt, 1882'.

1883 Lanarkshire Volunteer founds Boys' Brigade on military lines.
1885 Yeomanry embodied for local service because of regular Army commitments in Egypt.
1886 First Volunteer medical unit, Volunteer Medical Staff Corps, formed at Maidstone.
1887 Victoria's golden jubilee, part-time troops in royal review at Aldershot.
1888 Defence Act empowers War Office to embody Yeomanry for service anywhere in Britain.
1892 Volunteer Long Service Decoration (VD) instituted for officers.
1894 Volunteer Long Service Medal instituted for other ranks.
1895 Army reorganisation: Duke of Cambridge resigns after 39 years as C-in-C; succeeded by Lord Wolseley, with curtailed powers.
1896 Volunteer Engineers, Fortress and Railway Force, RE, become RE(Volunteers); Martini–Metford carbines issued to Yeomanry.
1897 Princess Christian's Army Nursing Service Reservists formed; troops celebrate Victoria's diamond jubilee.
1899 Start of South African War; call for Volunteers.
1900 First big wave of Yeoman and Volunteers to serve in field; CIV and IY in South Africa.
1901 Death of Victoria; Edward VII presents Yeomanry and Volunteers with South African medals at London parade; 'Imperial' added to Yeomanry title; Militia Reserve abolished.
1902 War ends; 1,300 women nursing officers have served overseas; WO sets new training commitment for Volunteer Force: six days' camp and more drill nights, but regulation has opposite effect to that intended and numbers fall.
1903 Reserve for Militia formed (old Militia Reserve had been reserve for regular Army).
1904 Royal Commission on Militia and Volunteers reports critically on both forces; War Office (reconstitution) Committee reports critically on administration; strength of Volunteers 250,226, and of Militia 93,873; office of C-in-C of Army abolished, and Empire's most famous soldier loses his job; C-in-C, WO Council and Army Board to be replaced by Army Council.
1906 General Staff increased to 72 members; War Office moves from Pall Mall to Whitehall; conference of Militia COs makes clear they do not want to be in TF.
1907 TFAs founded on New Year's Eve; FANY founded earlier in year.
1908 TF formed (of Yeomanry and Volunteers); Militia converted to Special Reserve and by end of year it has 67,740 reservists; TF Nursing Service formed.

1909 Army enters new age as Automobile Association and motor enthusiasts boost automobilism by transporting battalion from Crystal Palace to Hastings on St Patrick's Day; in May cars transport troops from Huddersfield to Meltham in mobilisation manoevres; VADs to supplement TF medical units; General Staff becomes Imperial General Staff; on 19 June the Monarch presents colours to qualified TF battalions.

1910 Death of Edward VII; VADs enlarged to include members from Scotland and St John Ambulance Brigade enabling personnel to serve as ambulance nursing auxiliaries.

1911 George V's coronation, Territorials on parade.

1912 VADs serve in Balkans fighting.

1914 Embodiment and baptism of fire for TF; 7th Bn Middlesex Regiment first to volunteer to go overseas as complete unit, followed immediately by four Royal Fusiliers battalions; they form garrisons in the colonies to relieve regulars; VADs in Belgium and Brittany by August and some captured in Brussels; FANYs staff 200-bed *Hôpital* Lamarck for Belgian troops in September; in September London Scottish first TF battalion to land in France; on 5 October Queen's Own Oxfordshire Hussars first Territorials to engage enemy; on 31 October London Scottish first Territorials to fight major battle (sustaining 640 casualties); Germans using irritant gas; first bar to any VC is earned by Territorial, Lieutenant Col Arthur Martin-Leake, VC, 5th Field Ambulance, RAMC.

1915 Germans use poison gas.

1916 British Army's most devastating day, 1 July on Somme, 57,470 casualties, nearly 20,000 fatal; 15 September, first tanks in action; conscription introduced.

1917 WAAC formed; second double VC is Territorial Captain Noel Chavasse, VC, MC, RAMC.

1918 Armistice and victory at cost of 129,806 Territorials' lives; WAAC becomes Queen Mary's Auxiliary Army Corps.

1919 Territorials, QMAACs, VADs and FANYs march with regulars in victory parade; treaty of Versailles signed.

1920 TF reconstituted as TA; bounty £5 for trained man, £4 for recruit; dramatic change for Yeomanry, half of whose 53 regiments convert to RA; only 14 retain cavalry role and although they had been mounted infantry since 1901, are re-equipped with swords; one regiment goes to signals and one to infantry; Cenotaph in Whitehall unveiled, Unknown Warrior buried in Westminster Abbey.

1921 QMAAC disbanded; Defence Force set up (for a few months) to counter threat of mine and rail strike coincidentally with unrest in Ireland while many Army units are occupying former enemy territory.

1923 Tank Corps becomes Royal.

1924 Supplementary Reserve formed.

1926 TA embodied for 90 days, to help cope with general strike; FANYs drive cars and lorries for Army and police.

1927 Armoured formation adumbrates tactics of future when Experimental Mechanised Force, about brigade strong, of medium and light tanks, armoured cars and infantry in carriers, using air support, in Salisbury Plain exercise show superiority over complete infantry division plus cavalry brigade supplied by horse waggons; German military observers note how traditional force was outmanoeuvred; Army halts recruiting for AA units in TA to save money; FANY recognised officially by WO and appears in *Army List*.

1928 Fifteen nations, including Germany, sign Kellogg–Briand Pact outlawing war; ultimately 50 others sign.

1930 Army Council designates this Territorial Year.

1931 First use of wireless to command large formation of tanks in Salisbury Plain demonstration.

1932 TA camps cancelled as economy, but FANY pursuing independent path, attend camp and take part in regular Army exercise.

1934 Army gets first tank brigade – of four RTC battalions.

1935 Mechanisation of Army starts, decade after CIGS announces intention to begin it, with emphasis on tanks; AA pilot scheme, Southern Division, formed from London TA infantry battalions.

1936 Death of George V; Army Estimates provide only £2m for mechanisation, mainly on lorries for infantry.

1937 AA defences strengthened, largely through TA; six TA infantry battalions convert to RTC as part of expansion of tank arm; Northern Ireland gets its first TA units, heavy battery of artillery and fortress company of engineers; Territorials at coronation of George VI; FANY title changes to Women's Transport Service (FANY).

1938 ATS formed; TA anti-aircraft units embodied and stand by to protect Britain in crisis; Army gets its first Mobile Division, located in Egypt; first TA unit to mount guard at Buckingham Palace, HAC.

1939 Militia returns as six-month compulsory full-time conscription for men, but before first intake is due to be released force is subsumed into Army; Couverture operation means Territorials spend month, unit by unit to man AA gunsites from end of May; RAC formed; TA embodied just before declaration of war, but AA units at their guns 10 days earlier; Armed Forces Act makes all auxiliary forces full-time and part of regular forces; home defence battalions of regiments and Auxiliary Military Pioneer Corps formed for older men.

1940 FANY-ATS unit formed but some remain 'Free FANYs'; LDV formed, name later being changed to Home Guard; AA sites in intense action in Battle of Britain and Blitz; AA gunners shoot down 357 enemy aircraft in Battle of Britain.

1941 ATS given full military status as part of armed forces; its members already doing more than 100 different types of job compared with five at start of war; Army's last cavalry engagement – in Syrian campaign and Yeomanry units take part.

1942 Conscription of women into services; last horsed Yeomanry regiment, Yorkshire Dragoons, parts with mounts.

1943 ATS strength 200,000; Allies invade Europe via Pantellaria, Sicily and Italy.

1944 Second European front opens; Territorials in Britain in action against V-1 flying bomb.

1945 Britain's armed forces and auxiliaries total 5,090,000; war is won; but postwar internal security problems start immediately in South-East Asia and Palestine; last TA unit up to present day to be on operations, 2/7th Middlesex, in anti-terrorist patrols in Judaea and peace-keeping at Giv'at Hayyim; older Territorials go home.

1946 Demobilisation of TA completed.

1947 Recruiting for reconstituted TA; Britain's armed forces and auxiliaries down to 1,292,000.

1948 Royal review of TA in Hyde Park.

1949 ATS becomes WRAC; QAIMNS becomes QARANC.

1950 Korean War starts; first large-scale use of helicopters in battle; national service Territorials report to drill halls for 3½ years part-time service.

1951 Home Guard reconstituted.

1952 Death of George VI; TA strength 198,500 at calendar year's end.

1953 Korea ceasefire; prisoners return; many livery companies revive tradition of supporting part-time soldiers; TA at coronation.

1954 Korean War formally ends.

1955 AA Command disbanded.

1956 TA reorganisation; RAC amalgamations; £20 bounty offered for extra commitment.

1958 TA's golden jubilee; national parades in Belfast, London and Edinburgh; many local parades.

1959 First TA unit guards Tower of London, 8th Bn Royal Fusiliers.
1961 National service conscription ends on New Year's Day; conscripts who have completed full-time service are transferred to Z reserve instead of 3½ years in TA.
1962 TA Emergency Reserve founded
1963–64 Last national servicemen demobilised, some having had release delayed because of Army commitments.
1964 TA's strength 116,500 at calendar year's end.
1965 Selective call-out of TAER to Aden mainly as composite company of Royal Sussex but individuals reinforce corps; some reservists fall.
1966 RE take over airfield damage repair role from RAF.
1967 TA and AER replaced by T&AVR; TA&VRAs cut to 14; Territorials and AE Reservists cut by nearly two thirds; many battalions reduced to companies, others stay as cadres; new type of TD and TEM replace awards for TA and AER.
1968 First calendar year since start of Second World War that army has not suffered casualty on active service; T&AVR's strength 54,800 at end of its first year.
1969 Rise in Northern Ireland violence.
1970 T&AVR strength drops to 47,589 by third year.
1971 Expansion of T&AVR establishment; four new Yeomanry regiments, Wessex, Mercian, Queen's Own and Duke of Lancaster's Own among new units founded or reformed.
1975 Recruiting in Northumberland, 6th Bn RRF formed; countrywide Ex Inside Right tests mobilisation procedures.
1978 Shapland committee sits; Ex Griffins Galore tests TA units in Germany.
1980 Ex Crusader in Germany tests Territorials.
1981 Expansion of T&AVR establishment from 70,000 to 86,000 eventually; average number of permitted training days raised from 38 to 42; women command mixed units, signals being followed by general hospital.
1982 T&AVR becomes TA; South Atlantic War, Falklands Defence Force becoming last colonial part-time troops up to present day to be deployed operationally; HSF pilot scheme starts.
1983 TA's 75th birthday.
1984 Ex Lionheart in Germany tests Territorials. TA airfield damage repair units formed.
1985 Countrywide Ex Brave Defender tests Territorials in home base.
1986 Expansion of TA announced: aim is 90,000 members by 1992; National Employers Liaison Committee formed with £2m annual

budget for five years to persuade employers TA training can help civilian workforce; TA gets first independent helicopter unit, 666th Squadron, AAC (V).

1987 Ex Keystone tests TA units in Germany.

1988 8th Queen's Fusiliers formed 16 May: A and B companies retain Queen's cap badge, C (City of London) Company retains Fusilier cap badge, and HQ Company is mixed: the CO will be found from each regiment in alternate postings; 101st (London) Engineer Regiment (Explosive Ordnance Disposal) (V) formed 1 June; unit provides first TA WRAC member to qualify as bomb disposal officer.

1989 Bounty is £445.

1990 TA is 75,425 strong against establishment of 90,344; *Options for Change* announced; bounty is £600; Alyson Keane, WRAC (V), of 2nd Yorkshire Volunteers, becomes first servicewoman to qualify as helicopter rigger marshaller; in November 34 nations sign in Paris biggest arms reduction treaty in history; at end of month, Army asks selected Territorials, mainly medicals, to volunteer for Gulf force during Kuwait invasion crisis; other corps invited to volunteer for other theatres to release regulars.

1991 Bounty is £775; by start of Gulf war more than 900 Territorials, men and women, mainly medicals are accepted for active service after volunteering for short engagements.

1992 Adjutant General's Corps formed; Princess of Wales's Royal Regiment (Queen's and Royal Hampshires) formed; Royal Irish Regiment formed; WRAC disbanded; HSF disbanded.

1993 Royal Logistic Corps formed; London Regiment reborn; TA strength drops to 67,812 (1 March) against establishment of 68,195.

1994 TA establishment 65,000.

1995–96 TA establishment scheduled to be 63,500.

Appendix 2

TA GUNNER REGIMENTS AT 1 SEPTEMBER 1939

At general embodiment of the TA on 1 September 1939, the Territorial artillery arm consisted of the regiments shown below. It will be remembered that Territorials of AA Command had already been embodied and were at their posts to defend the country.

Royal Horse Artillery

11	HAC and City of London Yeo	106	Lancashire Yeo
12	HAC	149	Lancashire Yeo
104	Essex Yeo	107	South Notts Hussars Yeo
147	Essex Yeo	150	South Notts Hussars Yeo

Field Artillery

51	Westmorland and Cumberland	61	North Midland
109	Westmorland and Cumberland	116	North Midland
52	Manchester	64	7th London
110	Manchester	117	7th London
53	Bolton	65	8th London
111	Bolton	118	8th London
55	Wessex	67	South Midland
112	Wessex	119	South Midland
57	Home Counties	68	South Midland
113	Home Counties	120	South Midland
58	Sussex	69	West Riding
114	Sussex	121	West Riding
60	North Midland	70	West Riding
115	North Midland	122	West Riding

71 West Riding
123 West Riding

72 Northumbrian
124 Northumbrian

74 Northumbrian
125 Northumbrian

75 Highland
126 Highland

76 Highland
127 Highland

77 Highland
128 Highland

78 Lowland
129 Lowland

79 Lowland
130 Lowland

80 Lowland City of Glasgow
131 Lowland City of Glasgow

81 Welsh
132 Welsh

83 Welsh
133 Welsh

85 East Anglian
134 East Anglian

86 East Anglian–Herts Yeo
135 East Anglian–Herts Yeo

87 1st West Lancs
136 1st West Lancs

88 2nd West Lancs
137 2nd West Lancs

90 City of London
138 City of London

91 4th London
139 4th London

92 5th London
140 5th London

94 QO Dorset Yeo
141 QO Dorset Yeo

96 Royal Devon Yeo
142 Royal Devon Yeo

97 Kent Yeo
143 Kent Yeo

98 Surrey & Sussex Yeo
144 Surrey & Sussex Yeo

99 Bucks and Berks Yeo
145 Berks Yeo

102 Pemb & Cardiganshire
146 Pemb & Cardiganshire

105 Bedfordshire Yeo
148 Bedfordshire Yeo

Medium Artillery

51 Midland
63 Midland

53 London
64 London

56 Highland
65 Highland

57 Lowland
66 Lowland

58 Suffolk
67 Suffolk

59 4th West Lancs
68 4th West Lancs

61 Carnarvon & Denbigh Yeo
69 Carnarvon & Denbigh Yeo

Heavy AA

8 Belfast
9 Londonderry
51 London
52 London
53 City of London
54 City of London
55 Kent
56 Cornwall
57 Wessex
58 Kent
59 The Essex Regiment
60 City of London
61 Middlesex
62 Northumbrian
63 Northumbrian
64 Northumbrian
65 Manchester
66 The Leeds Rifles (W Yorks Regiment)
67 York and Lancaster
68 North Midland
69 The Royal Warwickshire Regiment
70 3rd West Lancashire
71 Forth
72 Hampshire
73 Untitled
74 City of Glasgow
75 (Home Counties) (Cinque Ports)
76 Gloucestershire
77 Welsh
78 1st East Anglian
79 Herts Yeo
80 Berkshire
81 Untitled
82 Essex
83 Blythwood
84 Middlesex, London Transport
85 Tees
86 HAC
87
88
89
90
91
93
94
95
96
97 The London Scottish
98
99
100
101
102

Light AA

11 City of London
12 Finsbury Rifles
13
14 W Lothian R Scots
15 Isle of Man
17
18
19
20
23
24
25
26
27
28
29
30
31
36
51 Devon

52 East Lancs
53 KOYLI
54 Argyll & SH
55 Devon
56 East Lancs
57 KOYLI
58 Argyll & SH

Searchlight

56 Cameronians
57 Glasgow
59 Warwickshire
61 S Lancs Regt
62 The Loyals
70 Sussex
71 East Lancs
72 Middlesex
75 Middlesex

Anti-tank

51 West Highland
61 West Highland

52 (6th London)

53 Worcestershire Yeomanry
63 Worcs & Oxon Yeo

54 QO Royal Glasgow Yeo
64 QO Royal Glasgow Yeo

55 Suffolk & Norfolk Yeo
65 Suffolk & Norfolk Yeo

56 King's Own
66 King's Own

57 East Surrey
67 East Surrey

58 Duke of Wellington's
68 Duke of Wellington's

59 D of Connaught's – Hants
69 D of Connaught's – Hants

60 Royal Welch Fusiliers
70 Royal Welch Fusiliers

From March 1941 the Northumberland Hussars became 102 Regt Northumberland Hussars.

From November 1941 the following anti-tank regiments were formed:
86 Devonshire Regiment (from 5th Devons)
87 Devonshire Regiment (from 7th Devons)
88 Manchester Regiment (from 2/9th Manchesters)
90 King's Own Royal Regiment (from 9th KORR)
91 Argyll & Sutherland Highlanders (from 5th A&SH)
92 Gordon Highlanders (from 4th Gordons)
93 Argyll & Sutherland Highlanders (from 6th A&SH)
100 Gordon Highlanders (from 8th Gordons)

Heavy Artillery

(these became coast regiments in 1940):

Fife became:	504 Coast Regt and 502 Coast Regt
Tynemouth:	509 Tynemouth, 510 Tynemouth and 616 Tynemouth
Hampshire:	527 Hampshire, 528 Hampshire and 529 Hampshire
Devon:	566 Devon, 567 Devon and 568 Devon
Cornwall:	530 Cornwall
Kent & Sussex:	519 Kent & Sussex, 520 K & S and 521 K&S
Forth:	503 Forth, 505 Forth and 506 Forth
Thames & Medway:	516 T&M, 517 T&M and 518 T&M
Clyde:	538 Clyde
Suffolk:	514 Suffolk and 515 Suffolk
Lancashire & Cheshire:	524 Lancashire & Cheshire
Dorsetshire:	522 Dorsetshire
Glamorgan:	531 Glamorgan
East Riding:	512 East Riding and 513 East Riding
Pembroke:	532 Pembroke
Durham:	511 Durham and 526 Durham
The Princess Beatrice's (Isle of Wight) Rifles:	530 The Princess Beatrice's (Isle of Wight) Rifles
188 (Antrim) Heavy Battery:	525 Antrim (from March 1940)
Orkney:	533 Orkney, 534 Orkney and 535 Orkney

References and Notes

Chapter 1

1 James Boswell, *The Life of Samuel Johnson,LL.D.*, p 265, 1778.
2 In an order to his troops signed at Headquarters, Aix-la-Chapelle, 19 August 1914.
3 Report of the Norfolk commission (1904) (*vide* Bibliography).
4 *Ibid.*
5 *Ibid.*
6 Report of the Esher committee (1904) (*vide* Bibliography).
7 Archie Hamilton, Minister of State for the Armed Forces, in a statement to the House of Commons on 21 February 1991.
8 Campbell-Bannerman papers, British Museum; additional MS 41218, C-B to Sir Arthur Haliburton 27 February 1906; cited by W S Hamer, *The British Army Civil-Military Relations 1885–1905*. (Oxford (1970)).

Chapter 2

1 Francis Grose, *Military Antiquities Respecting a History of the English Army from the Conquest to the Present Day*, Vols I and II. (London (1786–88)).
2 This type of bow is in the National Army Museum, Chelsea; the exhibit, recovered from the Mary Rose, is 73in long and requires a pressure of 80lb to pull the string back 36in.
3 Colonel I B Gailey, Colonel W F Gillespie and Lieutenant Colonel J Hassett, *An Account of the Territorials in Northern Ireland 1947–1978*. (TA&VRA for Northern Ireland, Belfast (1979)).
4 Report of the Norfolk commission (1904) (*vide* Bibliography).
5 *Ibid.*
6 *Ibid.*
7 *Ibid.*
8 Colonel G J Hay, *An Epitomised History of the Militia (The Constitutional Force)*. (United Service Gazette, London (1905)).

Chapter 3

1. John Stow, *A Survey of London and Westminster* (1598).
2. Major G Goold Walker, *The Honourable Artillery Company 1537–1947*, p 41 (Gale & Polden, Aldershot (1954)).
3. William Skinner, *The Society of Trained Bands of Edinburgh*. (Pillans & Wilson, Edinburgh (1889)).
4. A D Galloway, *The Ward of Broad Street*, Lord Mayor's Show programme, (City of London Corporation (1988)).
5. Archives of the Working Men's College Corps.
6. Ditto
7. Archives of the Queen's Westminsters

Chapter 4

1. *The Queen's Own Royal Glasgow Yeomanry, 1848–1948*. (Private.)
2. Quoted by Christopher Hibbert, *The English: A Social History 1066–1945*, p 494. (Guild, London 1987)).
3. R G Gammage, *The History of the Chartist Movement* (1894).
4. Karl B Spurgin, *On Active Service with the Northumberland and Durham Yeomen, under Lord Methuen (South Africa, 1900–1901)*. (Walter Scott, Newcastle upon Tyne (1902)).
5. Lieutenant Colonel Sir Richard Verdin, *The Cheshire (Earl of Chester's) Yeomanry*. (Private (1971)).

Chapter 5

1. L S Amery, *The Problem of the Army*. (Edward Arnold, London (1903)).
2. AO 257 of 1 November 1906.
3. WO letter of 25 March 1931 68/Gen/5455/AG4 Medals.
4. Dame Irene Ward MP, *FANY Invicta*. (Hutchinson, London (1955)).

Chapter 6

1. *Military Operations France and Belgium*, Vol I, p 10.
2. Major W E Grey, *The 2nd City of London Regiment (Royal Fusiliers) in the Great War (1914–19)*. (Regimental, London (1929)).
3. Lord Hankey [the former cabinet secretary], *The Supreme Command, 1914–1918*, pp 138–9. (London (1961)).
4. Such volunteers were allowed to wear a white metal brooch over the right breast pocket of their uniform.

5 The film star Ronald Colman was among the wounded (*vide* chapter Famous Part-Timers).
6 Experienced by the author's grandmother and members of her family.
7 Major General Sir Frederick Maurice, Introduction to *The History of the London Rifle Brigade 1859–1919*. (Constable, London (1921)).
8 Lieutenant General Sir William Marshall, *Memories of Four Fronts*, pp 33–4. (Benn, London (1929)).
9 Percy Hurd, *London's Fighting Territorials*, Vol II. (Newnes London (1916)).
10 *Ibid.*
11 *The History of the London Rifle Brigade, op cit*, p 99.
12 Grey, *op cit*, p 69 (citing a letter originally published in *Draper's Record*).
13 *Ibid*, p 70.
14 Frederick P Gibbon, *The 42nd (East Lancashire) Division 1914–1918*, p 62. (Country Life, London (1920)).
15 *Ibid.*
16 *Ibid.*
17 H A Adderley, *The Warwickshire Yeomanry in the Great War*. (Regimental, Warwick (1922)).

Chapter 7

1 Sir Douglas Haig's Dispatches
2 General [Erich] Ludendorff, *My War Memories* Vol I. (Hutchinson London (1919)).
3 The author's father.
4 Major C H Dudley Ward, *The 56th Division*.
5 *Ibid.*
6 The author's father.
7 Sir Basil Liddell Hart, *The Tanks*. (Cassell, London (1959)).
8 David Lloyd George, *War Memoirs* (1936).

Chapter 8

1 Ludendorff's figure, *op cit*, Vol II p 602.
2 Ludendorff, *op cit*, Vol II, p 679.

Chapter 9

1 Salmond cited by General Sir Frederick Pile, *Ack-Ack*, p 57. (Harrap, London (1949)).
2 Verdin, *op cit*.

[3] In a statement to the House of Commons on 10 November 1932.
[4] In a letter dated 22 January 1937 sent by Sir Stenson Cooke to all AA staff.
[5] In conversation with the author.
[6] Pile, *op cit*, p 81.
[7] Quoted by P M Huggett, The Girls in Green and Grey, 75th anniversary issue *The Territorial Army Magazine*, 53(4). Council of TA&VRAs, London (1983)).
[8] In conversation with the author.
[9] Recalled by Major Herbert Sawyer, late the Rough Riders, to the author.
[10] R Blankley, quoted by George Forty, *A Pictorial History of the Royal Tank Regiment*, p 118. (Spellmount, Speldhurst (1989)).
[11] Recalled by Captain Peter Erwood to the author.
[12] *Ditto,* comment.
[13] Quoted by Pile *op cit*, p 91.
[14] *Ibid* p 92.

Chapter 10

[1] Told by him to the author.
[2] Ditto.
[3] Ditto.
[4] Told by her to the author.
[5] Canon Eric Gethyn-Jones, *A Territorial Army Chaplain in Peace and War*, p 8. (Gooday, East Wittering (1988)).
[6] Told by him to the author.
[7] Ditto.
[8] Ditto.
[9] Verdin, *op cit*, p 205.
[10] Huggett, *op cit*.
[11] Kenneth Oliver, *Chaplain at War*, (Angel Press, Chichester (1989)).
[12] Told by him to the author.
[13] Hugh Gunning, *Borderers in Battle*, p 48.(Private (1949)).
[14] Major L F Ellis, *The War in France and Flanders 1939–40*, p 326, cited by Brigadier Peter Young, *The British Army.* (Kimber, London (1967)).
[15] Pile *op cit*.
[16] *Ibid.*
[17] In conversation with the author.

Chapter 11

[1] Pile, *op cit*, p 227.
[2] *Ibid*, p 228.

[3] Lindsay, *op cit*.
[4] Northcote Parkinson, *Always a Fusilier*, p 110. (Sampson Low, London (1949)).

Chapter 12

[1] Pile, *op cit*.
[2] *Ibid*.
[3] Described by him to the author.
[4] Gethyn-Jones, *op cit*, p 178.
[5] Told by him to the author.

Chapter 13

[1] The author was in the group.
[2] Dates are from the statutes of the Most Excellent Order of the British Empire for creating additional members.
[3] (Ed) P K Kemp, *The Middlesex Regiment(DCO)*, pp 243–5. (Gale, Aldershot (1956)).

Chapter 14

[1] All these quotations were made at a meeting of the officers' mess of Headquarters 47 Infantry Brigade at the Duke of York's Headquarters, Chelsea, and noted by the author at the time.

Select Bibliography

Official Publications

Report of the Royal Commissioners Appointed to Enquire into the Civil and Professional Administration of the Naval and Military Departments and the Relation of those Departments to Each Other and to the Treasury. Cd 5979 (1890) (the Hartington commission)

Report of His Majesty's Commissioners Appointed to Inquire into the Military Preparations, and Other Matters Connected with the War in South Africa. Cd 1789 (1904) (the Elgin commission)

Report of the Royal Commission on the Militia and Volunteers. Cd 2061 (1904) (the Norfolk commission)

Report of the War Office (Reconstitution) Committee, Pt i. Cd 1932 (1904), *Pt ii,* Cd 1968 (1904), *Pt iii,* Cd 2002 (1904) (the Esher committee)

Militia Act, 1757

Militia Act, 1797

Volunteer Act, 1863

Territorial and Reserve Forces Act, 1907

Territorial and Militia Act, 1921

Territorial Army Regulations, HMSO (various years)

The New Annual Army List (Hart's) (various years)

The Army List (various years)

Official handbooks of all the TA&VRAs

General

L S Amery, *The Problem of the Army.* (Edward Arnold, London (1903)) (First published that year under the same title as an anonymous series of articles in *The Times*)

Harold Baker, *The Territorial Force.* (Murray, London (1909))

Major R Money Barnes, *The Soldiers of London.* (Seeley, London (1963))

Major Peter Bateman, *The 8th Queen's Fusiliers.* (Private (1988))

Pat Beauchamp, *FANY Went to War.* (Routledge, London (1940))

Colonel John K Dunlop, *The Development of the British Army, 1899–1914.* (Methuen, London (1938) (accepted as Ph D thesis))

J K (Colonel John K) Dunlop, *The Territorial Army Today.* (Black, London (1939))

George Forty, *A Pictorial History of the Royal Tank Regiment.* (Spellmount, Spelhurst (1989))

Colonel I B Gailey, Colonel W F Gillespie and Lieutenant Colonel J Hassett, *An Account of the Territorials in Northern Ireland, 1947–78.* (TA&VRA for Northern Ireland, Belfast (1979))

Frederick P Gibbon, *The 42nd (East Lancashire) Division 1914–18.* (Country Life, London (1922))

The Register of the George Cross. (*This England*, Cheltenham (1988))

Michael Glover, *The Fight for the Channel Ports 1940.* (Leo Cooper, London 1985))

Major W E Grey, *The 2nd City of London Regiment (Royal Fusiliers) in the Great War (1914–19)*. (Regimental, London 1929))

Hugh Gunning, *Borderers in Battle.* (Private (1948))

W S Hamer, *The British Army Civil-Military Relations 1885–1905.* (Oxford (1970))

R E Handley, *The 1st Londons, 1939–45.* (Littledown, St Margaret's Bay, Dover (1986))

Captain Sir Basil Liddell Hart, *The Tanks*, Vols I and II. (Cassell, London (1959))

Colonel G J Hay, *An Epitomised History of the Militia (The Constitutional Force)*. (United Service Gazette, (London (1905))

History of the London Rifle Brigade, 1859–1919. (Constable, London (1921))

Percy Hurd, *The Fighting Territorials*, Vols I and II. (Newnes, London (1916))

(Ed) David Keir and Bryan Morgan, *Golden Milestone.* (Automobile Association, London (1955))

(Ed) P K Kemp, *The Middlesex Regiment (DCO)*. Gale, Aldershot (1956))

Canon Eric Gethyn-Jones, *A Territorial Army Padre in Peace and War.* (Gooday, East Wittering (1988))

T M Lindsay, *Sherwood Rangers.* (Burrup, Mathieson, London (1952))

General [Erich] Ludendorff, *My War Memories*, Vols I and II. (Hutchinson, London (1919))

Lieutenant General Sir William Marshall, *Memories of Four Fronts.* (Benn, London (1929))

Colonel A R Martin, *Historical Record of the London Regiment*. (Private, undated)

(Ed) Alan H Maude, *The History of the 47th (London) Division 1914–1919.* (Amalgamated Press, London (1922))

C Northcote Parkinson, *Always a Fusilier.* (Sampson Low, London (1949))

General Sir Frederick Pile, *Ack-Ack.* (Harrap, London (1949))
Records of the 24th Middlesex (formerly the 49th), the Post Office Volunteers, 1868–1896. (Private)
The Queen's Own Royal Glasgow Yeomanry 1848–1948. (Private)
Captain G A Raikes, *The History of the Honourable Artillery Company.* (London (1879))
Major G W Robertson, *The Rose and the Arrow.* (136th Field Regiment, RA OCA (1988))
B E Sargeaunt, *The Royal Monmouthshire Militia.* (RUSI, London, (1910))
Colonel E O Scaife, *Short History of the Royal Welch Fusiliers.* Gale & Polden, Aldershot (1940))
William Skinner, *The Society of Trained Bands of Edinburgh.* (H & J Pillans & Wilson, Edinburgh (1889))
Major D A D Smith, *A Brief History of 39th(City of London) Signal Regiment(Volunteers).* (Regimental (1975))
Karl B Spurgin. *On active Service with the Northumberland and Durham Yeomen, under Lord Methuen (South Africa, 1900–1901).* (Walter Scott, Newcastle upon Tyne (1902))
The Times Guide to the House of Commons. (*The Times*, London (various editions))
Sir Richard Verdin, *The Cheshire(Earl of Chester's) Yeomanry 1898–67.* (Private (1971))
The Register of the Victoria Cross. (This England, Cheltenham (1987)
(Ed) D Collett Wadge, *Women in Uniform.* (Sampson Low, London (1946))
Major G Goold Walker, *The Honourable Artillery Company, 1537–1947.* (Gale & Polden, Aldershot (1954))
Edgar Wallace. *Kitchener's Army and the Territorial Forces.* (Newnes, London (1916))
Dame Irene Ward, *FANY Invicta.* (Hutchinson, London (1955))
The Reverend R W Weir, *The History of the 3rd Battalion King's Own Scottish Borderers 1798–1907.* (Courier and Herald, Dumfries (1907))
Ray Westlake, *The Rifle Volunteers.* (Picton, Chippenham (1982))
Dame Leslie Whateley (director ATS 1943–46), *As Thoughts Survive.* (Hutchinson, London (1948))
Whitaker's Almanack. (London (various years))
Who's Who. (London (various years))

Index